Catalogue of Irregular Greek Verbs

A CATALOGUE

OF

IRREGULAR GREEK VERBS,

WITH

ALL THE TENSES EXTANT,

THEIR

FORMATION, MEANING, AND USAGE.

By PHILIP BUTTMANN, LL.D.,

LATE PROFESSOR IN THE UNIVERSITY OF BERLIN, AND LIBRARIAN OF THE ROYAL LIBRARY.

TRANSLATED AND EDITED,

WITH EXPLANATORY NOTES AND A VERY COPIOUS INDEX,

By the Rev. J. R. FISHLAKE,

Late Fellow of Wadham College, Oxford; Translator of "Buttmann's Lexilogus."

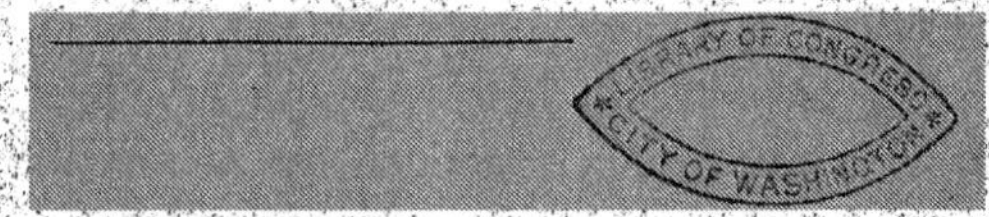

LONDON:

JOHN MURRAY, ALBEMARLE STREET.

1837.

PRINTED BY RICHARD AND JOHN E. TAYLOR,
RED LION COURT, FLEET STREET.

INTRODUCTION.

The Irregular Greek Verb, though all acknowledge its importance and difficulties, has been hitherto confessedly neglected. On this point both our Lexicons and Grammars are particularly defective and unsatisfactory. In their excuse however it may be fairly alleged, that no work can do justice to so extensive a subject, unless it be confined to the examination of that subject only. I have been frequently struck with the truth and the force of these considerations when consulting the second volume of Buttmann's large Greek Grammar (Ausführliche Sprachlehre), which is dedicated to the examination of the Irregular Verbs, and contains a very extensive catalogue of them. In that catalogue I found all the prominent irregularities of the Greek Verb so fully and fundamentally investigated, that I was convinced a translation of it would prove a most valuable assistant to every lover and student of Greek literature, whether he should be satisfied with a mere superficial knowledge of this part of the language, or might wish to see it traced and explained with the deepest and soundest criticism: and as the catalogue constitutes a distinct part of the original Grammar, there was little difficulty in forming it into a separate work.

In this Catalogue Buttmann professes to have two objects in view; first, to enumerate all the *primitive* verbs, whether regular or irregular, which are in general use, particularly in prose, specifying in each the actual usage of the best writers: secondly, to give a list of all verbs, and all forms of verbs, which are anomalous or irregular. On the former of these points little need be said. In some respects its importance is not at all inferior to the latter, particularly for the composition of Greek prose; but in extent it is comparatively inconsiderable. The regular verbs occurring in this Catalogue are so few, (almost every Greek verb having an irregularity in some part of its formation,) that their occasional appearance does not alter the general character of the work; and I have therefore given it a title corresponding with its great leading object, which is, to examine and explain those verbs (with their tenses and persons,) which are properly irregular. If it be asked what verbs Buttmann considers to be properly irregular, I answer in his own words, those which do not follow some general analogy. In accordance with this idea, he has omitted in his Catalogue one numerous class of verbs ending in -άζω, -ίζω, -αίνω, -ύνω, -εύω, -όω, -άω and -έω, because they are derived from other words (not verbs) according to a fixed analogy, because they are all formed in the same simple way, have all a perfect active in -κα, and are invariably defective in the aor. 2. active and passive. For the same reason he has excluded those also which are formed in -ω with the preceding syllable of the radical word strengthened; consequently those ending in -αίρω, -λλω, -πτω, -ττω, and -σσω*. Where, however, we find a verb with either of the above terminations not derived from a noun or other word, but only a lengthened form of some simple stem or root, it is manifestly a deviation from ge-

* Of these ἀλλάσσω only has an aor. 2, consequently is placed in the following Catalogue as an exception to a general analogy.

neral analogy; and as an aor. 2. may be formed from the original root,—e. g. in ἀλιταίνω, aor. 2. ἤλιτον; in κτυπέω, aor. 2. (from ΚΤΥΠΩ) ἔκτυπον,—such verbs have a place in the following Catalogue; as have also all those ending in -άνω, that termination being invariably of the same kind. Within these and the like restrictions almost every irregular verbal form occurring in any known writer will be found, either expressly mentioned or sufficiently referred to in the present work.

In the prosecution of Buttmann's first object, all verbs, whether regular or irregular, which are common in the best prose writers, are distinguished in this Catalogue by a larger type, so that the pure Attic usage of each verb is seen at one view. But any point requiring a more minute disquisition, anything which seldom occurs in prose, which belongs to the language of poetry or to the dialects, is added in a smaller character and in a separate paragraph. Those verbs also whose whole usage brings them under this second class are inserted in the same smaller type.

All themes and forms not actually occurring in any known writer, but which must be supposed in order to class with precision different verbs according to their respective families, are distinguished by *capital letters*, that the eye may not become accustomed to such unusual forms by seeing them printed in the common character. And, to spare the ear as much as possible the formation of these verbal stems into a present in -ω, they are generally distinguished merely thus, ΑΔ–, ΛΗΒ–, &c. If a theme however occurs but once in any genuine remains of antiquity, it appears in the Catalogue in the common character. At the same time it must be understood, that such an appearance does not necessarily prove the actual occurrence of the first person singular of the present. If there be found in actual usage any person of the present, or even of the imperfect (at least in most cases), it is considered quite sufficient to warrant this grammatical use of the whole or any part of the present tense.

The object of this Catalogue requires, strictly speaking, that the usage of every verb inserted in it should be given, wherever it does not follow of itself, at full length. As yet however this has been done very imperfectly; and it must therefore be premised, that wherever in the present work no future, aorist or perfect is expressly mentioned, the common fut. active, the aor. 1. or the perf. 1. (as the regular formation of the verb), is presumed to be in use, at least there is nothing to prove that it is not so. But as soon as, instead of either of the above, an aor. 2., or a perf. 2., or a fut. middle occurs, such tense is added by name. The word "MIDD." standing alone, means that the middle voice of that verb is in use. The expression "Att. redupl." shows that the perfect has the Attic reduplication. Where it is said that "the pass. takes σ," it is to be understood as referring to the perf. and aor. 1. passive; this expression is however used only where that circumstance does not follow of itself. The frequent references to Buttmann's Lexilogus are to the English translation published in 1836.

The deponents are generally noticed as such, although properly speaking that point comes within the province of the Lexicon. When however they take in the aorist the middle form, they belong to this Catalogue, and the anomaly is marked by "Depon. midd."; whilst "Depon. pass." added wherever the meaning appears to require the remark, shows that the verb still adheres to the passive formation.

Single forms occurring in any writer are generally referred back to the first person singular of the indicative of the particular tense. Occasionally however a person of the plural, a conjunctive or a participle, is quoted alone; and this is done in many of the Epic and rarer forms for the sake of greater accuracy and certainty; because it does not necessarily follow from the occurrence of any certain form, that the first person singular of the indicative of that tense must have been in use. And in general it is much more advantageous to the student, who has made a little progress in the language, that some forms actually occurring should be laid before him, which he understands grammatically, and which he may remember to have met with in the course of his reading, than that he should find one indicative grammatically framed, without being able to see to what forms of known and actual occurrence it is intended to lead him.

Whatever meaning—active, passive or middle, transitive or intransitive—is given to the present, the same is supposed to belong to every succeeding tense not expressly marked with a different meaning. If, for instance, under βούλομαι we find the fut. βουλήσομαι from the middle, and the aor. ἐβουλήθην from the passive, this shows that these are the only two forms which occur in the sense of the present βούλομαι, and consequently that there is no instance of an aorist ἐβουλησάμην, or of a future βουληθήσομαι.

The insertion, in their alphabetical places, of supposed verbal stems or roots is intended less for the accommodation of the student, than to complete the plan of the work: and this may be said not only of those which must necessarily be supposed in every methodical treatise of this kind, as ΛΗΒ- for λήψομαι, ἔλαβον, but of many which are merely apparent, i.e. where a change, for which there is no foundation in the regular inflexion, but which has been effected by the operation of syncope or metathesis, is referred back to a root formed by that same figure; e. g. KMA- relates to Κάμνω.

As long as a form shall occur in any of the genuine remains of ancient Greek literature which is not to be found classed or explained in this Catalogue, it will not have attained that completeness which ought to be its aim. On the other hand, whatever occasional information may be gathered from dialects not used by any authors extant, belongs to the plan of this work no further than as it may elucidate the connection between forms and dialects.

The attempt, however, to make this Catalogue etymologically complete might in some particular cases produce confusion; as, for instance, when certain verbs, springing from the same stem or root with different yet cognate meanings, are placed together as belonging to one and the same verb. In such cases it is rather the province of grammar to keep separate what usage has already separated. Thus it is certain that χάσκω, χάζομαι, χανδάνω are etymologically the same, and yet each must be preserved distinct from the others, to render the explanation of each the more clear and intelligible; χαδεῖν must be confined to the sense of *containing*, χάσασθαι to that of *yielding*, and χανεῖν to that of *standing open*; in order that, where it is not sufficiently clear from the context which of these different senses a form has, we may not be led to give it a meaning which does not belong to it.

I have extracted most of the preceding remarks and directions from Buttmann's Grammar, in which they form a kind of introductory chapter to his Catalogue of Verbs: to these I have prefixed a few observations explanatory of the work, and of my object in undertaking it; thus making them perform the double office of introduction and preface.

Of the work itself I need only add, that, like the Lexilogus, of which I offered to the public a translation about two years ago, it is a most extraordinary specimen of Buttmann's extensive research, and deep yet sound criticism. In some instances, indeed, he has only sketched an outline of the inflexions of a verb, which Passow in his Greek and German Lexicon has filled up. In these cases, or where-ever else I found that the latter had added any valuable information, I have availed myself of it, and, where it was possible, have attached the name of the author. When however that could not be so easily done, from the shortness of the quotation or from its breaking into the middle of a paragraph, I have merely inserted it within brackets. Beside a few occasional remarks, entirely explanatory, and always distinguished by "Ed.," I have myself added nothing: it would have been indeed the height of presumption in me to imagine that I could improve, by adding to or taking away from, a subject which has been handled in so masterly a manner by Buttmann and Passow.

J. R. FISHLAKE.

Little Cheverel, Nov. 1837.

[illegible]

[illegible]

[illegible]

[illegible]

IRREGULAR VERBS.

A.

'Αάω, *I harm, lead into error.* Of this verb Homer has the 3. pres. pass. ἀᾶται *, the aor. 1. act. ἄασα, contr. ἆσα (Od. λ, 61.), and of the pass. and midd. ἀάσθην, ἀασάμην, ἄσασθαι. Both alphas are common. Verbal adj. ἀατός, whence with ἀ priv. ἀάατος (⏑–⏓⏑) *inviolable.*

Immediately from ἀάω comes the subst. ἄτη with α long; and from this latter, but with α short †, come two new forms, viz. 1.) ἀτάω synonymous with ἀάω, found only in the pres. and imperf. pass.; ἀτῶμαι, *I suffer harm*, used by the Attic poets: 2.) ἀτέω, with intrans. meaning, found only in Il. υ, 332. and Herodot. 7, 223. in the particip. ἀτέοντα, ἀτέοντες, *senseless, desperate.*

It may perhaps be thought that ΑΩ is the original form of this verb, and ἀάω, ἀάσω a resolution of it: but general analogy is contrary to the idea of a resolution, unless where there has been previously a contraction. As little disposed am I to consider ἀτάω the original, and that the τ was dropped afterwards. The true original form is ΑϜΑΩ, as is evident from the Pindaric αὐάτα (Pyth. 2, 28.), and the Laconian ἀάβακτος (Hesych.) for ἀάατος. On the other hand the meaning of *to satiate* is classed under ἄω, because in that meaning the double α is rare and even suspicious. This is the only way of marking clearly the distinction between the two Homeric epithets ἀάατος (ἀάω) *inviolable*, and ἆτος (ἄω) *insatiable.*

"ΑΑΩ, *I satiate.* See "Αω.

'Αγάλλω ‡, *I deck, adorn:* fut. ἀγᾰλῶ; aor. ἤγηλα, ἀγῆλαι

[* used in an active sense; but see Lexilog. p. 8 and note.—Ed.]

[† I find the α in ἀτάω marked long both in Maltby's Lex. Prosod. and in Passow's Gr. and Germ. Lex. I know of only two passages where the word occurs, viz. Soph. Aj 269. and Eurip. Suppl. 182. The former is decisive in favour of the length of the α, in the latter it is uncertain.—Ed.]

[‡ The active does not occur in Homer, Hesiod or Herodotus. Pindar is the earliest writer in which it is found.—Ed.]

(Eurip. Med. 1027. Lex. Seguer. p. 328.).—Midd. ἀγάλλομαι, *I pride myself on, delight in*: the aor. of this voice is nowhere found.

Ἄγαμαι, *I admire*: Depon. Pres. and imperf. like ἵσταμαι, Od. ζ, 168; fut. midd. ἀγάσομαι; aor. ἠγάσθην, Eurip. Herc. F. 845. Epist. 3, 8., part. ἀγασθείς; Epic ἠγασάμην, but found also in Demosth. pro Cor. 59. and Aristid., and in Il. γ, 181. ἠγάσσατο.

This family of verbs has in the Ionic dialect the collateral sense of *to envy, to be indignant*; but in the pres. it is only in the form ἀγάομαι in the Epic poets (Hes. θ. 619. ἀγώμενος, Od. ε, 119. 122. ἠγάασθε); ἀγαίομαι has it in Ionic prose also. The other tenses have both meanings in common, e. g. Il. ρ, 71. ἀγάσσατο, *he envied*; Od. σ, 71. ἀγάσαντο, *they admired.*

Ἄγαμαι is used by all writers in a *good* sense. The above induction appears sufficient to confine ἀγῶμαι to the other meaning; to which one passage only, Od. π, 203., seems at first sight to be an exception. But ἀγάασθαι in that passage would be utterly superfluous, if we understand it in the sense of merely admiring (Οὔτε θαυμάζειν περιώσιον οὔτ' ἀγάασθαι). Hence I think that the idea of admiration is heightened to the collateral idea of envy, i. e. Ulysses represents the excessive admiration of his son as bordering on envy or jealousy.

Ἀγγέλλω, *I announce*: fut. ἀγγελῶ; aor. 1. ἤγγειλα.—Midd.

Besides the aor. 1. we find not unfrequently both in act. and pass. the aor. 2. also; this tense however is not free from suspicion, as it depends on a single letter. Thus in Eurip. Androm. 1242. (ἀπαγγέλῃ), in Iph. A. 353. (διήγγελον), and in Thuc. 8, 86. (ἀπήγγελον) both the sense and the manuscripts are decidedly in favour of restoring the pres. and imperf.; and a little further on in the same chapter of Thucydides the aor. 1. ἀπήγγειλεν is actually restored to the text from the best manuscripts. The same has been done in Xen. Anab. 3, 4, 14. where, contrary to Xenophon's usage, παρήγγελε formerly stood. But in Lycurg. 18. p. 150, 8. and 87. p. 158, 26. the manuscripts offer no alternative for ἀπήγγελεν, ἐξήγγελε, but the imperfect, which does not suit the context*: and so in Plat. Meno 2. ἀπαγγέλωμεν, though otherwise weakly

* Bekker has however, following the majority of his manuscripts, placed it in the text at the former of these passages; in which I think he has acted less judiciously than at 15. p. 149, 32. of the same work, where he has adopted from one manuscript the imperfect in the place of ἀπήγγελον, which is evidently incorrect.

supported, may be defended by the sense against the present, which is found in a great majority of the manuscripts. In Soph. Œd. T. 955. the reading ἀγγελῶν is from Triclinius only; the Codd. and the old editions have ἀγγελών, which the glosses in the Cod. Lips. explain to be the aorist (see Hermann *), a tense much more natural in that passage than the future. Compare also the various reading ἀγγέλωμεν in Eurip. Or. 1539 (1533 Matth.) and my note on Demosth. Mid. 11, 2. Least of all should I have thought of altering παρήγγελε † in the Ionic writer Herodotus 9, 53, where Schweighäuser has adopted from the single Florentine manuscript an imperfect for which there are no grounds in the context. The aor. 2. pass. occurs in Eurip. Iph. T. 932. (ἠγγέλης) without any various reading, although ἠγγέλθης ‡ would be admissible. In Æl. V. H. 9, 2. occurs διηγγέλη. In Plut. Galb. 25. ἀπηγγέλη.—In εἰπεῖν and ἐνεγκεῖν the two aorists are so easily confounded, that great caution appears to me advisable in this verb also. Nor is it unworthy of consideration, that a form which undoubtedly existed, (for this I think is proved by the number of instances adduced,) should never have been branded as objectionable by any Atticist.

Ἀγείρω, *I collect together*: Att. redupl.—MIDD.

Of the aor. 2. midd. the Epic language has ἀγέροντο, ἀγερέσθαι, and the syncopated part. ἀγρόμενος.—Compare Ἐγείρω.

From ἠγερέθομαι an Epic sister-form of the perf. and imperf. midd. come ἠγερέθονται, -οντο; to which we may without doubt refer the reading of Aristarchus ἠγερέθεσθαι, Il. κ, 127. instead of the common reading ἠγερέεσθαι.—Compare ἠερέθονται under Ἀίρω.

We may certainly feel some hesitation in explaining ἀγέροντο Il. β, 94. to be an aorist, and ἠγείροντο β, 52. an imperfect, as there is no appearance of anything in operation but Epic prosody, and Epic indistinctness between imperfect and aorist. But if the grammarian is not to be deterred in a similar case from distinguishing at Il. β, 106. 107. ἔλιπεν and λεῖπε (at least according to form) as aor. and imperf., as little must he hesitate here. And when at Il. β, 52. we read τοὶ δ' ἠγείροντο μάλ' ὦκα, and at Od. ξ, 248. θοῶς δ' ἐσαγείρατο λαός, we have a similar identity of sense, while the tenses are unquestionably different. We must also recollect, that not only the accents, but even the very turns of thought, adapt themselves to the metre. At Il. β, 52. ἠγείροντο at the side of ἐκήρυσσον is a very natural imperfect, and at v. 94. ἀγέροντο,

* [Hermann says this aor. is never used in tragedy—perhaps never at all by the older writers. On referring to the passage in question in Sophocles, the sense so plainly requires the future, that I feel certain Buttmann must have confounded this with some other passage.]

† [Yet Schweighäuser has retained ἀπήγγελον in Herodot. 4, 153.]

‡ [Dindorf reads ἠγγέλθης.]

it is true, stands in the midst of imperfects. But when it is said οἱ δ' ἀγέροντο. Τετρήχει δ' ἀγορή, it is quite as natural to render it, "And now they were assembled [not *assembling*]: the crowd heaved restlessly." Besides, as ἀγρόμενος (by syncope for ἀγερόμενος) is undoubtedly an aor. particip. *assembled*, so ἀγέροντο must in every instance be considered an aorist also. Nor is there anything in Od. β, 385. to prevent our accenting, with Barnes and Porson, ἀγερέσθαι, as this form is in all its relations a common aor. 2. (compare ἀλιτέσθαι), and the silent traditionary accent on an infinitive occurring but once can be of no authority.—Compare Ἐγρέσθαι.

Ἄγημαι. See Ἡγέομαι.

Ἀγνοέω, *I am ignorant of*: fut. ἀγνοήσομαι, but also ἀγνοήσω, Demosth. c. Zenoth. p. 885. Conon. p. 1266. Theocrin. p. 1337. whence the passive sense of ἀγνοήσεσθαι in Demosth. pro Cor. p. 310. is less surprising. [Vid. Hemsterh. ad Thom. Mag. in v.]

Ἀγνώσασκε Od. ψ, 95. has a various reading ἀγνώσσεσκε as old as itself. These iteratives are sometimes formed from the aorists, sometimes from the imperfect; thus ἔτυπτον becomes τύπτεσκον; ἔτυψα—τύψασκον; ἔλιπον—λίπεσκον: and there are a few which take in the Epic poets α instead of ε after the characteristic of the present, as ῥίπτασκον, κρύπτασκον, in which case they correspond in meaning with those formed from the aorists. Now there is nothing in the sense of Od. ψ, 95. to induce us to prefer either form. If we take ἀγνώσσεσκε, it must be from the imperf. of ἀγνώσσω: if we decide in favour of the aorist, nothing appears more natural than ἀγνώσασκε for ἀγνοήσασκε, as Homer uses elsewhere the verb ἀγνοέω only, and this explanation is supported by the ἀλλόγνωσας of Herodot. 1, 85.

Ἄγνυμι, *I break* (trans.): fut. ἄξω*: the past tenses have the syllabic augment: aor. act. ἔαξα (Il. η, 270. contr. ἦξα, Il. ψ, 392. Od. τ, 539.), aor. pass. ἐάγην with α long: the perf. 2. ἔαγα (Sappho), Ion. ἔηγα, has the passive or intransitive sense, *I am broken*†.—Midd.

The α in this verb is originally long, as shown particularly in its derivatives ἀγή, ἀαγής, which are connected with ἐάγην in the same way as πληγή is with ἐπλήγην, and ἐνιπή with ἐνένιπον. Hence the α of the

* Formed according to the general rule of verbs in μι from the obsolete ἄγω, like ΔΕΙΚΩ, δείκνυμι, δείξω, &c.

† As the perf. 2. generally gives the preference to the intrans. sense, we find in a great number even of transitive verbs

root is long in the aor. 2. pass. ἐάγην, as we see from some passages of the Attics, (Brunck on Aristoph. Ach. 928.) and from Il. λ, 558. But it is also found in Epic poetry short; although, by the disappearance of the digamma, which belonged originally to this verb, as will be seen below, we cannot now ascertain in some passages the true Homeric form of this tense. See Heyne on Il. γ, 367., who tries to establish, and not without probability, the digamma and the long α uniformly. In the later poets, as Theocr. 22, 190. it is most certainly short. Compare πλήττω, of which the aor. 2. pass. retains its original length, but shortens the syllable when used in one particular sense.

The digamma, whence the irregular augment comes, is proved beyond a doubt to have originally belonged to this verb by the Hesiodic form καυάξαις (ε, 664. 691.), which can be explained in no other way. That is to say, ϜΑΞΑΙ became in composition ΚΑϜϜΑΞΑΙ, as βάλλω καβ-βάλλω. This spiritus, thus doubled and united by the metre, was of necessity retained here, while the digamma disappeared everywhere else. But by the intimate affinity, and in some respect identity, of the sounds U and V, Υ and Ϝ, it passed over into υ, and consequently with the α into the diphthong αυ. See the same process in εὔαδεν, under Ἁνδάνω.

This makes the occurrence of ἦξε for ἔαξε twice in Homer (Il. ψ, 392. Od. ι, 539.) the more remarkable. In the same way Hippocrates has κατῆξα (Epidem. 5, 13.); but as he writes the substantives also κάτηξις, κάτηγμα (De Artic. 16. 17. De Fract. 16. 28.), it would appear that in the Ionic dialect the whole formation, with the exception of the pres. and aor. 2. pass., had the η in the root: in Homer on the other hand, who elsewhere invariably uses ἔαξα, and, dropping the augment, ἄξαντο; Il. ζ, 40. π, 371. (see below the same form under Ἄγω), ἦξα can be only the augment. If however we compare ἄτη, which comes from ΑϜΑΤΑ, we shall be the less surprised at ἦξα as a contraction from ΕϜΑΞΑ.

It is far more astonishing to find that in this verb the augment is carried on even to forms in which it is naturally inadmissible, and that this takes place in very old writers. Thus Hippocrates has very com-

this form only with the immediate meaning, which in almost all cases is of an intransitive nature: thus—

ἄγνυμι—ἄγνυμαι, *I break* (intrans.); perf. ἔᾱγα, *I am broken.*

δαίω—δαίομαι and δέδηα, *I burn* (intrans.).

ἐγείρω—ἐγείρομαι, *I wake* (intrans.); ἐγρήγορα, *I am on the watch.*

ἔλπω—ἔλπομαι, and ἔολπα, *I hope.* See also κήδομαι κέκηδα, μαίνομαι μέμηνα, οἴγω ἀνοίγομαι ἀνέῳγα, ὄλλυμαι ὄλωλα, πείθομαι πέποιθα, πήγνυμαι πέπηγα, ῥήγνυμαι ἔῤῥωγα, σήπομαι σέσηπα, τήκομαι τέτηκα, φαίνομαι πέφηνα, φθείρομαι ἔφθορα, γίγνομαι γέγονα. Compare also δέρκομαι, μείρομαι and προβέβουλα under βούλομαι. From this its connexion with passive or middle forms arose the improper appellation of the perfect midd.

monly κατεαγῇ, κατεάγεις, as for instance in De Artic. 35, bis. Vectiar. 1. 2.—Apollon. Rh. 4, 1686. has ἐξεαγεῖσα, which metrical passage, in a poet of some antiquity, and a learned grammarian, is of great weight. The passages quoted from the Attic writers must be left for future criticism: Plat. Gorg. p. 469. e., see Heind. and Bekker; Lysias c. Sim. p. 99, κατεάγεις, according to Bekker's MSS. καταγείς; ib. p. 100, 5, κατεάξαντες without any various reading.

In the other verbs which have this kind of augment, and which were in common use quite as much as the above, this irregularity is not found until a very late æra; for instance, ἀπεωσθέντος in Pæanius 9.; ἐξεώσεις in Theod. Prodr. p. 17.; ἐωνησαμένην in an inscription of a still later time in Chishull's preface to his Travels, p. 6; and this gives additional importance to the antiquity of the examples from ἄγνυμι, in which verb this irregularity was probably introduced and sanctioned by usage earlier than it was in others, in order to avoid confusion with ἄγω and ἅπτω.

Of the later forms ἄσσω and κατάσσω for ἄγνυμι, Schneider in his Lexicon quotes the Schol. Hom., Celsus ap. Orig. 7. p. 368., Hesych. v. ἄγνυτον and ἐνιῆλαι., Artemid. sæpe; and from Æsop. August. F. 3. 55. and 213. the form κατεάσσω.

Ἀγνώσσασκε
Ἀγνώσασκε } See Ἀγνοέω.
Ἀγνώσσεσκε

Ἀγορεύω. See Εἰπεῖν.

Ἀγρέω, *I take*; imperat. ἄγρει, ἀγρεῖτε, used often in Homer as common interjectional particles, like *age* in Latin and *tenez* in French. The rest of the verb disappeared before αἱρέω, leaving some derivatives. One instance of the indic. remains in a fragment of Archil. in Br. Anal. 1, 41. For a more detailed account see Buttm. Lexilog. p. 20, &c.

Ἄγχω, *I choke*, transitive. Midd. intransitive.

Ἄγω, *I lead*; fut. ἄξω; takes in the aor. 2. the reduplication, ἤγαγον, ἀγαγεῖν*; perf. ἦχα, common form ἀγήοχα†; aor. 1. act. ἦξα, imperat. ἄξετε, Hom.; aor. 1.

* Thus we find in prose the similar form ἤνεγκον, ἐνεγκεῖν (see φέρω); and the following poetic aorists: ἤραρον, conj. ἀράρῃ &c.; see ΑΡΩ. ἤκαχον, ἀκάχων &c.; see ΑΧΩ. ἤπαφον, ἀπάφων; see ἀπαφίσκω. ἄλαλκον (Hom. for ἤλαλκον), ἀλαλκεῖν &c.; see ἀλέξω. ὤρορε, 3. pers.—see ὄρνυμι (perf. ὄρωρα). ἐνένιπον (ἐνένιπτον); see ἐνίπτω. If we compare these forms with ἤγαγον, λέλαθον, πέπληγον, we shall see that they are undoubted aorists, notwithstanding all which has been said to the contrary.

† With ἀγήοχα we may class some other anomalous forms which change their vowel to ο in both perfects: ἔρρωγα (perf. intransit.) from ῥήγνυμι. πέπτωκα from ΠΕΤΩ, πίπτω. εἴωθα for εἶθα from ἔθω. ἄωρτο plusq. perf. pass. for ἦρτο or ἤερτο, from αἴρω or ἀείρω. ἕωκα, ἀφέωκα, Dor. (whence in N. T. ἀφέωνται) for εἶκα, ἀφεῖκα, ἀφεῖνται, from ἀφίημι. ἐδή-

midd. ἠξάμην, seldom in the Attic, but its compounds frequent in Herodotus: perf. pass. ἦγμαι.—MIDD.

For a full account of ἀγήοχα see Buttm. Lexilog. pp. 116. 139. The use of this form in the letter of Philip and in the resolution of the people in Demosth. pro Cor. p. 238. 249., in Lysias ap. Phrynich. p. 121. and in Aristot. Œcon. 1, 7. shows that it was an old and familiar form, which, being in no respect worse than ἐδήδοκα, recommended itself for use instead of the indistinct ἦχα, as ἐδήδοκα took the place of ἦκα. The Attic writers, however, preferred the shorter form. See προῆχα in Reisken's Ind. ad Demosth. συνῆχας in Xen. Mem. 4, 2, 8. note. In general the perfect was avoided as much as possible; and hence the later grammarians sometimes marked ἦχα as obsolete, sometimes rejected ἀγήοχα as bad Attic. See Dorv. ad Charit. p. 481. (494.) Lob. ad Phryn. p. 121.

An aor. 1. ἦξα, ἆξαι was also in use, but rejected by the Attics. It is found however in προσῆξαν, Thuc. 2, 97., in ἆξαι, Antiph. 5, 46. p. 134. in τοὺς φυγάδας κατάξαντες, Xen. Hell. 2, 2, 20. (12.), in ἦξαν, ἄξας, Batrachom. 115. 119., in ἄξασθε, ἄξαντο, Il. θ, 505. 545. with many other passages which need the examination of the critic. See Lobeck ad Phryn. p. 287. 735. In Aristoph. Ran. 468. ἀπῆξας is from ἀπάττω; hence the latest editors have distinguished it by the ι: see ἀΐσσω.

The Epic imperat. ἄξετε, like ἔπεσον, ἐβήσετο, λέξεο, ὄρσεο, ἀείσεο, is one of those aor. 2. which take the characteristic σ of the aor. 1., but are commonly mistaken for anomalous derivatives of the fut. 1. Homer uses it instead of ἀγάγετε, which would not be admissible in the hexameter; ἄγαγε he does use at Il. ω, 337. With this form we may join ἀξέμεν, Il. ω, 663. as inf. aor. for ἄξαι or ἀγαγεῖν.

'ΑΓΕΟΜΑΙ. The reading ἀγεόμενον in Herodot. 3, 14. might be adopted without hesitation, if Schæfer's opinion, that this too is corrupted from ἀγινεόμενον, were not still more probable. See also ἡγέομαι.

'Αδῆσαι, *to feel dislike.* Of this verb Homer has in the Odyssey the forms ἀδήσειεν and ἀδηκότες, which are generally connected with τὸ ἄδος, Il. λ, 88.; and as this last has the first syllable short, but the two others have it always long, they are written, according to the example of some of the grammarians, ἀδδήσειεν, ἀδδηκότες. See this point discussed in Lexilog. p. 22: see also ἆσαι, *to satiate*, under "Αω.

"Αδω, (old and poet. ἀείδω*), *I sing*: fut. ᾄσομαι, ἀείσομαι,

δοκα, and in Hom. pass. ἐδήδομαι, from ἔδω. ἐνήνοχα from ΕΝΕΚΩ. And the very defective Epic perfects ἄνωγα, ἀνήνοθα, ἐνήνοθα.

* [Homer always uses ἀείδω, ἀείσομαι. "Ασομαι is properly Attic (see Markl. Eurip. Suppl. 932. Brunck, Aristoph. Vesp. 1228. Fr. 1294.), but is found in

The future midd. is Attic (Aristoph.); see Piers. ad Mœr. p. 38.: ἀείσω, ᾄσω, is in other dialects, Theogn. 4. Theocr. 7, 72. 78. The imperative ἀείσεο is one of those aor. 2. which take the characteristic σ of the aor. 1. See above ἄξετε, under Ἄγω.

Hermann has very properly defended ἀείσεο in the 17th Hom. Hymn against ἀείδεο; (in Hymn 20, where ἀείδεο stands without any known various reading, it must remain,) for ἀείδομαι as active is an unheard-of form. Now as the aor. midd. of ἀείδω and ᾄδω is equally unknown, this ἀείσεο may be an imperative formed from the future ἀείσομαι. But there are as little grounds in common usage for the Epic aorist ἐβήσετο as for the one in question; and as that stands in the same relation to ἔβην and βήσομαι (tenses in common use) as ἀείσεο does to ᾖσα and ᾄσομαι, it appears that the aor. midd. of some verbs, as well as the fut. midd., had in the old language a purely active meaning. See also Lexilog. p. 226. note.

ΑΔ-. See Ἀνδάνω.

Ἀείδω. See Ἄδω.

Ἀείρω. See Αἴρω.

Ἀέξω. See Αὔξω.

Ἄημι. See Ἄω.

Αἰδέομαι, *I feel shame*: fut. αἰδέσομαι; perf. ᾔδεσμαι; aor. 1. pass. ᾐδέσθην; aor. 1. midd. ᾐδεσάμην. The aor. pass. and midd. have the same meaning; but in the Attic language αἰδέσασθαι refers to the person who has committed a shameful action with the meaning of *to pardon*. [See Demosth. Aristocr. 72.]

An old poetical form of the present is αἴδομαι*, from which arose the one in common use. It never has the augment: αἴδετο. Of the fut. αἰδήσομαι for αἰδέσομαι see the note to Μάχομαι.

Αἰνέω†, *I praise*: fut. αἰνέσω‡; aor. ᾔνεσα; perf. act. ᾔνεκα; perf. pass. ᾔνημαι; aor. 1. pass. ᾐνέθην. Also αἰνήσω, ᾔνησα, in the Epic poets and Pindar.

Αἰνίσσομαι, *I speak enigmatically*: Depon. midd.

Hom. Hymn. 5, 2. Less pure is the fut. ᾄσω, but found sometimes in the Attics, as in Eurip. Herc. F. 681. Dor. ἀσῶ, Theocr. 1, 145. Ἀείσω is used by the non-Attic poets, and is found in Hom. Epig. 14, 1. attributed by Pollux to Hesiod.—Passow.]

* [Homer uses in the present both αἴδομαι and αἰδέομαι, but forms all his tenses from the latter, which is also the prevailing form in prose.—Passow.]

† [In good prose writers we seldom if ever find αἰνέω, always ἐπαινέω.—Passow.]

‡ See note under Δέω, *I bind*.

Αἴνυμαι, *I take*. Only pres. and imperf.: without augment therefore, αἴνυτο. [Hom. and Hes.]

Αἱρέω, *I take*: fut. αἱρήσω; perf. ᾕρηκα, Ion. ἀραίρηκα; perf. pass. ᾕρημαι, Ion. ἀραίρημαι; aor. 1. pass. ᾑρέθην*; fut. pass. αἱρεθήσομαι; aor. act. εἷλον, ἑλεῖν, from ἝΛΩ.—Midd.—Verbal adj. αἱρετός, -έος. Compare Ἁλίσκομαι.

A less frequent future is ἑλῶ; thus we find περιελῶ, Aristoph. Equ. 290., καθελεῖ, Antiphil. Epig. 15., ἀφελοῦμαι, Com. ap. Antiattic. Seguer. p. 80, 12., and occasional examples down to the latest writers.

The aor. 1. ᾕρησα too is found in the common language; and even in Aristoph. Thesm. 760. we have ἐξῃρήσατο, which cannot be rejected as a false reading. See Lobeck ad Phryn. p. 716.

The Ionians have a peculiar reduplication for the perfect, ἀραίρηκα, ἀραίρημαι with the spir. lenis, the usual form in Ionic prose for the common ᾕρηκα, ᾕρημαι. Compare ἀλαλύκτημαι from ἀλυκτέω, ἀλάλημαι from ἀλάομαι, ἀκάχημαι for ἀκήχεμαι, and ἐληλίγμαι from ἑλίσσω.

Εἶλα, ἕλαι, and εὗρα from εὑρίσκω, forms occurring in the later writers, as the Alexandrine, the Orphic poems, &c., are regular aor. 1. by virtue of the characteristic; but as only the aor. 2. of these verbs, εἷλον, εὗρον, was in common use elsewhere, it is plain that these are instances of the change of termination from the aor. 2. to the aor. 1. which took place in some unformed dialects. Other terminations beside the 1. pers. sing., as for instance the 2. pers. in ας, the infin. in αι, the part. in ας, are seldom found, but in their place the regular terminations of the aor. 2.† Hence it is clear that the indiscriminate use of εἶπον and εἶπα, of ἤνεγκον and ἤνεγκα, in the oldest and best writers, arises from the same change: all which tends to prove the original identity of the two aorists.—In the aor. 2. midd. εἱλάμην, -ω, -ατο, -αντο, &c., in εὑράμην, &c., in ἐπαυράσθαι for -έσθαι, in the Dor. γενάμενος, and in ὤσφραντο for ὤσφροντο, Herodot. 1, 80, 26., we have the same mixture of termination; of this the later writers furnish most frequent instances, but the older Ion. dialect is not without them. On these two forms, and the 2. pers. εἶλω, see Lobeck ad Phryn. p. 139. 183. The Homeric γέντο will be found in its alphabetical place.

Αἴρω (Att. and poet. ἀείρω, *I raise*) is formed regularly

* See note under Δέω, *I bind*.

† Not a few instances of the others are however to be found in the dialects; ἀφέλαι, Inscr. ap. Chishull. p. 138. l. 5.—ἐκβάλαι in Maittaire from a Byzantine writer, and the part. ἀγάγας in Hesychius. In the above examples we must not overlook one thing, that only the terminations of the aor. 1. are adopted; the formation of the root remains the same, otherwise it would be ἀφεῖλαι, ἐκβῆλαι.

according to the rules of verbs having as their characteristic one of the liquids λ, μ, ν, ρ.—MIDD. Compare Ἄρνυμαι."

The Attics were enabled to use the α of the fut. long because ἀρῶ is contracted from ἀείρω. As the same thing is expressly mentioned by one of the grammarians with regard to φαίνω φανῶ, there is no doubt of it in the present instance, although most of the cases that occur are still under the consideration of the critic. In many passages, where for instance the text has the present of αἴρω or αἱρέω, all becomes correct by adopting some form of ἄρῶ: and in Eurip. Iph. T. 117. the emendation of ἀροῦμεν is indeed confirmed by all the manuscripts*. In Æschyl. Pers. 797. ἀροῦμεν is likewise the old and acknowledged reading: and in Eurip. Heracl. 323. ἀρῶ, in Iph. A. 125. ἐπαρεῖ, and in Tro. 1148. ἀροῦμεν are, according to this analogy, placed beyond a doubt both by sense and context†. This however need not make us doubt the correctness of the form ἀρῶ with α short; as in Soph. Aj. 75. ἀρεῖς, and in Œd. Col. 460., ἀρεῖσθε stand in the Iambic place.

The aor. 2. active is never used in any of its forms; but in the middle, Homer has the aor. 1. in the augmented indicative only (ἠράμεθα, ἤρατο), and without the augment the aor. 2. ἀρόμην; in all the other moods the aor. 2. only, ἄρωμαι (α short), ἀροίμην, ἀρέσθαι. The Tragedians were able to use the same moods when the metre allowed it (e. g. in Soph. El. 34. ἀροίμην), otherwise they have always the aor. 1. of which the α is long.

For ἄωρτο see note on ἀγήοχα under Ἄγω, and Lexilog. p. 135. &c.

Ἠερέθονται, -οντο, for ἀείρονται, comes from the Epic ἠερέθομαι, lengthened from ἀείρομαι, with the quantity of the root changed. Compare ἠγερέθομαι under Ἀγείρω.

And lastly by resolution into -έω comes the form αἱρεύμενος for αἱρόμενος in Hes. ε. 474., where however it has been hitherto obscured by a mistaken reading in almost all the manuscripts of βιότοιο ἐρεύμενον, and still more by the present βιότου αἱρεύμενον. The poet is speaking of the vessels being all full, and he then says, καί σε ἔολπα Γηθήσειν βιότου αἱρεύμενον ἔνδον ἐόντος, i. e. "when thou takest from the stores which are therein:" this is the only natural construction of αἱρεσθαι. But αἱρεύμενον stands for αἱρόμενον, as is sufficiently certain by comparing it with

* The sense of this passage has however been obscured by all the editors before Seidler, by misunderstanding the construction of μέν—δέ.

† Porson (on Eurip. Med. 848.) first introduced this spondaic future, but by a slight mistake he thought to be able to form αἰρῶ also from ἀίρω, in order to approach nearer to the text as handed down: and thus this barbaric form actually crept into some later editions. Elmsley (on Eurip. Heracl. 323.) corrected it.

both the earlier and later Ionisms πιέζευν, πιεζεύμενος, πινεύμενος, &c. And this, which is the only true reading, is actually preserved in the Etym. M., but in an article disfigured by mistakes*.

Αἰσθάνομαι, *I perceive*: Depon. midd. Imperf. ᾐσθανόμην; fut. αἰσθήσομαι; aor. ᾐσθόμην†. [Later writers have also a passive form αἰσθηθῆναι, as the LXX.]

Αἴσθομαι also must have been in use, as some grammarians have wished to distinguish it from αἰσθάνομαι; see Lex. Seguer. pp. 183. 216. 359: and in Plat. Rep. 10. p. 608, a. Bekker has adopted from the manuscripts αἰσθόμεθα instead of αἰσθώμεθα, which does not suit the passage. See also Isocr. Nicocl. p. 28. Steph. according to Bekker's reading; Fronto, Epist. ad Marc. 1, 8, 4. where see the Add.

Ἀΐσσω (in Hom. a depon. pass. also), *I rush, hasten.* In the Attics a dissyllable, and even in the Tragedians ᾄσσω or ἄσσω, commonly ᾄττω or ἄττω, and so also ᾖξα, ᾆξαι with and without the iota‡.

From the subst. ἄϊκες we may conclude that the ι in the complete form is long by nature, and therefore the infin. aor. must be accented ἀΐξαι. The pretended syncopated form συναΐκτην in Hes. α, 189. must now yield to the true form συναΐγδην, as Gaisford reads it.

Αἰσχύνω, *I make ashamed, treat in a shameful manner:*

* This is the article Αἰρεύμενον; for so it is now written, and the spiritus is repeated several times, until the grammarian quotes the form again; and then, as well as in the verse of Hesiod which is subjoined, it is expressly written αἰρεύμενον. But the beginning of the article, until we come to one grand mistake, is quite correct in the old Venetian editions, of which I will here transcribe the whole: Αἰρεύμενον, αἴροντα, λαμβάνοντα. παρὰ τὸ αἰρῶ τὸ σημαῖνον τὸ λαμβάνω, κατὰ πλεονασμὸν αἰρῶ, αἰροῦμαι, αἰρούμενον· καὶ τροπῇ Αἰολικῇ αἰρεύμενον. Ἡσίοδος, &c. In Sylburg's edition the first word and the three which follow πλεονασμόν have the aspirate; whence arose the unintelligible sentence, αἱρῶ ... κατὰ πλεονασμὸν αἱρῶ, which Sylburg himself confessed he did not understand. It must be αἴρω ... κατὰ πλεονασμὸν αἰρῶ, and the pleonasm consists in the circumflex, i. e. in the ε concealed under it, from which now comes αἰρούμενον or αἰρεύμενον. Whether the reading of the Hesiodic manuscripts from which Grævius quotes be αἰρεύμενον, or whether it be αἱρεύμενον, which he rejected without mentioning it, is uncertain.

† Verbs of three or more syllables in άνω and some in αίνω come from a radical form without the alpha, which supplies it with some tenses as formed from έω: thus αὔξω and αὐξάνω; βλαστάνω, aor. ἔβλαστον, fut. βλαστήσω: see also ἁμαρτάνω, ὀλισθάνω, αἰσθάνομαι &c.—ἀλφάνω and ἀλφαίνω; ἀλιταίνω, ἤλιτον, ἀλιτήσω; ἐρυθαίνω, κερδαίνω, ὀσφραίνομαι.

‡ Most probably the iota subscript in the Attic forms may be ascribed to the accuracy of the grammarians. See Hemst. ad Plut. 733. Valck. ad Phœniss. 1388. and compare the various readings of the passages there mentioned. In pronunciation it was naturally distinguished by lengthening the *a*.

pass. *I am ashamed*; perf. pass. ᾔσχυμμαι*; part. ᾐσχυμμένος, Il. σ, 180. with a genuine various reading ᾐσχυμένος.

Αἰτέω, *I ask.*—Midd.

Αἰτιάομαι, *I accuse*: Depon. midd.

Ἀΐω, *I hear*. Used only in pres. and imperf.

Verbs beginning with α, αυ, and οι, followed by a vowel, have no augment, as ἀΐω, ἄημι, ἀηδίζομαι· αὐαίνω, οἰόω, οἰακίζω, οἰωνίζομαι: but the α if short becomes long, therefore ᾇον &c.—Οἴομαι and ἀείδω are exceptions; as is also ἐπήϊσα, (from ἐπαΐω, Herodot. 3, 29. Heind. Plat. Hipp. Maj. p. 289. E.) Herodot. 9, 93. Apoll. Rhod. 1, 1023. 2, 195. with the augment and ι short.

[Passow in his Lexicon marks ἀΐω – ◡ –, and says that in Hom. the first syllable is *short* whenever the third is *long*. In the Tragedians it is common, Seidl. Eurip. Tro. 156. The iota is much oftener short than long, Heyne Il. ο, 252. Spohn Hes. ε, 215.]

1 Ἀκαχίζω, transit. *I grieve, vex any one.* The theme ΑΧΩ gives the following forms: ἤκαχον, ἀκαχεῖν†, from which is formed the present in common use. From the same aor. as a new theme‡ came the fut. ἀκαχήσω, Hymn. Merc. 286., and again an aor. 1. ἀκάχησε, Il. ψ, 223.—Midd. ἄχομαι or ἄχνυμαι, *I grieve (myself)*; aor. ἠκαχόμην. Perf. pass. (*I am grieved*) ἀκήχεμαι§, ἀκηχέμενος, Il. σ, 29., and transposing the quantity, ἀκάχημαι, ἀκαχήμενος, Il. τ, 312. infin. ἀκάχησθαι. Ἀκηχέδαται, Il. ρ, 637. is most probably a corruption of ἀκηχέαται, which is a various reading, is regular, and supported by ἀκαχείατο, Il. μ, 179., (while for the δ there are no grounds whatever.—To the same intransitive meaning of the middle belongs also the part. pres. act. ἀχέων, -ουσα, *grieving, lamenting.*

Ἀκαχμένος, *sharpened, pointed.* Hom.—If this perf. part. pass., (the only part of the verb which occurs) be compared with the substantive ἀκή and ἀκωκή, *a point*, it leads us to a verb ΑΚΩ (*acuo*), because the

* Before the termination μαι of the perf. pass. the ν undergoes three changes:

1. Into μ in ᾔσχυμμαι; in ἐξήραμμαι (ξηραίνω), Athen. 3. p. 80., and in σέσιμμαι (σίνω), σεσιμμένος, Inscr. Chish. p. 130.

2. Generally into σ, as in πέφασμαι, μεμίασμαι, μεμόλυσμαι, &c.

3. The ν is rejected and the vowel remains long, τετραχυμένος, Aristot. H. A. 4, 9. This takes place very rarely.

† See note on ἀγαγεῖν under Ἄγω.

‡ From the aor. 2. act., as being a most necessary and consequently a most ancient tense, were taken very naturally new forms. Thus from εὗρον, ἔτυχον, infin. εὑρεῖν, τυχεῖν were formed εὑρήσω, τυχήσω, not from εὑρέω, τυχέω, which were never in existence.

§ The perfect passive, as well as the other perfects, is intimately connected with the present; and as the terminations are similar in the infinitive and participle, this affinity can only be shown by adopting the accent of the present; thus ἐλήλαμαι, ἐλήλαμενος; ἀρήρεμαι, ἀρηρέμενος, and many others.

χ of the perf. act. before the μ is not changed into γ. For the α instead of η in the second syllable see below, note (*).

Ἀκέομαι, *I heal, cure*: Dep. midd. Fut. ἀκέσομαι; the perf. takes the σ. [The act. is found once in Hippocr. Loc. in Homin. c. 5. The aor. pass. ἀκεσθῆναι has a pass. sense in Pausan. 2, 27, 3. Ἀκειάμενος is a false reading for ἀκειόμενος, from ἀκείομαι, Epic sister-form of ἀκέομαι, Od. ξ, 383. Il. π, 29.—Passow.]

Ἀκήδεσεν. See Κήδω.

Ἀκούω, *I hear*†: fut. midd. ἀκούσομαι; perf. Att. ἀκήκοα, Dor. ἄκουκα, later ἤκουκα; plusq. perf. ἠκηκόειν. The pass. takes σ, and the perf. pass. is formed without reduplication, ἤκουσμαι, ἠκούσθην.

Ἀκροάομαι, *I hear*: Depon. midd. The fut. is ἀκροάσομαι, not -ήσομαι, an exception to the general rule. Of this verb the 2. pers. ἀκροᾶσαι, ἠκροᾶσο, for ἀκροᾷ, ἠκρρῶ, was also in use among the Attics: the former occurs in Lex. Seguer. p. 77, 22., and the latter at p. 98. is quoted from Antiphanes. See Piers. ad Moer. p. 16. Lex. Seguer. p. 18, 10.

Ἀλαλάζω, *I shout*: fut. -ξω, &c.

Ἀλαλκεῖν. See Ἀλέξω.

Ἀλαλύκτημαι. See Ἀλυκτέω.

Ἀλάομαι, *I wander*: Depon. pass. [Imperf. ἠλώμην; aor. ἠλήθην, poet. ἀλήθην.—Passow.]

The Epic form ἀλάλημαι, ἀλάλησθαι, ἀλαλήμενος, with the meaning of a present, is supposed to be a form in μι, according to the analogy of ἄημαι, δίζημαι: but there are no grounds for such an idea; for the accent of the present in these forms is no proof, being found also in such undoubted perfects as ἀκήχεμαι, ἐλήλαμαι, and others (see note on ἀκήχεμαι under Ἀκαχίζω); and the meaning of the present is so similar to

(*) In forming the Attic reduplication the temp. augm. of the second syllable is sometimes neglected; for instance in ἀκαχμένος, ἀλάλημαι, ἀλαλύκτημαι, ἀκάχημαι, ἀραίρηκα, ἀραίρημαι.

† [No pure Attic writer has the fut. act. ἀκούσω, Schæf. Greg. p. 1063. It first occurs three times in Lycophr., then in the LXX and the N. T., and more frequently in later writers, as Dion. Hal., Lucian Navig. 11. Jacobs' Anth. Poet. vol. i. p. l., vol. 3. pp. 552. 580. 1024. and particularly Schæf. Appar. Demosth. vol. 2. p. 232.—Passow.]

that of the perfect, that usage is constantly confounding them. See Buttm. Lexilog. pp. 112. and 202, note.

'Αλδαίνω*, *I make large and strong.* The present is found in the later Epic poets, as Nicand. Alex. 402. Homer has ἤλδανε, Od. σ, 70. ω, 768. where, particularly in the second passage, it appears to be completely an aorist. At Il. ψ, 599. stands the intransitive ἀλδήσκω†, *to grow, increase.* Other forms are not found in the older poets; Schneider in the Supplement to his Lexicon has collected those which occur in the later‡; among them is the intransitive ἄλδομαι in Nicander, for which undoubtedly he had an older precedent: compare ἄλθομαι, ἀλθαίνω. From this came the verbal adj. ἀλτός, whence in Homer ἄναλτος, *insatiable,* literally *whom nothing fills and nourishes,* Od. ρ, 228. σ, 113, 363.

'Αλείφω, *I anoint*: [fut. -ψω, aor. ἤλειψα; aor. pass. ἠλείφθην; aor. 2. conjunct. ἐξαλιφῇ, Plat. Phædr. p. 258, B. as restored by Bekker from the best manuscripts. Midd. ἀλειψάμην, ἀλείψασθαι, ἀλειψαμένος, Hom. The perf. ἤλοιφα, the Att. ἀλήλῐφα (Demosth. in Callipp. 29.), and the pass. ἀλήλιμμαι were in post-Homeric use.—Passow.]

In the Attic reduplication ἀλείφω, like ἀκούω, takes a short vowel in the third syllable, even shortening the vowel of the root: ἀλείφω, ἀλήλῐφα, ἀλήλιμμαι; ἀκούω, ἀκήκοα. There occurs also frequently ἀλήλειπται; but whether this be a correct form, or a false reading for ἀλήλιπται or ἤλειπται, is uncertain.

'Αλέξω, *I ward off*, and in the midd. *I ward off from myself*; fut. act. ἀλεξήσω, fut. midd. ἀλεξήσομαι; aor. midd. ἠλεξάμην, ἀλέξασθαι, ἀλεξάμενος, as from ΑΛΕΚΩ.

See Schneid. on Xenoph. Anab. 1, 3, 6. From the aor. 1. act., formed according to the analogy of the future, come the Homeric ἀλεξήσειεν and ἀπαλεξήσαιμι. There are no grounds in Pind. Ol. 13, 12. for a present ἀλεξεῖν. The pres. ἀλέξομαι, which sounds so like a future, and is

* [Akin to ἄλω, ἄλδω, ἄλθω, ἄρδω, *alo*.—Passow.]

† One can hardly help suspecting that this, by a very common mistake, is corrupted from ἀλδίσκω: but the great unanimity of authorities forbids it. [Passow marks ἀλδίσκω in his Lexicon as very doubtful. Schneider gives a transitive sense of ἀλδήσκω from Schæf. Theocr. 17, 78.]

‡ ['Αναλδήσκοντες, Apollon. Rhod. 3, 1363. 'Αλδήσκουσαι, Eratosthenes, where Scaliger reads ἀλδίσκουσαι. 'Αλδίσκω, Suid. 'Αλδαίνουσι, Nicand. Al. 402. 'Εναλδόμενον, Nicand. Al. 532. 'Εναλδήνασα, transit. 409. 'Αλδήσασκεν, from ἀλδέω, Orph. Lith. 364. 'Αλδύνηται, Quint. Sm. 9, 473. where Rhodomannus reads ἀλδαίνηται. 'Αλδυνομένους, Suid.—Schneid. Suppl.]

thought suspicious (see Schneid.) in Xenophon, appears certain in Sophocl. Œd. T. 171. and particularly 539.

The Poets have in the active the aorist ἤλαλκον, ἀλαλκεῖν, ἀλαλκών*, with the reduplication† from ΑΛΚΩ, whence ἀλκτήρ and ἀλκάθειν. Hence (according to the note on ἀκαχεῖν, ἀκαχίζω) came a new future ἀλαλκήσω.

A present ἀλέκω appears to have been actually used by the epigrammatic poet Diodorus (Epig. 1. Anthol. 6, 245.), although it is only as a conjecture instead of the ἀλέγοις of the manuscript. Still however the early existence of this theme would not even then be proved, as these later poets occasionally made a form from analogy. But this ἀλέκω bears the same relation to the forms which we have seen above from the root ΑΛΚ–, as ὀρέγω does to ὄργυιά, ὀργή: see also Buttm. Lexilog. p. 132. From the aorist of this verb ἀλέξαι was formed the present in common use ἀλέξω, which then took again its own proper inflexion ἀλεξήσω. In the same way the similar verb ἀέξω, αὔξω, arose from the root ΑΕΓ– ΑΥΓ–, which beside that has produced only the Latin verb.

Ἀλέω ‡, *I bruise or stamp to pieces, grind*: fut. ἀλέσω, Att. ἀλῶ; imperf. ἤλουν; perf. act. Att. ἀλήλεκα; perf. pass. ἀλήλεσμαι, [altered by Bekker in Thucyd. 4, 26. to ἀλήλεμαι, but still an undoubted form in Amphis ap. Athen. 14. p. 462, A. and in Herodot. 7, 23.—Passow.] The later writers used in the present ἀλήθω, which however was still an ancient form. See Piers. ad Moer. p. 17. Lobeck ad Phryn. p. 151.

Ἀλέομαι or ἀλεύομαι, *I avoid*: Depon. midd. An active ἀλέω is doubtful. From this present we find ἀλεῦμαι for -οῦμαι, Theogn. 575. ἀλεύμενος, Simon. de Mul. 61. ἀλέοντο, ἀλέοιτο, Hom. ἀλευόμενος, Hes. ε, 533. ὑπαλεύεο, ib. 758. The aorist is the aor. 1. without σ: ἀλέασθαι and ἀλεύασθαι, ἠλεύατο, ἀλέαιτο, ἀλευάμενος, &c. The conjunctive therefore is as to form undecided between the pres. and aor. At Od. ξ, 400 ἀλεύεται is the conjunctive shortened according to the custom of

* Ἀλαλκών is, as far as I know, always correctly written thus, and with the infin. ἀλαλκεῖν will therefore prove ἤλαλκον, ἄλαλκον to be undoubted aorists; although the only Homeric passage of this indicative (Il. ψ, 185.) requires the imperfect. But then in Hes. θ, 527 it is as plainly an aorist. This single exception in Hom. may quite as likely arise from a false reading having crept in during the transmission of those very ancient poems, as from an indistinctness of tense: and as ἀμύνοι is a various reading for ἀλάλκοι at Il. φ, 138. 539., so may ἄμυνε have been the true reading in Il. ψ, 185.

† See note on ἤγαγον under Ἄγω. And Buttm. Lexilog. pp. 132 548.

‡ [Its root seems to be akin to ἔλω, ὀλαί, οὐλαί, *mola*, *molere*. Buttm. Lexilog. p. 259.]

the Epic poets*; and at *ω*, 29. the same form standing instead of the future may serve for the pres. indic. as well as the conjunctive.

In the Attic poetry occurs also an act. ἀλεύω with the regular aorist (ἤλευσα) ἀλεῦσαι. Its exact causative meaning, as deduced from that of ἀλεύομαι, is *to snatch away, protect*; and in this sense it is quoted from Sophocles in Lex. Seguer. 6. p. 383, 4. (ἀλεύσω, φυλάξω). In Æschyl. Sept. 141. also nothing is wanting to ἄλευσον but to supply ἡμᾶς: while ib. 88. and Suppl. 544. have the accus. of the evil *to be warded off*; and at Prom. 567. with ἄλευε either sense is admissible.

An Epic present is ἀλεείνω†, but with the meaning of the middle ἀλέομαι. Compare ἐρεείνω.

Ἀλῆναι, ἀλήμεναι. See Εἴλω.

Ἄλθομαι, *to heal*, i. e. *become healed*: [there is no known instance of the pres. act. or pass.—Passow.] imperf. pass. ἄλθετο, Il. ε, 417.; fut. ἀλθήσομαι, Il. η, 405.; but in this latter passage there are doubts both of the sense and reading: see Heyne. To this intransitive sense was added a causative one, *I heal*, i. e. *I cure*, which assumed different forms; ἀλθαίνω, ἀλθίσκω or ἀλθήσκω, ἀλθάσσω or ἀλθέσσω‡, whence the fut. ἀλθέξω, &c.; which forms are found in the Ionic prose of Hippocrates and others, but still need the help of the critic. See Foës. Œc. Hippocr.

Ἀλίνδω. See Κυλίνδω.

Ἁλίσκομαι, *I am taken*: imperf. ἡλισκόμην. Of this verb the *active* is not in use, but its place is supplied by αἱρεῖν, of which again ἁλίσκομαι is used as the passive, and always in the same or a cognate sense. It forms its other tenses from ἉΛΟΩ (compare ἀμβλίσκω), and with the additional irregularity, that *aorist* and *perfect* have the passive sense in the active form§: aor. ἥλων (Herodot. 3, 15. Xen. Anab. 4, 4, 21.), Att. ἑάλων‖, with α long; the other moods with α short, as opt. ἁλοίην (Il. χ, 253.), and Ion. ἁλῴην (Hom. sæpe), conj. ἁλῶ, ῷς, &c., infin. ἁλῶναι, part. ἁλούς;

* The Epics frequently shorten on account of the metre the long vowel of the conjunctive, changing *ω* and *η* back again into *ο* and *ε*; instances may be found in Il β, 440. ξ, 87. υ, 173. Od. α, 41. δ, 672. κ, 355.

† [It is generally used with an accus. but also with infin. Il. ζ, 167. ν, 356.—In Apoll. Rh. 3, 650. ἂψ ἀλεείνειν is intransit. *to retire*.—Schneid. and Passow.]

‡ [We find ἀλθίσκω twice in Hippocr. 7, 563. D. Ἀλθάσσω, Aretæus p. 61. B. Συναλθάσσω, Hippocr. p. 758. Ἀλθέσσω, Aret. 3, 13. Ἀλθέξεται, Aret. p. 42. C. Ἀλθεξις, Aret. 2, 1. and a various reading in Hippocr. 758. E.—Schneider.]

§ Thus the perfects ἔαγα, ἔρρωγα, *I am broken, torn*; in later writers πέπληγα, *I am struck*; in Hom. τετευχώς; and in the Lat. *vapulo*. See note p. 5.

‖ See note under Γιγνώσκω.

Perf. ἑάλωκα with α short [the usual form in Thucyd. and Demosth.]; Ion. and Att. ἥλωκα. The fut. is from the middle voice, ἁλώσομαι.—See Ἀναλίσκω.

The augment of ἑάλων deserves particular attention. It is not merely the syllabic augment before the vowel of the root, but, as this vowel is long in ἑάλων while it is short in ἁλῶναι, &c., the length of the α must be looked upon as a parallel case to the ω in ἑώρων. Besides, in ἥλων the regular augment is as old as the other, and as early as Homer (Od. χ, 230.) and Herodotus (7, 175. ἥλωσαν); while ἑάλων is properly the Attic form. In the perfect this is reversed; ἥλωκα is a strict Atticism; and ἑάλωκα the common form. See Dawes Misc. p. 315. and Piers. ad Moer. p. 178. But this ἑάλωκα is distinguished from ἑάλων by the quantity of the α, the reason of which it is difficult to ascertain*. Compare ἑόρακα and note under Ὁράω.

Homer has once (Il. ε, 487.) the long α in a form which has not the augment, the part. ἁλόντε, which appears to be the original quantity: compare ἀνᾱλίσκω.

Ἀλιταίνω, *to commit a fault, sin against*: fut. ἀλιτήσω; aor. act. ἤλιτον †, aor. mid. ἀλιτόμην. The act. and mid have the same meaning. [Homer uses only the above two aorists.]

The Epic language has also a participle used like an adjective, ἀλιτήμενος‡ in an act. sense, *sinning*, Od. δ, 807. Hes. α, 91 §. This form may be considered as a shortened perf. (for ἠλιτημένος) or a syncopated aorist (like βλήμενος): as regards its active sense we may compare it with the similar passive part. πεφυγμένος, ὀλόμενος.

* These, like many other irregular forms, had originally the digamma, and were therefore Ἐ-ϜΑΛΩΝ ϜΕ-ϜΑΛΩΚΑ, Ἐ-ϜΕΣΣΑΤΟ ϜΕ-ϜΕΣΤΟ. But when the digamma was changed to the aspirate, they took the augment according to the analogy of other aspirated verbs, consequently ἑ-άλων, whence ἥλων, as ἥρμοζον was formed from ἁρμόζω.

† See note on Αἰσθάνομαι.

‡ [Passow calls it a part pres. from an obsolete verb ἀλίτημι, ἀλίτημαι.]

§ I hope to defend ἀλιτήμενον Εὐρυσθῆα in this second passage against ἀλιτήμερον, which has been taken from the Scholium of Tzetzes and the Etym. Mag. v. ἠλιτόμενος. See Hermann in Add. ad Greg. Cor. p 879. The reading of the text has been always so generally preferred, that the emendation can be offered as nothing more than a various reading. But considered accurately I cannot acknowledge it to be such. The utmost we can draw from the Schol. of Tzetzes is that some old grammarians thought there was meaning enough in the common reading ἀλιτήμενον to explain it as synonymous with ἠλιτόμηνον, which Homer uses with reference to the same Eurystheus,) but not as an epithet,) so that ἀλιτόμηνος or ἀλιτήμενος might be each formed from μήν according to the difference of the rhythm. Let any one read now the gloss in the Etym. M. and he will see at once that the statement there given is the same, and that ἀλιτήμερος is an error of transcription: for in the whole passage nothing is mentioned but the derivation from μήν, whereas if the etymologist had really used the other word, he must have given his reasons for it.

'Αλίω. See Κυλίνδω.

ΑΛΚ-, ἀλαλκεῖν. See Ἀλέξω.

'Αλλάσσω, -ττω, *I change.* [Aor. 1. pass. ἠλλάχθην, always in Herodot., frequently in the Traged., sometimes in Aristoph.] Aor. 2. ἠλλάγην, common in Attic prose.

"Αλλομαι, *I leap.* Usage seems balanced between the two aorists, ἡλάμην, ἅλασθαι (with α long), and ἡλόμην, ἁλέσθαι (with α short): but the forms ἥλατο, ἁλάμενος and ἁλέσθαι, ἅλοιτο, appear to have the preference*.

The Epic language has the syncopated aorist, which takes the lenis, and from which come the 2. and 3. pers. ἆλσο, ἆλτο; part. ἄλμενος, ἐπάλμενος and ἐπιάλμενος†. The long α of the indicative of this form, which is shown by the circumflex, is an augment after the Doric manner; whence ἐπᾶλτο, not ἔπαλτο. The conjunct, which does not admit of such a syncope, is the conjunct. of the regular aor. 2. ἅληται, and this shortened (according to note on 'Αλέομαι) becomes ἅλεται, which some of the Grammarians have likewise written with the lenis, but on false grounds‡.

'Αλοάω, *I thrash*: fut. ἀλοήσω, and in the older Attics -άσω. The greater number of examples are in -ήσω: see

* See Fisch. ad Well. iii. a p. 29. On the 2. pers ἧλω and ἧλου see Erf. ad Œd Tyr. 1310. where Hermann now reads the imperf., which is very harsh in that passage.

† The Grammarians accounted for this lenis by the consonant following the λ; see Lex. de Spirit. p. 210. Valck. Their rule, like everything similar, is bad but when we consider that the same takes place in the metathesis ἁμαρτεῖν, ἤμβροτον, ἀβροτάζω, we see at once, without following the process throughout, that such changes had an influence on the aspirate; other changes of the same nature, though the reverse of the above (i. e. from the lenis to the aspirate), we may see in ἄρω, ἁρμόζω, in ὄρω, ὁρμάω, &c: see Buttm. Lexil. p. 300. No one with common sense will suppose that a grammatical caprice can have produced this old and fixed tradition.

‡ While the orthography of ἆλτο has been handed down invariably the same, that of ἅληται has been uncertain from the oldest times, as is clear from the Scholia on the Homeric passages (Il. λ, 192. φ, 536.) and the copies of the Grammarians In this however it is to be observed, that those who wrote ἄληται derived the word, inverting the usual way, from ἀλῆναι, although they could not decide between the two spiritus; see Schol. on both the above passages:—but those who classed the word with ἅλλεσθαι, did not change the aspirate; see Eustath. and Schol. Min. ad λ, 192. Now as the grounds for the spiritus of ἆλτο, which were touched on in the last note, cannot (look at them in what light we will) be applicable to ἄληται, so neither is there anything throughout to direct us to ἄληται with the lenis; and analogy therefore requires us to write ἅληται, and to join it to the regular aor. 2, which had as good a title, through that ἆλτο, to be admitted into the Epic language, as ὤρετο (to which belongs ὄρηται) has through ὦρτο. Beside the above, Homer has also once the aor. 1. ἐσήλατο, Il. μ, 438.

Valck. ad Ammon. 1, 4. p. 21. s. Lex. Seguer. p. 379, compared with p. 16. p. 270, 27. and Thom. Mag. in voc. [Att. ἀλοάω; Poet. ἀλοιάω.—Passow.]

'ΑΛΟΩ. See 'Αλίσκομαι and 'Αναλίσκω.

'Αλυκτέω and (Il. κ, 94.) ἀλαλύκτημαι, *I am uneasy, full of anxiety.* Beside Homer, Hippocrates, according to Erotian, used this present (compare Foes. Oec. Hipp. v. ἀλύζει); and ἀλυκταίνω (Etym. M.), ἀλυκτάζω (Herodot. 9, 70.), are analogous sister-forms. We abandon therefore all analogy when we attempt to make ἀλαλύκτημαι a present; while as perf. pass. it can still have the sense of the present increased in force; compare κεχάρημαι, τέτυγμαι, δεδακρυμένος; see also note on 'Ακαχμένος.—Quintus Sm. 14, 24. has also ἀλάλυκτο, which, if we may trust to a form of such a poet, is a nearer approach to the original theme. This verb must not however be classed with ἀλύσκω, ἀλύξω, but rather with ἀλύω and ἀλύσσω, which also mean a confusion and uneasiness of mind.

'Αλύσκω, *I avoid*: fut. ἀλύξω, &c. [Homer generally uses the fut. and aor. 1. ἤλυξα; in Hes. Fr. 22. we find ἄλυξεν; the midd. occurs only in Hes. ε, 365.—Passow.]

This verb is evidently formed from ἀλεύομαι. the κ therefore is not a radical letter with σ inserted, as in λάσκω, τιτύσκω; but it is the appendant verbal form in -σκω (as in φάσκω, &c.), which in its inflexion rejects the σ, as in διδάσκω.

The lengthened form ἀλυσκάζω* is a frequentative like ῥιπτάζειν, ἑρπύζειν. But this idea does not suit the aorist ἀλύσκασε, which has been the general reading of Od. χ, 330.; and Wolf was therefore right in adopting (from the Lex. of Apollon. and the Harl. MS.) the reading ἀλύσκανε; for the context requires the imperfect, and ἀλυσκάνω is lengthened in a perfectly analogical manner without any change of meaning.

'Αλύω, *I am beside myself*†, has only the pres. and imperf.

* [Homer uses the pres. and imperf., which thus supply the place of those tenses in ἀλύσκω.—Passow.]

† The only meaning of this verb is *to be beside oneself—either with grief or joy*; those who give it the sense of ἀλᾶσθαι are in error. in the two passages quoted by Schneider in his Lexicon (Il. ω, 12. Apoll. Rh 4, 1289.) as instances of this meaning, there is a verb of such a sense (δινεύεσκε, ἑρπύζοντες), but ἀλύειν refers only to distraction of mind.—On the doubtful aspirate, ἀλύειν, ἀλύειν, see Lex. Seguer. 6. p 380. [Passow calls ἀλύειν the Attic form, but says that the later Atticists kept to the older form ἀλύειν, Locella Xen. Eph. p. 172.]

This verb must not be confounded with the former one, as its meaning is always decidedly different. But the Homeric present ἀλύσσω, (Il. χ, 70.) appears to belong to it, although with some deviation or additional force of meaning.

'Αλφάνω or ἀλφαίνω, *I find, obtain.* It forms its tenses from ἄλφω (see note on Αἰσθάνομαι); thus aor. 2. ἦλφον, ἄλφοιμι, Hom. [Passow has both ἀλφαίνω and ἀλφάνω as presents, and cites in proof of the latter Eurip. Med. 301., the only passage of the Tragedians in which it is found; adding, on the authority of Elmsley, that it is more frequent in the Comedians. The Grammarians have also ἀλφάζω, ἀλφαίω, ἀλφάω, ἀλφέω, ἄλφω, Dor. ἀλφάδδω.]

'Αμαρτάνω, *I err*: fut. ἁμαρτήσομαι; perf. ἡμάρτηκα; aor. ἥμαρτον, infin. ἁμαρτεῖν; [the fut. act. ἁμαρτήσω is found only in the Alexandrians; the aor. 1. ἡμάρτησα only in later writers, Lobeck. Phryn. p. 732.—Passow.]

For ἥμαρτον the Epic language has often ἤμβροτον, ἀπήμβροτον, formed by transposition, by the change of α to ο, and the necessary insertion of β. See Buttm. Lexilogus, p. 82. &c. On the change of the spiritus compare the note on 'Αλτο.

'Αμάω, *I (mow and) collect together, bind up in sheaves.* —Midd.

The first α is long (Il. σ, 551. Hes. ε, 390.) and short (Il. γ, 359. Hes. ε, 763.), but the augment is always regular, ἤμων, &c. [According to Passow the first α in Hom. is long in the act. and short in the midd., while in later writers, as in Theocr. 10, 7. 10, 16. 11, 73. it is common.]

'Αμβλίσκω, *I have an abortion, miscarry*: fut. (formed from the less frequent ἀμβλόω) ἀμβλώσω; aor. 1. ἤμβλωσα; perf. ἤμβλωκα.

Euripides, among the older writers, has the pres. ἀμβλόω in Androm. 356.; and from this passage, viewed on one side of the question only, εἰ σὴν παῖδα φαρμακεύομεν Καὶ νηδὺν ἐξαμβλοῦμεν, ὡς αὐτὴ λέγει, arose the supposition that ἐξαμβλόω had a causative meaning with reference to the female, *to cause to miscarry*. But if we compare together the different passages of the simple and compound verb, the result is such a variety of relations, that a distinction so decided as the above disappears at once. The most common meaning is that where the female about to bring forth is the subject, as Plat. Theæt. p. 150. e. *ἀπελθόντες δὲ* (metaphorically transferred to scholars) *ἐξήμβλωσαν διὰ πονηρὰν συνουσίαν*. In Æl. V. H. 13, 6, 3. *βουλόμεναι ἀμβλῶσαι*, *wishing to miscarry*. In Plut. Lycurg. 3. *οὐκ ἔφη δεῖν ἀμβλίσκουσαν αὐτὴν—κινδυνεύειν*. But one who helps or injures may also be the subject, and then the production is generally the object expressed. In Plut. Arat. 32. metaphorically spoken of the fruits of the field, *καρποὺς ἀπαμβλίσκειν*. In Æl. ap. Suid. v. *ἐξήμβλωσεν*: *ἡ ἐλπὶς ἐξήμβλωτο αὐτῇ*. In Aristoph. Nub. 137. *ἐξήμβλωκας* (*ἡμῖν*) *φροντίδα*, and immediately afterwards *τὸ ἐξημβλωμένον*; again in Plat. Theæt. 149. d. *ἀμβλίσκειν* and *ἀμβλίσκουσιν* seem to have the midwives as their subject. And so in the passage of Euripides the phrase *ἐξαμβλοῦν τὴν νηδὺν* is very intelligible, particularly as a poetical expression, without its following as a necessary consequence that *ἐξαμβλοῦν γυναῖκα* had been also made use of. However, in all the passages quoted above, and also in the common meaning *to have an abortion*, the verb may be considered as a causative, if we imagine to ourselves an immediative sense, *to miscarry*, whose subject shall not be the mother, but the child; and as such we actually find an aor. 2. (or by syncope) in Suid. v. Ἤμβλω with a fragment of Ælian, *ἐξήμβλω ἡ ἔννοια τῷ ἀνοσίῳ**; which again is strongly confirmed by Pollux, in whose collection of the terms relating to this subject (II. c. 2.), instead of the untenable *ἀμβλῦναι*, *ἀμβλῶσαι*, we must read from the manuscripts *ἀμβλῶναι*, *ἀμβλῶσαι*.

Ἀμείβω, *I exchange*.—Midd. [The act. is seldom used by Homer, more frequently by the Attic writers.—Passow.]

Ἀμπέχω and Ἀμπισχνοῦμαι. See under Ἔχω.

Ἀμπλακίσκω, *I commit a fault*, *err*: fut. *ἀμπλακήσω*; aor. 2. *ἤμπλακον*, *ἀμπλακεῖν*†. The Doric dialect has *ἀμβλακίσκω*, &c.‡

Ἀμύνω, *I ward off*. The perf. is wanting both in the act.

* Under Ἐξήμβλωσεν we find, it is true, these same words with the form *ἐξήμβλωτο*; but beside that the pluperf. does not suit the context when completed as it is under Ἤμβλω, even this very Ἤμβλω speaks plainly in favour of the amended *ἐξήμβλω*.

† Verbs in *έω* sometimes have a present in *ισκω*, although their tenses are formed from the infin. of the aor. 2. in *εῖν*, as *εὑρίσκω*, *ἀμπλακίσκω*, *ἀπαφίσκω*, *ἐπαυρίσκομαι*.

‡ The present in *ισκω* occurs in Theagenes ap. Stob. Serm. 1. Schow. p. 22., where this editor has corrupted the old reading to *ἀμπλακέοντι*. Gaisford has given the whole paragraph from his manuscripts with *ἀμβλακίσκῃ* (for so he reads it) three times; but in the first-quoted passage *ἀμπλακίσκοντι*. The form *ἀμβλακεῖν* is also in Archilochus, 30. As to the other forms, *ἀμπλακεῖν* and some that come from it, found in the Tragedians with the first syllable *short*, are now written in such passages *ἀπλακεῖν* &c., in some measure from the representations of the old Grammarians. See Erf. ad Soph. Œd. T. 474. ed. min. Matth. ad Eurip. Iph. A. 124.

and pass.—MIDD.—Ἀμύναθον, ἀμυνάθειν, ἀμυναθοίμην, are formed from ἀμυνάθω, a lengthened form of ἀμύνω, like διωκάθειν, εἰργάθειν.

On these forms Elmsley (ad. Eurip. Med. 186.) was the first to observe that the pres. indic. in -άθειν never occurs; but he was hasty in adding that they are always aorists, and must therefore be accented in the infin. -εῖν. It is true that the examples quoted by him of ἀμυνάθειν have the momentary meaning of the aorist, but διωκάθειν, Plat. Euthyphr. p. 15. d. and ἐδιώκαθες, Gorg. p. 483. a. are quite as plainly in duration the pres. or imperfect. This particular formation belongs therefore to those cases in which the preterit was not clearly separated into imperfect and aorist, and which consequently in this relation take a direction according to the nature of the verb; as for instance the idea of διώκειν contains the duration in itself*.—More certain is it, that ἔσχεθον is always an aorist, and the same as ἔσχον; and the accentuation of the infinitive of this verb σχεθεῖν is confirmed by the Homeric σχεθέειν. But I do not therefore think we are justified in writing σχεθών, σχεθόντες, Pind. Pyth. 6, 19. Soph. El. 744; nay πέφνων (see observations on this verb in its place) ought to check such an arbitrary proceeding, and teach us not to hazard a decision on these traditionary points. See Elmsl. ad Eurip. Heracl. 272. Herm. ad. Soph. El. 744.

Ἀμφιέννυμι [and ἀμφιεννύω: fut. ἀμφιέσω, Att. ἀμφιῶ; aor. ἠμφίεσα, Poet. ἀμφίεσα.—Midd. ἀμφιέννυμαι, aor. ἠμφιεσάμην, whence 3. plur. ἀμφιέσαντο, Il., and imperat. ἀμφιέσασθε, Od.; perf. pass. ἠμφίεσμαι, less frequently ἀμφιεῖμαι. In prose the compound is more used than the simple.—Passow.] See Ἕννυμι.

Ἀμφισβητέω, *I am of a different opinion, dispute.* [Herodot 4, 14.: imperf. ἠμφισβήτουν; aor. ἠμφισβήτησα, Demosth.—Passow.]

As ἀμφισβητεῖν is compounded of ἀμφίς and βαίνω, ἠμφισβήτουν,

* Elmsley quotes, as an authority of the old Grammarians in favour of the aorist, the single gloss of Photius, ἠμύναθον, ἤμυναν; while he passes over in silence the great number of instances in all glossographers of such forms explained to be pres and imperf. But even if all these forms were really aorists, the accentuation of εῖν, ὼν must be a doubtful point, unless there be a precedent for it in the old Grammarians, as these aorists form a very peculiar analogy, which we are not justified in joining with the aor. 2. merely on account of the termination in ον.—As to that part of Elmsley's observation that the pres. indic. of these forms was not in use, the non-occurrence of those in particular, when the others are so frequent, is certainly of great weight; for of the other forms in θω the pres. indic. is found pretty frequently, for instance of πελάθω, the α of which belongs to the root, πελάθεις, -θει, in Eurip. Rhes. 557. Aristoph. Ran 1265. Thesm 58.

-ησα, -ηκα are regular formations; but the custom generally observed in compounds with ἀμφί caused quite early a false separation in the word, whence ἀμφεσβήτουν, and with double augment ἠμφεσβήτουν. Whether ἀμφεσβήτουν actually occurs I know not, but ἠμφεσβήτουν has been uniformly restored to the text of Plato by Bekker from the best manuscripts, and in the Etym. Mag. p. 94, 37, it is quoted from Plato, though altered by Sylburg without authority. And further, in the passage quoted there from Andocides de Myster. p. 4, 38. ἠμφεσβήτουν is the undoubted reading; for the whole context shows that it was so in both passages; as also Fischer ad Well. ii. p. 296. has observed, only that he, taking the words of the Grammarians still more literally, reads ἀμφεσβήτουν.

Ἀναίνομαι, *I refuse*: [imperf. ἠναινόμην, Poet. ἀναινόμην, and in later authors like Agathias, frequently ἀνηνόμην.—Passow.] aor. ἠνηνάμην, ἀνήνασθαι, conjunct. ἀνήνηται.

This is a verb in αἰνω formed from the negation ἀν (see Buttm. Lexil. p. 118.); its aorist is therefore quite regular, like ἐλυμηνάμην. The other tenses are not in use; for in Il. ι, 510. Theocr. 25, 6. where ἀνήνηται is quoted as a perfect, it is the aor. conjunct.

Ἀναλίσκω, *I employ; expend, consume*: imperf. ἀνήλισκον. The older form ἀναλόω is found in Thucyd. and the dramatic poets: imperf. without augm. ἀνάλουν, Thucyd. 8, 45. The other tenses are formed entirely according to the old form, as fut. ἀναλώσω, while the aor. and perf. have sometimes the augment, sometimes not; thus the Att. aor. is ἀνάλωσα, without augm. (Herm. Soph. Aj. 1028.), in the non-Attic writers sometimes ἀνήλωσα, sometimes ἠνάλωσα; in the same way the Att. perf. is ἀνάλωκα, the non-Att. ἀνήλωκα and ἠνάλωκα, Valck. ad Phœn. 591*. Perf. pass. ἀνάλωμαι, aor. pass. ἀναλώθην and ἀνηλώθην. The pres. ἀναλόω is rare.

This verb is distinguished from ἁλίσκομαι by the second α being invariably long†. And thence arises also the uncertainty of the augment, as the long α was sometimes read without any (see Ἀδῆσαι). Which of

* In Æschin. c. Timarch. p. 8. 9. ἀνάλωσε, ἀνηλωκώς, have a various reading, but one of no great authority.

† Notwithstanding this distinction, the similarity of meaning in ἁλίσκεσθαι *sumi* and ἀναλίσκειν *consumere*, and the relation of the aorists prove the actual identity of the root. The active form of ἁλῶναι, ἑαλωκέναι, shows for instance that the passive sense gave a neuter idea, as in the similar case of *vapulare*; and so the relation which the aor. 1. in ἀναλῶσαι bears to the above is causative, according to the leading analogy which I have drawn

the two forms was pure old Attic has been always a disputed point among the Atticists themselves, and one not easily to be decided: although among modern critics ἀναλ- was long the favourite. See Thom. Mag. with Hemsterh. note; Moeris. p. 25. Valck. ad Phœn. 591. Fischer ad Well. iii. p. 33 sqq. On the other side see Elmsl. and Herm. ad Soph. Aj. 1049 (1028.). In Isocrates Coray uniformly wrote, contrary to the preponderating authority of the manuscripts, ἀναλ-; and Bekker, following the Codex on which he places most reliance, has uniformly restored ἀνηλ-. For ἠνάλωσα in this semi-compound form there appears to be no authority whatever; but κατηνάλωσεν in Isocr. Euag. 22. (Bekker, 73), and κατηναλωμένα, Nicocl. 9. (Bekker, 37.), are established firmly by the same manuscript.

Ἁνδάνω, *I please*: imperf. ἑάνδανον, Herodot. 9, 5.; ἑήνδανον and ἥνδανον in Homer; aor. ἕαδον, Herodot. 1, 151. 4, 145. 153.*, εὔαδον, Hom. and ἅδον, Poet.; infin. ἁδεῖν, &c., all with α short; fut. ἁδήσω, Herodot. 5, 39.; perf. ἕᾱδα†. A passive voice does not occur; but in the Doric dialect is found a synonymous middle ἁδέσθαι in Fragm. Pythagor. p. 749, Gale. [We find also ἁνδάνεται, Archias Epig. 16.—This verb is mostly Ion. and Poet.—Passow.]

The Homeric aor. εὔαδον is to be explained by the digamma E-FAΔON ἔ-ἅδον ἕαδον. But F might be doubled on account of the metre, EFFAΔON, and, as it could not therefore entirely disappear from the verse, it passed over into the cognate υ, εὔαδον, as in καυάξαις under Ἄγνυμι‡.

The double augment ἑήνδανον follows the analogy of ἑώρων and ἑάλων, and therefore undoubtedly there were grounds for it in the old language, though hardly in the Homeric, in which the aor. was EFAΔON, EAΔON, AΔON. This was caused by the uncertainty of tradition in the old times of those dialectic forms; and from the same cause arose the confusion of ἑάνδανε and ἥνδανε in Herodotus. The pure Homeric forms, as soon as the digamma disappeared, were without doubt ἑάνδανεν, and, where ἥνδανε now stands, ἅνδανε; while that of Herodotus was ἥνδανον, according to the analogy of ὥρων.

We have merely to add that this verb, which is used only in the dialects and poets, is properly the same as ἥδω (compare λανθάνω, λήθω),

out in my Grammar; that is to say, to the analogy of δύω, ἔδυσα, δύσω,—ἔδυν, δέδυκα, δύσομαι, belongs, ἉΛΟΩ (I take), ἀναλόω, ἀνάλωσα, ἀναλώσω—ἑάλων, ἑάλωκα, ἁλώσομαι.

* In these three passages incorrectly quoted as a perfect by Fischer, 3. p. 21.

† On ἕᾱδε, Theocr. 27, 22. suspected as to tense, quantity, and accent, I can come to no decision.

‡ The idea of this form signifying *well-pleased*, is not to be entertained for a moment, as the above analogy proves. Had this been the case, we must have met with such expressions as ἅδεν εὖ, εὖ γὰρ ἅδεν.

and distinguished from it by nothing more than a slight deviation of meaning and a difference of construction.

Ἀνέσει [3. sing. fut. of ἀνίημι, Od. σ, 265. ; ἄνεσαν, 3. plur. aor. 2., Il. φ, 537 ; ἀνέσαιμι, opt. aor. 1. act., Il. ξ, 209.—Passow.]. These Epic forms compounded with ἀνά, and which, if we judge by their meaning, can be joined only with ἀνίημι, have this peculiarity, that they take ε instead of η in the future, with which they unite the regular formation of the aor. 1. in σα instead of κα. This form however appears to be used only where the preposition has the meaning of *again, back*, as *to bring back, send back*; while at Il. β, 276. ξ, 362. ἀνήσει, ἀνῆκεν have merely the sense of *to excite.* [Ἀνέσαντες, Il. ν, 657. is called by the best of the old Grammarians the part. aor. 1. act. of ἀνέζω, although both in form and meaning it belongs to the above.—Passow.]

Ἀνήνοθα, *I press forward*: a perfect with the sense of a present, the third person of which was also used as an aorist*. For its theme we must take ΑΝΘΩ or ΑΝΕΘΩ, a detailed account of which see in Buttm. Lexil. pp. 110. 133. &c.

Ἀνιάω, *I grieve or vex any one*: fut. ἀνιάσω, Ion. -ήσω. Passive with fut. midd. *I grieve or vex (myself)*. [Ἀνιῴατο, 3. plur. opt. pres. pass. in Herodot. 4, 130. This form is more frequent in prose than ἀνιάζω. In Homer the ι is always long, in later writers short also. The α of the penult. in pres. is always short, in fut. &c. always long; whence by the Ionic writers it was changed to η.—Passow.]

Ἀνοίγω. See Οἴγω.

Ἀντάω, *I meet*. In prose its compounds only are used, particularly ἀπαντάω, ἀπαντήσομαι (Xen. Hell. 1, 6, 3.), ἀπήντησα, &c.

For the Homeric ἤντεον we must not suppose any form in έω†: like μενοίνεον, ὁμόκλεον, it is Ionic for ἤντaον.—Of the barytone form in ω we find only the passive ἄντομαι, ἤντετο, with the same meaning as ἀντάω, but with no other tenses.

* Thus γέγωνα, *I call*, 3. pers. γέγωνε(ν), *he calls*, Od. ζ, 294., whence a new form in ον gives a 3. pers. ἐγέγωνε(ν), which, by dropping the augment, becomes again γέγωνε(ν); see Il. ξ, 469. ω, 703. Herein it is very conceivable that the meaning of this form fluctuates between the imperf. and aorist. Of this kind we have in Homer the following:
δείδιε pres. Od. π, 306.—imperf. Il. σ, 34.
ἄνωγε pres. Il. ω, 90.—aor. Od. ε, 276.
ἀνήνοθε pres. Od. ρ, 270.—imperf. Il. λ, 266.
ἐνήνοθε pres. Od. θ, 365.—imperf. Il. β, 209.

† [Passow however has ἀντέω, Ion. for ἀντάω.]

'Ανύω, Att. ἀνύτω*, *I complete*: fut. ἀνύσω, &c. The pass. takes σ.—MIDD.—[The α and υ are always short.—Passow.]

A more restricted Atticism was ἁνύω with the aspirate, καθανύω. See Piers. ad Moer. v. ἥνυσα. Lex. Seguer. p. 14. Hesych. v. καθανύσας.

Theocritus, 7, 10. has a syncopated form (or, which comes to the same, one formed from ἄνυμι,) ἄνῡμες, imperf. act., and at 2, 92. ἄνῡτο, imperf. pass. or midd. To the same formation belongs also the opt. pass. ἄνῡτο, on which see the following.

"Ανω, an older form of ἀνύω: used only in pres. and imperf. ἄνειν, Plat. Cratyl. p. 415. a. ἦνον, Od. γ, 496. ἄνοντος, Aristoph. Vesp. 369. ἄνομαι, *I draw to a close*, Il. κ, 251. Æschyl. Choeph. 788. (795.) Valck. Herodot. 7, 20. ἤνετο, Herodot. 8, 71.

This verb, with regard to quantity, is a solitary exception to the general rule, having its α uniformly long. Hence ἔργον ἄνοιτο, Od. σ, 473. must be left as an instance of Epic uncertainty: compare ἀμάω. But the opinion of Barnes is more probable, that the various reading ἄνῡτο is the true reading, as optat. of ἄνυμαι (see the preceding), like δαίνῡτο, Il. ω, 665. from δαίνυμαι: compare Od. π, 373. ἀνύσσεσθαι τάδε ἔργα.

"Ανωγα, *I command*; an old perfect, but which never has the augment of the perfect. Of the sing. are found only the 2. and 3. pers.; of the plur. only the 1. pers. with syncope, ἄνωγμεν, Hymn. Apoll. 528.—Pluperf. with the force of an imperf. (ἠνώγειν) ἠνώγεα, 3. pers. ἠνώγει.—To the perf. belong, according to the general analogy of perfects, other moods, as ἀνώγῃ, ἀνώγοις; infin. ἀνωγέμεν for ἀνωγέναι, and the imperat. ἄνωγε, Eurip. Or. 119. Callim. Fr. 440. But the more common imperat. is ἄνωχθι, formed from ἄνωγμεν as κέκραχθι from ἐκέκραγμεν; and again, by a similar formation, from ἀνώγετε (Od. ψ, 132.) and ἀνωγέτω (Od. β, 195.) came, by imitating the passive termination, ἄνωχθε (Hom.) and Eurip. and ἀνώχθω (Hom.)†.

The sense of the present introduced also the inflexion of a present; thus Homer and Herodotus (7, 104.) have 3. sing. pres. ἀνώγει, and Homer (Il. δ, 287.) has ἀνώγετον as indicative. Again ἤνωγον (Il. ι, 578.) or ἄνωγον (Il. ε, 805. Od. ι, 331.) is imperf. or rather aor., of which

* 'Ανύτω (like ἀρύω, ἀρύτω,) is the common form in the older Attics, so that for this dialect we may form ἀνύτω, ἀνύσω. But as ἀνύω, ἀνύσω, was the usual formation in the oldest Epic, as well as afterwards in the common language of the day, we had better take this as the leading form, and the other as a sister-form used only in pres. and imperf., just as γλύφω and γλύπτω. On these verbs, as well as on the false way of writing them in -ύττω, see Koen et Schæf. ad Greg. Cor. in Att. 26., Hemst. ad Plut 607., and the notes to Thom. Mag.

† See ἐγρήγορθε and note under 'Εγείρω.

the 3. pers. ἤνωγε stands full and complete in Hymn. Cer. 298. and Hes. ε, 68.; elsewhere it is always without an augment, consequently like the present (or perfect) ἄνωγεν or ἄνωγε, Herodot. 3, 81. To these were added a fut. ἀνώξω and aor. ἤνωξα, Od. π, 404. κ, 531. Hes. α, 479.

It were unnecessary to suppose a theme ἀνωγέω, from which to form the 3. sing. imperf. ἠνώγει; for this belongs to ἠνώγεα: but at Il. η, 394. we read also the 3. pl. ἠνώγεαν. This form however certainly crept into the text after the digamma, which followed in εἰπεῖν, had ceased to be perceived; whence Bentley proposed the simple alteration to ἤνωγον*.

A striking want of symmetry, and at the same time an uncertainty, but probably not attributable to the old poet, arises from the usage of the *third person* as it now exists in his writings. For we find not only as a pres. sometimes ἄνωγε(ν) from ἄνωγα, sometimes ἀνώγει (Il. ζ, 439. η, 74.) from a theme in ω, but also as a preterit either ἄνωγε(ν) from ἤνωγον, or ἀνώγει (Il. β, 280. δ, 301.) for ἠνώγει from ἠνώγεα. To reduce all this to uniformity and rule would be perhaps now impossible without some very arbitrary proceeding. At the same time there are strong grounds for suspecting ἀνώγει as a pres to be not Homeric, as it stands (without any reason for it) in the same expression and the same part of the metre as ἄνωγεν, e. g. θυμὸς ἄνωγεν, Il. ξ, 195. θυμὸς ἀνώγει, χ, 142., and in every instance it can be changed for ἄνωγεν, which has the oldest and surest analogy in its favour, and which in many cases is the reading of the manuscripts instead of the other, for instance in Il. ο, 180. σ, 176.†

Among the singularities of this verb we would call attention to its striking analogy with οἶδα. Both unite the sense of the present with the form of the perfect, neither of them has the augment, ἄνωγα, -ας, -ε, like οἶδα, -ας, -ε; the 1. plur. ἄνωγμεν answers to ἴδμεν, and in the imperat. ἄνωχθι, -θε, -θω answer to ἴσθι, ἴστε, ἴστω, only changing the τ into θ in the latter. The pluperf. with the force of an imperf. is (ἠνώγειν) ἠνώγεα, 3. sing. ἠνώγει, ἀνώγει, answering to ᾔδειν, ᾔδεα, ᾔδει. All these are original forms; the transitions to the pres. and imperf. (ἀνώγει; imperf. ἤνωγον, ἄνωγον; ἤνωγεν, ἄνωγεν, &c.) are of later usage. Ἄνωγα is therefore without doubt in sense as well as form an

* But whoever examines the whole context of that passage will perhaps agree with me in thinking it still more probable that ἠνώγει, supported by the same digamma, was copied from v 386. and used again here (v. 394) where Priam's words are repeated from v. 375.

† There would then remain of the pres in ω nothing in Homer but the above-mentioned ἀνώγετον, which again is very suspicious, as it is scarcely to be supposed that a writer who did not make use of ἄνωγας should have used ἀνώγατον

old perfect like οἶδα, although it may be impossible to disentangle it etymologically from the present, and discover from which sense of the present it comes. See Buttm. Lexil. p. 135.

'Απαντάω. See 'Αντάω.

'Απαυράω. See ΑΥΡ-.

'Απαφίσκω, *I deceive*: fut. ἀπαφήσω; aor. ἤπαφον, ἀπαφεῖν*: conj. ἀπάφω, &c.: the middle has the active sense, as in the opt. aor. ἀπάφοιτο, Od. ψ, 216. These aorists are reduplications from 'ΑΦΩ, whence ἀφή and ἅπτομαι, properly *to handle, stroke down, caress, palpo.* From these aorists was formed the present ἀπαφίσκω (Od. λ, 217. Hes. θ, 536.), as εὑρίσκω from εὗρον, εὑρεῖν; see note on 'Αμπλακίσκω: but of a new formation arising out of the same aorist (according to the rule laid down in a note on 'Ακαχίζω) nothing has been preserved except the aor. 1. ἐξαπάφησεν, Hymn. Apoll. 376. All the rest disappeared before the new verb ἀπατάω, ἀπατήσω, ἠπάτησα, which are now the only forms in Homer†.

'Απολαύω, *I enjoy*: [fut. ἀπολαύσω in Dion. Hal. and Lucian, but more generally] ἀπολαύσομαι, Xen.; aor. 1. ἀπέλαυσα, and aor. 2. ἀπέλαυον, Thucyd. and Xen.: but in later writers these aor. took, in addition to the syllabic, the temporal augment, thus ἀπήλαυον, ἀπήλαυσα‡, Isocr. ad Demon. c. 3. Ælian. V. H. 12, 25. Alciphr. 3, 53. It is true that Herodian in Hermann, p. 315., disapproves of these latter aorists; but when we see the other forms which that writer objects to, it only shows that these were very old and in common use. [An aor. midd. ἀπελαυσάμην nowhere occurs. The perfects are formed regularly, and are in Attic usage. A simple λαύω is not found; and probably ἀπολαύω comes from the same root as λαμβάνω, λαβεῖν.—Passow.]

'Απούρας. See ΑΥΡ-.

* As these are aor, not imperf., the correct accentuation of the part. is ἀπαφών (not ἀπάφων) as we find it in Hymn. Ven. 38. Eurip. Ion 705.: and other passages ought to be corrected according to these. As to the reduplication see note on ἀγαγεῖν under "Αγω.

† Nothing however is more probable than that these forms expelled at some later æra the old and genuine ἀπαφήσω, ἀπάφησεν. Homer certainly had only the subst ἀπάτη, which was formed by itself from 'ΑΦΩ, ἀφάω (see Buttm. Lexil. p 117), and from which again came the new verb ἀπατᾶν used in prose.

‡ See note under Βούλομαι.

Ἅπτω*, in both its senses, *I set fire to* and *I fasten*, is regular. From ἀφή we see that its characteristic letter is φ. Its second meaning is the causative one of *to hold firm*, which is the proper sense of the middle ἅπτομαι (Il. θ, 67.), and from which came the common meaning, *to touch*.

Ἑάφθη, or ἐάφθη (for the aspirate is doubtful), which occurs twice in Homer, viz. Il. ν, 543. ξ, 419., appears to belong to this verb; for if we compare at Il. β, 15. η, 402. φ, 513. the perf. ἐφῆπται (necessity, evil, death) *is fixed upon*, we must then take for ἐπὶ—ἐάφθη in both passages the physical meaning of *inflicta est*, *was struck upon*. But there are objections to this sense; and a very strong one as regards the form is this, that the separate augment εα is found in those verbs only which had the digamma, of which there is nowhere any trace in ἅπτω, ἅπτομαι. This form requires therefore a further examination. [It is fully examined in Buttm. Lexil. p. 242—246.]

Ἀράομαι, *I pray*, *curse*. The first α in the Epics is long, in the Attics short †.—Depon. midd.

There is one instance, Od. χ, 322., of an act. infin. ἀρήμεναι, which, as the context requires a past tense, like Od. δ, 378. and ξ, 134., must be an aorist. And the only way in which I can arrive at such a one is by supposing an old depon. pass. from the simple root (ἄρομαι), of which there remains nothing but this solitary instance of the aor. 2. pass. ἀρῆναι (with long vowel like ἐάγην) for ἀρήσασθαι; just as Homer uses elsewhere both the aor. pass. and aor. midd. of other deponents, of αἰδέομαι for instance.—Ἀρημένος is a very different word: see it in its alphabetical place.

Ἀραρίσκω, *I fit*. The simple theme ΑΡΩ is one of the most fruitful of the Greek radical verbs: from it are derived immediately the following, —ἀρέσκω, ἀρτάω, ἀρτύω, ἀρύω, αἴρω, ἁρμόζω, ἄρνυμαι. The pres. ἄρω never occurs. Its meaning is both transit. and intransit. according to which the tenses may be thus divided:

* [From an obsolete root ἄπω, answering to the old Latin *apo*, whence *apiscor*, *capio*, *capto*, and *apto*. Some (but without any grounds) consider ἅπτω, *I set fire to*, a different word from ἅπτω *I fasten*, deriving it from αὔω.—Passow.]

† The same holds good of the subst. ἀρά. But in Homer a regular distinction is observed between ἀρή with α long, meaning *a prayer* or *curse* (as at Il. ο, 598. Od. ρ, 496.), and ἀρή with α short, in the sense of *evil*, *destruction* (as at Il. μ, 334.) We must however remark that a third Homeric form ἀρειή, *harsh words*, *threatening* (Il. ρ, 431.) has α short. [Passow makes the above difference depend not on the meaning but on the position of the word in the verse; viz. in the *arsis* long, in the *thesis* short.]

1. *Transit.*—Act. fut. ἀρῶ, Ion. ἄρσω; aor. 1. ἦρσα, Ion. ἄρσα, infin ἄρσαι, part. ἄρσας, Hom. More used than the aor. 1. is the aor. 2. ἤραρον*, Ion. ἄραρον (˘˘˘), infin. ἀραρεῖν, part. ἀραρών, Hom. passim; and from this aor. 2., which in Hom. is twice intransit. also, comes the transit. pres. ἀραρίσκω (see note on ἀμπλακίσκω), which we see in the imperf. ἀράρισκεν, Od. ξ, 23.—Pass. perf. ἀρήρεμαι, to which may be joined both in formation and sense the new pres. ἀρέσκω; aor. 1. ἤρθην, of which Homer has only 3. plur. ἄρθεν for ἤρθησαν, Il. π, 211. Of the midd. we find the aor. 1. part. ἀρσάμενος, Hes. α, 320.

2. *Intransit.*—This sense, as arising from the continuity of action represented by the perfect, belongs to that tense almost exclusively; ἄρᾱρα†, (˘¯˘), Ion. and Ep. ἄρηρα‡, part. ἀρᾱρώς, Ion. and Ep. ἀρηρώς, fem. ἀρᾱρυῖα, but in the Epics ἀρᾰρυῖα§, with the second syllable short; pluperf. ἠράρειν (ᾱ), Ion. and Ep. ἀρήρειν or ἠρήρειν. The perf. has generally the sense of a present, the pluperf. that of an imperfect. But beside the perfect we have also two instances of the aor. 2 with an intransit. meaning, viz. Od. δ, 777. ἤραρεν ἡμῖν, *was pleasing to us*; and Il. π, 214., where we find both the meanings of this form within a line of each other, Ὡς ὅτε τοῖχον ἀνὴρ ἀράρῃ—Ὣς ἄραρον κόρυθες. In both passages we must not overlook the *momentary* sense of the aorist; in the former passage, "the proposal which was pleasing to us all," that is to say, *recommended itself* at the time of consultation: and in the latter it is a mere repetition of ἄρθεν which is in the preceding line, and which would have been literally repeated but for the intentional repetition of ὡς ἀράρῃ—ὣς ἄραρον; consequently the sense is, "so the helmets *fitted themselves* to each other" (compare Il. μ, 105. οἱ δ' ἐπεὶ ἀλλήλους ἄραρον); and the description then follows correctly in the imperf. ἀσπὶς ἄρ' ἀσπίδ' ἔρειδεν, &c.

Ἄρμενος, *fitting, suited,* is a syncopated aor. 2. midd, used as an adjective, exactly like the part. ἀρηρώς, Hom.—And in the same way as ἄρμενος and ἄρθεν with a passive formation had an intransitive or reflective meaning, there was also a perfect ἀρήρεμαι, (like ἀκήχεμαι and ὀρώρεμαι,)

* Formed with the reduplication; see note on ἀγαγεῖν under Ἄγω.

† The temporal augm. of the second syllable is sometimes omitted. In the poetical verb ἄρᾱρα however, which, from the mere formation of the perf. 2 and without any regard to the augment, ought to have the η in its middle syllable, and is therefore written in Ionic poetry ἄρηρα, the α in the Attic form is only a consequence of the ρ preceding (compare the termination ρα of the 1. declension, the contractions like ἀργυρᾶ, the fut in -ράσω), and the augment is therefore not so much omitted as invisible.

‡ At Od. ε, 248. we find ἄρηρεν transitive, but from the Scholia it is evidently a false reading for ἄρασσεν.

§ The lengthened vowel of the perf 2. may be shortened again, of which we have examples in the Epic participles σεσαρυῖα, μεμακυῖα, τεθαλυῖα, etc., where the ᾰ is restored in place of the η. In Hes. θ, 607. ἀρᾱρυῖαν is undoubtedly false for ἀρηρυῖαν.

of which we find the part. ἀρηρέμενος* with the accent thrown back on the antepenult. according to the note on ἀκήχεμαι under Ἀκαχίζω. The same perf. as a midd. with transit. meaning occurs in Hes. ε, 429. προσαρήρεται.†

For the aor. part. ἀρηράμενος see the last note.

The Greek verb, like the German *fügen* [*to fit*, and not unlike the English *to fit* and *to be fitting*], makes a metaphorical transition to the mind, with the meaning of *to be pleasing*. Thus Od. δ, 777. ὃ δὴ καὶ πᾶσιν ἐνὶ φρεσὶν ἤραρεν ἡμῖν. Soph. El. 147. ἐμὲ...ἄραρε φρένας. Il. α, 136. ἄρσαντες κατὰ θυμὸν, where we must understand ἐμὲ τῷ γέρᾳ, and compare it with πώμασιν ἄρσον ἅπαντας (τοὺς ἀμφορέας) Od. β, 353. and ἤραρε θυμὸν ἐδωδῇ, ε, 95. It is clear therefore that ἀρέσκω, ἀρέσω, which is used in the same sense, comes from this ΑΡΩ with the inflexion -έσω.

Ἄρδω, *I water*: fut. ἄρσω, &c. It has no perf., and in the passive neither perf. nor aor. For its meaning see Buttm. Lexil. p. 157.

Ἀρέσκω, *I please* (compare Ἀραρίσκω): fut. ἀρέσω [midd. ἀρέσομαι, Poet. ἀρέσσομαι; aor. 1. ἤρεσα, midd. ἠρεσάμην, Poet. ἄρεσσα, ἀρεσσάμην; aor. pass. ἠρέσθην]; perf. ἤρεσμαι. —Midd.

Sextus (adv. Gr. 10, 266.) quotes the perf. act. ἀρήρεκα as in common use.

Ἀρημένος, *hurt*, *injured*: a solitary part. perf. with α long, Od. ι, 403. σ, 53, &c. [The ancients explained it by βεβλαμμένος. It is of

* This participle occurs three times in Apollon. Rh. 1, 787. 3, 833. 4, 677. where Brunck changed it into an aor ἀρηράμενος, which was a reading of the first passage in some manuscripts. Now from ἄρηρα it may be allowable to derive a pres. ἀρήρομαι; but for an aor 1. formed again from this pres. or immediately from the perf. I know neither proof nor authority. for I do not reckon as such Quintus Sm., who has this ἀρηράμενος frequently, and read it so in Apollonius. In the first of the three passages quoted above the aor. 1. would be unnatural.

† The word however is suspicious in this passage. That is to say, its construction there depends on εὖτ' ἄν, and it is therefore conjunct for προσαρήρεται. But in such a context as "after he...has fitted together," the perf. of the conjunct is in Greek contrary to all analogy, and only the conjunct. aor. (εὖτ' ἂν...ἀράρῃ) is admissible. In this case ἀρήρεται must therefore be the conjunct of ἀρηράμην, which Brunck indeed thought he had found in Apollonius, though he had not only no grounds for it, but the sense was intransitive. If we look for an aor. which might supply the place of ἀράρῃ in the metre, a comparison of ἀρσάμενος in Hes Scut. 320. used likewise of fitting a piece of workmanship, will furnish us with ἄρσηται, ἄρσεται. Perhaps therefore the old reading was πρὸς ἄρ' ἄρσεται ἱστοβοῆι. Some Codd of Lanzi have προσαρήσεται.

doubtful origin: the derivation from ἀράω, ἀράομαι is very uncertain, but its connection with ἀραιός undoubted.—Passow.]

Ἀριστάω, -ήσω, &c. Of this verb we find two remarkable forms used in familiar Attic quoted from some lost comedies by Athenæus (10. p. 423.), ἠρίσταμεν, ἠριστάναι, and from δειπνεῖν two, δεδείπναμεν, δεδειπνάναι, which appear to have been formed similarly because they were words of similar meaning; for the α in δεδειπνάναι cannot be regularly derived from δειπνέω, δεδειπνηκέναι. See Mus. Antiq. Stud. I. p. 249.

Ἀρκέω, *I suffice*: fut. ἀρκέσω, &c. The passive, which has the same meaning as the active, takes σ.

Ἁρμόττω, and ἁρμόζω, *to fit*: fut. ἁρμόσω, &c.—Midd.

Many verbs with σσ or ττ have for their characteristic letter a labial instead of a palatic, which in most of them can only be known by their taking in the inflexion a single σ instead of the ξ, γ, κ, χ of the other verbs in σσω. The principal verbs of this kind in prose are πλάσσω, πάσσω, πτίσσω, ἐρέσσω, βράσσω, βλίττω, and ἁρμόττω, for which last ἁρμόζω is also used. In poetry κορύσσω, ἱμάσσω and λίσσομαι. To these we may add two which partake of both characteristics, viz. νάσσω, fut. νάξω, &c.; but perf. pass. νένασμαι; verbal adj.ναστός,—and ἀφύσσω, an Epic word of which Homer has the fut. ἀφύξειν, but in the aor. ἤφυσα, &c.

Ἀρνέομαι, *I deny*: depon. pass. with fut. midd. ἀρνήσομαι (Eurip. Ion. 1026.), and aor. pass. ἀρνηθῆναι; the aor. midd. ἀρνήσασθαι is generally Poet. but occurs also in Herodot. 3, 1. Æschin. Ctesiph. 81.

Ἄρνυμαι, *I acquire, gain by my exertions*, a lengthened form of αἴρω, as πτάρνυμαι is of πταίρω: it is a defective deponent, used only in the pres. and imperf., and takes its other tenses from αἴρομαι, fut. ἀροῦμαι: compare Il. ζ, 446. with σ, 121., and χ, 160. with ι, 124.

Ἀρόω, *I plow*: fut. ἀρόσω, &c.; but, contrary to analogy*, it takes no σ in the passive. It has the Att. reduplication. The Ionic perf. pass. is ἀρήρομαι, part. ἀρηρομένος, Hom. and Herodot. The Ionic inf. pres. is ἀρώμεναι, ἀρόμεναι, or ἀρόμμεναι, Hes. ε, 22.†

* Verbs which do not lengthen their vowel in the future take a σ in their perf. passive, as τελέω, έσω—τετέλεσμαι, ἀνύω, -ύσω—ἤνυσμαι, -σπάω, -άσω—ἔσπασμαι.

† The text and many MSS. have ἀρόμ-

Ἁρπάζω, *I carry off by violence*: fut. Att. ἁρπάσω, Xen. Mag. Eq. 4, 17., also fut. midd. ἁρπάσομαι, Xen. Cyr. 7, 2, 5. Aristoph. Pac. 1120.; aor. 1. act. ἥρπασα, aor. 1. pass. ἡρπάσθην. Also in common use, but later than the former, a fut. ἁρπάξω, aor. 1. act. ἥρπαξα, aor. 2. pass. ἡρπάγην. Homer has both formations.

A form ἁρπάμενος (according to the analogy of οὐτάμενος, κτίμενος, &c.) is found in the later poets, as in Nonnus and the Anthologia (Cod. Vat. pp. 462. 516.).

Ἀρτάω, *I hang, fasten on*: fut. ἀρτήσω, &c.—Midd.

Ἀρύω, Att. ἀρύτω, *I draw* or *dip up*: fut. ἀρύσω, &c. See note under Ἀνύω. The pass. takes σ.—Midd. The υ is always short.

Ἄρχω, *I am the first, take the lead, command.* The midd. has the same meaning; but in the Attics (with the exception of Soph. El. 522.) that voice alone has the sense of *to begin*. The act. is common in Homer, Hesiod, Herodotus and Pindar.

ΑΡΩ. See Ἀραρίσκω.

Ἀσάομαι, *I feel disgust* or *dislike*: generally a depon. pass. [The aor. 1. pass. ἀσηθῆναι occurs in Herodot. 3, 41., the aor. 1. midd. ἄσασθαι φρένα in Theogn. 567.] The act. ἀσάω is more rare, Theogn. 593, Bekker. Galen. ap. Foes. in voc. Ἀσσάομαι, Hippocr.

Ἀσπάζομαι, *I greet*: fut. ἀσπάσομαι, &c.—Depon. midd.

Αὐδάω, *I speak*: fut. -ήσω, Att. -άσω. The tenses principally in use are the imperf. 3 pers. ηὔδα as aorist, and the aor. 1. αὐδῆσαι. Pindar (Ol. 2, 166.) uses αὐδάομαι as a depon. midd., as does Soph. Aj. 772. Phil. 130. 852.

μεναι, many have also ἀρόμεναι, which was the only reading of the Scholiasts, who *merely recommend* its being read and written in the former way. This ἀρόμεναι is by syncope for ἀροέμεναι, and may be therefore classed with ἔδμεναι and εἰρύμεναι. But a great number of the MSS. have according to Lanzi ἀρώμεναι, and it was and still is a question for the critic in what way the oldest writing ΑΡΟΜΕΝΑΙ is to be read. Now surely the same criticism, which in Homer from καλέω, καλέσω wrote κἀλήμεναι, could not in Hesiod from ἀρόω, ἀρόσω write ἀρόμεναι or ἀρόμμεναι. The reading ἀρώμεναι, which undoubtedly came from some old critic, deserves therefore, on account of its analogy with those Homeric forms, our maturest consideration.

As the Doric dialect is not used by Herodotus, αὐδάξασθαι, ηὐδάξατο in Ionic prose must be formed from a pres. αὐδάζομαι. The act. αὐδάζω, -άξω, occurs in Lycophr. 892.

Αὔξω, and αὐξάνω, *I increase, add to*: fut. αὐξήσω, &c.: see note under Αἰσθάνομαι. Pass. with fut. midd. *I increase, grow.* [Passow says the act. has a transit. sense, but in the Poets frequently intransit. Musgr. Soph. Œd. T. 1085. Erf. and in N. T. e. g. Luc. i. 80. The fut. midd. has a pass. meaning. The regular fut. act. αὐξανῶ is found only in the LXX.]

In the Epic language the sound of this αὔξω is ἀέξω; but it occurs only in the pres. and imperf. See 'Αλέξω, toward the end.

ΑΥΡ-. To this root, with the original idea of *to take*, belong two compounds*:

1. ἀπαυράω, *I take away*. Of this verb we find only the imperf. (with the meaning of an aorist) ἀπηύρων, ἀπηύρας, ἀπηύρα, all three in Homer; and (from a theme ΑΥΡΩ) an aor. 1. midd. ἀπηύρατο, Od. δ, 646., but with a various reading ἀπηύρα. Connected by meaning with the above forms are also the participles aor. 1. act. ἀπούρας, and midd. with a passive sense ἀπουράμενος, (Hes. α, 173.) by a change of vowel which never occurs elsewhere†.

2. ἐπαυρίσκομαι, *I reap advantage or disadvantage from, enjoy*; depon. midd.: fut. ἐπαυρήσομαι, Il. ζ, 353.; aor. act. ἐπηῦρον, Dor. ἐπαῦρον, Pind. P. 3, 65. [of this aor. Homer has only 3. pers. conjunct. ἐπαύρῃ, Il. λ, 391. ν, 649. and infin. ἐπαυρεῖν, ἐπαυρέμεν, Il. λ, 573. σ, 302. Od. ρ, 81.]; aor. midd. ἐπηυρόμην, Eurip. Hel. 476. [of this aor. Homer has only the 2. pers. conjunct. ἐπαύρηαι, ἐπαύρῃ, Il. ο, 17. Od. σ, 107. and 3. plur. ἐπαύρωνται, Il. α, 410.]; infin. ἐπαυρέσθαι, Eurip. Iph. T. 529. and in non-Attic writers ἐπαύρασθαι‡, Hippocr. Jusjur. 3. and elsewhere.

* See both examined more at length in Buttm. Lexil. p. 144. &c.

† If I am right in my conjecture (Lexil. p. 145. &c.) we may add a future also in the various reading ἀπουρήσουσιν (Il. χ, 489. where the common reading is ἀπουρίσσουσιν,) from a verb, which does not occur again in Homer, ἀφορίζω; under which some of the Grammarians, contrary to all analogy, place also the acknowledged form ἀπούρας.

‡ See last paragraph under Αἱρέω.

The infin. pres. ἐπαυρίσκεσθαι (Il. ν, 733.) occurs frequently in Hippocr. The pres. ἐπαύρομαι, which was supposed for some other purpose, (whence the accentuation ἐπαύρεσθαι,) does not occur; ἐπαύρωμαι is conjunct. aor. The pres. act. ἐπαυρίσκω is found only in Theogn. 115.: no pres. ἐπαυράω or ἐπαύρω exists. Hesiod. ε, 417. has ἐπαυρεῖ from ἐπαυρέω. The active forms are found only in the Epic and Lyric poets; the midd. passed over to the usage of the Attics also.

Compare the different tenses of this verb and its meaning with the verb εὑρίσκω, which differs from it only in the diphthong, as εὔχομαι and αὐχέω.

Αὔω, *I call out, sound aloud.* This present occurs only as a dissyllable; but the other tenses (as if formed from ἀΰω) are fut. ἀΰσω, aor. ἤϋσα, infin. ἀῦσαι, with υ long. From the subst. ἀϋτή, *a cry*, comes in the Epic and Tragic poets a new pres. ἀϋτέω, also with long υ.

Αὔω, *I kindle*; Att. αὔω; αὔοι, Od. ε, 490. Αὔηται, *takes fire*, Arat. 1035. (Diosc. 333.) Thence in prose

Ἐναύω, *I kindle*. Herodot. 7, 231. Xen. Mem. 2, 2, 22. The pass. probably takes the σ, whence ἔναυσμα.—MIDD. Ἐναυσάμενος, Ælian.

This compound has, I believe, no augment, a point however not proved by the instance from Herodot. 7, 231. οὔτε οἱ πῦρ οὐδεὶς ἔναυε.

This verb is incorrectly supposed to be the same as αὔω, or αὔω, *I roast*, but which in the common language was εὕω: see this verb. Akin to αὔω is αὐαίνω*, *I dry*; and therefore this third αὔω must be considered as a separate verb from the two others.

Ἀφάω or ἀφάω, *I handle*: ἀφόωντα, Il. ζ, 322.; but in the later Ionic writers ἀφάσσω, as we find the part. pres. ἀφάσσουσα, and the aor. 1. 3. pers. ἤφασε, imperat. ἄφασον, Herodot. 3, 69. A pres. ἀφασσάω, and some other forms which have not yet been examined critically, occur in Foes. Œc. Hippocr. in voc.—Compare Ἀπαφίσκω.

Ἀφύσσω, *I draw off liquor*, &c.: fut. ἀφύξω; aor. 1. ἤφυσα, Od. ι, 165.; poet. also ἄφυσσα; aor. midd. ἠφυσάμην, Od. η, 286. For the rule of formation see Ἁρμόττω.

Ἄχθομαι, *I am loaded*, metaph. *vexed*: pass. without any act. in use; generally with fut. midd. ἀχθέσομαι, Aristoph.

* Verbs beginning with α, αυ, οι, followed by a vowel, do not take the augment; as ἀΐω, ἄημι, ἀηδίζομαι, αὐαίνω, οἰόω, οἰακίζω, οἰωνίζομαι: but the α if short becomes long, as ἄϊον, αὐαίνετο, οἰάκιζεν, &c.—By ἐπαφαυάνθην, (Aristoph. Ran. 1089.), we see that αὐαίνω in the Attic pronunciation had the aspirate.

Nub. 865. 1432. Av. 84., but sometimes ἀχθήσομαι; aor. 1. ἠχθέσθην (Od. ο, 457.), whence also the pass. fut. ἀχθεσθήσομαι: see Piers. ad Moer. p. 21.

ΑΧΩ, ἀχέω. See Ἀκαχίζω.

Ἄω. This theme appears under four different meanings:—

1. *I blow*. 3. pers. imperf. ἄεν, Apollon. Rh. 1, 605. But the pres. ἄημι is more usual, of which 3. sing. ἄησι, Hes. ε, 514., infin. ἀῆναι, ἀήμεναι, part. ἀεὶς, ἀέντος; imperf. 3. sing. ἄη, Od. μ, 325. but at ε, 478. τ, 440. we find διάει. Midd. ἄημαι, ἀήμενος; 3. sing. imperf. ἄητον. In the dual pres. ἄητον (Il. ι, 5.) and the infin. pres. we find the η retained, contrary to the analogy of τίθημι. This passive form has the active sense except at Od. ζ, 131. where it means *to be blown through*.

In the Etym. M. is quoted 3. pl. ἄεισι, and the explanation of its being Æolic for ἀεῖσι is proved by reference to Hes. θ, 875. Much the same is said by the Schol. Il. ε, 526., in Heyne vol. 5. p. 712. Ἄλλαι ἄεισι was therefore an old-established reading there (see the various readings), and ἄεισι without doubt a genuine form.

2. *I sleep*: aor. ἄεσα, contr. ἆσα, Od. τ, 342. π, 367. [This verb is the root of αὔω, ἰαύω, ἀωτέω.—Passow.]

3. *I satiate*. From the pres. come the following infin. act. ἄμεναι, (Il. φ, 70.) contr. from ἀέμεναι for ἄειν; 3. pres. pass. ἆται (Heysch), and by resolution ἄαται, Hes. α. 101., where it stands as a future*. Fut. ἄσω, aor. ἆσα, infin. ἆσαι; with the midd. ἄσεσθαι, ἄσασθαι; although the active form also occurs in the intransitive or middle sense, *I am satiated*, like the above-mentioned ἄμεναι and ἆσαι, Il. ο, 317. ψ, 157, &c. Verbal adj. ἀτός, and with α priv. ἄατος, contr. ἆτος, *insatiable*. On these forms see Buttm. Lexil. p. 2.

By old grammatical tradition the conjunct. ἑῶμεν or ἕωμεν (Il. τ, 402.) is attached to this verb, consequently it is for ἄωμεν or ὦμεν: see Etym. M. v. ἄδην, and Buttm. Lexil. p. 26.

There are no grounds for adopting the radical ΑΔ- as is generally done; on which, and on the relations of this verb to ἀδῆσαι, see Buttm. Lexil. p. 22, &c

4. *I hurt*; aor. 1. ἆσα. See Ἀάω.

Ἄωρτο. See Αἴρω.

* There are sufficient grounds for this future, but some doubts about the resolution. see Buttm. Lexil. p. 142 where he has enlarged on the probability of the ἆται of Hesych. being taken from this passage.

B.

Βάζω, *I speak*: fut. βάξω; and 3. sing. perf. pass. βέβακται, Od. θ, 408.

Βαίνω, *I go*: fut. βήσομαι, Dor. βᾱσεῦμαι; perf. βέβηκα (whence the syncopated forms βεβάασι, βεβᾶσι); infin. βεβάμεν, part. βεβαώς, βεβαυῖα, contr. βεβώς, βεβῶσα, βεβώς; which forms are rare except in the poets: Homer has the Epic βεβάᾱσι, part. βεβᾰώς, βεβᾰυῖα, infin. βεβάμεν. The aor. 2. ἔβην* is like ἔστην, therefore ἔβημεν, &c., imperat. βῆθι, conjunct. βῶ, optat. βαίην, infin. βῆναι, part. βάς, βᾶσα, βάν. [Homer has also βάτην (ᾰ) for ἐβήτην; and in 3. plur. βάν and ἔβαν for ἔβησαν†. Aor. midd. ἐβήσετο, more rarely ἐβήσατο.] Some compounds have also a passive, e. g. παραβαίνω, παραβέβαμαι, παρεβάθην. Verbal adj. βατός.

The pluperf. ἐβεβήκειν has in Homer almost always the sense of *went*, for which as imperf. the plainest passages are Il. ζ, 313. 495. 513. π, 751. Od. ρ, 26.; while at Od. ν, 164. it must be understood as an aorist; and the only clear instance of its pluperfect sense is in the expression ἄιδόσδε βεβήκει, Od. γ, 410. ζ, 11. Compare Heyne ad Il. δ, 492.

In addition to the perf. pass. παραβέβαμαι we must mention παραβέβασμαι in the spurious oration of Demosth. De Fœd. Alex. p. 214. extr., and in later writers βήσω, ἔβησα, in a causative sense and also in the common language; e. g. ἐπιβῆσειν, Lucian Dial. Mort. 6, 4.

On the unusual particip. pres. of βάω we have only to say, that it occurs in anapæstic verse in Cratinus (προβῶντες), and in a causative sense in the Doric treaty in Thucyd. 5, 77. (ἐκβῶντας).

The 2. pers. imperat. of the aor. 2. was also shortened by the Attics in the compounds (as in ἵστημι, ἀνάστα) κατάβα, Aristoph. Vesp. 979. πρόβα, Acharn. 262.

The Epic forms (βέβαα) βεβαώς, βεβαυῖα, and the 3. plur. βεβάασι are formed from the perfect by omitting the κ, as in κεκαφηώς, τετιηώς, κεχαρηώς, βεβαρηώς, τετληώς, πεπτηώς, τετμηώς, κεκμηώς: this must therefore have been a rule in the Ionic language, as it is not done on account

* See note under Γιγνώσκω.

† For the short α in βάν and ἔβαν see Διδράσκω toward the end and note.

of the metre: and in the cases of βέβηκα, ἕστηκα, πέφυκα, the vowel is also shortened. These and other abbreviated forms of this verb (βέβᾰμεν for βεβά-αμεν, infin. βεβάναι with α short for βεβα-έναι, &c.) are seldom found except in the dialects and poets. The conjunct. βεβῶσι, part. βεβῶσα, occurs in Plat. Phædr. p 252. (ἐμβεβῶσι) 254.; the infin. συμβεβάναι, ἀποβεβάναι, are found in Herodot. 3, 146. 5, 86.

In the aor. 2. Homer has some forms with α instead of η short, βάτην for ἐβήτην, ὑπέρβασαν for ὑπερέβησαν; with these we may compare many other words in which the Ionians changed the η into short α, as πάρη* for πήρα, ἀμφισβᾰτέω, ἀμφισβᾰσίη, for -ητέω, -ησία, and μεμᾰκυῖα from μέμηκα. On the other hand βᾰτε in Æschyl. Suppl. 206. in the iambics is one of the solitary instances of a Doricism† in the Tragic language. In Theocr 15, 22. βᾰμες for βῶμεν is an unusual Doricism. The 1. sing. aor. 2. conjunct. βέω and βείω for βῶ, and 3. pers. βήῃ for βῇ, &c. are Ionic and Epic resolutions, like στείω, στήῃς, στήητον, &c., θείω, θείωμεν, &c., δαμείω, &c.

Beside the fut. midd. the Epics have also the aor. midd. in the same sense, but varying in form, ἐβήσατο and ἐβήσετο‡, imper. ἐπιβήσεο. Of these the second would appear to be the only correct form in Homer, according to a note in Buttm. Lexil. p. 226.; the first might have been used in a causative sense for ἔβησεν, but for this I find no other authority in Homer than ἀναβησάμενοι, Od. ο, 474.

See the form βέομαι, βείομαι, in its place.

This verb has in the Ionic dialect and the Poets the causative sense also *I cause to go*, i. e. *bring, carry, remove*, a meaning which otherwise belongs to βιβάζω. The fut. act. and the aor. 1. are the only tenses which have this meaning; but in the compounds it appears to belong also to the aor. 1. midd., as νὼ ἀναβησάμενοι, *taking us into his vessel*, Od ο, 475. Of other forms I know of only two instances, ἐπιβῆτον, Od. ψ, 52., and καταβαίνει, Pind. Pyth. 8, 111: for βαίνω πόδα and such kind of expressions (see Seidler on Eurip. El. 94.) appear to me only a liberty taken with the syntax, in which the Greek poets occasionally indulged themselves, and no change of meaning in the verb βαίνω. The Epic sister-form βάσκω has also both senses; βάσκ' ἴθι, *go*; ἐπιβασκέμεν, *to bring into*, Il. β, 234.

The Epic language has also the form βιβάω, βίβημι, which it uses in the sense of *I stride*, of which however we have only the pres. βιβᾷ (Hymn Merc. 225), and the part. βιβῶν, βιβῶσα, (Il. γ, 22. Od. λ,

* See Heraclid. ap. Eust. Il α, 24. p. 22, 14. Od. μ, 89. p. 478, 12. Basil.

† We always find for instance in the Tragedians Ἀθάνα, ποδαγός, κυναγός, and sometimes ναός, the Doric gen. of ναῦς.

‡ See ἐδύσετο toward the end of Δύω.

539.) βιβάς (Il. η, 213). [To these Passow adds ἐβίβασκε, Ion. imperf. Hymn. Apoll. 133.] Now if we take this as a present instead of βαίνω, the whole verb corresponds exactly in formation with ἵστημι, and both have the fut. and aor. 1. in the causative sense.

Βάλλω, *I throw*: fut. βαλῶ, and sometimes (but not in the early writers) βαλλήσω, Aristoph. Vesp. 222. 1482. with the aor. 1. ἐβάλλησα; the usual aorist is the aor. 2. ἔβαλον, midd. ἐβαλόμην; perf. βέβληκα, perf. pass. βέβλημαι*, Epic βεβόλημαι also; aor. 1. pass. ἐβλήθην.—Midd.

Βαλλέειν is an Ionic resolution of βάλλειν; thus we find ὑπερβαλλέειν, συμβαλλεόμενος, Herodot.

From a syncopated aor.† ἔβλην come the Epic forms ξυμβλήτην (Od. φ, 15.), ξυμβλήμεναι infin. for -ῆναι, (Il. φ. 578.); pass. ἔβλητο, &c., βλῆσθαι, βλήμενος; conjunct. βλήεται for βλήηται, Od. ρ, 472.; optat. βλείμην, βλεῖο‡, &c.; and a future βλήσομαι, Il. υ, 335.

All these forms, beginning with the perfect βέβληκα, arise from the metathesis of ΒΑΛ to ΒΛΑ§; nor is it any objection to this that the optat. has the diphthong ει, as we see the same change from the vowel of the root α in other cases, for instance in a precisely similar one under πίμπλημι and in χρή (χράω). Besides in the verb before us the old original form was ΒΕΛ (by metath. ΒΛΕ), as shown in the derivative βέλος, and more particularly in the verbal adjective βελέτης in ἑκατηβελέτης. Compare τέμνω τάμνω, τρέπω τράπω, and σκέλλω.

From the same old stem or root too, by that change of vowel which is the most usual, come the verbal substantive βόλος, and the common Epic perf. pass. βεβόλημαι.

Βάπτω, *I dip*: fut. βάψω; perf. pass. βέβαμμαι; aor. 2. pass. ἐβάφην. The characteristic letter is φ.

* We know that in general there is no conjunct. or optat. of the perf. pass., partly from the difficulty of forming them, partly from their being seldom wanted, but that they are made up of the participle and a tense of εἶναι. There are cases however where, for the sake of greater expression, of clearness, or of conciseness, such moods are *formed*. Thus διαβέβλησθε, Andocid. p. 22, 41. ἐκτέτμησθον, Plat. Rep. 7. p. 564. c.

† See note under Γιγνώσκω.

‡ The various reading βλῇο arises from a twofold opinion of the old Grammarians; ἐβλήμην, optat. βλῄμην or βλείμην; but the connection of these passive with the corresponding active aorists, as shown in a note near the end of Γιγνώσκω, and the prevailing form of the optative σβείην, βαίην, γνοίην, are decisive in favour of βλεῖο. Compare πλείμην under Πίμπλημι.

§ As in θνήσκω, θανοῦμαι, ἔθανον, τέθνηκα (ΘΑΝ, ΘΝΑ): in θρώσκω, θοροῦμαι, ἔθορον (ΘΟΡ, ΘΡΟ): in βλώσκω, μολοῦμαι, ἔμολον, μέμβλωκα (ΜΟΛ, ΜΛΟ).

Βάρυνω, *I load*, takes in the pass. the perf. of the otherwise non-Attic βαρέω, βεβάρημαι, *I am loaded*, Plat. Symp. 203. b., for which Homer uses intransitively the act. βεβαρηότα, βεβαρηότες*: see the article on Βαίνω, paragraph 6.

Βαστάζω, *I bear or carry*: fut. βαστάσω, &c.; but in the pass. it changes its formation, and makes the aor. 1. ἐβαστάχθην. Compare διστάζω, νυστάζω.

ΒΑΩ, βίβημι. See Βαίνω.

Βέομαι, or βείομαι, 2 pers. βέῃ, an Epic future, *I shall live*, which there are quite as strong grounds for our explaining to be a real but irregular future, (like πίομαι or like κέω, κείω,) as there are for our calling it a conjunctive, for βέωμαι, used like a future. A more important question is, whether it belongs to an old verb ΒΕΙΩ, whence βίος and βιόω; or whether the passive of βαίνω took in more ancient usage the sense of *I walk*, i. e. *live*, in which case βείομαι will correspond with the active βείω for βῶ. This investigation will therefore prevent the necessity of altering, as Wolf has done, the traditionary form βιόμεσθα, (Hymn. Apoll. 528.) to βεόμεσθα.

Βιάζομαι, *I force*: depon. midd., from which however is not only formed with a passive meaning the aor. pass. ἐβιάσθην, as in many similar verbs †, but the other tenses (for instance the pres. and imperf. frequently, and the perf. perhaps always,) are used passively.

The active is used sometimes by the poets, as Od. μ, 297. Alcæus ap. Anecd. Bekk. p. 86. For the passive use of βιάζομαι see the passages of Thucyd. in Popp. Prolegg. 1. p. 184. and those of Xenoph. in Sturz. Lexicon. See also Hymn. Cer. 68. Soph. Ant. 66.

The Ionians have the form in -άομαι; e. g. in Herodot. βιᾶσθαι, βιᾶται, βιώμενος, imperat. βιῶ; aor. 1. ἐβιήσατο, and also as pass. βιηθείς. Homer has βεβίηκεν actively.

Βιβάω, βίβημι. See Βαίνω.

Βιβρώσκω, *I eat*. From this synonym of the verb ἐσθίω

* See Græv. ad Lucian. Solœc 7. Tho. M. v. βαρύνειν, where the intrans. βεβάρηκα is given as the genuine Attic form, and the rhetorician Aristides quoted in confirmation of it, but his words appear to be an intentional imitation of Homer. With respect however to the authority quoted above from Plato for βεβάρημαι it has been observed, and not without reason, that the words in that passage sound very poetical.

† There are many deponents of which the poets use an active form with the same meaning, as βιάζω for βιάζομαι, δωρέω for δωρέομαι, μηχανάω for μηχανάομαι.

was formed in the Attic and common language neither future nor aorist. In the active voice the only tense in use was the perfect, in the passive all the tenses, βέβρωκα, βέβρωμαι, ἐβρώθην*.

The future midd. βρώσομαι was used only by the later writers; see Lobeck. ad Phryn. p. 347. The future pass. βεβρώσομαι occurs in Od. β, 203. The Epic language had also a syncopated aor.† ἔβρων, Hymn. Apoll. 127. From the perf. part. βεβρωκώς was formed by syncope βεβρώς, βεβρῶτος‡, Soph. Antig. 1010.

The Homeric form βεβρώθοις, Il. δ, 35. is not a perf. but comes from a poetic pres. βεβρώθω, *I feed upon, devour*, in which the stem or root ΒΡΟΩ is formed in -θω, like κνάω κνήθω, ἀλέω ἀλήθω, and the reduplication prefixed to increase the force of the word, as in τετραίνω from τράω, τιτράω and τετρεμαίνω from τρέω.

We find some forms from ἔβρωξα; viz. καταβρώξασαι, Apollon. Rh. 2, 271., καταβρώξειε, Dionys. Perieg. 604. But in these passages the Harpys are described as swallowing a whole meal at once, and the sea-monsters as devouring whole ships with their crews; while all the forms which come from ΒΡΟΩ have simply the sense of eating up with mastication, and, where they are used metaphorically, of the consumption or waste of property. Hence Struven's emendation, καταβρόξασαι, καταβρόξειε, in the Supplement to Schneider's Lexicon is very probable (see under ΒΡΟΧ-); particularly as Dionysius had undoubtedly in his mind the καταβρόξειεν of Od. δ, 222. For as all the Homeric forms with ο are used to express the swallowing or gulping down of fluids, they were the more calculated for the above sense, as we see from the analogy of καταπιεῖν§.

Βιόω, *I live*, is but little used by the Attics in the pres. and imperf.; these they borrow from ζῶ, which again does not often occur in its other tenses. We find then in common use the fut. βιώσομαι; aor. 1. ἐβίωσα rare; aor. 2. ἐβίων‖, optat. βιῴην (not -οίην), conjunct. βιῶ, ῷς, ῷ, &c.,

* On the analogy of this verb with some others by metathesis of the stem or root ΒΟΡ, ΒΡΟ, see note under Βάλλω, and Buttm. Lexil. p. 84.

† See note under Γιγνώσκω.

‡ Like πίπτω, perf. πέπτωκα, part. πεπτωκώς, by syncope πεπτώς and πεπτεώς.

§ There is one other instance, viz. κατέβρωξεν in Schol. Pind. Ol. 1, 38., of the eating up the shoulder of Pelops. It is difficult to say whether this should be suffered to remain as the incorrect form of a faulty writer, or altered to κατέβρυξεν, upon a supposition that it was copied from an older narrative of the story.

‖ See note under Γιγνώσκω.

infin. βιῶναι, part. βιούς; perf. βεβίωκα, and perf. pass. in the expression βεβίωταί μοι.

The pres. βιόω, which is very common in Lucian (see Reitz. Ind.) and others, occurs but rarely in the older writers; we do meet with τῶν ἀσελγῶς βιούντων, Æschin. 1, 5. p. 1. ζητῶν βιοῦν, Eurip. Fr. Archel. 30. From the time of Aristotle it is found more frequently. In Herodotus 2, 177. the MIDDLE has the sense of *I subsist upon, victum habeo*; and in Aristotle's Ethics 10, 10. p. 105. f. Duv. (10, 9. Wilkinson.) the more expressive meaning of *I lead a certain kind of life.*

[The fut. act. βιώσω is used by Diog. Laert.—Passow.]

Somewhat more singular is the very common use of the infin. aor. 2. βιῶναι (beside its own natural usage) for the infin. pres., i. e. for βιοῦν or ζῆν. Thus ἔτι γάρ νύ μοι αἶσα βιῶναι, Od. ξ, 359., ἀνάγκη ἐγένετο αὐτῷ μετὰ τὴν κρίσιν τριάκοντα ἡμέρας βιῶναι, Xen. Mem. 4, 8, 2., πῶς πέφυκε; δεινῶς λέγειν, κακῶς βιῶναι, Æschin. Ctes. p. 97, 33. And this usage may perhaps extend to the other moods; as the optat. in Plat. Gorg. p. 513. extr. σκεπτέον τίν' ἂν τρόπον τοῦτον ὃν μέλλει χρόνον βιῶναι ὡς ἄριστα βιῴη.

I find but one instance of the aor. 1. in the pure Attic times, viz. in Xen. Œc. 4, 18. εἰ ἐβίωσεν, *if he had lived.* But in the participle this tense (βιώσας, Hippocr. Coac. vol. 1. p. 559.) appears to have taken the place of the cases of βιούς (-όντος, &c.) which never occur: thus we find βιούς, Plat. Phæd. p. 95. e. and οἱ ὁσίως βιώσαντες, p. 113. d. In the older language the aor. 1. had probably, according to the analogy of ἔστησα, ἔβησα, &c., the causative sense of *I make to live, preserve life,* and, to express that meaning, a present βιώσκω, according to the analogy of μεθύσκω, πιπίσκω. This supposition is confirmed by the pres. βιώσκεσθαι, *to be brought to life, revive,* Aristot. Meteor. 1. c. 14.; and the aor. 1. (though in the middle voice like ἐβήσατο, ἐστήσατο) does actually occur in this sense at Od. θ, 468, σὺ γάρ μ' ἐβιώσαο, *thou hast preserved my life.*

Βιόμεσθα, Hymn. Apoll. 528. Wolf has altered to βεόμεσθα. See under Βέομαι.

The compound of this verb with ἀνά has only the aor. ἀνεβίων, ἀναβιῶναι to express the intransitive sense of *I revive*; the causative meaning, *I resuscitate,* is expressed by the aor. 1. midd. ἀνεβιωσάμην, Plat. Phæd. p. 89. b. Hence the pres. ἀναβιώσκομαι, being both passive and middle, has both senses; as passive, *I am brought to live again, I revive*, ἀναβιώσκεσθαι, -οιτο, ibid 72. c. d.; as middle, *I bring to life again, resuscitate*, οἱ . . . ἀναβιωσκόμενοι ἄν, Crito p. 48. c.

The active voice in this causative sense, ἀναβιώσκω, is found in Schol. Eurip. Alcest. init.*, and ἀνεβίωσα in Palæph. 41.

Apollon. Rh. 1, 685. has βώσεσθε for βιώσεσθε, an absorption of the iota which takes place also in σωπᾷν for σιωπᾷν, and perhaps in πέπωκα also.

Βλάπτω, *I hurt, harm*: fut. βλάψω; aor. 1. ἔβλαψα; fut. midd. in passive sense βλάψομαι, Thucyd. 6, 64.; perf. pass. βέβλαμμαι†; aor. 1. pass. ἐβλάφθην, Thucyd. 4, 73. Antiph. p. 61., but more generally aor. 2. pass. ἐβλάβην. The characteristic of this verb is therefore β.

From the aor. 2. arose a new present βλάβω of which we find only the 3. sing. βλάβεται in Homer.—Compare δρύφω for δρύπτω, στενάχω for στενάζω.

Βλαστάνω, *I germinate*: fut. βλαστήσω; perf. ἐβλάστηκα‡, Eur. Iph. A. 594.; aor. 2. ἔβλαστον, see note under Αἰσθάνομαι.

The aor. 1. ἐξεβλάστησε occurs in Hippocr. De Alim. 1. and in the later writers, for instance Aret. 6, 3. In Æschyl. Cho. 585. we read βλαστοῦσι, which, if the reading be good in other respects, must undoubtedly be accented βλάστουσι, which brings it into analogy with αὔξω and αἴσθομαι: compare also δαρθάνω.

Βλέπω, *I see*: fut. βλέψω, &c. The aor. 2. pass. is irregular §. This verb is not found in Homer.

Βλίττω, *I take the bees from the hive*: fut. βλίσω, Ion. βλίσσω: see Ἁρμόττω. Of this verb I have never found an

* Perhaps from Pherecydes, who is mentioned there, and from whom the story is quoted in Schol. Pind. p. 3, 96. with the expression ἀναβιοῦν ἐποίει.

† See following note under βλαστάνω.

‡ All verbs beginning with γν, and some with γλ, βλ, take in the perfect, instead of the reduplication, the syllabic augment ε. Of verbs beginning with βλ, the only one which I find with the reduplication is βλάπτω, βέβλαμμαι; and of those beginning with γλ, γλύφω is doubtful; for we have ἐξεγλυμμένος, Plat. Rep. 10, p. 616. d. Διέγλυπται, Athen. 3. p. 93. c. Διαγεγλυμμένος, Ælian. V. H. 3, 45.

§ Some verbs, whose radical vowel is ε, do not change their vowel in forming the aor. 2. pass: thus from φλέγω, βλέπω, λέγω we find ἐφλέγην, and the participles βλεπείς, συλλεγείς; compare also λέπω, πλέκω, ψέγω.

instance of the present with σσ, probably because it was originally a pure Attic word. See Buttm. Lexil. pp. 84, 189.

ΒΛ–. See Βάλλω.

Βλώσκω, *I go.* This verb comes by metathesis from the root ΜΟΛ– (see Βάλλω with note, and Buttm. Lexil. pp. 84, 189.), whence the fut. μολοῦμαι; aor. ἔμολον, μολεῖν, μολών; perf. μέμβλωκα. Of these tenses Homer uses the aor. and perf., the Tragedians the future, Æschyl. Prom. 694. Soph. Œd. C. 1742.

That βλώσκω is the real present to those tenses we have proofs enough in the indexes of Homer, Aristophanes, and Euripides. Wherever the present μολέω occurs it is suspicious: see Schæfer on Soph. Œd. C. 1742.

Βοάω, *I cry out*: Attic fut. βοήσομαι.

The Ionians always contract the οη of this verb to ω, making in the fut. βώσομαι, and throw back the accent, as aor. 1. ἔβωσα*. The same takes place in νοέω. For that this is the correct explanation of these verbs may be learnt from comparing them with βωθεῖν for βοηθεῖν, ὀγδώκοντα for ὀγδοήκοντα, &c. The throwing back of the accent takes place in other similar cases In the passive voice βοάω inserts the σ in the aor. 1. of this contraction, but not in the perfect; βεβωμένος, ἐβώσθην, Herodot. 3, 39. 6, 131.

ΒΟΛ–. See Βάλλω and Βούλομαι.

Βόσκω, *I feed* (in its active sense): fut. βοσκήσω†, according to which the other tenses are formed.—Midd. *I feed* (in its intransit. sense).

Βούλομαι, *I wish*: depon. pass.; with fut. midd. βουλήσομαι (see note under Βόσκω); perf. pass. βεβούλημαι; aor. 1. ἐβουλήθην, also Att. ἠβουλήθην‡.

* We find also in Aristoph Pac 1154. βώσατο, and in the Etym. M. νένωται is quoted from a satirical piece of Sophocles.

† Of all the changes which take place in forming the different presents of verbs, the easiest is that of ω into έω, as ῥίπτω and ῥιπτέω, κύω and κυέω, γαμέω from ΓΑΜΩ Hence as often as the regular inflexion of a verb presented any difficulty, sounded badly, or caused obscurity, it was inflected as if the present had been in έω.

‡ In the three verbs βούλομαι, δύναμαι, and μέλλω, the Attics very commonly increase the syllabic augm of the imperf. and aor. by the addition of the temp. augm, and use both ἐδυνάμην and ἠδυνάμην, ἐδυνήθην and ἠδ-, ἐβούλετο and ἠβ-, ἐβουλήθην and ἠβ-, ἔμελλον and ἤμ-. The aor. ἐμέλλησα, which is found only in the sense of *delaying*, has never this augment. Nor is it confined to the Attics, but occurs in the Epic and Ionic dialects; see Hes. θ, 478, 888. Herodot. 1, 10. It does not however preponderate until the times of the later Attics, as it is never found in the Tragedians, and but little in the older prose or Aristophanes. Compare Poppo on Thucyd. vol. 1. p. 225.

Homer has also a perf. *βέβουλα* in the compound *προβέβουλα*, *I prefer*: see note under Ἄγνυμι. On the form *βόλομαι*, *βόλεσθαι*, which occurs twice in Homer, see Buttm. Lexil. p. 196.

BO–. See Βοάω.

Βράζω; more commonly *βράσσω*, -*ττω*, *I boil* (in its intrans. sense), *I ferment*, *I throw up* (as the sea does), *I winnow*: fut. *βράσω*; aor. 1. *ἔβρασα*. The passive has again frequently the intrans. sense.

Some wish to confine the sense of boiling and fermenting to the pres. *βράζω*, but all the different meanings run too much into each other for this to hold good: *βράττω* appears to be the Attic form for all. See Ruhnk. Tim. p. 64., Stephan. Thesaurus and Schneider's Lexicon* with the Supplement and the compounds with *ἀνά*, *ἀπό*, and *ἐξ*.

Βραχεῖν, *ἔβραχον*, an Epic aor. with the meaning of *to rattle*, *to crack*, *to roar* (as the sea or a wounded combatant is said to do).

Βρέμω and *βρέμομαι*, *fremo*, *I roar* (as the sea or thunder does), *I resound*. Used only in pres. and imperf.

Βρέχω, *I wet*: fut. *βρέξω*, &c. Pass. *I am wet*, *βρεχόμενοι πρὸς τὸν ὀμφαλόν*, Xenoph. It has the aor. 1. *ἐβρέχθην*, and the aor. 2. *ἐβράχην*.

Pindar has the perf. pass. *βεβρεγμένος*, Ol. 6, 92.—The doubtful

* [I compile from that untranslated Lexicon the following:

Intrans.—*to boil up*, *foam*, *ferment*; *τοῦ πότου λαμπρῶς βράζοντος*, Heliod. p. 193. where Jacobs conjectures *βρυάζοντος*. *Οἶνος βράζων*, *fermenting*, Alex. Aphrod. Probl. p. 282. *Βράζων νόος*, *a turbulent spirit*. It also expresses the *roaring* of the bear, Pollux 5, 58. Its compound is used for the *rushing forth* of fire, *πολλὴ πυρὸς ἐξέβρασε ζάλη*, Apollod. 1, 6.

Trans.—*to throw up with violence* (as boiling water or a tempestuous sea does), *εὖτε βράσσηται πάμφυρτος ἀφυσγετός*, Oppian. Hal. 1, 779. *Ὀστέα βέβρασται παρ' ἠόνι*, Antip. Thess. Epig. 61. *Ἔβρασεν ἐς ἠιόνα*, Laur. Tull. Epig. 2. *Τὰ μὲν ἔβρασεν ἤλιθα νηδὺς πνεύματα*, Nicand. Al. 25. *Τὰ δ' ἀθρόα νειόθε βράσσαις*, ib. 137. In the same sense is used the compound *ἐξεβράσσοντο*, of vessels *cast on shore*, Herodot. 7, 188. Again *ἑαυτὸν ἐξέβρασε*, Ælian. H. A. 6, 15. Also, *to throw up and shake corn* in order to winnow it, Ruhnk. Tim. p. 64. *Μόσχος θηλῆς χύσιν βράττει*, *sucks by pushing and shaking the teat*, Meand. Al. 359. Lycophr. 461. And in the passive, *βρασσόμενος ὑπὸ γέλωτος*, *shaking with laughter*, Lucian 5, p. 213. Anecd. Bekk. 1, 66. The passive voice has also the intrans. sense in *θάλασσα πνεύματι βρασσομένη*, Leonid. Tar. 57. Apoll. Rhod. 2, 323. *Πόθοισι βρασσόμενος*, Greg. Naz. Carm. 20, 4. But the compound *ἀναβράττω* has an active sense, *to boil up*, *κρέα*, Aristoph. Batr. 510. Pac. 1197. Ach. 1005. *Ἀνάβρασον ὑποκαίων*, Dioscor.; and so has the other compound *ὁ φάρυγξ αἵματος θρόμβους ἐκβράσσεται*, Hippocr. 531, 20.—Ed.]

perf. *βέβροχα* or *βέβρῡχα* see under Βρυχάομαι; as also the root ΒΡΟΧ–, below.

Βρίζω, *I slumber*: fut. *βρίξω* (never *βρίσω*); aor. 1. *ἔβριξα*, Eurip. Rhes. 825., infin. *βρῖξαι*, part. *ἀπόβριξας*, Od. ι, 151. μ, 7. The pres. is found in Il. δ, 223. Hesychius has *βρισθείς*.

Βρίθω, *I am heavy*: fut. *βρίσω*; aor. 1. *ἔβρῑσα*, infin. *βρῖσαι*.

The Poets have also *βρίθομαι* and *βέβριθα*, both with the same meaning as the pres. active.

ΒΡΟ–. See Βιβρώσκω.

ΒΡΟΧ–: a stem or root from which we find only some forms of the aor. 1. act. and aor. 2. pass. in the Epics with the meaning of *to suck in, to swallow up*, *καταβρόξειεν*, *ἀναβρόξειεν*, *ἀναβροχέν* (*swallowed up again*), Od. δ, 222. μ, 240. λ, 586. See Βιβρώσκω; and *ἀναβέβροχα* under Βρυχάομαι. These forms are also treated of more at length in Buttm. Lexil. p. 200, &c.

Βρύκω and Βρύχω* are generally distinguished by the former meaning *to bite, feed on*, the latter *to gnash the teeth*; but the distinction is not sufficiently certain: see Buttm. on Soph. Phil. 745. and compare *ῥέγκω* and *ῥέγχω*. Of these two verbs no other tenses are found† except that Hesychius has *βρῦξαι, δακεῖν*. [In Buttm. Lexil. p. 203. will be found a detailed account of these verbs as well as Schneider's articles (translated from his Lexicon) on *βρύκω, βρύχω, ἀναβρύχω, βρῡχάομαι* and *ὠρύω, ὠρύομαι*.]

Βρῡχάομαι, *I roar*; depon. pass.; with fut. midd. and aor. pass. but we sometimes find also the aor. midd., Plat. Phæd. p. 117. d. Βρυχηθείς, Soph. Œd. T. 1265.

Of the more simple form the perf. *βέβρῡχα* with the sense of a pres. is used by the poets: for that this tense belongs here, and not to *βρύχω*, *frendeo*, is proved in Buttm. Lexil. p. 200. &c. Compare the similar of *μυκάομαι* and *μηκάομαι*.

A very difficult form occurs in Il. ρ, 54. *ἅλις ἀναβέβρυχεν ὕδωρ*. The short υ in this perf. is contrary to the general analogy of the perfect 2, in which all the vowels except ο are long. This form also is

* [According to Moeris *βρύχω* was the common form, *βρύκω* the Attic: in opposition to which see Herm. Soph. Phil. 735. —Passow.]

† [Yet I find in Passow's Lexicon, under Βρύκω, *ἀλὶ βρυχθείς*, Phil. Thes. Epig. 77. Βρῦκον στόμα, Nicand. and aor. 2. *ἔβρῠχε*, Epigr. Adesp. 418.—under Βρύχω the perf. *βέβρῡχε*, *βεβρῡχώς*, pluperf. *ἐβεβρύχει*. In addition to which the aor. 1. *ἔβρυξε*, Eryci. Epig. 2. *βρύξας*, Diodor. 16.—Ed.]

treated of fully in Buttm. Lexil. p. 200., and the alternative left of considering it either a mere onomatopœia βέβρυχε, *it spouts forth*, or an anomalous change of vowel ἀναβέβρυχε for ἀναβέβροχε (itself an old reading) from ἀναβρέχειν, which also may mean *to spout forth*.

Βρύω, *I am full*, appears only in the pres. and imperf.

[Ἔρνος ἀνθεῖ βρύει, Il. ρ, 56. With gen. Soph. Œd. C. 16. But it has also a transit. sense, χάριτες ῥόδα βρύουσιν, *produce in plenty*, Anacr. 37, 2.—Passow.]

Βυνέω, *I stop up*, makes fut. βύσω, aor. 1. ἔβυσα with υ long; but the passive takes the σ.

The pres. βύω was not used by the Attics. In Aristot. H. A. 9, 37, 3. Schneider's Codd. have βυνοῦσιν, and in Aristoph. Pac. 645. the general reading of the text ἐβύουν is now from the best sources corrected to ἐβύνουν. Herodot. 2, 96. has διαβύνεται, and 4, 71. διαβυνέονται. Compare κυνέω, and δύνω, ἐνδυνέουσι, under Δύω.

Γ.

Γαμέω, *I marry*, i. e. *take a wife*, forms from ΓΑΜΩ a future of similar sound with the present; thus, Ion. fut. γαμέω, (Il. ι, 391.) Att. fut. γαμῶ, (Xen. Cyr. 5, 2, 12.); aor. ἔγημα, infin. γῆμαι, part. γήμας; perf. γεγάμηκα, &c. —Pass. *I am married*, i. e. *taken to wife* (ἐγαμήθην).—Midd. *I marry*, i. e. *take a husband*.

The fut. γαμήσω and aor. 1. ἐγάμησα belong to the later writers. The older future (from ΓΑΜΩ) was γαμέσω*, fut. midd. γαμέσομαι, whence γαμέσσεται, Il. ι, 394., which however has in that passage the causative meaning of *to give a woman in marriage*, in which sense Menander used also the aor. 1. ἐγάμησα: see Schol. Ven. ad Il. ι, 394. Lobeck. ad Phryn. p. 742. Meineke Menand. Fr. 303. p. 274. Buttm. in Friedem. and Seeb. Misc. Crit. 2, 4. p. 712. Compare also Reisig De ἂν Partic. p. 127. The γαμεθεῖσα of Theocr. 8, 91., for the aor. 1. part. pass. γαμηθεῖσα, is grounded on the old future γαμέσω.

Γάνυμαι, *I am glad*: depon. Beside the pres. and imperf. it has a fut. γανύσσομαι [used only by the Epics and Anacr. 8. and formed from an

* See note under Δέω, *I bind*. [But Passow gives it as his opinion that wherever this form occurs there are reasons for suspecting it to be spurious.]

obsolete verb *γανύω*, which occurs only in the perf. pass. *γεγανυμένος*.—Passow.] consequently it does not follow the general analogy of verbs in *νυμι**.

ΓΑ–. See ΓΕΝ–.

Γέγωνα, a perf. 2. with the meaning of a present†, *I call aloud*: infin. *γεγωνέμεν* (for *-έναι*); part. *γεγωνώς*; conjunct. *γεγώνω* (Soph. Œd. C. 213.); imperat. *γέγωνε*, used by the Tragedians. The 3. sing. perf. 2. *γέγωνε* is in Homer both pres. and aor. (see Ἀνήνοθα and note.) The other tenses are inflected as from a pres. in *-έω*, formed from the above perf. 2., as the infin. pres. *γεγωνεῖν* (Il. μ, 337. Eurip. Hippol. 586.) and the imperf. *ἐγεγώνευν* (Od. ι, 47. &c.). Hence then the 3. sing. *ἐγεγώνει* is to be classed with these, although it may with the same sense be the pluperf. also. The fut. *γεγωνήσω* is used by Euripides; the aor. *γεγωνῆσαι* by Æschyl. Prom. 989., and the verbal adj. *γεγωνητέον* by Pind. Ol. 2, 10. Even Xen. Ven. 6, 24. has the imperat. *γεγωνείτω*. And lastly was formed a pres. *γεγωνίσκω*, used by the Tragedians and also by Thucyd. 7, 76.

Γελάω, *I laugh*, with fut. midd. *γελάσομαι*, more rarely *γελάσω*, Monk Eurip. Alc. 158. Popp. Xen. Cyr. 1, 4, 16. Bornem. Xen. Conviv. 1. 16. The α is short in the inflexion. The pass. takes σ.

The regular aor. 1. is *ἐγέλασα*, Poet. *ἐγέλασσα*: but as the Dorics form all verbs in *-ζω* with a fut. in *-ξω*, we have the Dor. fut. *γελάξω* and the Dor. aor. *ἐγέλαξα*.

The regular contr. part. is *γελῶν*, plur. *γελῶντες*, but in some contracted verbs the ω is resolved into ωο: which takes place only where a syllable long by position follows the ω, or it has the ι subscript, in which latter case ῳ is resolved into ωοι; e. g. *ἡβώοντες*, *ἡβώοιμι*, for *ἡβῶντες*, *ἡβῷμι* (from *-άοντες*, *-άοιμι*), and for *γελῶντες* may stand according to the metre *γελόωντες* or *γελώοντες*, Od. σ, 40. 110‡.

* There are three verbs which do not follow the general analogy of verbs in *νυμι*, viz. *ἀνύω*, *τανύω*, *γάννυμαι*, all three with υ short.

† See Buttm. Lexil. p. 202. note.

‡ At Od. υ, 347. 390. we find however another form, *γελοίων* for *ἐγέλων*, and the part. *γελοίωντες*, although in both passages the text is uncertain, from their being various readings without the diphthong. In itself it is very conceivable that, as the resolution of οω is by far the most usual, and the most common mode of lengthening a syllable was by changing it into οι, like *ἀλοιάω*, *ἠγνοίησεν*, so *γελόων* became *γελοίων* whenever the verse required it (Eust. adv. 347.). But in that case we must read *γελοίωντες* at Od. σ, 110. also, where there is no such various reading. We are led to view the word however in another light by the meaning of *γελοιήσασα* at Hymn. Ven. 49. where the context points not to mere *laughing*, but rather requires *laughing and joking*, (γε-

ΓΕΝ-. This stem or root, which answers to the Lat. verb. *gigno, genui,* unites in Greek the causative meaning *to beget,* with the immediate or intransitive *to be born, to become.* The forms are mixed together anomalously. Of the active voice the perf. 2. γέγονα is the only tense in use; all the others, in both meanings, belong exclusively to the middle. The whole may be classed from usage under the following two presents :—

1. γείνομαι has the proper and simple sense of *to be born*; its present, which belongs to the Epic poets only, is used in both meanings, *to be born* (Il. κ, 71.), and *to beget* (Od. υ, 202. where we have γείνεαι the 2. sing. conj. aor. 1. midd. for γείνηαι). The aor. 1. midd. ἐγεινάμην, infin. γείνασθαι, is transitive, *to beget, bring forth,* and belongs to both prose and poetry.

2. γίγνομαι, old and Attic; in the common language γίνομαι, with ι long; fut. γενήσομαι; aor. ἐγενόμην; perf. γεγένημαι, or in the active form perf. 2. γέγονα*. All these forms are without exception intransitive, not only in their proper meaning *to be born,* but also in the general sense *to become, fieri,* and in which they are most commonly used. To these we may add the meaning of *to be,* as ἐγενόμην and γέγονα serve at the same time for preterites of the verb εἰμί†. Not unfrequently however the perf. γέγονα may be also taken as a present, *I am*; yet so that the meaning always comprehends the more exact idea of *I have been, I have been born*‡. Compare πέφυκα.

λοίησασα εἶπεν); therefore γελοιᾷν from γέλοιον. And this meaning is most suited to Od. υ, 390., where the suitors get ready for their banquet γελοίωντες, *laughing and joking*; which therefore, according to this second analogy must be written γελοιῶντες. On the other hand at σ, 110. (γελώοντες) we want nothing more than simple laughing, and so at υ, 347. instead of γελοίων we must restore the old reading γελώων for ἐγέλων.

* For an account of the meaning of this form see note under Ἄγνυμι.

† Instances of this use of γέγονα are, οἱ πάντες βασιλεῖς γεγόνασι, *who have all been kings,* Plat. Alcib. I. 41. c. p. 124. εἰ ἄρα τις γέγονεν ἐραστής.. οὐκ, ἠράσθη, ib. 55. a. p. 131.

‡ For instance, in Plat. Phæd. p. 76. c. ἀφ' οὗ ἄνθρωποι γεγόναμεν, *since we are men,* i. e. *have been born men* Hence ἑξήκοντα ἔτη γέγονα, *I am sixty years old,* i. e. *have been born sixty years.*

With these we may join the verb *γεννάω*, which takes entirely the causative meaning *to beget*, as well as its more general sense *to produce*; while the above-mentioned aor. *ἐγεινάμην* is used only with the strict and simple idea of begetting and birth, and for that sense is the higher and better expression.

From the root ΓΕΝ- arise in strictness of analogy no other presents than *γείνομαι*, like *τείνω* from ΤΕΝ-, and *γίγνομαι*, like *μένω*, *μίμνω*. The form *γίνομαι* might indeed, as *ει* and *ι* were in very ancient times almost the same, be reckoned identical with *γείνομαι*; but the analogy of *γινώσκω* shows that it arose in the course of pronunciation from *γίγνομαι*. That grammatical decision appears therefore to have been correct, according to which the old Epic poets admitted those two forms only, and used *γείνομαι*, on account of the established usage of *γείνασθαι*, in the sense of *being born*, *γίγνομαι* in that of *to become*. With regard to Attic usage, the Atticists decide between *γίγνομαι γιγνώσκω*, or *γίνομαι** *γινώσκω*, in favour of the former orthography; see Valck. ad Phœn. 1396.: but we learn from Athenian inscriptions that the other mode of writing these verbs was likewise an old and Attic usage.

In the Doric dialect the verb *γίγνεσθαι* was a depon. pass., therefore *ἐγενήθην* was used for *ἐγενόμην*; see Lobeck ad Phryn. p. 108. and Archyt. ap. Gal. p. 674. (*γενάθημεν*); and thence it came into the common language of the later writers. But the future *γενηθήσεσθαι* (occurring twice in Plat. Parmen. p. 141. e.) presents difficulties of another kind; see Heind.

Callimachus (in Cer. 58.) uses *γείνατο* in the exact sense of *ἐγένετο*, *facta est*. With this I join the particip. *γενάμενος*, which Archimedes has frequently, p. 48, 28. 35. 38. p. 127, 23. The form which Callimachus uses is therefore nothing more than an Epic lengthening of *γένατο*, and the same kind of formation as *εἰλάμην*, *εὕρατο*, &c.

The aor. *ἔγεντο*, *γέντο*†, by syncope for *ἐγένετο*, is used by Hesiod, Pindar and other poets. Theognis, 640. has *ἐπέγεντο*.

For *γέγονα* we find a poetical form (*γέγαα*) plur. *γέγαμεν*—*γεγάασιν*;

* [*Γίνομαι* was unknown not only to Homer but also to the Tragedians.—Passow.]

† These passive aor. are formed from the simple present of the verb; and when that pres. is the one in common use, they are distinguished from the imperf. and the moods of the pres. merely by this syncope. Hence they are exactly like the perfect and pluperfect pass. of those verbs, but without the reduplication; and may therefore be compared, but must not be confounded, with them. In meaning, whether active, passive or middle, they follow their pres. in *μαι*; and they belong only to the oldest period of the language. e. g.—

δέχομαι—*ἐδεδέγμην*, *ἐδέδεξο*, &c., *δε*-

infin. γεγάμεν (for -άναι); part. Ep. γεγαώς, γεγαῶτος*, (for -αότος), γεγαυῖα, Att. γεγώς, -ῶσα, -ώς. See βέβαα, &c. under Βαίνω.

With these are united three other forms: 1.) γεγάᾱτε, Batrach. 143. Hom. Epigr. ult. for γεγᾰᾰτε, on account of the metre, perhaps formed according to a false analogy from γεγάᾱσι: see Buttm. Lexil. p. 142.— 2.) ἐκγεγάονται, *they will be born*, Hymn. Ven. 198., a future which bears the same relation to γέγαα as τεθνήξομαι does to τέθνηκα, is used like the latter as a simple but express future, and formed without the σ like πίομαι, ἔδομαι, and the Epic futures in -ύω for -ῠσω, viz. ἐρύουσι Il. λ, 454., τανύουσι Od. φ, 174. &c.—3.) Dor. infin. γεγάκειν (for -έναι), Pind. Ol. 6, 83., which supposes the existence of the more complete perfect γέγηκα (as βέβηκα, βέβᾰα) of which Hesychius quotes the conjunct. γεγάκω.

Γέντο, *he took*, an old verb in Homer, of which we find only this one form. It appears to be a dialect of ἕλετο, as κέντο for κέλετο is quoted from Alcman by Eust. ad Il. ι, 756, 32. Rom. (658, 29, Bas.) The γ instead of the aspirate is preserved in many glosses of Hesychius and others.

Γεύω, *I cause to taste, give to taste*: Midd. *I taste, enjoy*: Perf. pass. γέγευμαι, Eurip. Hipp. 663.: aor. 1. pass. probably with σ; for though we find γεῦμα, we say also γευστέον, γευστικός, &c.; and some verbs have the σ in the aor. pass. although they have none in the perf., as παύω, πέπαυμαι, ἐπαύσθην; μνάω, μέμνημαι, ἐμνήσθην, &c.

In Theocrit. 14, 51. we meet with a singular form γεύμεθα, which unless forced can only be called a perfect without the reduplication: and as there are few or no undisputed instances of the reduplication (i. e. the real syllabic reduplication) being omitted in the pure times of the language, this form arose most probably from the faulty language of common life; as the similar one ἔλειπτο, Apoll. Rhod. 1, 45. and 824. (which can be nothing but a pluperf.) is perhaps to be ascribed to an inaccurate imitation of the old Epic language.

Γηθέω, *I am glad*, fut. γηθήσω, &c. The perf. γέγηθα is the same as the present, only in more common use, and that not merely in Homer (who always has the former, never the latter,) but in prose also (Plato).

δέχθαι.—aorist syncop. (ἐδέγμην) ἔδεξο, ἔδεκτο, infin. δέχθαι, imperat. δέξο.

μίγνυμι, ΜΙΓΩ—(ἐμίγμην) μίκτο.

λέγομαι—ἐλέγμην, λέξο, λέκτο, λέχθαι.

πάλλω—(ἐπάλμην) πάλτο.

ὄρνυμι, ΟΡΩ—ὤρμην, ὦρτο, infinit. ὄρθαι, particip. ὄρμενος, imperat. ὄρσο: and some others, as ἔγεντο, εὖκτο, ἆλτο, ἐλέλικτο, ἵκμενος, ἄρμενος.

* The Epics allowed themselves the liberty of pronouncing the accented ο in the oblique cases of the part. perf. *long*, as τετριγῶτας for -ότας.

There is no authority for a present γήθω*; consequently none for γήθει, a various reading of γηθεῖ at Il. ξ, 140., on the other hand we have ἐγήθεον in Hom., γαθεῦσι in Theocr. We see the same in ῥιγέω ἔρριγα, δουπέω δέδουπα, of which no pres. in -ω is in use. Yet Eustathius quotes γηθόμενος, which is found also in the later Epics† who probably had some older precedent for it: this however proves nothing in favour of the active form having been used; compare ἀχέω ἄχομαι, ἐρέω ἔρομαι, κυρέω κύρομαι.

Γηράω and γηράσκω, *I grow old*: fut. γηράσομαι ‡; it is inflected regularly according to the first form; only the Attics have in the infin. aor. beside γηρᾶσαι a syncopated form γηρᾶναι §, preferred by the Atticists.

This infin. either comes from an aor. 2. or is formed by syncope similarly to διδράσκω, ἔδρᾱν, δρᾶναι; therefore ἐγήραν, -ας, -α, &c. γηρᾶναι, &c. In the older language this was undoubtedly the only aorist; hence also in the Epics the part. γηράς (Il. ρ, 197.), γηράντεσσιν (Hes. ε. 188.): and certainly the 3. pers. ἐγήρα (Il. ρ, 197.), and κατεγήρα (Herodot. 6, 72.), are not imperf. but this same aorist; for in both passages the sense requires, to make it complete, that "he did grow old in it:" whilst in Herodot. 2, 146. κατεγήρασαν may quite as well be the 3. plur. of ἐγήραν. The long α ‖ in ἐγήρα and γηρᾶναι answers to that in ἔδραν, and corresponds as in all ¶ such aorists with the vowel of the perfect.— A particip. in εις, έντος, consequently as coming from a sister-form in έω, is quoted in the Etym. M. from the later Ionic poetry of Xenophanes. Compare the note on Πίμπρημι.

The aor. 1. ἐγήρασα occurs in Æschyl. Suppl. 901. in a causative sense, *to make a person grow old*; while the infin. γηράσαι is used in Xen. Mem. 3, 12, 8. as intransitive. According to Passow there are doubts of the reading in Æschylus; but even supposing it to be true, there are many instances of the aor. 1. having a causative sense, while

* [Passow has the form γήθω as a pres. not in use, from which he deduces the perf. γέγηθα.]

† [The earliest writer in which it occurs is Quintus Smyrn.—Passow.]

‡ In Simonid. 1. (Gnom. Brunck) the active form γηρασσέμεν occurs, in which the double σ at all events is false. but it is possible that the true reading there was γηρασκέμεν. Οὔτε γὰρ ἐλπίδ' ἔχει γηρασκέμεν, οὔτε θανεῖσθαι.

§ See note under Γιγνώσκω

‖ It is true that the only historical evidences in favour of this quantity are the circumflex on γηρᾶναι in correct editions (see Oud ad Tho. M. in v.), and the α in both the iambic verses quoted by Pierson ad Moer. in v. falling in the place where a long syllable is admissible: but the above analogy makes it certain.

¶ Thus βέβηκα ἔβην, ἔκτᾰκα ἔκτᾰν ἔκτα, δέδρᾱκα ἔδρᾱν. φθάνω is the only exception, which see.

the pres., was intransitive, and *vice versa*: for instance μεθύω, *I am drunk*, πλήθω, *I am full*; aor. ἐμέθυσα, *I have intoxicated*, ἔπλησα, *I have filled*; thus also ναίω and ἔνασσα, κύω and ἔκυσα; and instances of the opposite kind we have in τρέφω, *I nourish*, ἔτραφον, *I am well fed, fat*; στυγέω, ἔστυξα; ἀραρίσκω, ἦρσα; ὄρνυμι, ὦρσα, &c.—With regard to the reading of the infin. γηράσαι in Xen. Mem. [both Moeris and Tho. M. prefer γηρᾶναι, and] certainly nothing was easier than the change of this latter word to the common form, as in Herodot. 7, 114. γήρασαν might have been easily corrupted to the present reading γηράσασαν. See a similar case in the aor. of διδράσκω.

Γίγνομαι, γίνομαι. See ΓΕΝ—.

Γιγνώσκω, old and Attic, in the common language γινώσκω (compare γίγνομαι); *I know*: fut. γνώσομαι; aor. ἔγνων (plur. ἔγνωμεν), imperat. γνῶθι, γνώτω, &c.; optat. γνοίην, infin. γνῶναι (Epic γνώμεναι); part. γνούς*; perf. ἔγνωκα; perf. pass. ἔγνωσμαι; aor. 1. pass. ἐγνώσθην, infin. γνωσθῆναι; part. γνωσθείς. Verbal adj. γνωστός, old form γνωτός, γνωστέος.

The ω in ἔγνων corresponding with the vowel of the perfect (according to the preceding note) continues through the aorist with the exception of the optat. and participle. Indeed γνοίην is become the established reading even in Homer, where however we find ἁλώην (see Ἁλίσκομαι). Hence συγγνῴη in the old Atticism Æschyl. Suppl. 230, deserves our attention. In the later Attics this is again found; see Lobeck ad Phryn. p. 347.—The 3. plur. ἔγνων for ἔγνωσαν is (if the reading be correct) an exception: for when the syllable -σαν is abbreviated to -ν, the vowel preceding is always shortened; thus βάν for ἔβησαν is short, ἔδρᾰν for ἔδρᾱσαν (see Διδράσκω), ἔδῠν for ἔδῡσαν. In Pind. Pyth. 9, 137. Isthm. 2, 35. ἔγνων stands without any various reading; but as

* Many verbs have a syncopated aorist which must be either compared with the aor. 2. or reckoned as such. The 1st pers. of this aor. always ends in ν, and the vowel preceding it is (with the single exception of φθάνω) the same as that of the perfect; thus it corresponds exactly with the aor. 2. of verbs in μι in all its moods and its participle: thus—

σβέννυμι, ΣΒΕΩ, ἔσβηκα—ἔσβην, ἔσβημεν, σβῆναι, σβείην.

βαίνω, ΒΑΩ, βέβηκα—ἔβην, ἔβημεν, βῆναι, βαίην, βάς.

διδράσκω, δέδρᾱκα—ἔδρᾱν, ἔδρᾱμεν, δρᾶναι, δραίην, δράς.

κτείνω, ἔκτᾰκα—ἔκτᾰν, ἔκτᾰμεν, κτάναι, κταίην, κτάς.

γιγνώσκω, ἔγνωκα—ἔγνων, &c.

Other instances equally or even more complete may be seen under ἁλίσκομαι, βιβρώσκω, βιόω, δύω, πέτομαι, σκέλλω, τλῆναι, φθάνω and φύω; while single forms of this aorist will be found under βάλλω, γηράσκω, κλάω, οὐτάω, πλέω, πτήσσω; and some imperatives, as βῆθι, δρᾶθι, γνῶθι, δῦθι; plur. βῆτε, δῦτε, &c.

the syllable is long in both cases by position, we cannot in either of these instances attain perfect certainty from the metre. [Passow however, in his Lexicon, quotes at once ἔγνον as from Pindar, without stating whether on any authority.] In Æschyl. Pers. 18. ἔβαν is by its position in the anapæstic metre long. See Lachm. de Chor. Syst. p. 28.—The occurrence of the passive aor. opt. συγγνοῖτο*, and of the active aor. συγγνῷη, both in the same passage of Æschylus (230. 231.), and in the same active sense, is very singular.

The compound ἀναγιγνώσκω has, beside its common meanings, the sense of *to persuade*, particularly in the Ionic writers (see Hemst. ad Tho. M. in v. and Koen. Greg. p. 503.); and in this alone, as being a causative meaning, do we find the aor. 1. ἀνέγνωσα, Herodot. 1, 68. 87. and in many other passages of this author †.

Γλύφω, more rarely γλύπτω, Eurip. Troad. 1306. On the augment of the perf. see note under Βλαστάνω.

In this verb, as in φρύγω φρύσσω (Theocr.), in δρέπω δρέπτω (Mosch.) &c., the former, which is the more simple present, is the more usual, while the latter, which is the more forcible one, was indeed formed but not in general use.

Γοάω and γοάομαι, *I bewail*. Epic infin. γοήμεναι, for γοᾷν, Il. ξ, 50.; aor. ἔγοον, Il. ζ, 500. [which Passow calls an imperf.]

Γράφω, *I write*.—Midd. The aor. 2. pass. ἐγράφην is formed, not regularly from the aor. 2. act., but from the imperf. ἔγραφον, as ἐτρίβην (with ι short) from ἔτριβον, φρῠγῆναι from ἔφρῠγον; in all which the rule of the aor. 2. is preserved, that the long vowel becomes short.

Beside the perf. γέγραφα there was also in use γεγράφηκα (see Archim. De Spiral. Procem. extr.) which, when occurring in the common language of the time, is censured by the Grammarians: see Phot. v.

* With the syncopated act. aor. described in the last note may be classed a passive aor. in μην, σο, το, &c., corresponding therefore with the regular aor. 2. midd., in which however three things may be remarked: 1. that most of the instances of this aor. have a completely passive sense; 2. that they follow the vowel of the perfect passive; 3. that they belong only to the language of the older poets. Some of them do indeed serve as passive to the above-mentioned active aorists, for instance, ἐβλήμην optat. βλείμην—from ἔβλην (ξυμβλήτην): see Βάλλω.

ἐκτάμην, κτάσθαι, κτάμενος—from ἔκταν: see Κτείνω.

See also οὐτάμενος, and κλῦθι with the old particip. κλύμενος.

† The quotation of the aor. 2. in this sense by some of the Grammarians (see Hemst. Hesych. Erot. Galen.) arises from false readings in Herodot. and Hippocr.—See Steph. Rec. Voc. Herod. in v. and Fœs. Œc. Hippocr. in v.

πεπύχηκα, who quotes it from Theopompus, Herodian ap. Herm. p. 317, Lob. ad Phryn. p. 764.*

Γρηγορέω. See Ἐγείρω.

ΓΩΝ–. See Γέγωνα.

Δ.

ΔΑ–, ΔΑΙ–. The verbs belonging to these roots have four leading senses; *to divide, to give to eat, to burn, to teach.*

1. δαίω, *I divide*, has in this form and meaning the pres. and imperf. only, and is exclusively poetical. To the same sense belong, from the root ΔΑ–, the fut. δάσομαι, the aor. ἐδασάμην with α short, both used *in prose* as well as verse, and the perf. δέδασμαι with a passive meaning, *I am divided*, (Il. α, 125. Herodot. 2, 84.) of which the 3. pl. on account of the sound follows again the root ΔΑΙ–, δεδαίαται, Od. α, 23. The analogy† of μαίομαι μάσασθαι, ναίω νάσασθαι, shows that the Lexicons have no occasion to bring forward a pres. ΔΑΖΟΜΑΙ from which to form δάσομαι, &c. This pres. is nowhere found, but another poetical one does occur, δατέομαι (see it in its place), which bears the same relation to those forms as πατέομαι does to πάσασθαι.

2. δαίνυμι, *I receive at my table, give to eat.* Midd. δαίνυμαι, *I eat at table as a guest, feast on* (δαῖτα, κρέα, &c.), forms according to the analogy of all verbs in νυμι its tenses from δαίω, which however in the pres. never has this meaning. Therefore fut. act. δαίσω, aor. 1. ἔδαισα (Herodot. 1, 162.), fut. midd. δαίσομαι, aor. 1. ἐδαισάμην, &c. As to whether we may add ἐδαίσθην also see note on Δαΐζω.—The Ionics, without any contraction, omit the σ in the second pers. sing.; thus imperf. δαίνυο‡, imperat. μάρναο, φάο, θέο, &c. [Callimachus has δαινύω, –⏑–.—Passow.]

3. δαίω, *I burn, set fire to*§. Midd. *I burn, am on fire.* [Of the act. the pres. and imperf. only are in use.—Passow.] Of the midd. we find the pres. and imperf., the aor. 2. ἐδαόμην, whence 3. sing. conjunct. δάηται, Hom. The perf. and pluperf. δέδηα‖, ἐδεδήειν, Poet.

* The two passages from Demosth. c. Dionysod. pp. 1291. 1293. are quoted erroneously, as they come from the verb παρασυγγραφεῖν, *to act contrary to agreement.*

† The verbal termination of αιω for αω in the Epic language is not, like ειω for εω, a mere help to the metre; for αω is seldom used without the contraction, and the α might be long of itself: but αἰω, like ἄζω and ἄγνυμι, is a mode of strengthening in the pres. the α which is short in the inflexion: beside the above-mentioned see μαίομαι, ἀγαίομαι, λιλαίομαι, κεραίω, κεδαίω, σκεδάννυμι, and in prose κναίω, ψαίω.

‡ This form occurs indeed only in Il. ω, 63. Δαίνυ' ἔχων, where there is a various reading Δαίνυσ': but it is one so little worthy of credit, that it is justly disregarded: compare ἔσσυο.

§ The intrans. sense, *to blaze*, has been given to the active voice from a misinterpretation of Il. ε, 4. and 7. Compare Il. σ, 206. 227.

‖ See note under Ἄγνυμι.

δεδήειν, belong to the intrans. meaning of the middle, with the sense of the pres. and imperf. The future, which is nowhere found, appears, according to the analogy of καίω, to have been δαύσω, whence δεδαυμένος, *burnt*, in Simonid. ap. Etym. M. v. δαύω, and (by a very good emendation) in Callim. Epig. 53. (28.)

4. ΔΑ–, with the ideas of *to teach* and *learn*. To the former belongs the aor. 2. act., of which ἔδαε occurs in Theocr. 24, 27. Apollon. 4, 989., and the same form with the reduplication δέδαε is found occasionally in the Odyssey*. The perf. has the sense of *to learn*, of which Homer has only the particip. δεδαώς (*one who has learnt*), other writers have δεδάασι†. To this we may add the aor. pass. ἐδάην (*I was taught, I learned*); from which comes, according to the note under Ἀκαχίζω, a new formation δαήσομαι, δεδάηκα or δεδάημαι (*I have learnt*). Another Homeric form δεδάασθαι, *to try and learn, inquire into, examine*, (Od. π, 316.) can only be a pres. in -άομαι formed from δέδαα (just as from γέγαα comes γεγάονται, only that this occurs as a future); excepting which we find no other trace of the present of this merely poetical verb; though it is the stem from which branches the common verb διδάσκω, having its own proper inflexion: see below.

The Epic future δήω (δήεις, δήομεν, δήετε) belongs to this stem or root ΔΑΩ, *I learn*‡, consequently has the meaning *I shall learn, find out*, and comes undoubtedly from the future δαέω by contraction of the two first vowels, as the similar Epic future κείω or κέω is formed from κεέω§: see Κεῖμαι.

Δαΐζω, *I divide, cut in two, kill*: fut. δαΐξω, &c.

In Eurip. Heracl. 914. stands δεινᾷ φλογὶ σῶμα δαϊσθείς, whilst everywhere besides, even in the Tragedians, we find δαιχθείς, δαΐξας, &c. Elmsley reads, to answer with the verse in the antistrophe, δαισθείς, thinking to form it from δαίω, *I burn*, but which appears to me contrary to the above analogy. Nor are there any grounds for forming δαισθείς from δαΐζω, as there was nothing to hinder the use of δαιχθείς, like δεδαιγμένος in Pind. Pyth. 8, 125. (see Hermann and Boeckh on that passage.). If then we read δαισθείς, I can place it only under δαίνυμαι; and I see no reason why the language of Lyric poetry might not have formed from the transitive sense of this middle voice, *to eat, consume*, an aor. passive, *was consumed*.

* This last is generally but erroneously given to δέδαα with the other meaning. That it was the old aor. is shown by the gloss in Hesych. Δέδαον· ἔδειξαν, ἐδίδαξαν.

† See for this formation βέβαα, &c. under Βαίνω.

‡ According to the Etym. M. v. δῆλος, Alcæus had a pres. δέω, *I find*; which coincides with our adoption of δάω.

§ An exactly similar contraction we find in one of the declensions of nouns, viz. κλεῖα, σπῆι, for κλέεα, σπέεϊ.

Δαίρω. See Δέρω.

Δάκνω, *I bite*: from ΔΗΚΩ come the fut. δήξομαι, perf. δέδηχα, &c.; aor. ἔδακον*, infin. δακεῖν. [In the passive the perf. δέδηγμαι is the tense most in use.—Passow.]

Δακρύω, *I weep*, has no passive; but the perf. pass. δεδάκρυμαι takes the idea of *I am weeping, I am in tears*, Il. π, 7., δεδάκρυνται, (the eyes or cheeks) *are suffused with tears*, Il. υ, 204. χ, 491.; part. δεδακρυμένος, *weeping, in tears*, Plut. Paul. Æmil. 10. See the note on Πεφυγμένος.

Δαμάζω, δαμάω, δαμνάω. See Δέμω.

Δαρθάνω, *I sleep*: fut. δαρθήσομαι; perf. δεδάρθηκα; aor. 2. ἔδαρθον. See note under Αἰσθάνομαι.

The Poets transpose the letters of the aorist, making ἔδραθον.

We find also in the shape of an aor. pass. καταδαρθέντα, Aristoph. Plut. 300., and καταδαρθῶμεν (which however depends entirely on the accent) Thesm. 794. Again κατέδραθεν for -ησαν, Apollon. Rh. 2, 1229. We may suppose these forms (as Bekker does in his criticism on Wolf's Homer) to have taken a passive shape merely from mistaking the θ. But as they occur principally in the compound with κατά†, the aor. of which certainly has in itself something of a passive nature, as in German *ich habe geschlafen*, and *ich bin eingeschlafen*, in English *I have been asleep*, and *I was fallen asleep*; I would rather suppose this to be the true reason: and κατεδάρθην will then be the perfectly regular form of the aor. 2. pass.; and thus the traditionary reading καταδραθῶ (Od. ε. 471.) appears to me unobjectionable, i. e. I believe it to have been the reading in the time of the Attics‡.

In Aristoph. Nub. 38. the Scholiast quotes καταδάρθειν, instead of -εῖν, as the Attic mode of writing. I would observe that the aorist certainly does not appear to suit that passage, which requires the idea of duration; whence also τὶ is added. The natural idea of a person disturbed in his sleep is not, 'let me fall asleep a little,' but 'let

* In forming a new present ν is sometimes inserted before the termination; as δάκνω, aor. ἔδακον: compare κάμνω, τέμνω.

† Little importance can be attached to quotations like ἐδάρθη and ἐδράθη in Hesychius; and ἀποδαρθέντα, quoted from a Comic writer in Lex. Seguer. p. 349., will, as to meaning, stand pretty much on the same ground as the compounds of κατά.

‡ I think that the account which I have given above is one which may fairly stand valid as long as no historical grounds can be adduced to the contrary, and notwithstanding the mere unsupported objection of Porson on the passage of Plutus.

me sleep a little.' Καταδάρθειν may therefore very possibly be an Attic sister-form of καταδαρθάνω, like αἴσθομαι or αὔξω.

Δατέομαι, depon., used only in pres. and imperf., while the other tenses are taken from Δαίω, No. 1., which see. Hesiod ε, 795. has the aor. 1. infin. of this verb without the σ, δατέασθαι, like ἀλέασθαι, ἀλεύασθαι from ἀλέομαι.

Δέαται, it appears, occurs only once, Od. ζ, 242. δέατο. But to this verb belongs also the aor. with its vowel changed δοάσσατο, conj. δοάσσεται (for -ηται). In that passage of the Odyssey the common reading was δόατο, but the unanimous consent of Grammarians and manuscripts has now restored δέατο. Both forms however indisputably belong to each other, as ε—ο is a common change of vowel. Apollonius uses the 3. optat. act. δοάσσαι and δοάσσατο personally, and writes also δοιάζειν, -εσθαι; as he, with the majority of the Grammarians, derived the Homeric verb from δοιή; *doubt*, and understood it in the sense of *to conjecture, reflect*. But in the Homeric passages either there is no doubt, or, if there is one, it lies in the former part of the sentence; and δέαται, δοάσσατο, answer exactly to the verb ἐδόκει, ἔδοξεν. See a full account of these forms in Buttm. Lexil. p. 212, &c.

Δεδίσσομαι, -ττομαι, *I affright*: depon. midd. [Poet. for δειδίσσομαι; but the part. aor. midd. δεδιξάμενος is found in Demosth. de Fals. Leg. 291.—Passow.]

In Homer we have δειδίσσομαι frequently, and in a transitive sense; but once it occurs intransitively, *to be afraid*, Il. β, 190. The verb comes from δεῖσαι, δέδια, δείδια. Another form is δεδίσκομαι (see Piers. ad Moer. p. 119.), which must not however be confounded with the Homeric δειδίσκομαι, δεδίσκομαι, on which see the note to Δείκνυμι.

Δεῖ. See Δέω.

Δείδω. See Δεῖσαι.

Δείκνυμι, and δεικνύω, *I show*: fut. δείξω; aor. 1. ἔδειξα.

The Ionians spoke all the forms which came from the simple root with ε only; as, δέξω, ἔδεξα, ἀπεδέδεκτο, Herodot. 3, 88., ἀπεδέχθη id. 7, 154.*. That is to say, all these forms preserve their original length by position, like μέζων, κρέσσων. Compare also πείκω.

The midd. δείκνυμαι has in the Epics (Il. ι, 196. Hymn. Ap. 11.) the additional meaning of *to salute, welcome, drink to*†. Consequently to it

* Though many passages still have δεῖξαι, at least among the various readings, and even taken from good manuscripts, this ought not to militate against the correctness of restoring δέξαι universally. Compare Kœn. Greg. Cor. in Ion. 36. Schweigh. Lex. Herodot. in δείκν. and ἀποδείκν.

† [In this sense Homer uses only the perf. and pluperf.—Passow.]

belongs the perf. δείδεγμαι, which has the same meaning, and is used as a present: 3. plur. δειδέχαται, 3. sing. pluperf. (as imperf.) δείδεκτο. The syllable of reduplication δει is found here, merely because δει is also the syllable of the stem or root, as in δεῖσαι*.

Δειπνέω, -ήσω, &c. On the Att. perf. δέδειπνα, infin. δεδειπνάναι, see Ἀριστάω.

Δεῖσαι, *to fear*: aor. 1. ἔδεισα; fut. δείσομαι [the act. fut. δείσω is found only in Aristid. 2. p. 168.—Passow.]. Homer has the present δείδω, but only in its first person: instead of it we find the perfect (with the meaning of the present), with two forms in use, δέδοικα and δέδια, the choice of which depended on the one or the other sounding more agreeably to the ear†. Of δέδια and its pluperfect the plural takes the syncope; thus δέδιμεν, δέδιτε, for δεδίαμεν, -τε; and pluperf. ἐδέδιμεν, ἐδέδιτε, ἐδέδισαν, for ἐδεδίειμεν, -τε, ἐδεδίεσαν; imperat. δέδιθι.

The infin. is not formed according to this analogy, but remains δεδιέναι; the Epics however form it in -ιμεν, δειδίμεν (see below); compare the same formation in the pres. of εἶμι, I go.—In the indicative the unsyncopated forms, as δεδίαμεν, and particularly ἐδεδίεσαν, belong to the later writers: whence however they have frequently been transferred to the copies and editions of Attic authors. See Lobeck ad Phryn. p. 180.

In Homer the δ is always doubled after the augment or the preposition in composition, as ἔδδεισε, περιδδείσας. Now as this verb, with its compounds and derivatives, very frequently makes the preceding short

* That is to say, many bring the form δείδεκτο under δέχομαι, by which they hope to deduce the meaning of *to receive*, *welcome*, with greater facility. But the above forms ought not to be separated from the present δείκνυμαι, which occurs in a similar sense, nor from its sister-form δεικανᾶσθαι; and to these again belong the synonymous presents δειδίσκομαι, δεδίσκομαι; whence also Apollonius 1, 558, might say δειδίσκετο πατρὶ in the common sense of ἐδείκνυε. The original idea is indisputably the *stretching out* and offering of the hand, the cup, &c., with which that of *pointing* with the finger, or showing, corresponds very well.

† The form δεδιυῖα deserves our attention, which the Antiatticist p. 90, 1. quotes from the Comic writer Eubulus, and which Bekker from evident traces in the manuscripts has restored to the text of Plat. Phædr. p. 254. extr. But the form of the *optative* δεδιείη, which that critic has adopted from nearly the same manuscripts, at p. 251. a. of the same work, I cannot admit. If the optative be there indispensable, analogy requires δεδιοίη, like πεφευγοίη, ἐληλυθοίη, ἐδηδοκοίη, πεποιθοίη. But the syntax of the common reading, εἰ μὴ δεδίει (imperf.)...θύοι ἄν... appears to me admissible.

syllable in the cæsura of the old hexameter long (e. g. Il. λ, 10. ξ, 387.); and the δ of its stem or root is scarcely ever* preceded by a short syllable, it is clear that there must have been something peculiar in the old pronunciation of this verb to have produced such a general coincidence: and Dawes with great probability suspects this to have been the digamma after the δ (*dw*), to supply the place of which the δ was afterwards doubled. See Dawes Misc. Crit. pp. 165. 168. and Buttm. Lexil. pp. 355. 375.

The Epics pronounced (with the diphthong) δείδοικα, δείδια, ἐδείδιμεν, the reason of which was, as in δείδεκτο under δείκνυμι, that the diphthong was in the stem or root†. Now as the fem. particip. of δείδια could not be admitted into an hexameter, Apollonius Rh. (3, 753.) has, and undoubtedly not without a precedent from some older poet, δειδυῖα‡. There arose also a regular present δείδω, which however is found only in its first person§.

On the 3. pers. of the perf. δείδιε used as imperf. see Ἀνήνοθα and note. Δεδοίκω is a Doric pres. formed from the perf. in Theocr. 15, 58., like ἑστήκω in the Ionic epigram of Posidippus ap. Athen. 10. p. 417, e.

Δέδοικα is formed from the theme ΔΕΙΩ, with the change of vowel usual in the perf. 2.; and δέδια is shortened from it, as πεφύασι is from πέφῡκα, ἴδμεν from οἶδα. But that theme also was still in existence in

* The only exceptions to an immense number of instances are ὑποδείσατε, Od. β, 66. ἀδειής, Il. η, 117. δεδίασιν, Il. ω, 663., the last of which, as being taken from ω, is of no weight.

† And thus it includes δεῖσαι, according to the statement here given of it. But when we consider the peculiarity of this verb, as noticed above, according to which the δ in its stem or root was originally equivalent to *dw*, it follows that in Homer's pronunciation the first syllable of both δέδοικα and δέδια must have been also long by position. After the disappearance of the digamma the syllable δει discharged the same office in these forms as the double δ did in ἔδδεισε. This is the most accurate and detailed account which I can give of these perfects.

‡ This form is a clear proof how firmly the length of the augment-syllable had established itself in the old Epic; otherwise they would have said δεδιυῖα, the sound of which could have been no objection to those who used πεφυυῖα. The form δεδίασιν in Il. ω, 663. has been already touched on in the last note but one.

§ In the epigram of Antagoras, Cod. Vat. p. 379. n. 147. (in Brunck. Simonid. 62.) we ought undoubtedly to read δείδιτε instead of δείδετε. Compare the various readings δειδίμεν, δειδέμεν, Od. ι, 274. As the verse can in every instance dispense with the form δείδω, the poets appear to have been swayed in their preference of that or δείδια by merely metrical reasons. Compare Il. κ. 39. with φ, 536.—On δείδω we have only further to observe that in many Lexicons [Schneider's and Passow's for instance] it serves as the theme for the whole verb: but our statement must have made it sufficiently clear that it originally took its rise from δείδια. And it is equally clear from the above-mentioned δειδυῖα, (as a substitute for which δείδουσα must have been at once apparent,) and from δεδίασιν in so old a poet as the author of Il. ω. must at all events have been, and who would therefore certainly have used δείδουσι, that this present was unknown to those old writers further than in its first person.

the Epic language in this its shortened form, whence Homer has more than once the imperf. δίε (ἐδίε), e. g. Il. λ, 556. ρ, 666.*

This Epic δίω contained also the idea of *to fly, run*, δίον Il. χ, 251. Hence the causative idea of *to frighten away*; but this is expressed in Homer, contrary to the analogy of other writers, by the passive form δίεσθαι, δίωμαι, &c. (Il. μ, 276. η, 197.). But there must have been also an active transitive δίημι†, pretty nearly corresponding in meaning with this, from which two Homeric forms come: 1. ἐνδίεσαν, *they urged* (the dogs) *on*, Il. σ, 584. 2. δίενται, pass. or midd. with a neuter sense, *they run*, Il. ψ, 475. Hence the infin. δίεσθαι may belong to both forms and both meanings, as in Il. μ, 276. and 304.

In Æschyl. Pers. 697. 698. (in both which verses the present reading is δέομαι, a theme formed without any authority,) the old editions and the majority of the manuscripts have δείομαι, contrary to the metre. But three manuscripts, according to Hermann, give δίομαι; which must therefore be the true reading concealed under the above corruption; and what in Homer is expressed by δίω is thus represented in Æschylus by δίομαι, which with δέδια has in its favour the analogy of κήδομαι κέκηδα, ἔλπομαι ἔολπα, and the like.

ΔΕΚ—. See Δείκνυμι and Δέχομαι.

Δέμω, *I build*, and midd. δέμομαι: aor. 1. ἔδειμα; midd. ἐδειμάμην; perf. 1. δέδμηκα‡, perf. 2. δέδομα, perf. pass. δέδμημαι.

The pres. and imperf. are rare even in the poets. The pres. is found only in the part. δέμοντα, Hymn. Merc. 188.; the imperf. δέμον in Od. ψ, 192.; but the aor. act. and midd. occur in the Ionic writers, and later in common prose. The perf. pass. is used by Herodot. 7, 200. The form δείμομεν, Il. η, 337. is the conjunct. aor. 1. act. shortened from δείμωμεν.

Of the sister-form§ δομέω we find principally the aor. and perf., but their usage is also limited; see Lobeck ad Phryn. p. 587. sqq. The common language used οἰκοδομέω, e. g. ᾠκοδόμησε τεῖχος, and the like.

* Nay the theme exists unshortened, but in a poem which can hardly be quoted with such a view as this, in Orph. de Lapid. 335. δειέμεν, where however Hermann has adopted (I see no reason why) Tyrwhitt's correction δειδέμεν. See the preceding note.

† The pretended verb δίημι, said to have the same meaning as διαίνω, *to water*, and which is so described in Schneider's Lexicon, is erroneous. All the forms of that kind belong to διίημι: see Riemer's Lex. and Lobeck ad Phryn. p. 27. [Passow places the different forms διεὶς, διέμενος, &c. under δίημι, which he says is contracted from διάημι.]

‡ It may be doubted whether this perf. be formed by metathesis like βέβληκα (see Βάλλω and note), or by a mere syncope: on the former hypothesis, it will run thus, δέμω (ΔΕΜ, ΔΜΕ) δέδμηκα; by the latter, like νέμω νενέμηκα, δέμω (δεδέμηκα) δέδμηκα.

§ Many dissyllable barytone verbs, which have ε in the syllable of the stem or root, make sister-forms by changing the ε to ο, and taking the termination έω; as, φέρω φορέω, τρέμω τρομέω, φέβομαι φοβέομαι, &c.

The same stem or radical word Δέμω has also the meaning of *to tame* in the following forms; perf. δέδμηκα; perf. pass. δέδμημαι; aor. 1. pass. ἐδμήθην, part. δμηθείς; aor. 2. ἐδάμην*, part. δăμείς. Beside these was formed the present in the following manner: 1. δαμάζω and δαμάω. 2. by the insertion of the syllable να, δάμνημι and δαμνάω†. Of these δαμάζω has become the usual form in prose as well as verse, and is inflected regularly through all its tenses like the derivative verbs in άζω: δαμάω, as a present, is the Epic sister-form of δαμάζω (like ἀντιάω for ἀντιάζω), Il. α, 61.; but its forms are at the same time the Ionic and Attic future of δαμάζω; e. g. δαμάᾳ, Il. χ, 271. δαμόωσιν, Il. ζ, 368. ‡. Midd. δαμάζεσθαι, δαμάσασθαι, Eurip. Hom. &c. δάμνασθαι, Hom. Hes.

Δέρκομαι, or perf. with the meaning of the pres. δέδορκα, (see Buttm. Lexil. p. 202. note,) *I see, look*. Aor. by transposition ἔδρăκον, which act. form is used particularly by the Epics; the other poets use the two aorists belonging to the deponent δέρκομαι, viz. ἐδέρχθην, Soph. Aj. 425. and ἐδράκην, Pind. On the short α in ἔδρακον see Πέρθω.

There are no grounds for a pres. act. δέρκω. The perf. δέδορκα has in Pindar (Ol. 1, 153, &c.) a pass. or intrans. meaning also, φέγγος, φάος δέδορκε, *is seen, shines*.

Δέρω, *I skin, I beat*, is inflected regularly according to the rules of verbs whose characteristic letter is one of the four liquids, λ, μ, ν, ρ. Thus it has no fut. 1. but a fut. 2. δερῶ; its aor 1. is not formed in σα but in α, as ἔδειρα; its perfect 1. is (with the change of ε to α, like πείρω, περῶ, πέπαρκα,) δέδαρκα and its perf. 2. δέδορα. In the pass. it has a fut. 2. δαρήσομαι, and an aor. 2. ἐδάρην §.

An Attic sister-form of the present is δαίρω, [whence the infin. aor. δῆραι,] Aristoph. Nub. 442, Av. 365. See Heind. ad Plat. Euthyd. 35. Passow mentions also a later Ionic pres. δείρω, as probably formed from the aor. ἔδειρα. Verbal adj. δαρτός, Ep. δρατός.

* Beside these two synonymous aorists there has been quoted a syncop. aor. ἔδμητο; the only authority for which is Antim. Fragm. 19. ap. Pausan. 8. p. 651.; where however the reading γ' ἔδμηθ' is false. The manuscripts have δ' ἔδμηθ' contrary to the context. But Schellenberg saw that the true reading is, Ὅς ῥα τότ' Ἀδράστῳ τριτάτῳ δέδμηθ' ὑπ' ἄνακτι.

† Like περνάω πέρνημι from περάω; and with the change of ε into ι, κιρνάω κίρνημι from κεράω (κεράννυμι), πίλνημι, πίτνημι and σκίδνημι from πελάω, ΠΕΤΑΩ, ΣΚΕΔΑΩ. These derivatives occur mostly in the dialects and poets.

‡ Thus we have as futures τελέει, Il. θ, 415. τελεῖ, Plat. Protag. p. 311. b. καλεῖ, Xen. Symp. 1, 15. καλεῖσθε, Demosth. Lept. 5. κορέεις, Il. ν, 831. These futures in έω—ῶ, and άω—ῶ, with a similarly sounding present, are not very numerous. Compare ἐλαύνω and περάω.

§ The aor. 1. also did however exist; see δαρθείς in Lex. Seguer. 2. p. 89, 5.

Δεύω, *I wet*, is inflected regularly. The Epic *δεύομαι* see under Δέω, *I am wanting*.

Δέχομαι, Ionic (but not Epic) *δέκομαι*, *I receive*; depon. midd.: fut. *δέξομαι*, also *δεδέξομαι*, Il.; aor. 1. *ἐδεξάμην*.—Pass. perf. *δέδεγμαι*; pluperf. *ἐδεδέγμην*; aor. *ἐδέχθην*, part. *δεχθείς*, (in a pass. sense) *taken*.

The perf. *δέδεγμαι* has in the Epics another peculiar sense of a present, *I wait*, e. g. *δεδεγμένος εἰσόκεν ἔλθῃς*, Il. κ, 62. Also, *I receive*, particularly of one who stands to receive an attack, or waits for game; e. g. *δεδεγμένος ἐν προδοκῇσιν*, Il. δ, 107. Imperat. *δέδεξο*, Il. ε, 228. υ, 377., to which belongs with a similar active sense the fut. *δεδέξομαι*, Il. ε, 238. But *δείδεγμαι*, *I welcome*, similar as that idea may seem to be to the above meaning, belongs to *δείκνυμι*, as we have shown under that verb.

The syncop. aor. (*ἐδέγμην*) *ἔδεκτο*, *δέχθαι*, imperat. *δέξο*, has been mentioned before in a note under the root ΓΕΝ–. According to the analogy there laid down it has the sense of an aorist, and therefore means *received*, exactly synonymous with *ἐδεξάμην*; compare Il. ο, 88. with α, 596. It happens however that the 1. sing. *ἐδέγμην* does not occur in this meaning but only with that of an imperf., *I was waiting for, expecting*, (e. g. Od. ι, 513.) and in the same way the particip. *δέγμενος*, *ποτιδέγμενος*, has only the sense of *waiting, expecting* (e. g. Il. ι, 191. η, 415.), that is to say, the sense of the perf. *δέδεγμαι* as given in the last paragraph; in which therefore these forms differ from the analogy of the syncopated forms laid down in the above-mentioned note under ΓΕΝ–. But since at Il. μ, 147. *δέχαται*, which is not an historical form, is used in speaking of the waiting for an attack, consequently in the exact meaning of *δεδέχαται*, it is clear that the perf. *δέδεγμαι* in this its peculiar sense (as a present), which sense the *present* *δέχομαι* *never* has, was able to throw off the reduplication,—a rare occurrence, of which we find but two or three instances, and those in the later writers*; we must therefore lay down for *δέχομαι* in the old Epic writers a twofold usage: viz.—

δέχομαι, *I receive*; sync. aor. (*ἐδέγμην*) *ἔδεκτο*, &c. *received*.

δέδεγμαι or δέγμαι (whence δέχαται) *I wait for, expect*; pluperf. (with the force of an imperf.), *ἐδεδέγμην* or *ἐδέγμην*, part. *δεδεγμένος* or *δέγμενος*.

From the form *δέκομαι* would come (see the second note under Δέμω†)

* See Γεύω.

† That is to say, according to the analogy laid down in that note from *δέκομαι* might be formed *δοκέομαι*, from which would come regularly *δεδοκημένος*.

also the Epic perf. δεδοκημένος, Il. ο, 730. Hes. α, 214. in the sense of the above-mentioned δεδεγμένος. We find in Apollon. Lex. δεδοκημένος· ἐκδεχόμενος, ἐπιτηρῶν: which is therefore to be distinguished from the Attic δεδόκημαι under δοκέω.

Δέω, *I bind*: fut. δήσω; aor. 1. ἔδησα; perf. δέδεκα*; perf. pass. δέδεμαι; aor. 1. pass. ἐδέθην.—MIDD. The fut. 3. (or paulo-post fut.) δεδήσομαι generally supplies in Attic writers the place of the non-Attic fut. 1. pass. δεθήσομαι, which however is occasionally found, e. g. Demosth. c. Timocr. 126. 131. 190.—Dissyllable contracted verbs do not in general take the contraction, except in ει: thus we have τρεῖ, πνεῖν, but τρέομεν, πνέουσι, &c.: δέω, *I find*, is however an exception; for we find τὸ δοῦν, τῷ δοῦντι, Plat. Cratyl. (ὁ) ἀναδῶν, Aristoph. Plut. 589. διαδοῦμαι, &c.; in which respect it differs from δέω, *I am in want of*, which makes τὸ δέον, δέομαι, and even sometimes δέεται.

On the above-mentioned usage of the future see Moeris and Thom. Mag. in v. We will only remark that it is not to be considered as an aberration of the pronunciation from δ to θ, for the future 3. is used in some other verbs in the same way: see particularly Πιπράσκω.

Instead of δέω the older Ionic and Attic language had a present of a more distinct and intelligible sound, δίδημι; e. g. imperf. δίδη, Il. λ, 105. διδέντων, Od. μ, 54. according to the reading of Aristarchus; διδέασι, Xenoph. Anab. 5, 8, 24. as taken from the most credible sources. See Porson. ad Schol. Od. *l. c.*

Δέω, *I am in want of*, *I fail*: fut. δεήσω; aor. ἐδέησα, for which Homer has once δῆσεν, Il. σ, 100. This verb is generally impersonal; δεῖ, *it is wanting*, *it is necessary*, (*il faut*), conjunct. δέῃ (contr. δῇ), optat. δέοι, infin. δεῖν, part. δέον, Att. δεῖν; imperf. ἔδει; fut. δεήσει; aor. 1. ἐδέησε. Pass. δέομαι (as depon. *I am in want of*), δέῃ or δέει, δεῖται, &c.; fut. midd. δεήσομαι; aor. 1. pass. ἐδεήθην. This voice is never impersonal.

* This verb, like αἰνέω, αἱρέω, ποθέω, and many others, inflects some of its tenses regularly with η, e. g. its future and aor. 1., but others with ε, viz. its perfects and aor. passive.

This verb, with respect to its contraction, differs from the preceding merely in the forms which in δεῖν, *to bind*, are contracted to ου*. But the contraction also to ει, which is regularly found in all verbs of this kind, was partly omitted in the one before us; for instance in the 2. pers. sing. (which is of rare occurrence) τοσούτου δέεις, Isocr. Busir. 5, p. 222.; and Xenophon uses δέεται, δέεσθαι, perhaps always, as it is still preserved in many passages†.

The conjunctive of the impersonal is frequently found in verse as a monosyllable, because, according to some δέῃ though written as two syllables, was pronounced as one. See Meineke on Menand. Fr. Inc. 28. and 39., and a fragment of Philetærus ap. Athen. 10. p. 416. f. But there is an old precept, well deserving attention, according to which δεῖ and similar monosyllables are said to have had at the same time the force of conjunctive as well as of indicative. See Reisig on Aristoph. I. p. 44.‡

The Grammarians mention as a contraction of a peculiar kind the neut. part. of the two verbs δεῖν, *to be in want of*, and δοκεῖν; that is to say for δέον (which is otherwise never contracted) δεῖν, and for δοκέον δοκεῖν, the same in sound as their infinitives, and which they

* Compare the preceding verb, particularly toward the end of the first paragraph.

† Δέεσθαι, Mem. 1, 6, 10. Anab. 7, 7, 31.; δέεται, Anab. 7, 4, 8.; δέεται and προσδέεται three times in Mem. 3, 6, 13. 14.; ἐδέετο, Hell. 6, 1, 18. In some of these passages no manuscript can be quoted against this reading, in others very few; notwithstanding which, the common form has been of late introduced by the editors into all; while in another passage (Mem. 4, 8, 11.) this was done long ago, although the old editions and four manuscripts have προσδέεται. Eight passages in a single author, while not one is quoted from any of the older writers, are sufficient to warrant our attributing with certainty to this author at least, an Ionicism, of which the existence is very probable at that æra of the Atticism and in that particular verb; while we can see no reason for this form, which was unknown to the other Attics, having been foisted into this one writer by copyists or grammarians. In addition to this we have the gloss of the Antiatticist in Bekker p. 94. Ἐδέετο ἀντὶ τοῦ ἐδεῖτο, which merely proves the great probability of what was most probable before. The only usage of later writers and Grammarians (see Schæfer ad Greg. p. 431.) at a time when certainly every one pronounced δεῖσθαι, is a single affected imitation of Xenophon. Among the instances of similar resolution in other verbs mentioned by Lobeck ad Phryn. p. 220. sqq. are only two from pure writers of πλεῖν, which may be seen under that verb. These make it probable that the Ionicism was still familiar enough in those short verbs, to cause it to be preferred in the case before us.

‡ Dobree (on Aristoph. Plut. 216.) rejects much too disdainfully this precept given in the Hort. Adon. 187. b., for the truth of which I certainly cannot answer, but which is undoubtedly taken from one of the older Atticists: for this writer quotes (exactly as Phrynichus often does, e. g. pp. 70. 84. 120. 250. Lob.) the ῥήτορες, that is to say the later ones, as using the common form. If now we compare δηλόει δηλοῖ, we have an analogy for δέῃ δεῖ. The passages quoted by Reisig from Aristophanes Plut. 216. Ran. 265., where the reading in many, and those the best manuscripts, is κἂν δεῖ, "and even if it must be," give the above-mentioned precept great weight. Still this usage, if I have stated it correctly, cannot be the same as a similar one in κεῖμαι, as μὴ διάκειμαι does not arise from contraction.

even call *Attic* forms. See Greg. Cor. in Att. 72. with the notes. Apollon. de Adv. p. 542, 33., and the Exc. Paris. at the end of Schæfer's Gregorius, p. 678. Phavor. vv. δεῖν and πλεῖν. But there are no instances quite free from doubt; which warrants our suspecting that the existence of these forms arose entirely from the syntax of the sentences being mistaken, and that the forms are really infinitives standing elliptically or used as substantives*.

Homer has this verb with the stem or root ΔΕΥ- instead of ΔΕ-, very frequently as a passive δεύομαι, ἐδεύετο, δευήσομαι, and once as active ἐδεύησεν, Od. ι, 540.; both voices in the sense of *to be wanting*; so that the poet, in speaking of a momentary event, appears to have used the aor. act. instead of the common prose form δεηθῆναι. In the midst of this great unanimity of meaning in the root ΔΕΥ-, we find two passages which are very striking: 1. Il. ι, 337. which has the impersonal δεῖ, whereas in all the other passages χρή is used in a similar sense: 2. Od. σ, 100. ἐμεῖο δ' ἔδησεν in the sense of the above-mentioned ἐδεύησεν, where the common form ἐδέησεν therefore is shortened in a way which we meet with nowhere else.†

* In the first place, it is very remarkable that the Lexicons of Atticists and rhetoricians which have come down to us, and which do not overlook the comparative πλεῖν for πλέον, have not the two forms in question: beside which, some of the manuscripts, even that of Gregory, mention only πλεῖν, and have not the addition of δεῖν ἀντὶ τοῦ δέον: while δοκεῖν depends entirely on the most uncertain authorities, Phavorinus and the above-mentioned Exc. Paris. Hence it is highly probable that some of the very late Grammarians were the first to make use of the well-known case of the comparative πλεῖν for πλέον, in order to understand δεῖν and δοκεῖν in certain phrases as participles. Whence under the word Δεῖν in the Etym. M. we find after that explanation the following, ἢ ἀπὸ τοῦ δέειν, δεῖν. The gloss itself may be compared with those on Δεῖν ψήθην and Δεῖν in Hesychius. And how suitable the article is to the infinitive τὸ δεῖν, τὸ δέον, in the latter Lexicographer, is clear. Under these circumstances the example from Lysias c. Alcib. 1. p. 140. 12. (the only one which has been hitherto adduced,) is of no weight, as the passage is otherwise corrupted, and those manuscripts which are well known have only δεῖ, while δεῖν as well as δέον is an arbitrary correction: one of these we must choose, and our choice will of course be regulated by a consideration of all that has been brought forward. As to δοκεῖν, I have no doubt that it depends entirely on a comparison of the expression ἐμοὶ δοκεῖν with ἐκείνῳ δοκοῦν; but this comparison is most uncertain; for the meaning of the latter is, "*since it seems good and pleasing to him*," that of the former "*as it appears to me*," which in Herodotus is evidently an infinitive, ἐμοὶ δοκέειν (see Herm. ad Vig. not. 204.). We have now therefore to consider the contraction as stripped of all analogy; for πλεῖν, if that be the only instance, is sufficiently explained as shortened from πλεῖον, which in a phrase of daily occurrence like πλεῖον ἢ μύριοι is very conceivable. But in πλεῖον the pure sound of the stem or root is ει, which in δέον or δοκέον is unheard of even in the Ionic dialect. Further, the name Κλεισθένης, which the Grammarians introduce also in the comparison, is compounded not of Κλεο- but of Κλεει-, from κλέος, as ὀρείνομος from ὄρος; and, not to omit anything bearing on the question, the name Νείλεως is not from Νεόλεως, but a dialect from the old name Νηλεύς, the head of the family of that old colonist.

† If criticism were not bound to consider as sacred whatsoever the old rha-

ΔΗΚ–. See Δάκνω.

(Δήω. See ΔΑ–4.)

Διαιτάω, *I arbitrate*: pass. with fut. midd. *I live in a certain way, lead a certain kind of life.* The only irregularity in the formation of this verb is in the augment, as it makes sometimes ἐδιαίτησα, sometimes διῄτησα, and has even the double augment κατεδιῄτησα. Compare the following.

Διᾱκονέω, (and διᾱκονέομαι depon. midd.) *I serve.* Like the preceding verb its irregularity consists in the augment: thus ἐδιακόνησα and διηκόνησα, δεδιακόνηκα and δεδιηκόνηκα.

On the derivation of this word, which is indisputably not compounded of διά, see Buttm. Lexil. p. 231.

Διδάσκω, *I teach*, loses the σ in the formation; thus fut. διδάξω; aor. 1. ἐδίδαξα; perf. δεδίδαχα; perf. pass. infin. δεδιδάχθαι, Il. λ, 831. &c.—Midd.

It comes from ΔΑΩ, and is exactly like ἀλύσκω, which may be compared with it. In the poets we meet with another future διδασκήσω, e. g. in Hes. ε, 64. Hymn. Cer. 144.

Δίδημι. See Δέω, *I bind*.

Διδράσκω, *I run away*, generally occurs in composition with ἀπό, ἐξ, or διά: fut. δράσομαι; perf. δέδρακα; all with ᾱ long; hence Ion. διδρήσκω, δρήσομαι, &c.—Aor. 2. ἔδρᾱν, -ᾱς, -ᾱ, -ᾱμεν, -ᾱτε, ἔδρᾱσαν and ἔδρᾰν; conjunct. δρῶ, -ᾷς, -ᾷ, &c.; optat. δραίην; imperat. δρᾶθι; infin. δρᾶναι; part. δράς, δράντος (not δρᾶντος); Ion. ἔδρην, -ῆναι, &c.: but δραίην, δράς retain the α, according to the analogy of ἔστην.

psodists and critics have handed down as the text of those primæval monuments of antiquity, it would be easy to alter the one passage to χρῄ, and the other to ἐμεῦ δ' ἐδέησεν. If however the Homeric formation δευήσω be compared with the common δεήσω, there will be great probability in the conjecture of some moderns, that this verb had originally a digamma, which in some cases produced the diphthong ευ, as in εὔαδεν; while in others it was entirely omitted, as in δεήσω, ἕαδεν. Hence also we may find it easier to explain how δέεσθαι, &c. remained longer than others in a state of resolution; and to bring πλέει within the same analogy we may adduce the formation ἔπλευσα. But the steps by which we advance here are not so sure as in εὔαδεν and καυάξας: we will therefore content ourselves with merely pointing out the probability.

The form ἀποδιδράναι in Thucyd. 4, 46., which would come from δίδρημι, Bekker has now amended (from the reading of several manuscripts) to ἀποδρᾶναι; but in Dio Chrysost. to. 1. p. 52. we read ἀνάγκη μισεῖν, αὐτὸν καὶ ἀποδιδρᾶναι* θέλειν, which might very well have been grounded on such a precedent as the above passage of Thucydides.

The aor. 1. ἐδρᾶσα, which is the regular aorist of δράω, *I do*, was also that of διδράσκω in the common dialect, and after the time of Aristotle in the written language; here and there it is found also in some copies of the earlier authors†.

The formation of the aor. 2. in ᾱν, &c. detailed above not only arises completely from the analogy laid down in the note under Γιγνώσκω, but is also expressly given in the same way by Phrynichus in the Appar. Sophist. p. 11. Two instances of the 1. sing. occur also in Lex. Seguer. 6. p. 419, 31. The quantity of the ᾱ is evident from the Ionicism ἔδρην, and from the following conclusion of an anapæstic verse of Aristoph. in Herodian (Piers. p. 465.), δεῦ|ρο δ' ἂν οὐκ | ἀπέδρα|μεν: with which we may join the unquestionable amendment of Reiske in Eurip. Heracl. 14. ἐξέδρᾱμεν for ἐξέδραμον. Compare Γηρᾶναι. But that the α in the 3. plur. ἔδραν should be short, is only according to the general rule of the aor. 2. of verbs in μι, with which this aorist corresponds‡. We have only to add one remark, that according to the grammarians Phrynichus and Herodian this form must have been used by the Attics also; Thucydides and Xenophon however have only the regular ἀπέδρασαν.

Δίδωμι, *I give*: fut. δώσω; aor. 1. ἔδωκα§; perf. δέδωκα; aor. 2. ἔδων; perf. pass. δέδομαι; aor. midd. ἐδόμην.

Homer has in the pres. 2. and 3. sing. διδοῖς, διδοῖ, as formed from διδόω, Il. ι, 164. 519., which forms occur also in Herodot. and Hippocr. But δίδοισθα, or rather διδοῖσθα, is found only in Homer, e. g. Il. τ, 270. The following forms are also Homeric only; the imperat. pres. δίδωθι (Od. γ, 380.), the infin. pres. διδοῦναι (Il. ω, 425.), the fut. διδώσειν, δι-

* The circumflex need not excite our suspicion against this form; not only because we find it so often erroneously placed over the termination in άναι, but because the radical long α in this verb might certainly produce a present in ᾱμι, ᾶναι.

† Thus it is easy to conceive that ἀποδράσας and -άσασα, wherever they are now met with in Attic writers, are corruptions of ἀποδράς and -ᾶσα. See Bekker on Andoc. Myst. 125. Lys. c. Andoc. 28. and compare Γηράω.

‡ Thus the Dorics and Epics use ἔθεν, ἔστᾰν, ἔδον, ἔδυν, for ἔθεσαν, ἔστησαν, &c. The same takes place in other anomalous aorists, as ἔτλᾰν, βάν, for ἔτλησαν, ἔβησαν, Hom.

§ This irregular aorist in -κα is principally used in the sing. in good writers; in the plur., particularly in 1 and 2 pers., the Attics generally preferred the aor. 2. There are neither moods nor participles of the form in -κα, except the participle of the middle, which however with its indicative belongs to the Ion. and Dor. dialects. Except this indic. and particip. the other moods of the middle are never met with. In Attic prose we find, of the middle, the aor. 2. only.

δώσομεν (Od. ν, 358. ω, 314.), and the aor. 2. *δόσκον* for *ἔδων* (Hom.).*—The imperat. pres. *δίδοι*, as from *δίδοιμι*, is an unusual Doricism for *δίδου*, in Pind. Ol. 1, 136. The infin. pres. *διδῶν*† (Theocr. 29, 9.) is also Doric. Instead of *ἐδίδοσαν*, the Dorics and Epics used *ἔδιδον*, *δίδον*, Hymn. Cer. 328, 437. On the unusual accentuation of the conjunct. pass. *δίδωται* and the opt. pass. *ἀπόδοιντο*, which look like Atticisms, (Fischer quotes some instances from Ionic writers,) see the second paragraph under *Δύναμαι*.

The form *δόθι*, and *θέτι* from *τίθημι*, are never used. The former was once the reading in Nicand. Th. 562., but is now rejected by the discovery of better manuscripts. *Δῷσι* is 3. sing. of the conjunct. for *δῷ*, as *ἱστῆσι* is for *ἱστῇ*. As the conjunctive arises from contraction, it is again resolved by the Ionics; thus for *διδῶ*, *δῶ*, *δῶς*, &c. they use *διδώω*, *δώω*, *δώῃς*, *δώωμεν*, *δώητε*, &c.: and in this resolved form the Epics shorten the vowel, thus *δώομεν* for *δώωμεν*, &c.

Δίζημαι, *I seek*, an Ionic depon. midd. according to the formation in *μι*, but retaining the *η* in the passive: thus *δίζημαι*, *ἐδίζητο*, *ἐδίζηντο*, *δίζησθαι*, *διζήμενος*, Herodot.; *δίζηαι*, Od. λ, 100.; *ἣν δίζῃ*, Callim. Epig. 11. The shortened forms *δίζεαι* (Theocr. 25, 37.) and *δίζεο* (in an hexameter in Etym. M. v. *ἀσελγαίνειν*) are perfectly regular. But the forms of the proper theme in *-ομαι*‡ are also frequently found. In Herodotus however those in *-εται*, *-ετο*, *-εσθαι*, are now, according to the manuscripts, universally changed into those with *η*: and in Callim. Epig. 17., where hitherto has stood *δίζονται*, Jacobs has adopted from the Vatican manuscript (vii, 459.) *δίζηνται*, so that the other formation in general, at least in the older writers, may be doubted§. Fut. *διζήσομαι*, Od. π, 239.; aor. 1. *ἐδιζησάμην ἐμεωυτόν*, Heraclit. ap. Plut. adv. Colot. 20. p. 1118.

The verb *δίζω*, which occurs in Il. π, 713. and in an oracle in Herodot. 1, 65. with the meaning of *to doubt*, is supposed to be the same stem or family as *δίζημαι*. Compare *Ἐξέδισεν* preserved in Suidas from some lost writer.

Δικεῖν, infin. to *ἔδικον*, *I threw*; a defective poet. aorist [found in the lyric and tragic poets, with no other tenses, except the aor. 1. *ἔδιξε* in Simmias Br. Anal. 1, 208. In Lycophr. 531. is *πήδημα λαιψηρὸν δικών*.]

* On this iterative see *δύσκεν* toward the end of *Δύω*.

† See Mus. Ant. Stud. 1. p. 242. sqq.

‡ In Brunck's Anal. 3, 216. is *διζομένη*.

§ In Apollon. 1, 1208. the reading *δίζετο κρηναίης* has been preferred perhaps a little too hastily, on account of the rare occurrence of *δίζομαι*. But *ἐδίζετο* in Moschus 2, 28. stands undisputed, as it does in the following fragment, perhaps of Callimachus, in Suid. v. *ἄγκος*; *ποσσὶδ' ἀνελθεῖν Ἄγκος ἐς ὑψικάρηνον ἐδίζετο*: not to mention (see Ind. Gesn.) the Orphic poems.

Διστάζω, *I doubt*, (like βαστάζω and νυστάζω,) seems to partake of the two formations of verbs in -ζω; its future is διστάσω, and though I know of no examples of the formation in -ξω, -γμαι, &c., yet the verbal substantive is δισταγμός, and still we find δίστασις.

Διψάω, *I thirst*; fut. διψήσω; infin. διψῆν, never διψᾶν.

Δίω. See Δεῖσαι.

Διώκω, *I pursue*, has the fut. διώξω in Xen. Cyr. 6, 3, 13. Anab. 1, 4, 8. and Demosth. p. 989.; but the general Attic fut. is διώξομαι, Aristoph. Equ. 368. Elmsl. Ach. 278. Plat. Theæt. p. 168. a. On ἐδιώκαθον, διωκάθειν, from διωκάθω, see Ἀμύνω and note.

ΔΜΕ-. See Δέμω.

Δοάσσατο, δόαται. See Δέαται.

Δοκέω, *I seem*, *appear*; also *I think*: it forms its tenses from ΔΟΚΩ, as fut. δόξω, aor. 1. ἔδοξα; but takes its perf. from the passive δέδογμαι, *I have seemed*.

The regular formation δοκήσω, aor. 1. ἐδόκησα, belongs to the poets. Thus δεδόκημαι in Pind. Nem. 5, 36. Eurip. Med. 761. Aristoph. Vesp. 726. (also Herodot. 7, 16, 3.) must be distinguished from the Epic δεδοκημένος under Δέχομαι.

For a full account of the supposed neut. part. δοκεῖν for δοκοῦν, see Δέω, *I am in want of*, with note.

Δουπέω, *I sound heavily*, *I fall*: fut. δουπήσω; perf. δέδουπα; aor. 1. ἐδούπησα and (Il. λ, 45.) ἐγδούπησα from a stem or root ΓΔΟΥΠ-, which appears to bear the same relation to δουπέω as κτυπέω does to τύπτω*.

Δράσσω, Att. δράττω, *I seize*, *grasp*; but the middle is more usual in the same sense.

Hence the 2. pers. perf. pass. δέδραξαι is used in Eurip. Tro. 745. as a middle. [So also δεδραγμένος, Il. ν, 393. Soph. Antig. 235.—Passow.]

* I suppose, for instance, that γδουπ- and κτυπ- are essentially the same onomatopœia for the sound proceeding from a heavy body, whether striking or struck; and hence that δουπεῖν came to signify the falling of such a body, τύπτειν the beating it.

Δράω, *I do*, is inflected regularly with α long; hence the perf. δέδρᾱκα is common to this verb and to διδράσκω.

Beside δέδρᾱμαι we find δέδρασμαι; see Thucyd. 3, 54. Hence the verbal adj. δραστός, δραστέος.

[Δρώοιμι is an Epic form produced from the optat. pres. act. δρῷμι, (Od. ο, 317.), and the only instance in Homer of this verb in its simple form: it was most frequent in the Doric dialect, in which it was used like the Attic πράττω, Aristot. Poet. 3, 6.—Passow.]

Δρέπω, *I pluck*, is inflected regularly; thus fut. δρέψω, &c. The midd. is frequent: [αἷμα δρέψασθαι is an unusual expression in Æschyl. Sept. 720. Verbal adj. δρεπτός.—Passow.]

In Pind. Pyth. 4, 234. δραπών is the particip. of the aor. 2., and perhaps the only part of that tense to be met with: but such solitary forms are not unusual in this aorist. Δρέπτω is less common than δρέπω; we find it in Moschus 2, 69. The middle δρέπτομαι is of more frequent occurrence; δρεπτομέναν, Anal. 1, p. 241. No. 81. Compare Γλύφω.

Δρύπτω, *I tear the flesh, scratch*, is inflected regularly: fut. δρύψω; perf. δέδρῡφα; perf. pass. δέδρυμμαι; aor. 1. midd. δρυψάμενος, Od. β, 153.

That ἀποδρύφοι in Il. ω, 21. cannot be an aorist, as some have explained it to be, is evident from the construction of the sentence. It must therefore be the pres. optat. of a sister-form ἀποδρύφω; and we know that it is not unusual for the more simple form of a verb to have been retained in the poets only, or formed by them on account of the metre, while the other passed into general use*.

Δύναμαι, *I can*, forms the pres. and imperf. like ἵσταμαι; depon. with fut. midd. δυνήσομαι; aor. 1. pass. ἐδυνήθην†, ἠδυνήθην, or ἐδυνάσθην, which last form (more Ionic than the others) never takes the augment; aor. 1. midd. ἐδυνησάμην, Hom.; perf. δεδύνημαι. Verbal adj. δυνατός, *possible*.

In the passive of all verbs in μι there are instances in the common language of a formation in the conjunctive and optative moods, by which they assimilate, sometimes in sound but always in accent, to the common conjugation. Instances in τίθεμαι, ἵσταμαι, δίδομαι may be seen under

* Thus βλάβεται in Hom. for βλάπτω, λίτομαι in the Hom. Hymns for λίσσομαι, στενάχω Epic for στενάζω.

† On the double augment see Βούλομαι and note.

their respective verbs: in the present case we have as proparoxytons, the optat. *δύναιτο* and the conjunct. *δύνωμαι*, (Ion.) *δύνηαι*, *δύνηται**, which have undoubtedly been introduced into Homer from the common language.

The shortening of the 2. pers. sing. *-ασαι* by the Attics into *-ῃ* does not apply to this verb, which took rather the Ionic form *δύνῃ*† (Ion. *δύνεαι*) and was used thus by the Tragedians (Eurip. Hec. 253. Androm. 238. Soph. Phil. 798. ed. Buttm. with the notes). In prose *δύνασαι* only was in use. But in the imperf. the Attics preferred even in prose the form *ἐδύνω*, *ἠδύνω*, to that in *-ασο*. Moeris, p. 182. Xen. Anab. 7, 5, 5.

Of the three forms of the aor. 1. pass. *ἐδυνάσθην* is the only one in Homer: it is preferred by Herodotus (see Wessel. on 7, 105.), and is frequent in Xenophon. The Attics prefer the double augment *ἠδυνάμην*, *ἠδυνήθην*; the former occurs also in Herodot. 1, 10. But in Thucyd. and Xenoph. the simple augment is the more common. Homer generally uses the aor. midd. *δυνήσατο*.

Δύω. Of this verb some tenses have the immediate meaning *to go into*, and others the causative meaning *to put into, envelope in*; while in all essential points it follows the examples of *ἵστημι* and *φύω*, and the analogies laid down in sect. 113. of my Grammar‡. The pres. act. *δύω*, *καταδύω*, &c. has the causative meaning *to envelope in*, *to sink anything*, and retains it in the fut. and aor. 1. act. *δύσω*, *ἔδῡσα*. Pass. *ἐδύθην* with *υ* short§. The Midd. *δύομαι*, *δύσομαι*, *ἐδυσάμην* has therefore the meaning *to wrap oneself up in*, which then very naturally makes a transition to the intransitive or immediate sense, *to go into*, *go under*, *sink under*. But this again takes a transitive meaning, e. g. *to put on*

* Notwithstanding *δύναμαι* as a proparoxyton is the only form in use, according to which we find *δύνηαι* (Il. Ζ, 229.) accented in the same way, yet the Ionians admit the resolution and write *δυνέωμαι*; e. g. in Herodot. 4, 97. — Compare Ἐπίσταμαι.

† [Yet Passow says that *δύνῃ* is in good writers conjunctive only, though it does occur in Eurip. Hec. 257., and that the Att. and Dor. is *δύνᾳ*, Schæf. Soph. Phil. 798.]

‡ [That is, of Buttmann's large detailed Grammar (*Ausführliche Sprachlehre*), of which this Catalogue forms part of the second volume. The section referred to, consisting of twelve pages, is of course too long to be inserted here, and to make extracts or an abridgement would be most unsatisfactory.—Ed.]

§ Like *ἐλύθην*, *ἐτύθην*, and the perf. pass. *λέλῠμαι*, although from *λύω*, *δύω*, *θύω*, fut. *-ύσω*, &c., all with *υ* long. See Δέω, *I bind*, with note; also Τείνω.

(a garment). All these meanings belonging to the immediate sense join with the middle voice the *active* perf. δέδυκα and the aor. 2. ἔδυν*. In addition to the above comes a new active form δύνω, which properly speaking is synonymous with the middle δύομαι, as ἔδυν is with the midd. ἐδυσάμην; yet so that in certain constructions and in the compounds these active forms are preferred.

Such is the foundation of the usage in this verb; the modifications arising out of the various deviations of its sense, particularly in the compounds, belong to the lexicons and lexicographers.

The aor. 2. of this verb ἔδῡν, like ἔφῡν, retains the υ long through all its persons (ἔδῡμεν, &c.); but the 3. plur. ἔδῠν, shortened by the Epic and Doric writers for ἔδῡσαν, has the υ short according to the regular analogy. See ἔδραν, &c. under Διδράσκω with note. Of the conjunctive and optative moods we must however make particular mention. To form a conjunct. according to the analogy of ἔστην, στῶ, is not possible, but it may follow that of the resolved form στέω or στείω, στῇης: and thus we find a conj. δύω, δύῃς, δύῃ from ἔδυν, not only in Homer, (e. g. Il. ρ, 186. ι, 604. λ, 194.) but even in Attic prose, ἐπειδὰν ὁ ἥλιος δύῃ, Plato Cratyl. 64. p. 413. b.; which forms therefore must not be derived from the present δύω, nor must we attribute to this latter an immediate sense. Of the optat. δύην (ῡ for υι) I can produce but one example, viz. ἐκδῦμεν† for ἐκδυίημεν (like σταίην – σταῖμεν) in Il. π, 99. But according to Bekker's observation, the construction in Od. ι, 377. σ, 348. υ, 286. requires the optative, and consequently in those passages instead of δύῃ we must write δύη.

The Epic δύσκεν, Il. θ, 271. is the 3. sing. aor. 2 act. for ἔδυ, and formed according to the regular analogy of iteratives, like στάσκον, δόσκον, &c. consequently it means, *he drew back each time*.

The Epic sister-forms of the aor. 1. midd. ἐδύσετο‡, imperat. δύσεο, (like ἐβήσετο, imperat. βήσεο,) are some among many instances of the aor. 1. taking the termination of the aor. 2., or, which is the same thing, the aor. 2. taking the characteristic σ of the aor. 1., of which the most complete instance is the well-known aor. ἔπεσον, πεσεῖν, &c.

* For an account of this aorist see note under Γιγνώσκω.

† See Buttm. Lexil. p. 425 and note.

‡ Amidst the uncertainty which prevails in Homer's text between ἐδύσατο and -ετο, it is very probable that the form in -ατο crept into it from common analogy, and that the true reading in the Epic poets is always ἐβήσετο, ἐδύσετο. At the same time it is possible that usage might have attached a distinct meaning to each form, and that Homer might have said in every instance δύσετο ὅμιλον, δύσετο ἠέλιος, &c., but δύσατο τεύχεα, χιτῶνα, &c.

See Buttm. Lexil. p. 226. note. The Epic participle δυσόμενος, used in the sense of a present in Od. α, 24. Hes. ε, 382., is certainly not a future; and as it does not describe one in particular, but the general setting of some of the heavenly bodies, it may be explained as coming from the common expression δύσετο δ' ἠέλιος.

Later writers form from δύνω an aor. 1., at least in the participle, ἡλίου δύναντος, μετὰ ἥλιον δύναντα, Æl. V. H. 4, 1, 1. Paus. 2, 11. ; Herodotus inflects the form δύνω, as he does many other barytones*, as if it were a pres. in -εω; thus 3, 98, ἐνδυνέουσι, *they put on*.

E.

Ἐάφθη. See Ἅπτω.

Ἐάω, *I permit*, &c. : fut. ἐάσω ; but in the augment it changes the ε not into η, but into ει†, e. g. imperf. εἴων ; aor. 1. εἴασα, &c.

The Ionics leave out the augment ; thus imperf. ἔων for εἴων, [ἔασα for εἴασα; Hom. who has also a pres. εἰάω, εἰῶ, Il. δ, 55. The fut. midd. ἐάσομαι is used in a passive sense, Thucyd. 1, 142.—Passow.]

Ἐγγυάω, *I give as a pledge* ; Midd. *I pledge myself*. This verb is inflected regularly, but is uncertain in its augment : thus we have in general use the imperf. ἠγγύων, and the aor. 1. ἠγγύησα, yet the perf. is equally common as ἐγγεγύηκα ; and again we find without any augment at all ἐγγυήσατο, ἐγγυηκώς‡, &c.

Ἐγείρω, *I waken (any one)* : fut. ἐγερῶ ; aor. 1. ἤγειρα ; perf. with Attic redupl. ἐγήγερκα ; perf. pass. ἐγήγερμαι. Midd. *I waken (myself)* ; to which we must add the syncopated aor. ἠγρόμην.

* Thus we find συμβαλλεόμενος, ὑπερβαλλέειν, ἐῤῥιπτέον, πιεζεύμενος, Herodot.

† The following verbs do the same : ἔχω, ἕρπω and ἑρπύζω, ἕλκω, ἐθίζω, ἑλίσσω, ἑστιάω, ἕπω and ἕπομαι, ἐργάζομαι.

‡ See Reisk. Ind. in Isæum. It is remarkable too that the aor. 1. ἐνεγγύησα, ἐνεγγυησάμην occurs frequently : see Budæus p. 76. 77. Stephan. Thesaur. and Lucian. Lexic. v. ἐνεγγυᾷν. Budæus explains this to be merely the augment; which is singular, as analogy would require ἐνεγύησα. Others place it as without the augment under ἐνεγγυᾷν. I consider it to be an anomaly in the augmentation ; and that daily pronunciation, deceived by ear and sense, strayed from ἐνεγύησα into the double compound ἐνεγγύησα.

This aorist has been mistaken by the Grammarians, at least the later ones, who, as we see in Thom. Mag., supposed a present ἔγρομαι. Such a one however is never met with, and the remaining forms are in every instance plainly aorists, e. g. ἔγρετο δ' ἐξ ὕπνου, Il. β, 41. κἂν ἔγρῃ μεσημβρινὸς, οὐδείς σ' ἀποκλείσει, Aristoph. Vesp. 774. In the same way the infin. also expresses universally the moment of waking: and hence it was a very easy step to substitute the accentuation of ἐγρέσθαι, and ascribe ἔγρεσθαι to the above-mentioned mistake of the Grammarians. But in a form which has always remained in the common language, and of which the infin. for instance occurs frequently (Od. ν, 124. Apollon. Rh. 4, 1352. Lucian Dial. Mar. 14, 2.), more than usual circumspection is necessary. In a similar case under ἀγείρω, where ἀγέροντο, ἀγερέσθαι occurred only in the old Epic language, and the latter but once, grammatical decision was necessary, and the perfectly regular aorist form required the accent agreeably to the general rule. Here on the contrary it is possible that the form being altered by syncope had caused a deviation from analogy even in the earlier times, an instance of which we shall see in the unquestionable and very similar aorist ἕζεσθαι under Ἵζω. Compare also Πέφνων.

The perf. 2. ἐγρήγορα,

whose anomalous reduplication was probably caused by the sound of ἠγρόμην, ἔγρεσθαι, belongs, like that aorist, to the immediate meaning, and expresses the being in a certain state or situation, *I am watching**. The pluperf. ἐγρηγόρειν has the force of an imperfect.

That no other part of the verb but this perfect (with the force of a present) occurs in the Attic writers, with the meaning of *to watch*, has been sufficiently proved by Fischer (iii. p. 65.), by Porson, by Schneider on Xenoph. Anab. 4, 6, 22., and by Lobeck ad Phryn. p. 119. From it however arose in the common language a present ἐγρηγορέω, and in the writers of the N. T. γρηγορέω. But we find as early as Homer (Od. υ, 6.) a participle ἐγρηγορόων, as if from an indicative in ῶ, ᾷς, ᾷ.†

In Homer we have further, in the place of the 2. plur. ἐγρηγόρατε, a form more convenient for the metre with a passive termination, ἐγρήγορθε‡; and to this we may join the corresponding infinitive ἐγρη-

* See note under Ἄγνυμι.

† The participle ἐγρηγοροῦσα in Hippocr. de Insomn. 1. is therefore defensible, although we find just before as a present, ἐγρήγορεν.

‡ In the same way from ἀνώγετε, ἀνω-

γορθαι. We find also in the same poet a very peculiar deviation in the active form of the 3. plur. (likewise with the θ), ἐγρηγόρθασιν.*

Ἐδω. See Ἐσθίω.

Ἐδοῦμαι. See Ἴζω.

Ἕζομαι. See Ἴζω.

Ἐθέλω and θέλω, *I wish, am willing*: fut. ἐθελήσω and θελήσω; but aor. 1. ἠθέλησα; imperf. ἤθελον; and perf. ἠθέληκα in good prose writers; τεθέληκα is an Alexandrine perf.; see Lobeck ad Phryn. p. 332.

[These two verbs are the same in meaning, and differ only in form: θέλω is not found in any Epic poet before the Alexandrine æra, ἐθέλω on the other hand never occurs in the iambic trimeter of Attic tragedy: the latter is the regular form in Attic prose, although the former is occasionally met with in the best writers, in such a combination as *εἰ θέλεις*, Lobeck ad Phryn. p. 7. Hence the Attics naturally preferred the imperf. ἤθελον and the aor. 1. ἠθέλησα, in which the augment comes regularly from ἐθέλω; consequently these forms are not to be compared with ἠβουλήθην, ἠδυνήθην, ἤμελλον. On the difference of meaning between βούλομαι and ἐθέλω see Buttm. Lexil. p. 194. &c.—Passow.]

Ἐθίζω, *I accustom*, is regularly inflected; e. g. fut. ἐθίσω, Att. -ιῶ, Xen. Cyr. 3, 3, 53.; but it takes ει for its augment, like ἐάω, which see with its note. Compare also the following.

Ἔθω. From this old present (of which we now find no remains in the Epic writers except the participle ἔθων, *being accustomed to*,) comes the very common perfect εἴωθα, *I am accustomed to*. The other tenses are furnished by the passive of ἐθίζω, of which the perf. pass. εἴθισμαι is nearly the same as εἴωθα.

γέτω, came ἄνωχθε, ἀνώχθω; and this seems the most natural way of accounting for the Epic πέποσθε (see πάσχω), viz. πέπονθα, πεπόνθατε, πέποσθε. See under Ἄνωγα.

* These forms do indeed appear in their external relations like a series of anomalies; but I think I can point out a general regularity running through the whole. The transition of ἐγρηγόρατε to the passive form ἐγρήγορθε was justified by the neuter meaning of ἐγρήγορα, which suited the perf. pass. quite as well as the perf. active, just as in ἀνέῳγα and ἀνέῳγμαι: but this passive might, according to the analogy of ἄωρτο (ἤορτο), retain the ο; and thus ἐγρήγορμαι, -ορθε, -όρθαι are regular. That the active form ἐγρηγόρθασι arose again from this ἐγρήγορθε, might have been only an appearance, but devoid of truth. As from ἀγείρω came ἀγερέθω, so from ἐγείρω might come ἐγερέθω and ἐγέρθω; of which latter theme the regular perf. 2. would be ἐγρήγορθα.

The perf. εἴωθα* is a lengthening of the stem or radical form, exactly as we see from εἴδω, ᾔδειν, ᾔδη, the lengthened form ἠείδη. The object in the formation of this perfect was to preserve both the augment and the change of vowel; it was therefore properly εἴοθα: hence arose, by transposing the quantities, the Ionic ἔωθα in Herodotus, and thence again came the common εἴωθα. The Doric writers had another formation, similar to the perf. 1. but with the change of vowel, ἔθωκα. See Buttm. Lexil. p. 138. Ἐώθεε (like ὀπώπεε) is according to the regular Ionic formation a pluperfect, and so it is used in Herodot. 4, 127.; but both are used also as perfects, the former in 2, 68. the latter in 3, 37. It has been wished to do away this irregularity by substituting in these cases the regular perfect in ε; but as we find also in Herodot. ἔψεε, ἐνείχεε, and ὤφλεε, it appears to me most probable that the Ionics, accustomed to insert their ε not according to well-known analogies, but from a dark and uncertain feeling, lengthened the historic forms ἧψε, εἶχε, ὦφλε, as well as these two perfects, contrary to true analogy. Compare Ἕψω.

Εἴδω, ἴδω, *video*, an obsolete verb, whose place has been supplied by ὁράω: the tenses formed from it compose two distinct families, of which one has the meaning of *to see*, the other exclusively the meaning of *to know*†.

1. *to see*: the only tense which retains this meaning is the aor. 2. εἶδον, and Epic without the augment ἴδον; infin. ἰδεῖν, Ep. ἰδέειν; conjunct. ἴδω, Epic ἴδωμι; part. ἰδών: all these forms are Homeric. The aor. 2. midd. has the same meaning, εἰδόμην, in Hom., more frequently without the augment ἰδόμην; infin. ἰδέσθαι; conjunct. ἴδωμαι; imperat. ἰδοῦ. See also Ὁράω.

2. *to know*: οἶδα‡, *I know*, to which we may add the part. εἰδώς; infin. εἰδέναι, Ep. ἴδμεναι and ἴδμεν; imperat. ἴσθι; conjunct. εἰδῶ, Ep. ἰδέω also; optat. εἰδείην; pluperf. ᾔδειν; fut. εἴσομαι, but less frequently and mostly Epic εἰδήσω. The aor. and perf. are supplied from γιγνώσκω.

Of the regular persons of οἶδα, the 2. sing. and the three persons of the plur. οἴδαμεν, οἴδατε, οἴδασι, occur but seldom, and, with regard to Attic usage, are disapproved of by the Atticists, while their places are supplied

* See note on ἀγήοχα under Ἄγω, and Buttm. Lexil. p. 136. &c.

† Those who attributed to εἴδω as a present the two meanings of *to see* and *to know* were guilty of an inaccuracy: εἴδω meant *I see, I see into it*; the perf. οἶδα, *I have seen into it*, and consequently *I know*.

‡ Properly the perf. 2. of εἴδω, with the augment thrown aside (like εἴκω, ἔοικα, Ion. οἶκα), but always used as a present, and consequently its pluperf. has the force of an imperfect. For the very remarkable analogy between the formation of this perf. and ἔοικα see last note but one under Εἴκω.

by syncopated forms: we will therefore first give the pure Attic usage of this verb in *οἶδα* and its pluperf. *ᾔδειν*.

ATTIC USAGE.

	S.	D.	P.
Pres.	οἶδα	—	ἴσμεν
	οἶσθα	ἴστον	ἴστε
	οἶδε(ν)	ἴστον	ἴσασι(ν)

Imperat.	Conj.	Optat.	Infin.	Part.
ἴσθι, ἴστω, &c.	εἰδῶ	εἰδείην	εἰδέναι	εἰδώς, -υῖα, -ός.

Imperf. S. ᾔδειν, Att. ᾔδη,
ᾔδεις, more generally ᾔδεισθα; Att. ᾔδης, more gen. ᾔδησθα,
ᾔδει; Att. ᾔδειν and ᾔδη;
D. ———
ᾔδειτον or ᾖστον,
ᾐδείτην — ᾔστην,
P. ᾔδειμεν — ᾖσμεν,
ᾔδειτε — ᾖστε,
ᾔδεσαν — ᾖσαν.*

Fut. εἴσομαι, less frequently εἰδήσω†.
Aor. (εἴδησα), εἰδῆσαι‡.
Verbal adj. (neut.) ἰστέον.

In both the Ion. and Dor. dialect we find the regular *οἶδας*, Od. α, 337.; in the Att. sometimes *οἶσθας*, Cratin. AB. 3. p. 1295. Piers. Moer. p. 283. Br. Aristoph. Fr. 143. Meineke Menandr. p. 122. The Ion. and Dor. use *ἴδμεν* for *ἴσμεν* §; and the Epics for *εἰδέναι* have *ἴδμεναι* and *ἴδμεν* as shortened from *εἰδέμεναι*. They have the same shortening of the radical vowel in the conjunct. *ἰδέω* (Il. ξ, 235. where however others read *εἰδέω* as a dissyllable), for *εἰδῶ*, and in the fem. part. *ἰδυῖα* for *εἰδυῖα*. We find also *εἴδετε*, 2. pl. conjunct. for *εἴδητε*, Od. ι, 17., *εἴδομεν* for *εἰδῶμεν*, Il. α, 363. For *ᾔδειν* the Epics have a lengthened form, by which the separation of the augment from the radical syllable is made more distinct (compare *ᾔειν* under Εἶμι, *I go*), and of which we find 2. pers. *ἠείδεις*, *ἠείδης*; 3. pers. *ἠείδει*, *ἠείδη*, Il. χ, 280. Od. ι, 206. Apoll. Rh. 2, 822., and Herodotus (1, 45.) has with the termination short *ᾔειδε* for *ᾔδει*‖. To these we must add a form as quoted in this verb only.

* On these syncopated forms of the dual and plural see Piers. ad Moer. p. 174.

† Isocr. ad Demonic. 4. *συνειδήσεις*; 5. *εἰδήσεις*; more frequently in the Ionic dialect.

‡ Hippocr. De Dec. Orn. 3. De Vict. Acut. 46. Aristot. Eth. 8, 3. Theophr. Procem. extr.

§ The Ion. *ἴδμεν* did not come from *ἴσμεν*; general analogy requires just the converse: *ἴδμεν* and the infin. *ἴδμεναι* belong evidently to *εἴδω*, and not to *ἴσημι*. See last note but one under *εἴκω*, *ἔοικα*.

‖ This shortened termination is certainly remarkable in a dialect which in other cases adds vowels without reason or ana-

ᾔδειν for ᾔδεσαν, Apollon. Rh. 2, 65. and lengthened to ἠείδειν, ib. 4, 1700. On the other hand Homer has (Il. σ, 405. Od. δ, 772.) the 3. pl. ἴσαν, in sound the same as the 3. plur. imperf. of εἶμι; and it is to be explained in the same way, for it bears the same relation to the syncopated form ᾖσαν for ᾔδεσαν, as ἴσαν from εἶμι does to ᾔισαν, ᾖσαν. Lastly Homer uses both futures, less frequently however εἰδήσω, Il. α, 546. The Epic infin. εἰδησέμεν, Od. ζ, 257.

In order to distinguish correctly where forms of this verb belong to the one or the other meaning, we must observe that many ideas which really relate to internal knowledge, but which we express by the sense of *seeing*, are given by the Greeks to the verb εἰδέναι. So in particular, ὡς εἰδῇς, ἵν' εἰδῆτε, in many combinations, where there is danger of our being influenced by custom to alter it to ἴδῃς, ἴδητε, e. g. in Demosth. Mid. 23. (p. 539. Rsk.) "I will lay it before you, ἵν' εἰδῆτε, ὅτι καὶ τούτων τὴν μεγίστην ὀφείλων δοῦναι δίκην φανήσεται:" and again at 24! (p. 541. init.): see other examples in Sturz. Lex. Xenoph. under εἴδειν 6.. To the above we may add also the verbal adj. ἰστέον, which is never used properly of seeing, though there are cases where we cannot translate it otherwise; see Heind. ad Plat. Theæt. 141. In the same way the Homeric conjunct. εἴδομεν, which always stands for εἰδῶμεν, (as at Il. ν, 327. Od. ζ, 257. where we should say "that we may see.., let us see...)" would be more accurately translated by *know*: nor can there be any doubt that the only passage where εἰδήσω according to the context might express the physical idea of seeing, Od. ζ, 257., belongs, like all the other cases, to εἰδέναι; "Thou wilt there know the most illustrious of the Phæacians." The later poets were the first, from misunderstanding perhaps the Homeric language, to use εἴδω in the exact sense of *to see*; εἴδομες, as a present, Theocr. 2, 25., or they formed from the aorist ἰδεῖν a new future, ἆρά γ' ἰδησῶ αὐτάν, ib. 3, 37.

But there is one part of the verb which really belongs to εἴδω, *video*, viz. the Epic middle εἴδομαι, εἰσάμην, used exactly as the Latin verbs *appareo* and *videor*, as at Il. θ, 555. α, 228. μ, 103.; and by a particular deviation it is joined with a dative in the sense of *to be like to*, εἰδόμενος Ἀκάμαντι, Il. ε, 462. εἴσατο υἷι Πριάμοιο, β, 791.

As εἴδω had originally the digamma, which we see in *videre* and the frequent hiatus in Homer before εἶδος, ἰδεῖν, εἰδέναι, &c., it had also the syllabic augment. This is the true explanation of the aor. εἶδον, ἰδεῖν, in the common language; thus εἴδω, ἔ—ιδον; ἰδεῖν, like λείπω,

logy. It is easy enough to conjecture that Herodot. wrote ἠείδεε: but the various reading ᾔδεε, from which this must be deduced, is very doubtful. The best manuscripts have ᾔειδε, the others εἶδε.

ἔλιπον, λιπεῖν; and (after the total disappearance of the digamma) by contraction εἶδον. This ει is therefore different from that in the pres. εἴδω, where it was added to strengthen the radical syllable ἰδ- as in λείπω from λιπ-. Hence in the Epic language the aor. εἰσάμην occurs with that augment ἐεισάμην. But Homer has also the particip. ἐεισάμενος, Il. β, 22., and Pindar (Nem. 10, 28.) ἐειδόμενος, for which it is necessary to suppose a theme ἐείδω, as such an ε is found in many verbs which had the digamma according to the analogy of ἐθέλω*.

Εἰκάζω, *I conjecture*, is regular, except in sometimes taking the augment, contrary to the analogy of verbs in ει: thus εἴκασα, εἴκασμαι, Att. ᾔκασα, ᾔκασμαι. See Moer. 182. and compare Ruhnk. ad Tim. v. εἰκάζων. In Plato it is found thus augmented in good manuscripts. See the following.

Εἴκω, *I yield*, is regular, and like other verbs in ει does not take the augment: thus imperf. εἶκον; aor. 1. εἶξα, where the place of the augment is supplied by the accent. The same is still visible in many compounds; thus ἄπειργε can only be the imperat. of ἀπείργω, the imperfect is ἀπεῖργε. But wherever in the written text of Homer the augment can be known only by the accent, it necessarily depended on the Grammarians whether to express it or not: and some of these appear to have been induced by an Ionic analogy to omit it entirely, writing ἵζε, ἔφιζε, ὑπόεικον; which last is the present reading of Il. π, 305. in Wolf's Homer, though he reads in every instance ἷζεν and ἐφῖζε. See Etym. M. v. καθῆστο.

Homer has the fut. midd. Il. α, 294. Od. μ, 117.; for at Il. δ, 62. ὑποείξομεν is the shortened conjunctive: in others we find the fut. act. as in Herodot. 7, 160. Xen. Hell. 5, 4, 45. Demosth. de Rhod. 197. ult. On εἴκαθον see ἀμύναθον under Ἀμύνω.

Εἴκω. We never find the present of this verb in the sense of *to be like to, to appear*, but the perf. 2. ἔοικα † with the force of a present is used in its stead; pluperf. ἐῴκειν,

* Thus ἐέλδομαι, ἐέλπομαι, ἐέργω, ἐίσκω.

† In the three perfects ἔοικα, ἔολπα, ἔοργα the ο is the usual change from the

and in Homer (Il. ν, 102.) once, 3. pl. ἐοίκεσαν; perf. infin. ἐοικέναι, part. ἐοικώς, -υῖα, -ός, beside which Homer has once εἰοικυῖαι, Il. σ, 418. The Attics preferred a sister-form of this part. εἰκώς, (like ἔοιδα, ἐοιδώς, εἰδώς,) particularly in its neuter εἰκός, although ἐοικός still remained always a good form. Homer has once εἰκώς, Il. φ, 254. and very frequently the fem. εἰκυῖα: the Ionics, but not Homer, always use οἶκα, οἰκώς, οἰκός. Fut. εἴξω (Aristoph. Nub. 1001.).

The same abbreviation which we find in εἰκώς takes place on account of the metre in other forms of this perfect; as, εἶκεν*, *he is like* (Aristoph. Av. 1298.), προσεικέναι (Eccl. 1161.); hence this infinitive is now written so in Nub. 185. and Eurip. Bacch. 1273., although it is possible that in all these passages it might have been written in the usual way and pronounced thus to suit the verse.

The Homeric εἶκε (Il. σ, 520.) is imperf., and the only instance of the pres. or imperf. of εἴκω.

Of the syncopated forms of this perfect we find ἔοιγμεν for ἐοίκαμεν in Soph. and Eurip., ἔικτον 3. dual for ἐοίκατον, Od. δ, 27., and ἐίκτην 3. dual pluperf. for ἐῳκείτην, Il. α, 104. This perfect made a further transition (without however changing its meaning) to the passive form†, of which Homer has only the pluperf. ἤϊκτο, and without the augm. ἔϊκτο, Il. ψ, 107.‡. The perf. ἔϊγμαι is found in composition in the post-Homeric poets, but with an irregular augment: thus προσῄξαι Eurip. Alc. 1066., προσῄικται Hesych.§.

radical vowel ε, and the ε at the beginning is the syllabic augment instead of the reduplication, like ἔαγα and some others; thus εἴκω ἔοικα, ἔργω ἔοργα, like δέρκω δέδορκα. Again in the three pluperfects ἐο- would by the temp. augm. be ἠο-, which again by Attic and Ionic analogy would become ἐω-, as χράομαι, Ion. χρέωμαι, νηός, Att. νεώς, and many others.

* [Whether the perf. εἶκα be a good Atticism or not, has been doubted; see Piers. ad Moer. p. 148. or Brunck Aristoph. Nub. 185.—Passow.]

† Compare the same thing in ἐγρήγορα —ἐγρηγόρθαι.

‡ In order to understand clearly the augment of the pluperf. in these forms ἐῴκει and ἤϊκτο, we must recollect that this is not the way of writing them which existed in Homer's time. Εἴκω is one of those verbs which had originally the digamma; the perfect therefore with the reduplication was ϜΕ-ϜΟΙΚΑ, consequently ἐῴκει was in his language ϜΕϜΟΙΚΕΙ, and ἔϊκτο, ἤϊκτο were ϜΕϜΙΚΤΟ, ΕϜΕϜΙΚΤΟ; which forms, if substituted for the others, suit the verse in every instance, by merely throwing aside occasionally a separable ν, as in Il. ψ, 107.

§ These forms appear to have arisen out of the old Epic ἤϊκτο by analogies imperfectly understood. For if it were wished to form at once from εἴκω, without going through the perfect ἔοικα, a perf. pass. ᾖγμαι, in order to resolve it into ἤϊγμαι, the leading analogy which

Lastly we have a complete deviation from the 3. plur. of the perf. in the Attic form εἴξασι, instances of which are collected by Ruhnk. ad Tim. p. 98. We have already shown in the Grammar* the exact similarity between this form and ἴσασι, and in so doing have refuted the short-sighted and incorrect explanations which have been given of both. The surest way appears to be this: to suppose that as in other inflected forms a σ sometimes appears and sometimes disappears between the stem of the verb and the termination, so the 3. plur. -αντι, -ᾶσι had a more complete ending -σαντι, -σᾱσιν, of which these two forms are chance remains†.

To this stem or root belong also ἴσκω, ἐΐσκω, which see in their places.

Εἰλύω, *I envelope*: fut. εἰλῡ́σω; perf. pass. εἴλῡμαι; aor. 1. part. εἰλυσθείς, Hom. Post-Hom. εἴλῠσα, Com. ap. Athen. 7. p. 293. d.

regulates such cases would be destroyed without sufficient reason. Whilst a language still exists in its vigour and purity, it is easy and not uncommon for an old analogy to be inaccurately understood: but to spin out new analogies on mere theory could have been only done by the later grammarian-poets.

* If we compare the different forms arising out of the two perfects ἔοικα and οἶδα, we shall find a very close analogy between them. From εἴκω, εἴδω, came ἔοικα, ἔοιδα; of the former a shortened form οἶκα is found in the Ionic dialect, of the latter οἶδα was in common use: the one has a part. εἰκώς, the other εἰδώς. Of ἔοικα the pluperf. (with the augm. after the analogy of ἑορτάζω, ἑωρτάζον) was ἐῴκειν; but there existed also the regular pluperf. with merely the οι shortened, as is clear from the 3. pluperf. pass. ἤϊκτο, (without the augm. εἴκτο,) which must come from a perf. εἶγμαι, pluperf. ἠΐγμην. In the same way from ἔοιδα came the pluperf. (ἠΐδειν) ᾔδειν. By syncope from ἔοικα were formed ἔοιγμεν and εἴκτην; from οἶδα—(οἶδ-σθα) οἶσθα, ἴδμεν, ἴσμεν, ἴστε; and in the pluperf. from ᾔδειν—ᾔσμεν, ᾔστε, ᾔσαν. From this ᾔσαν (for ἤδ-σαν) comes therefore the Homeric ἴσαν (for ἴδ-σαν) by the mere omission of the augment: so that it is not necessary to suppose for this single word that Homer was acquainted with ἴσημι, of which there is no other instance. And lastly,

ἔοικα— (οι into ι, εἴκ-σασιν) εἴξασιν;
οἶδα— (οι into ι, ἴδ-σασιν) ἴσασιν:

both Attic forms instead of the regular ἐοίκασιν, οἴδασιν; and both terminating in σιν, according to a mutual analogy, in which they differ from all other perfects. Whereas if this 3. plur. came from ἴσημι, why is it not accented like ἱστᾶσι, and lengthened in the Ion. dialect like ἱστέασι?

† The great difference between the terminations of the *principal* and of the *historic* tenses[a] is this, that by the augment ε and the consequent throwing back of the accent toward the beginning of the word, the terminations of the latter were shortened; e.g. τύπτ-οντι (Dor. for -ουσι) ἔτυπτ-ον; and consequently from the historic ending σαν we may conclude that there was in the principal tenses the ending -σαντι (-σᾶσι). In this remark I agree exactly with that acute philologist Landvoigt of Merseburg, who has thus resolved to my complete satisfaction a difficulty mentioned in my Grammar, in a note on the 3. plur. pres. indic. of the verbs in μι; namely, that in the most ancient mode of inflection the 3. plur. of the pres. and imperf. ended thus, τιθέ-σαντι, ἐτίθε-σαν. The σ in the former dropped out, leaving τιθέαντι τιθέασι, which were shortened to τιθεῖσι τιθέντι.

[a] [Buttmann in his Grammar divides the tenses of the verb into *principal*, viz. pres. perf. and fut., and *historic*, viz. imperf. pluperf. and aor.—Ed.]

Εἰλύομαι, *I drag myself along, crawl along*, Soph. The pass. ἐλυσθῆναι, used in Homer with the single ε, is distinct from the above, and means, 1.) *to compress or draw oneself up together*, Il. ω, 510. Od. ι, 433. 2.) *to be thrust* or *pushed*, Il. ψ, 393. The old Homeric language seems to have made a distinction between the forms beginning with εἰ and those with ἐ; using the former in the sense of *to envelope, cover up*, the latter in that of *to compress* and *to push*; but later poets confounded both forms and meanings. See Buttm. Lexil. p. 272.

Εἴλω, εἴλλω or εἵλλω, ἴλλω, and εἰλέω or εἱλέω, *I press together, shut in, envelope, roll up*: all the remaining forms, which occur in the common language, come exclusively from the form in έω; as, εἰλήσω, εἴλημαι, εἰληθείς.

It would be a difficult task to settle which of the various ways of writing and pronouncing this verb belonged to individual passages, as we find from the occasional remarks of the Grammarians that the same uncertainty prevailed among the ancients themselves. On these points, and on whatever concerns the meaning, see Buttm. Lexil. p. 253—271. The pronunciation with the aspirate was doubtless in this, as in many similar cases, confined principally to the Attics. In the older language the verb had the digamma, as is evident from many accompanying marks and many Epic forms which will be mentioned.

In Homer, beside the pres. and imperf. εἰλεῖν and the part. pass. εἰλόμενος, the rest of the formation comes from the simple stem or root ΕΛ-; as, the 3. pl. aor. 1. ἔλσαν, the infin. ἔλσαι, and (according to the analogy mentioned above in ἐεισάμενος*) ἐέλσαι; also the part. ἔλσας with the meaning of *to strike*, on which, and on the relation which this verb bears to ἐλαύνω, ἤλασα, see art. 44. in Buttm. Lexil. Perf. pass. ἔελμαι, ἐελμένος.

To this verb and to the same simple stem or root belong, according to all analogy, the aor. pass. ἐάλην and the 3. pl. without augm. ἄλεν (Il. χ, 12.), infin. ἀλῆναι, ἀλήμεναι, part. ἀλείς, ἀλέν. Compare στέλλω, ἐστάλην, and κείρω, ἔκερσα, ἐκάρην. Here also the aspirate is uncertain, and the editions and passages vary between the lenis and ἑάλην, ἁλῆναι†, &c.

The imperf. ἐόλει in Pind. Pyth. 4, 414. (according to Bœckh's undisputed emendation) and the pluperf. pass. ἐόλητο in Apollon. 3,

* See the conclusion of Εἴδω.

† Some of the Grammarians, principally the more modern, class these forms by themselves under a theme ΑΛΗΜΙ, which they join partly with ἀλέομαι partly with ἀλέες, *conferti*, &c.: but genuine grammatical tradition agrees with our statement. See Buttm. Lexilogus.

471. are sister-forms of εἴλει and ἔελτο with the meaning of *to press upon, disturb,* which bear the same relation to ΕΛΩ, εἴλω, as τρομέω does to τρέμω, ἐκτόνηκα to κτείνω, and other similar forms*.

To this place belongs, according to the writing of the word, the unusual verb with the meaning of *to use* or *treat ill,* προσελεῖν, as it was once written; or προυσελεῖν, as we find it in authorities on which we can depend. This latter pronunciation arose from the digamma which was originally between the σ and ε. There occur but two examples of it with the form of the present, viz. προυσελοῦμεν, Aristoph. Ran. 730., and προυσελούμενος, Æschyl. Prom. 435. For a full account of it see Buttm. Lexil. p. 494.

Εἵμαρται. See Μείρομαι.

Εἰμί, *I am,* a defective verb in μι, from a radical form ΕΩ. Beside the pres. and an imperf. ἦν, it has only a fut. ἔσομαι, Poet. ἔσσομαι; the other tenses are supplied by γίγνομαι; verbal adj. ἐστέον. From the middle comes the 2. sing. imperat. ἔσο, Epic and also Dor. ἔσσο; and the 1. sing. imperf. ἤμην, rejected indeed by the Atticists, but found occasionally in the older writers, and more frequently in the later†. Its other persons are never met with in any of the better authors. The most surprising is εἴατο for ἦντο, Od. υ, 106., where however others read εἶατο.

The 1. pers. sing. ἐμμί was Dor. for εἰμί: the 2. sing. pres. εἶς is only Ionic (Hom. and Herodot.), from which by leaving out the σ came the common εἶ: ἐσσί is Dor. and Ion., nor is it quite unknown to Attic poetry, Eur. Hel. 1246. The 3. pers. ἐντί is Dor. for both ἐστί and εἰσί. The 1. plur. εἰμέν is Ion. as εἰμές is Dor. for ἐσμέν, from which comes the unusual poetical form ἐμέν, Brunck. Soph. El. 21. The 3. plur. ἔασιν is Epic for εἰσίν: the Dorics have also ἔοντι.

In the Ionic dialect the part. the conj. and the optat. are formed from the theme ΕΩ, by which the part. has the same irregular accent as the part. ἰών from εἶμι, thus

Optat. ἔοιμι: conj. ἔω: part. ἐών.

This participle has in some Doric writers a particular feminine ἔασσα. The conj. is sometimes in the Epics strengthened by the diphthong ει, as εἴω, εἴῃς, εἴῃ (from which it is often confused with the optative), Il. ι, 245. σ, 88. Od. ο, 448. ρ, 586.; μετείω, Il. ψ, 47.‡. In the optative the

* These two forms (ἐόλει, &c) together with Bœckh's derivation of them are examined fully in Buttm. Lexil p. 63.

† This is a point which still requires critical examination see Piers ad Moer. p. 172. Fisch. 2. p. 502. Lobeck ad Phryn. p. 152. Schæf. ad Long. p. 423.

‡ Compare Herm. De Legg. quibusd. subtil. Serm. Hom. 1. p. 16. Matth. Gr. Gramm. p. 415. Schæf. Hes. Op. 538. 567. p. 238. Gnom. Gr.

abridged forms εἶμεν, εἶτε, are more rare than the others; εἶμεν is found however in Plat. Rep. 8. p. 558. d., and has been restored by Bekker in some other passages: εἶτε occurs in Od. φ, 195., and the dual εἴτην is found, according to Bekker, in several passages of Plato.

The 3. sing. of the imperat. ἤτω for ἔστω is found frequently in the N. T., e. g. 1 Cor. xvi, 22., and once in Plat. Rep. 2. p. 361. c. which is the more striking as he so frequently uses ἔστω. The 3. plur. has also an unusual sister-form (corresponding with the gen. plur. particip.) ὄντων, Plat. Leg. 9. p. 879. b. Ionic and Dor. ἐόντων, ἐόντω.

In the infin. we find in the old Ionic ἔμεν, ἔμεναι, ἔμμεν, ἔμμεναι; the last is the most common in Homer. The Dorics use ἦμεν or ἦμες, both which are at the same time 1. pl. imperf.—also εἶμεν, εἶμες, differing from 1. pl. pres. indic. only in the accent.

The *imperfect* has numerous sister-forms: e. g. from the radical form ΕΩ the 1. sing. ἔον for ἦν, Il. ψ, 643., but none of the other persons: ἔσκον, -ες, -ε, in Hom. is a mere imperf. as Il. η, 158, but in Herodot. a real iterative like the other forms in -σκον: and lastly the true Ionic form according to the formation in μι, ἔα, ἔας, and 2. plur. ἔατε; or lengthened ἦα, 3. sing. ἦεν*, Il. μ, 371.: ἔην occurs as 1. sing. in Il. λ, 762. only, where it is most probably false for ἔον; but as 3. sing. it is more common, and found in Ionic prose; Homer has also sometimes ἤην, and in 2. sing. ἔησθα for ἦσθα: the 3. plur. ἔσαν for ἦσαν occurs both in the older and later Ionic, as well as in the Doric dialect. In Hes. ε, 825. and θ, 321. ἦν also appears to stand for ἦσαν, but it is there rather a peculiarity of syntax†. From the Ionic ἔα arose the old Attic 1. sing. ἦ for ἦν, which with regard to the extent of its usage requires still further critical examination‡. For the 3. sing. ἦν the Dorics have by a particular anomaly ἦς. Poetical fut. ἔσσομαι for ἔσομαι, &c.; and from the Dor. ἐσοῦμαι comes ἐσσεῖται, Il. β, 393. ν, 317.

All the persons of the pres. indic. are enclitical except the 2. sing. εἶ, which always retains the accent; perhaps also εἶς, used enclitically by Wolf in Od. δ, 611.

Εἶμι, *I go*. The forms of this verb lead us to a root ʼΙΩ, with its radical vowel occasionally lengthened to ει; and connected with which are many irregularities both of form and meaning. Only the following moods and tenses are in use:

* This form has always the ν, whether before a vowel or consonant.

† As far as this is supposed to depend on prose authorities, it arises from entire misunderstanding: see Sturz. Lex. Xen. 2. p. 47. Herodot. 5, 12. where the nom. which follows it is not a plural but two singulars.

‡ See Fisch. 2. p. 498. 499. Heind. ad Plat. Protag. 5. In which it is particularly remarkable that Chœrobosc. (MS. ap. Bekk. fol. 242. v. and 348. v.) proves from Aristoph. Plut. 29. and Menander the usage of the 1. sing. ἦν.

INDICAT.	IMPERAT.	OPTAT.	CONJ.	INFIN.	PART.
Pres. S. εἶμι, εἶς, (generally* εἶ,) εἶσι(ν),	ἴθι, ἴτω,	ἴοιμι, &c.	ἴω, &c.	ἰέναι.	ἰών, ἰοῦσα, ἰόν
D. ἴτον, ἴτον,	ἴτον, ἴτων,	or			(always with the accent
P. ἴμεν, ἴτε, ἴασι(ν).	ἴτε, ἴτωσαν, or ἰόντων†.	ἰοίην, &c.			on the last syllable like the part. aor. 2. in other verbs).
Imperf. S. ᾔειν, Ion. ἤια, Att. ᾖα,					
ᾔεις or ᾔεισθα‡,					
ᾔει or ᾔειν,					
P. ᾔειμεν or ᾖμεν,					
ᾔειτε or ᾖτε,					
ᾔεσαν.					
(The dual follows the analogy of the 2. plur.)					

The Midd. (with the meaning of *to hasten*) is likewise used in pres. and imperf. ἵεμαι, ἱέμην, and (like ἵεμαι from ἵημι) makes the imperat. ἵεσο §, &c. Verbal adj. ἰτός, ἰτέος, or ἰτητός, ἰτητέος ‖.

* Homer has also εἶσθα, Il. κ, 450.

† Instead of ἴτωσαν Æschyl. Eumen. 32. has ἴτων, the same as the dual, a circumstance which otherwise occurs only in the passive formation. Compare in Εἰμί—ἔστων, and Elmsley on Markland's Iphig. T. 1480.

‡ Plat. Tim. p. 26. c. d. Euthyphr. p. 4. d. according to the present corrected text.

§ See this form in a verse in Lucian. Alex. 29. where the text incorrectly has ἴεσο.

‖ The longer form is merely a lengthening of the shorter one by a repetition of the reduplication, like ἔτυμος, ἐτήτυμος. In the simple verb the above verbals cannot well occur except in the neuter, ἰτέον, ἰτητέον. Perhaps the only instance of ἰτός is ἐξιτόν ἐστι, Hes. θ, 732. For ἰτητός see the compounds (εἰσιτητός, ἀνεξίτητος) in the lexicons.

[The middle voice of this verb is entirely rejected by some modern critics, as Elmsl. Soph. Œd. T. 1242. and L. Dindorf. Eurip. Supp. 699., who instead of it write ἵεμαι, ἵενται, &c. See however Schæf. Plut. 4. p. 326.—Passow.]

In meaning, this verb has the singular anomaly of its present having often the force of a future. In Homer it stands sometimes as a present, sometimes as a future; but in Ionic prose and in the Attic writers it is, with a very few exceptions*, a real future, *I shall go*: nor does it again take the force of a present until in such late writers as Pausanias and Plutarch. This however can only be said in its full extent of the indicative mood; the others are used sometimes as futures, sometimes they retain their natural meaning: and thus this verb supplies the place of some tenses of ἔρχομαι which are not much in use.

Homer has an infin. ἴμεν, and sometimes ἴμεναι, for ἰέναι: but εἶναι for ἰέναι is doubtful, as προσεῖναι in Hes. ε, 351. may come from εἰμί *I am*†. The 3. sing. opt. εἴη for ἴοι occurs in Il. ω, 139. Od. ξ, 496. The conj. εἴω for ἴω is quoted from the Doric writer Sophron in the Etym. M. p. 121, 29. and 423, 23. Homer has contracted the Ionic imperf. ἤϊα, 3. sing. ἤϊεν, ἤϊε, to ᾖε, Il., and in 1. plur. to ᾔομεν, Od.: beside which we find the 3. plur. ἤϊον in the Od., the 3. sing. ἴεν, ἴε, the 3. dual ἴτην, and the 3. plur. ἤϊσαν, which, though imperfects, have also the force of aorists. Lastly we find in the Epic poets a fut. midd. εἴσομαι; and from the aor. midd. εἰσάμην a 3. sing. εἴσατο, ἐείσατο, and a 3. dual ἐεισάσθην, Il. ο, 415. 544‡. A peculiar form, the 3. plur. pres. ἴσι for ἴασι, is found in Theogn. 716.

Εἰπεῖν, *to say*, an aorist: indic. εἶπον; imperat. εἰπέ§, compound πρόειπε, &c. Beside these the forms of the aor. 1. εἶπα were also in use; in the Attic language the most common were εἶπας, εἴπατε, εἰπάτω, but these were constantly exchanged for the forms with the ε, so that after all the speaker appears to have been generally guided by his ear. The most unusual are the 1. sing. εἶπα‖, which is rather

* See these exceptions in Herm. de Æschyl. Danaïd. p. 8.

† Two other passages quoted also in confirmation of it, (Herodot. 5, 108. Æschyl. Suppl. 300.) may be classed with that of Hesiod.

‡ I deduce διασειμένος (Apollon. Rhod. 2, 372.) rather from εἶμι, ἵεμαι, than from δίημι. A perfect εἶμαι from that verb is not more surprising than εἵσατο, καταείσατο, according to which it is formed.

§ On the accentuation of this imperat. see the second note under Ἔρχομαι. It is used also for εἴπετε, like ἄγε, particularly by Aristoph. see Elmsl. Ach. 328. Reisig Conj. p. 35. Demosth. Phil. 1. p. 43, 7. Cherson. p. 108, 13.

‖ Xen. Mem. 2, 2, 8. οὔτ' εἶπα οὔτ' ἐποίησα: the use of the aor. 1. is here evidently intentional. Ἔδειξα καὶ—εἶπα, Demosth. c. Euerg. p. 1151. Bekk. and Philem. Inc. 51. a., Eurip. Cycl. 101.

Ionic, and the 2. sing. imperat. εἶπον, which, with the optative*, is perhaps the rarest of all. The part. εἴπας, -ασα, -αν is peculiarly Ionic. The Midd., which however occurs only in the compound ἀπειπεῖν (*to refuse, to despair of*) in the same sense as the active, has always the form of the aor. 1. ἀπείπασθαι. Fut. ἀπεροῦμαι, Posidipp. Epigr. 2.

The 2. sing. imperat. εἶπον has been accented always in the grammars and generally in the text of different writers thus, εἰπόν; but it is proved in Buttmann's Excurs. 1. on Plat. Meno p. 70. that this latter accentuation was unknown to the pure Greek writers.

The generally acknowledged theme of this verb is ΕΙΠΩ, with the augm. ει; but then it is very unnatural for this augment to continue through all the moods, while it is never visible in ἐνέπω (see below). We certainly recognise the root ΕΠ- in the subst. ἔπος; but there is nothing to prevent the same root having been changed to ΕΙΠ-†.

According to this the verb has in common language no augment: originally it had the digamma, and hence in the Epics the syll. augm. ἔειπον. For the same reason the compounds have the hiatus, ἀποειπεῖν: see Buttm. Lexil. p. 130. note.

With this aorist εἰπεῖν usage has joined, so as to form but one verb, the Ion. fut. ἐρέω, Att. ἐρῶ, from the pres. εἴρω, which in the sense of *I say* is Epic; also the perf. εἴρηκα, perf. pass. εἴρημαι; and lastly the aor. pass. ἐῤῥήθην, pronounced also ἐῤῥέθην, but probably by those only who were not Attics‡. Verbal adj. ῥητός, ῥητέος. The fut. 3. (paulo-post fut.) εἰρήσομαι, from εἴρημαι, is used as a simple fut. pass. instead of ῥηθήσομαι§, which is found but seldom in Attic writers (Isocr. Philipp. init.).

The pres. εἴρω occurs in Od. λ, 137.: and thence undoubtedly comes

* In Plat. Soph. p. 240. d. εἴπαιμεν has been restored from the best manuscripts. So has also εἴπαιεν in Demosth. c. Nicostr. p. 1254. This opt. is more frequent in Aristotle. There is also an instance of εἴπειε.

† See Buttm. Lexil. p. 131. The occurrence of ἔπουσι (e. g. in Nicand. Ther. 738.) shows only the usage of a late grammarian-poet.

‡ This form is found written in various ways in the manuscript copies of the older writers: see Lobeck ad Phryn. p. 447. Bekker ad Æschin. 2, 34. 124. But the best manuscripts have it not unfrequently in its regular shape; see Plat. Gorg. 36. Theæt. 65.

§ This fut. appears to have been used only in its participle. Thuc. 8, 66. Plat. Phædr. 9.

the fut. ἐρῶ. But the aor. pass. ἐῤῥήθην points to a theme ΡΕΩ, to which we may refer the perf. εἴρηκα also, on account of the syllable ει which stands instead of the reduplication*. The Ionians and the common prose language had also εἰρήθην or εἰρέθην (see Schweigh. Lex. Herod. in ῥέειν), in the same way as from εἴλημμαι, διείλεγμαι crept into the non-Attic aorists εἰλήφθην, διειλέχθην†.

By some ἐρέω also is considered a present, but in the Epic writers it is always either a future, or, if a present, it is used with the sense of *to ask*, instead of ἔρομαι, which see‡. Yet Hesiod (θ, 38.) has a verb εἴρω produced to ἐώ, in which εἰρεῦσαι is the fixed traditionary reading, though the metre would admit εἴρουσαι quite as well.

Φημί was used as the present of this verb, but with certain limitations, which will be seen under it: in the compounds, however we find sometimes ἀγορεύειν (which properly means *to harangue*), e. g. ἀπαγορεύω *I forbid*, ἀπεῖπον *I forbade*; and sometimes λέγω, e. g. ἀντιλέγω, ἀντεῖπον §.

The expression with κακῶς, *to speak ill of*, was treated in this respect as a compound, for instead of εἰπέ με κακῶς, the present was ἀγορεύει με κακῶς.

The Epics have also an imperat. ἔσπετε, which is a sister-form with σ inserted, as in λάσκω from λακεῖν, ἴσκω from εἴκω.

The poetical verb ἐνέπω, or ἐννέπω, is shown in Buttm. Lexil. pp. 123. 131. to be no compound, but a strengthened form of the root or stem of εἰπεῖν (ΕΜΠ- ἐνέπω, like ΛΑΚ- ΛΑΕΚ-, ΟΡΓ- ὀρέγω). The imperf. (according to form) is ἔνεπον, ἔννεπον: the aor. ἔνισπον, ἐνισπεῖν, ἐνίσπω, ἐνίσποιμι; imperat. ἔνισπε; fut. ἐνίψω and ἐνισπήσω. Here the aorist as compared with the present is, by its long syllable, at variance with general analogy, but still not without example; see ἑσπόμην under Ἕπομαι.

* This syllable ει is found instead of the reduplication in the perf. of several verbs beginning with a liquid, in which case the pluperf. is the same: thus
εἴληφα from ΛΗΒΩ. See Λαμβάνω.
εἴληχα from ΛΗΧΩ. See Λαγχάνω.
εἴλοχα, εἴλεγμαι from λέγω.
εἵμαρται from μείρομαι.

† We may indeed, as many do, form εἴρηκα from εἴρω, or even from the fut. ἐρέω, as a new theme by means of the augm. ει; but by the method which I have followed above, the perf. pass., the aor. pass. and the verbals ῥῆμα, ῥητός, all agree together; and the grand analogy of the language is in favour of this plan.

‡ Struve has pointed out two passages in Hippocrates, viz. ὃ γὰρ ἂν . . . ἐρέω, *I say*, in Præcept. p. 64., and ἤρεον, *they said*, Epidem. 2. p. 691. If the syntax and reading of these passages are to be depended on (which I cannot take upon myself to assert positively) the two forms belong to the analogy of other Ionic presents sprung from the future, as μαχέομαι; and ἤρεον is then a proof that the augm. ει cannot be used in the way noticed in the preceding note.

§ Not that ἀπηγόρευσα, ἀντέλεξα, could not be used, but the compounds of εἶπον were far more common.

The circumflex over ἐνισπεῖν* shows too that in old grammatical tradition this form was considered an aorist. The future was formed, as is frequently the case, from this aorist, and that in two analogous ways: for in ἐνίψω the σ is dropped, as in the fut. of διδάσκω and ἀλύσκω†. From this future was formed again another present ἐνίπτω in Pind. Pyth. 4, 358., which however must be distinguished from the Homeric ἐνίπτω, *to revile*, which see hereafter.

The preterites ἔνεπον and ἔνισπον are always found without the augment, and where the metre would have required ἤνεπον, there ἔννεπον was introduced. The double ν in ἐννέπω is besides frequent in the Tragedians; but ἔννεπον seems not to occur, generally speaking, in their writings. We have supposed this preterite to be, according to form, an *imperfect*, like ἔφην under Φημί: but in usage they are both aorists, and the former is used in narration promiscuously with εἶπον and ἔνισπον: compare ηὔδα under Αὐδάω. Hence then we may explain the use of this form in the Hymn to Pan, 29., where ἔννεπον, answering to the preceding ὑμνεῦσι, stands for ἐνέπουσι. That is to say, as the indicat. of the aor. has in general, beside its meaning of a preterite, that of *doing a thing usually*, so this imperf. converted by usage into an aorist has the same secondary meaning, exactly like ἔκλυον, Il. α, 218.

The Grammarians deduce from ἐνισπεῖν a twofold imperative, ἔνισπε and ἐνίσπες. If this latter be genuine, we must suppose ἐνισπεῖν to be a compound‡, perhaps of ἐνί and σπεῖν, which would then correspond in form with σπεῖν from ἕπω, and of which the imperat. would be σπές, as from σχεῖν, σχές. See the Etym. M. v. ἔνισπεν, Schol. Od. ξ, 185. Some manuscripts have also ἔνισπες or ἐνίσπες (for the accent is uncertain) wherever the word stands at the end of the verse; on the other hand at Od. δ, 642. in the middle of the verse ἔνισπε could be the only reading. I would observe however that the aor. ἔνισπον as a compound is contrary to analogy, for in that case it ought to be ἐνέσπον, like ἐπέσχον; and further, that in the two passages of the Iliad, λ, 186. ξ, 470., where the Cod. Ven. has in the text ἐνίσπες, the scholium does not mention this reading, but has in the lemma (as far as

* See Od. γ, 93. Eurip. Suppl. 435. In Hes. θ, 369. the old accentuation must therefore be restored from the first edition. In Apollonius the modern editors have most arbitrarily rejected the circumflex; see Beck on Apoll. 1, 1333. and 3, 917.

† The same editors have given to Apollonius 2, 1165. from some manuscripts the non-Homeric form ἐνέψω.

‡ The above observation is grounded on this circumstance, that we find in the common dialects merely such monosyllabic imperatives as θές, δός, ἕς, σχές, φρές, with their compounds. To prove ἔνισπες to be no compound by comparing it with ζατές, ἀγές, in Hesychius, would throw that form into a most improbable dialect, which could only be justified by indications much surer than any we have to guide us.

the lemmata of Villoison are to be depended on) ἐνίσπε. I would not therefore recommend the adoption of this form with a view to strengthen the last syllable of the hexameter.

Εἴργω, *I shut out*, εἵργνυμι, *I shut in*, are distinguished from each other in their tenses merely by the breathing; thus, εἴρξω, εἶρξα: εἵρξω, εἷρξα. This verb, according to the analogy of verbs beginning with ει, does not take the augment, which is supplied by the accent: see Εἴκω, *I yield*. For εἰργαθον see Ἀμύνω, ἀμύναθον.

The Ionic form of this verb is ἔργω, ἔρξα, &c.*, which in the oldest language, as we shall see below, had the digamma, and consequently corresponded exactly with the same stem or root under ῥέζω. The distinction of *out* or *in* is not marked in Homer by the absence or presence of the aspirate, because in that early stage of the language the word had instead of the aspirate the digamma, the loss of which was supplied in the dialects by the one or other of the breathings; in the Epic language, according to general tradition, by the lenis; consequently the sense of Od. ξ, 411. was *to shut in*; τὰς μὲν (the swine) ἄρα ἔρξαν κατὰ ἤθεα. Originally therefore the meaning of the verb was undefined; it meant nothing more than *to separate*, *shut off*, and the context showed whether it was *in* or *out*. But in the Ionic dialect of Herodotus the distinction is observed, e. g. 3, 136. τοὺς Πέρσας ἕρξε ὡς κατασκόπους ἐόντας, and no doubt from old tradition: whence the same writer has ἑρκτῇ for the Att. εἱρκτή, *a prison*. In the Attic and in the common language it was also a standing rule: see Eust. ad Od. α, 27. (p. 14, 25. Bas.), and the directions of an old grammarian in Hermann (at the end of De Em. Gr. Gr.) p. 337.†. Nor is ἀπείργειν (with the exception of ἄφερκτος in the last note) ever found with a φ; on the contrary, the compound with κατά, the most usual in the sense of *to*

* It is singular to find this form in Thucyd. 5, 11. where περιέρξαντες is the reading of all the known manuscripts except one which has ει; for in all the other passages of this writer we find the diphthong. We may however compare with it ἄφερκτος in Æschyl. Choeph. 444.

† This is also proved in various instances by the manuscripts: compare for example the passages in Sturz. Lex. Xenoph. and Brunck's Index to Aristophanes, as well as Andoc. 4. p. 31, 27. 32, 36. There are however manuscripts which have εἴργω without exception (see Bekker on Thuc. 1, 35.); the reason of which was, that other grammarians ascribed εἵργω without distinction to the Attics, but εἴργω to the κοινοῖς (see Etym. M. 377, 48.), as is indeed the case in many other words. And certainly ἄφερκτος, *shut out*, quoted in the last note from Æschylus, leads to the same conclusion. If now we suppose (as was said before, and is certainly the more probable) that originally there was no distinction, but that one established itself by degrees, yet without ever becoming universal, all that can occur is satisfactorily explained.

shut in, is almost always written with the θ; while in Thucyd. 1, 76., where κατείργειν has the general sense of *to constrain, keep down by force*, the τ stands without a various reading. Further, that the sense of *shutting in* is expressed by the pres. εἴργνυμι, is evident from the grammarian above mentioned, who observes that "εἴργω in the present is not used;" for εἴργω is a very common present.

As to the digamma, the same conclusion results from the Epic augment in ἔεργον, ἐέργνυ, and again from the Epic sister-form (with its superfluous ε in the present) ἐέργω, in the same language, from which is contracted the common εἴργω*. The digamma is therefore very easily to be discerned in Od. ξ, 411. Τὰς μὲν ἄρα ἔρξας..., and in the Epic compound ἀποέργει. The Homeric perf. pass. ἔεργμαι, 3. plur. pluperf. ἐέρχατο does indeed seem by its syllabic augment to have the same marks of the digamma: but there is one point opposed to it; namely, that in both passages where it occurs the digamma with reduplication is inadmissible, because in Od. κ, 241. it is preceded by a consonant, in Il. ε, 89. by a shortened diphthong. These two passages belong however to the numerous instances where the digamma has disappeared from our Homer. The forms ἔρχαται, ἔρχατο, are much more striking, particularly in Od. ι, 221. κ, 283., where they begin the verse, and where consequently a slight emendation is not to be thought of. Here then the syllable of reduplication has quite disappeared, which in cases of the true syllabic augment (as if τεύχαται were put for τετεύχαται) is never the case. Hence in the history of the digamma, and its gradual disappearance, this verb would be a remarkable feature. The form ἔρχαται supposes the theme ἔργω to have the common lenis, and is therefore a regular perfect, but without the temp. augm.: and this too contrary to Epic usage, but as it occurs in a syllable long by position it is free from suspicion†.

Εἰρύω. See Ἐρύω.

Εἴρω. See Εἰπεῖν.

Εἴρω, *I string in a row*: aor. 1. εἶρα (Herodot. 3, 87. ἐξείρας, *exserens*) and ἔρσα (Hippocr. de Morb. 2, 33. διέρσας). Perf. pass. in the Epic poets ἔερμαι, ἐερμένος; in Herodot. 4, 190. ἐρμένος. In the former the digamma is not obliterated, for in the only two passages where the pluperf. ἔερτο, and the perf. ἐερμένον occur, (Od. ο, 460. σ, 296.) it is pre-

* Once in the text of our Homer we find εἴργω (Il. ψ, 72.), Τῆλέ με εἴργουσι, but it is indisputably a false reading: for as εἴργω is contracted from ἐέργω, it cannot have had the digamma, which the hiatus before the verb shows to have been in the verse; for ἐέργω, i. e. ΕϜΕΡΓΩ, has it not before the first ε; compare Il. β, 825. ἐντὸς ἐέργει. Bentley's emendation of this passage is therefore, certainly correct, μ' ἐέργουσι.

† The augment is occasionally omitted in syllables naturally long, as ἔντυε, ἕλκε, ἕλπετο, ἄρχε, ἅπτετο.

ceded by the separable ν. In Herodotus on the contrary we find the common form, but with the temp. augm. omitted, as is always the case in the Ionic dialect. Suidas quotes from some writer ἐνειρμένος πέδαις, consequently with the augm. ει; although it may be taken for the unchanged diphthong of the present; as in the verbal subst. εἱρμός; on the aspirate of which see Buttm. Lexil. p. 300. For ἀπόερσε see Ἔρσαι.

Εἶσα. See ἝΩ, 2.

Ἐΐσκω. See Ἴσκω.

Εἴωθα. See Ἔθω.

'ΕΛ–. See Αἱρέω.

'ΕΛ–. See Εἴλω.

Ἐλαύνω, *I drive*: fut. ἐλάσω with α short, Ep. ἐλάσσω; aor. 1. ἤλασα, Poet. ἔλασα, ἔλασσα; perf. ἐλήλακα, perf. pass. ἐλήλαμαι; aor. 1. pass. ἠλάθην: verbal adj. ἐλατός. In non-Attic writers the passive takes a σ, as ἐλήλασμαι, ἠλάσθην, ἠλαστός. The forms ἐλῶ, ἐλᾷς, ἐλᾷ, &c., infin. ἐλᾶν, are in the Attic prose a future, according to the analogy of verbs whose futures end in -ἄσω or -έσω, and which form a new Attic future by rejecting the σ and contracting the remaining termination, thus ἐλάσω, ἐλάω, ἐλῶ. See also last note under Δέμω.—MIDD.

The forms in -ῶ, -ᾷς, &c. occur also as presents from the simple theme ἐλάω. In prose however there is only one example, the imperat. ἀπέλα, Xenoph. Cyr. 8, 3, 32. In poetry there are several; ἔλων, Il. ω, 696., ἐλάαν, Od. ο, 50., ἐλᾷ, Pind. Nem. 3, 129., ἐκποδὼν ἔλα, Eurip. Herc. 819.

In Od. η, 86. is a 3. plur. pluperf. pass. ἐληλέδατο, for which Wolf writes ἐρηρέδατο, the reading of the old editions. This latter has however by far the fewest manuscripts in its favour, and it seems to me clear that the true reading must be some form of ἐλαύνω, as the expression is much the same as we find in v. 113. in Il. σ, 564. and Od. ζ, 9. But the reading ἐληλάδατο is likewise found in very few manuscripts, while by far the majority has ἐληλέδατο, and some ἐληλέατο. This last has been adopted by Alter; and when we consider that it is the regular Ionic form, according to the analogy of πεπτέαται for -ανται, and that it does not offend the metre, I cannot but think that it is the true reading of Homer.

In the Epic language we find some participles proparoxytons, as ἐληλάμενος, συνεληλάμενοι, Arat. 176., like ἀκηχέμενος (Il. σ, 29.), ἀκαχήμενος, and ἀλαλήμενος. See Herodian in Etym. M. v. ἀκαχήμενος and Thom. Mag. v. ἐληλάμενος. In Apollon. 2, 231. the modern editors have altered this accent, because it was not supported by a scholium, like the passage in Aratus. See note under Ἀκαχίζω.

Ἔλδομαι and ἐέλδομαι*, *I desire*; a defective depon. used only in pres. and imperf. It is found once in a passive sense, Il. π, 494. Both forms are exclusively poetical.

Ἐλέγχω, *I refute*: fut. ξω; perf. with redupl. ἐλήλεγχα; perf. pass. ἐλήλεγμαι.

Ἐλελίζω, *I turn round, tremble*: fut. ἐλελίξω; aor. 1. ἐλέλιξα, aor. 1. pass. ἐλελίχθην, midd. ἐλελιξάμενος, &c. Ἐλέλικτο (Il. λ, 39.) is a syncopated aorist. See Buttm. Lexil. p. 287.

ΕΛΕΥΘ–, ΕΛΘ–. See Ἔρχομαι.

Ἑλίσσω, -ττω, *I wind*: augm. ει†; perf. pass. εἵλιγμαι and ἐλήλιγμαι. In this last perf. three things are to be observed: 1.) that the simple augm. εἵλιγμαι was also in use: 2.) that the augm. ει does not take place with the reduplication: 3.) that the syllable of reduplication does not admit of the aspirate‡.

Ἕλκω, *I draw*: fut. ἕλξω; aor. 1. εἷλξα. It borrows also from a theme ἙΛΚΥΩ, which is not used in the pres. or imperf., and even in the fut. ἕλξω is preferred: see Piers. ad Moer. p. 134. But in the aor. εἵλκυσα, ἑλκῦσαι is far more common than εἷλξα, and in the passive εἵλκυσμαι, εἱλκύσθην are the only forms in use.—Midd.

The regular imperf. εἷλκον is never found in Hom. nor in Ionic prose, but always ἕλκον, ἕλκετο. The particular inflexion ἑλκήσω, ἥλκησα (with η as augment), ἑλκηθείς, has in Homer the stronger meaning of *to drag along*.

Ἔλπω, *I encourage to hope*: Od. β, 91. γ, 380. But it is generally used in the midd. ἔλπομαι, *I hope*; perf. ἔολπα with the force of the pres.; pluperf. ἐώλπειν with the force of an imperfect: see ἔοικα and note under Εἴκω; also the second note under Ἄγνυμι, and a note in Buttm. Lexil. p. 202. The Epic forms are ἐέλπομαι and ἐελπόμην: see Ἔλδομαι and note.

* Like ἐέλπομαι, ἐέργω, ἐειδόμενος, ἐΐσκω, which in the older language had the digamma.

† It is however to be observed that this diphthong is found also in the present, and even, though not frequently, in prose: see Lobeck ad Phryn. p. 30.

‡ In stating these rules we must however remember the rarity of this form, and that I know only some instances of it quoted by Maittaire from Pausanias.

'Ελύω. See Εἰλύω.

'Εμέω, *I vomit*, has ε in the inflexion and σ in the passive: it takes also the Attic reduplication.

[Æschylus has the fut. midd. ἐμοῦμαι in the sense of *to vomit*, while Xenoph. (Anab. 4, 8, 20.) has the imperf. act. in the same intrans. sense.]

'Εμνήμυκε. See 'Ημύω.

'Εναίρω, *I kill*: fut. ἐνᾰρῶ; aor. 2. ἤναρον, Eurip.: infin. ἐναρεῖν.—Midd. with aor. 1. ἐνηράμην, Hom. [This verb is not a compound: see Buttm. Lexil. p. 119.]

'Εναύω. See Αὔω.

ΕΝΕΓΚ–, ΕΝΕΙΚ–. See Φέρω.

'Ενέπω. See Εἰπεῖν.

'Ενήνοθα, a perf. with the force of a present, found in the Epic writers in composition only, and in the third person; used at the same time as aorist: thus ἐπενήνοθε, κατενήνοθε, *it lies* or *it lay thereon.* As a theme we must suppose ΕΝΘΩ, ΕΝΕΘΩ: see this more fully explained in Buttm. Lexil. p. 110. &c.

'Ενθεῖν, ἦνθον. See Ἔρχομαι

'Ενίπτω, *I reproach*, has in Homer two forms of the aor. 2, viz. 1.) ἐνένῑπον, for which two false readings ἐνένιπτον and (Il. ψ, 473.) ἐνένισπον have crept into the printed text of Homer, as I have shown in Buttm. Lexil. p. 123. &c. This form is the reduplicated aor. 2. with the radical vowel long, which we know from the subst. ἐνῑπή was long in the root also; 2.) the 3. sing. ἠνίπᾰπε, formed by a peculiar reduplication in the middle of the word, like ἠρύκακον, infin. ἐρυκακέειν from ἐρύκω.

Homer has another sister-form ἐνίσσω, which bears the same relation to ἐνίπτω as πέσσω to πέπτω. None of the forms, which are here placed together, ever stand absolutely in Homer with the meaning of *to say*, but they are sometimes used so with the sense of *to reproach*; they must therefore be distinguished from ἐνέπω, ἔνισπον, and the Pindaric ἐνίπτω (see under 'Ενέπω); while the long ι above mentioned makes it most probable that they belong to a particular family of verbs, of which a more accurate examination will be found in Buttm. Lexil. p. 123. &c.

Ἕννῡμι, or ἐννύω, *I put on, clothe*, forms its tenses from a theme ἝΩ; thus fut. ἕσω, Ep. ἕσσω; aor. 1 ἕσσα, infin. ἕσαι, fut. midd. ἕσομαι; aor. 1. midd. ἑσσάμην; perf. pass. εἷμαι, εἷσαι, εἷται, &c., whence 3. pl. pluperf. εἷατο (Il. σ, 596.), comp. ἐπιεῖμαι, ἐπιειμένος. From the pass.

ἕσμαι, ἕσμην, (which never occurs in its simple form in the first person,) come the 2. and 3. sing. of the pluperf. ἕσσο, ἕστο; and the compound ἠμφίεσμαι, &c. The forms with the syllabic augment (which takes the aspirate), ἑέσσατο (Il. κ, 23., Od. ξ, 519.) and ἕεστο (Il. μ, 464.), are Epic only.

The Ionics have another form εἵνυμι; for ἐπείνυσθαι in Herodotus proves that the ει in the Homeric εἵνυον (Il. ψ, 135.) is not the augment. The temp. augm. is found neither in the imperf. nor the aorist: the perf. only has the augment ει. Homer has not the temp. augm. in any tense, but the syllab. augm. only, which is to be accounted for by the digamma.

The simple ἕννυμι is never used in prose, but principally the compound ἀμφιέννυμι, which makes its fut. ἀμφιέσω, Att. ἀμφιῶ; fut. midd. ἀμφιέσομαι; and takes the augment in the preposition, ἠμφίεσα; infin. ἀμφιέσαι, pass. ἠμφίεσμαι, ἠμφίεσαι, ἠμφίεσται, &c. infin. ἠμφιέσθαι. Nor do the other compounds generally reject the vowel of the preposition before the ε, as ἐπιέσασθαι.

Ἐόλει, ἐόλημαι. See under Εἴλω.

Ἑορτάζω, *I celebrate, solemnize*: fut. ἑορτάσω; it takes the augm. in the second syllable ἑώρταζον, according to the analogy of ἔοικα, ἐῴκειν. See Εἴλω and note.

Ἐπαΐω, Herodot. 3, 29. See Ἀΐω.

Ἐπαυρεῖν, &c. See ΑΥΡ–.

Ἐπείγω, *I press*; pass. *I hasten*. For proof that this verb is no compound, see Buttm. Lexil. p. 118.

Ἐπίσταμαι, *I understand*, depon. pass. with fut. midd.; imperf. ἠπιστάμην: fut. ἐπιστήσομαι; aor. ἠπιστήθην; verbal adj. ἐπιστητός. In the optat. the accent sometimes follows the regular conjugation of barytone verbs, e. g. ἴσταιο, ἴσταιτο, ἴσταισθε, ἴσταιντο; but the conj. is always ἰστῶμαι, συνιστῆται, &c.*. See Δύναμαι with note, and Ἵστημι.

This verb is distinguished from ἐφίσταμαι, the proper compound of ἵσταμαι, by the π, by the augment, and by the aorist retaining the η of the formation before the θ.

Instead of the 2. sing. ἐπίστασαι the Attic poets have ἐπίστᾳ (Æsch. Eum. 86. 578.), the Ionics ἐπίστῃ (Theogn. 1043. or 1085. Bekk. 1081.)

* Yet the Ionic conj. is ἐπιστέωμαι, Herodot 3, 134.

Gaisf. See Buttm. on Soph. Phil. 798. The usual form in the imperf. is ἠπίστω and in the imperat. ἐπίστω, e. g. Xen. Mem. 3, 4, 9. Cyr. 3, 2, 16. See Moer. 163. 182. Homer has the imperf. without the augm. ἐπίστατο. The pres. and imperf. are conjugated like ἵσταμαι.

'ΕΠΩ, ἐνέπω. See Εἰπεῖν.

Ἕπω, *I am employed or busy about anything*: imperf. εἶπον, Poet. without augm. ἕπον; fut, ἕψω; aor. ἔσπον, infin. σπεῖν, part. σπών; compound ἐπέσπον, ἐπισπεῖν, μετασπών. The augment is ει, as περιεῖπεν, Xen. Mem. 2, 9, 5. This verb in its simple form is found only in Il. ζ, 321.*, but its compounds are used both in verse and in prose, περιέπω, διέπω, &c.

These aorists seldom occur except in poetry: though Ionic prose has frequently περιέσπε, Herod. 1, 73.; περισπεῖν ib. 115., and the passive of the same compound περιεφθῆναι, 5, 1. 6, 15., and περιέψεσθαι for περιεφθήσεσθαι, 2, 115. 7, 119.

Midd. ἕπομαι, *I follow*: imperf. εἱπόμην, and Poet. without augm. ἑπόμην; fut. ἕψομαι, infin. ἕψεσθαι. The aorist has this peculiarity that the augment is aspirated, ἑσπόμην, comp. ἐφεσπόμην (ἕσπου Plat. Polit. p. 280. b., ἐφέσπετο Eurip. Hipp. 1307.)†, and as a proof that it is merely the augm. it disappears in the other moods: infin. σπέσθαι, imperat. σποῦ, ἐπίσπου Plat. Theæt. p. 169. a., ἐπίσπεσθε Plat. Crit. p. 107. b. &c. The Ion. imperat. 2. pers. is σπέο, Ep. σπεῖο, Il. κ, 285.

If ἔσπον σπέσθαι and ἔσχον σχεῖν be compared with ἔπλε ἔπλετο and ἐπτόμην πτέσθαι, we see at once that the former arise from the same syncope as the latter. That is to say, the aspirate in ἕπω and ΕΧΩ (ἕξω) passed (as it does in so many other words) into a σ, which immediately attached itself to the consonants following, therefore ἔ-σπον, ἔ-σχον. This statement does not however militate against the insertion of a σ according to another analogy in the root 'ΕΠ, and thus ἑσπόμην, ἑσπέσθαι, ἕσπωμαι, ἑσπόμενος, became anomalous aorists. From

* [Yet Homer has frequently περὶ τεύχε' ἕπουσιν, e. g. in Il. ο, 555. ἀμφ' Ὀδυσῆα ἕπον, Il. λ, 483. and many other similar expressions, which Buttmann, it would seem, considered as compounds.—Ed.]

† A singular form is ἐπέσπουτο in Pind. Pyth 4, 237. which can hardly be joined with the Pindaric forms in the note following.

these, and not from the ἑσπόμην belonging to the former analogy, came the indicative which passed into the common language, while the other moods ἑσπέσθαι &c. remained in the usage of the Epics (Il. ε, 423. Od. μ, 349. Il. μ, 395. &c.). But from the very circumstance of ἑσπόμην being an aorist, the pres. ἕσπεται which is a various reading for ἔρχεται at Od. δ, 826. ought not to be allowed to displace the present old and unobjectionable reading of the text*.

Ἐράω, *I love*, is used only in the pres. and imperf.; having a regular passive ἐρῶμαι, ἐρᾶσθαι, ἐρώμενος. But the sister-form ἔραμαι, like ἵσταμαι, is a deponent synonymous with the active, and in the pres. solely poetical. The aor. pass. however, ἠράσθην, fut. ἐρασθήσομαι, with an active sense, is used in prose; part. ἐρασθείς.

The Epic language has instead of ἠράσθην the midd. ἠρᾰσάμην, whence ἠράσσατο, Hom. ἐράσσατο, Hes. and Pind. The perf. ἤρασμαι, Parthen. The 2. pers. pres. Epic with double σ, ἔρασσαι occurs in Theocr. 1, 78. The Dor. conj. ἔρᾱται for ἔρηται is accented according to the analogy of barytone verbs, Pind. P. 4, 164. compare ἐπίσταμαι and δύναμαι. Lastly ἐράασθε in an act. sense, Il. π. 208. is probably a false reading†.

Ἐράω is used only in its compounds, and with the regular aor. 1. ἐξερᾶσαι, κατερᾶσαι, *to pour* or *shoot out*, συνερᾶσαι‡ *to pour* or *throw together*.

Ἐργάζομαι, *I labour, work*, depon. midd.: fut. ἐργάσομαι;

* See the note in Buttm. Schol. Od. ad h. l. Bekker in his critique on Wolf's Homer has ventured a conjecture that all those Epic moods ἑσπέσθαι &c. have crept into Homer's poems by false readings, because in every instance the verse would admit δὲ σπομένοιο, ἅμα σπέσθαι &c., and that the later Epics, in whose verse this is not always the case, imitated the false reading. This view of the subject is much strengthened by the circumstance of the compounds being invariably written in Homer ἐπισπέσθαι, μετασπόμενος &c. However as the origin of such a reading, if there were no grounds for it in the language, is difficult to be conceived; and (which is the most important point) these forms are as fixed in Pindar (O. 8, 123. 9, 15. Isth. 4, 40.) as they are in the Alexandrine poets, there seems to be no doubt of a twofold ancient usage: at the same time it seems hardly possible that such a distinction as that between simple and compound could have existed in Homer's language. Bekker's supposition therefore, if confined to Homer, has great probability.

† That is to say, the depon. ἔρασθε is no more capable of resolution than ἵστασθε, δύνασθε &c.; and ἐρᾶσθε can be only passive. The reading must therefore necessarily be ἧς τοπρίν γ' ἐράσασθε. [Passow however seems to think it may be defended by supposing a theme ἐράομαι from which will come ἐρᾶται, Sappho Fr. 59. Theocr. 2, 149.]

‡ Isocr. Phil. p. 110 b. as restored by Bekker. Aristot. de Gen. Animal. 3, 1. extr.

perf. εἰργασμαι, Ion. ἔργασμαι. The augm. is ει. [The Ion. and Att. generally use the perf. pass. εἰργασμαι in the act. sense of the aor. midd. εἰργασάμην, Valck. Phœn. 1069. Lob. Soph. Aj. 21., but this tense is also found as a true passive, e. g. τὰ ἐργασμένα, Herodot. 7, 53. compare Plat. Charm. p. 173. c. Xen. Mem. 3, 10, 9. Conviv. 5, 4. Œcon. 19, 8., &c. And even the indic. of this perf. is found in a passive sense, at least in its compound ἀπείργασται, Plat. Legg. 4. p. 710. d. The fut. pass. ἐργασθήσομαι is seldom found with a really passive meaning which it has in Sophoc. Tr. 1218., Isocr. Epist. 6.—Passow.]

Ἔργω. See Εἵργω.

ἘΡΓΩ and ἔρδω, See Ῥέζω.

Ἐρεείνω. See Ἔρομαι.

Ἐρέθω, *I excite, irritate*, is used only in pres. and imperf., but we find in Mosch. 3, 85. the aor. with augm. ἤρεθον. Its derivative ἐρεθίζω is more used.

Ἐρείδω, *I support by placing one thing against another*: fut. ἐρείσω, &c. It has the Att. redupl.; thus perf. act. ἐρήρεικα, perf. pass. ἐρήρεισμαι; of this latter Homer has the 3. plur. ἐρηρέδαται for ἐρηρεισμένοι εἰσί, Il. ψ, 284; 329. Od. η, 86,95.; for which Apollon. Rh. uses ἐρήρεινται. Homer has the augm. only in ἠρήρειστο, but Hes. α. 362. has ἠρείσατο.—Midd. *I support myself*; ἐρειδόμενος, ἐρεισάμενος, &c. Hom.

Ἐρείκω, *I tear, break*: imperf. ἤρεικον; aor. 1. ἤρειξα. Midd. *I tear my clothes in pieces*. Pass. *I am torn* or *broken*; perf. ἐρήριγμαι, Hippocr.

To the intransitive sense of the pass. (e. g. Il. ν, 441.) belongs the Epic aor. 2. act. ἤρικον, Il. ρ, 295.* Compare the last paragraph of Γηράω.

Ἐρείπω, *I overthrow*: fut. ἐρείψω; aor. 2. ἤριπον; aor. 1. pass. ἠρείφθην; perf. 2. with Att. reduplication ἐρήριπα; perf. pass. ἐρήριμ-

* As this aor. 2. occurs in no other passage, it is not to be wondered at if later poets used it transitively: thus Euphor. Fr. 40. and Alex. Ætol. in Piers. ad Moer. p. 194. whose admirable emendation of the whole fragment was not understood by his neglecting in this verse to change καλόν into κακόν; διὰ μὲν κακὸν ἤρικεν ὄνσον.

μαι, and Ep. pluperf. 3. sing. ἐρέριπτο for ἠρήριπτο, Il. ξ, 15., but we find in Herodian Hist. 8. 2. κατερήρειπτο.

In this verb as in the last the passive makes a transition to the intransitive meaning *to fall over, fall down,* and this, as being the immediate sense, belongs to the aor. 2. act. ἤριπον, and the perf. ἐρήριπα (see note under Τεύχω), which however occur only in the poets*. In Pind. Ol. 2, 76. Boeckh has shown from the manuscripts and from Apollon. Synt. p. 277. that the part. aor. 2. pass. ἐριπέντι, not ἐριπόντι, is the true reading.

The Epic middle ἀνηρειψάμην belongs unquestionably to this verb, although in this compound its sense is somewhat different: Homer has frequently ἀνηρείψαντο, *they have torn away, carried off,* Il. υ, 234. Od. δ, 727. &c. and Hesiod θ, 990. has ἀνερειψαμένη, *having carried off*†.

Ἐρέπτομαι, *I feed, graze, eat,* occurs only in the pres. and imperf. Later writers use ἐρέπτω for ἐρέφω like γλύπτω for γλύφω, δρέπτω for δρέφω &c.: compare γλύφω. This form was long regarded with suspicion in Pind. P. 4, 240. but has been satisfactorily defended by Boeckh.

Ἐρέσσω, ττω, *I row*: fut. ἐρέσω; aor. 1. ἤρεσα, Poet. ἤρεσσα and ἔρεσσα, Il. ι, 361. Od. λ, 78. The compound διήρεσα occurs in Od. μ, 444. ξ, 351. From ἐρέτης and ἐρετμός we may conclude that its characteristic letter was τ.

Ἐρεύγω. See Ἐρυγγάνω.

Ἐρεύθω, *I make red*: fut. ἐρεύσω; aor. 1. infin. ἐρεῦσαι. Also ἐρυθαίνω, whence ἐρυθαίνετο, *he became red*: purely Homeric forms. The subst. ἐρύθημα comes from the formation in -ήσω, which belonged to ἐρυθαίνω as it did to ἀλιταίνω, in which the termination -αίνω is a mere extension of the original present, according to the analogy mentioned

* Of this aorist ἤριπον, which is frequent in the poets, we find one instance of a transitive meaning in the latest editions of Herodot. 9, 70. But the old reading ἤρειπον ought not to have been changed, even though the new reading had been favoured by manuscripts. A fixed line of distinction between imperf. and aor. is not possible in these older remains of antiquity. If Herodotus had intended to use the aor., we cannot but suppose that he would have said ἤρειψαν, as he has ἐρεῖψαι at 1, 164.

† There are no grounds for the theme ἀνερείπτω in the lexicons; nor must we be misled by the usage of this word in some later writers (ἀνηρείψασθε πόνον' *you have undertaken,* Orph. Arg. 292.). In the old Epic usage there is nothing to lead us decidedly from ἐρείπω. Whatever in the word ἀνηρειψάμην seems opposed to the sense of ἐρείπω lies merely in the preposition ἀνά and the midd. voice. The idea of a ῥιπή is in ῥίπτω, in ἐρείπω, and in ἀνηρειψάμην. What is *torn away,* falls to the ground; hence the simple ἐρείπω and ἤριπον contain in themselves this collateral meaning: if we add to this ῥιπή or tearing the sense of ἀνά in composition and the middle voice, we have ἀνηρειψάμην, *I have seized and carried up for myself,* a very proper verb to express such a transaction as the rape of Ganymede.

in note under Αἰσθάνομαι. On the other hand in the later form ἐρυθραίνω· -αίνω is a derivative termination from ἐρυθρός, as λευκαίνω is from λευκός with the regular flexion λευκᾶναι &c. And the Alexandrine poets treated ἐρυθαίνω in the same way, e. g. ἐρύθηνε, Apollon. Rh. 1, 791. Compare κερδαίνω.

Ἐρέφω, *I cover, crown*: fut. ἐρέψω; aor. 1. ἔρεψα. MIDD. Eur. Bacch. 323. Aristoph. Vesp. 1294. See also Ἐρέπτω.

Ἐρέχθω, *I torment, torture*; used only in pres. and imperf.

Ἐρέω. See Εἰπεῖν and Ἔρομαι.

Ἐρίζω, *I contend, dispute*: fut. ἐρίσω, Epic ἐρίσσω, Dor. ἐρίξω, &c. This verb has in the Epics a middle synonymous with the active, Il. ε, 172. Od. δ, 80. Hes. θ, 534., to which belongs the perf. pass. with Att. reduplication ἐρήρισμαι*; while ἐριδήσασθαι, Il. ψ, 792. probably does not belong to this verb but comes from the pres. ἐριδαίνω, according to the analogy laid down in note under Αἰσθάνομαι: only that ἐριδήσασθαι in the passage above mentioned has the second syllable long, whence it has been written with double δ†.

ἜΡΟΜΑΙ, *I ask*: fut. ἐρήσομαι; aor. ἠρόμην, imper. ἐροῦ (not ἔρου), Ep. ἔρειο; opt. ἐροίμην, conj. ἔρωμαι, infin. ἐρέσθαι (not ἔρεσθαι), part. ἐρόμενος. [This aor. is in common Attic use in all its moods, and the fut. is occasionally found in the best writers, Plat. Lys. p. 207. c. 211. d. Apol. p. 29. e. Xen. Hell. 4, 5, 6. but of the infin. pres. ἔρεσθαι there are great doubts, and even in Homer it is most probably the aor. and ought to be accented as such. The other tenses are supplied by ἐρωτάω.—Passow.] Ionic prose has on the other hand a present εἴρομαι, of which the imperf. εἰρόμην with its other moods εἴρωμαι, εἴρεσθαι, &c. are, like the above, used as aorists: fut. εἰρήσομαι.

* I know not whether this perf. occurs in any other passage beside the fragment of Hesiod ap. Clem. Alex. in Strom. p. 716. (603.) et in Cohort. p. 63. (48.) or No. 53. Gaisf.: but there, notwithstanding the faults of transcribers, its connexion with the context makes it unquestionable; and by comparing the two quotations it most probably ran thus, Αὐτὸς γὰρ πάντων βασιλεὺς καὶ κοίρανός ἐστιν, Ἀθανάτων τέ οἱ οὔτις ἐρήρισται κράτος ἄλλος.

† This way of writing it Wolf has very properly rejected: and thence we must conclude that the Greeks expressed this lengthening of the vowel, not by merely making it long (as from ἔρις ἔρῖδος), but by the accent or *ictus*. This however does not appear to me grounded on sufficient analogy: and it is therefore worth remarking, that the old Grammarians, according to the Scholium in Heyne, had another reading ἐριζήσασθαι. Compare the double way of writing ἀΐδηλος and ἀΐζηλος in Buttm. Lexil. p. 53. &c.

We often meet with the accentuation ἔρεσθαι, which is considered as a present; but as we nowhere find an indicative ἔρομαι, ἔρεται, &c., this is not conceivable. Now as the manuscripts frequently give us the aoristic accentuation ἐρέσθαι, ἐπερέσθαι, there is no doubt that this alone is the true way of writing it, and that the other arose from the grammatical custom of supposing a pres. ἔρομαι. Compare ἠγρόμην in ἐγείρω*. This supposition was very much supported by the actual existence of the Ionic pres. εἴρομαι, which was considered to be a mere Ion. production of the common ἔρομαι. But if we examine carefully all that is quoted on the subject and the analogy of the language, there can be no doubt of the Ion. εἴρομαι being the true theme, and ἐρέσθαι the regular aor. from it (compare ἀγερέσθαι), which thus takes its natural augment ἠρόμην. Now when we explain the Ion. εἴρετο &c. to be an imperf., it is not to be denied that we look to its exterior only, as with regard to the meaning there is no room for the exercise of any grammatical acuteness; because, as we see in the syntax, all these verbs belonging to the conversational narrative of the language stand very commonly in the imperfect, as ἐκέλευε, ἠρώτα, ἔννεπε, and thence also ἔφη. In Homer too we find εἴρομαι, εἴρεσθαι, εἰρώμαι &c. frequently enough; but sometimes we also meet with ἐρώμεθα, ἔροιτο, ἔρειο (for ἔρεο), ἔρεσθαι. Of the accentuation ἐρέσθαι being used in his poems I nowhere find any mention; and as the sense there is not more decisive than it is in Herodotus, we must consider the forms with ε and those with ει to be in the Epic language the same, and therefore leave the accentuation of ἔρεσθαι untouched. Again at Il. α, 513. φ, 508. we must remain in doubt between the reading of εἴρετο and ἤρετο; the best manuscripts are in favour of the former. Of this old verb therefore common prose has retained only the historic tense, which by the quantity of the stem and by the accent was pronounced as an aor. 2., whilst the present could be dispensed with on account of ἐρωτᾶν.

Later writers, mistaking the aoristic meaning of ἐρόμενος, have used ἐρησάμενος, Paus. 4, 12.† The fut. in the Ion. form εἰρήσομαι was liable to be confounded with the passive fut. εἰρήσομαι under εἰπεῖν; whence perhaps ἐπειρήσομαι was preferred.

The Ionic insertion of the ε in ἐρέεσθαι, ἐρέοντο &c. is found in Homer, and in ἐπειρεόμενος, Herodot. 3, 64., where those manuscripts

* That the Greek Grammarians supposed ἔρεσθαι to be falsely accented is clear from the Etym. M. v. Εἴρω and Λιτέσθαι, however faulty these articles may be in other respects.

† In that passage however Bekker proposes instead of ἐρησαμένοις δὲ ἔχρησεν to read χρησαμένοις.

which give ἐπειρόμενος are not deserving of attention. The Epic language had also in this formation the active ἐρέω, Il. η, 128. Od. φ, 31. λ, 229. which must not be confounded with the future ἐρέω from εἴρω, εἶπον: ἐρείομεν is 1. plur. conj. pres. for ἐρέωμεν, Il. α, 62. A lengthened present in the same language is ἐρεείνω. Compare ἀλεείνω.

Ἕρπω, *I creep along, go along*: fut. ἕρψω, &c. The augm. is ει. It is used only in pres. and imperf. [The latter meaning was the prevailing one in the Doric writers, Valck. Adon. p. 400. but not unknown to the Attic tragedians, Brunck. Eurip. Hipp. 561. Metaph. in Eurip. Cycl. 422. Passow.]

Ἔρρω, *I go forth* or *away*: fut. ἐρρήσω; aor. 1. ἤρρησα; perf. ἤρρηκα.

Ἕρσαι is an old aorist, of which we find in Hom. the compound ἀπόερσε, ἀποέρσῃ, ἀποέρσειε with the sense of *to wash away, sweep away*. Il. ζ, 348. φ, 283. 329. The present for this may be either ἔρρω with a causative meaning, or ΕΡΔΩ; see Buttm. Lexil. p. 156. &c.

Ἐρυγγάνω, *I eruct*: fut. ἐρεύξομαι*; aor. ἤρυγον.

The more simple theme ἐρεύγω does not occur in an active form; on the contrary Homer, Herodotus, and the non-Attic writers of a later period have ἐρεύγομαι, from which the latter formed ἠρευξάμην. Homer has, like the Attics, ἤρυγον. The meaning of this verb has modifications which may be seen in the Lexicons, in which however sufficient attention is not paid to the difference of the forms. See Lobeck ad Phryn. pp. 63. 64.

Ἐρυθαίνω. See Ἐρεύθω.

Ἐρύκω, *I hold back from*: fut. ἐρύξω; aor. 1. ἤρυξα, Æschyl. Sept. 1075. Ep. ἔρυξα, Il. γ, 113.

The Epics have also a peculiar aor. 2. with the reduplication in the middle of the word, ἠρύκᾰκον, Il. ε, 321. Infin. ἐρυκακέειν, Hom. Compare ἠνίπαπεν under Ἐνίπτω.

Ἐρύω and εἰρύω, *I draw*, a verb used only by the Ionics and Epics, has ῠ short in the inflexion. Ἐρύω has the fut. ἐρύσω, Ep. ἐρύσσω, but also ἐρύω, Il. λ, 454; perf. pass. εἴρυμαι. The Poet. and Ion. εἰρύω forms εἰρύσω, &c. The Midd. passes over to the meaning of *to save*; see Buttm.

* I have inserted this fut. without hesitation as it is the necessary result of the analogies laid down in my grammar, and it is by mere chance that I have not been able to find any instance of its actual occurrence.

Lexil. p. 303. &c., and in this meaning only we find a form without the ε, viz. ῥύομαι*. This verb is also used in Attic prose, and has in Attic poetry the υ always long in the inflexion, ἐῤῥῡσάμην. But in the Epic poets it is short even there, as ῥῠσάμην, Il. ο, 29.; hence, when the metre requires it long, this form also ought to be written by them with σσ: but the printed text has generally ἐῤῥύσατο, ῥύσατο, even where the syllable is required to be long†.

In the passive form of this verb it is sometimes difficult, particularly amidst the difference of meanings, to distinguish the tenses correctly. The perf. pass. has necessarily by virtue of the reduplication, even if it be formed from ἐρύω, the syllable ει as augment. To this tense belong, with some degree of certainty according to the sense, the forms εἴρυνται or εἰρύαται, pluperf. εἴρυντο, εἰρύατο, Il. ξ, 75. σ, 69. ο, 654. of the ships which *have been* or *were drawn up* on land. In the passage of Od. χ, 90. it may be doubted whether εἴρῡτο be pluperf. or syncop. aorist‡. In either case there is this certain result, at least for the Epic language, that as the radical syllable of the syncop. aor. always corresponds with that of the perf. pass., the 1. sing. of this last tense was not formed with the σ, but with the υ long§.

In the sense of *to save, watch over*, we frequently find ἔρυσθαι, ἔρυτο,

* Not that I mean by this expression, "without the ε," that this form is the later of the two; I rather think there are good grounds for concluding it to be the older, and that the ε was added afterwards as in θέλω, ἐθέλω.

† Because ῥῡσασθαι with υ long was usual in the Attic and common language, this quantity was supposed to be the ground of the Epic usage also, and ῥῠσάμην to be an Epic shortening of the syllable. Again in ἐρύσασθαι the earlier editors made a distinction between ἐρῠσασθαι, ἐρύσσασθαι, *to draw*, and ἐρῡσασθαι *to save*. See Buttm. Lexil. The justice of the conclusions which I have drawn both there and here is evident; and there is but one alternative, either to suppose with me a radical shortness through all the meanings, and to write the lengthened syllable in all instances with σσ, or to explain ῥῠσάμην to be a corruption (see Spitzner's Prosody, p. 68.), a mode of proceeding which the moderate critic will never wish to encourage. That the difference of quantity might have in time produced a difference of meaning is certain; and Attic usage shows it to have done so: but that it was not so at an earlier period is proved by the verbals ἔρῠμα, ἐρῠσίπτολις, &c. having the meaning of *to protect*, while ῥῡτήρ, ῥῡμός, &c. have the meaning of *to draw*. That the Epic language belongs to that period is in itself probable; the above-mentioned ῥῠσάμην gives it critical certainty.

‡ The passage runs thus, Ἀμφίνομος δ' Ὀδυσῆος ἐείσατο κυδαλίμοιο Ἀντίος ἀΐξας, εἴρυτο δὲ φάσγανον ὀξὺ, Εἴ πώς οἱ εἴξειε θυράων. Here εἴρυτο appears to stand in exactly the same situation as at Od. χ, 79. εἰρύσσατο φάσγανον ὀξύ. But we may understand the times of the action thus, "he rushed on Ulysses with the sword which he *had drawn*," and then εἴρυτο is the pluperf. of the same middle of which εἰρύσσατο is the aorist. If the poet had wished to use the aor., he might have said εἰρύσσατο δὲ ξίφος ὀξύ, as indeed he has done at δ, 530. If this argument be not conclusive, it will at least show that this is a solitary instance of the syncop. aor. εἴρυτο as a middle with transitive sense for εἰρύσσατο, whereas all other instances of those syncop. aorists have a completely passive meaning.

§ Of εἴρυσμαι, εἰρύσθην, as required by the grand analogy of verbs which

εἴρυτο, &c. with υ long; but they cannot be reckoned as perf. and plu-perf. according to sense, nor, where there is no long syllable for the augment, according to form. Aorists they could only be (i. e. syncopated aor.) where they meant a saving or snatching away completed in a moment; but the majority of these passages are decisive for the duration of the action. Thus εἴρῡτο, ἔρῡτο, 2. pers. ἔρῡσο are plainly imperf., Il. ω, 499. δ, 138. ν, 555. χ, 507. in all which instances the sense is *thou didst protect, he protected,* exactly corresponding with the undoubted imperf. in Il. ζ, 403. οἶος γὰρ ἐρύετο Ἴλιον Ἕκτωρ. In the same way εἴρυντο, ῥύατο are used of *protecting* bolts, walls, guards, Il. μ, 454. σ, 515. Od. ρ, 201.: and a similar meaning of duration is always found in the infin. εἴρυσθαι, ἔρυσθαι, ῥῦσθαι, e. g. Od. γ, 268. ι, 194. Il. ο, 141. It is clear therefore that all these forms belong to the *syncope of the pres. and imperf.*—εἰρύετο εἴρυτο, ἐρύεσθαι ἔρυσθαι. Nay, the indicative itself is used, not only by Apollon. 2, 1208. ἔρῡται, *he watches over,* but by Homer also, in as much as the 3. plur. εἰρύαται in the passages of Il. α, 239. Od. π, 463. stands in the sense of *to watch over, observe,* and consequently as it cannot in accordance with the above-quoted passages be explained from the meaning of the perfect, it can be only a present.

There remain some passages in which the sense of the aor. appears to suit better than that of the imperf., as ἔρυτο, Il. ε, 23. and 538. ἔῤῥυτο (lyric), Soph. Œd. T. 1352.: these however are sufficiently accounted for by the greater liberty taken in the older language in the use of the historic tense.

We have mentioned before in the last paragraph of the article on γένομαι and in Buttm Lexil. p. 305, that in the Epic language the future of ἐρύω becomes ἐρύω again*. We must consider in the same light the middle ἐρύεσθαι, Il. ξ, 422. ι, 248. υ, 195.; for Homer when speaking of a hope or intention to do some certain thing, never puts the verb following in the present, but always in the fut. or aor.; as we may see by comparing Il. σ, 174. χ, 351. where in a similar combination and meaning we find as in other cases the aor. ἐρύσασθαι.

There are still two other Hesiodic forms to be mentioned: 1.) ε, 816. infin. εἰρύμεναι with υ short, for ἐρύειν, *to draw*; therefore exactly analogous to the formation in μι, like δεικνύμεναι for δεικνύναι. 2.) θ,

shorten the vowel in the inflexion, I find no instance. Only in very late writers ἐῤῥύσθην is quoted from ῥύεσθαι, *to save.* See Stephan Thesaur.

* Some similar futures of verbs in -έω and -άω will be found in the last note under Δέμω, with which these Epic futures in -ύω correspond exactly; thus ἐρύω, fut. ἐρῦσω, and dropping the σ, ἐρύω—ἐρύουσι, Il λ, 454. τανύουσι, Od. φ, 174. Compare also σώω under Σώζω.

304. ἔρυτο likewise with υ short, and with a passive sense, *was watched, guarded.*

Ἔρχομαι, *I go*, borrows from ΕΛΕΥΘΩ its fut. ἐλεύσομαι, its aor. Ep. ἤλυθον, Att. ἦλθον* (from which all the other moods are formed, imperat. ἐλθέ†, inf. ἐλθεῖν, part. ἐλθών), its perf. ἐλήλῠθα; and verbal adj. ἐλευστέος (μετελευστέος):

The Epics lengthen the first and third syllable of this perf. thus, εἰλήλουθα‡, and in plur. this form suffers the syncope εἰλήλουθμεν, Il. ι, 49. Od. γ, 81. part. εἰληλουθώς, and once ἐληλουθώς, Od. ο, 81. Of the pluperf. Homer has only the 3. sing. εἰληλούθει, Il. In Hephæstion pp. 6. 7., quoted from some Comedian, we find two forms ἐλήλυμεν, ἐλήλυτε, in which the Attics transferred, it would seem, to the language of the common people the same syncope which they applied to ἐλήλυθα, ἐληλύθειν, but dropped the analogy of the perf. passive.

The Dor. ἦνθον, ἐνθεῖν for ἦλθον, ἐλθεῖν is analogous to βέντιστος, φίντατος for βέλτιστος, φίλτατος.

It has been mentioned under εἶμι, *I go*, that in usage it is connected with this verb. That is to say, instead of the collateral moods of the pres. of ἔρχομαι those of εἶμι are generally used; instead of the imperf. ἠρχόμην the imperf. ᾔειν or ᾖα; and instead of the fut. ἐλεύσομαι the indicat. pres. εἶμι: so that if we consider as the ground of our conjugation the almost universally prevailing usage, we shall join these two verbs together thus: pres. ἔρχομαι, imper. ἴθι, conj. ἴω, opt. ἴοιμι, infin. ἰέναι, part. ἰών. Imperf. ᾔειν or ᾖα; perf. and pluperf. ἐλήλυθα, ἐληλύθειν; aor. ἦλθον, ἐλθέ, &c.; fut. εἶμι, of which the other moods will be found under that verb.

* This distinction of ἤλυθον and ἦλθον into Ep and Att. is not quite accurate, as Homer has both forms; so has Pindar, but afterwards the latter became the one in general use.

† The 2. sing imperat. act of five verbs is an exception to the general analogy of accentuation; thus, εἰπέ, ἐλθέ, εὑρέ in the common, and λαβέ, ἰδέ in the Attic language.

‡ In this word the first production only is pure Epic, as in ἐμνήμυκε. The ου is nothing more than the proper sound of this perfect, which without the Attic reduplication would be ἤλουθα, the ου being the analogous change from the ευ which we see in ἐλεύσομαι. The supposed perfect ἤλυθα would therefore be contrary to analogy, and there can be no reason for introducing it into Hes. θ, 660. where the aor. is quite as good: the reading therefore of the old editions and of Gaisford's two manuscripts (Barocc. Medic.) should be restored to the text, ἠλύθομεν.

It is evident that the forms of εἶμι were preferred on account of their slightness (particularly in their numerous compounds) to the corresponding heavy-sounding forms of ἔρχεσθαι and ἐλθεῖν, in addition to which there was the ambiguity of ἠρχόμην. Still however the latter were never entirely obsolete, but always introduced where they contributed to the perspicuity or fullness of the sentence. Thus we find περιήρχετο, Aristoph. Thesm. 504. ἤρχετο, Arat. 102, 118. ἐλεύσεται, Soph. Œd. C. 1206. &c. See Elmsl. ad Eurip. Heracl. 210., Lobeck ad Phryn. pp. 37, 38.

To this mixture of forms we must add, in adapting it to the custom of other languages, a mixture of the meanings *go* and *come*. The forms of ἐλθεῖν have a decided preference for the meaning *come*, so that ἦλθεν for instance very seldom occurs in the sense of *going, going away**; and those of εἶμι are as seldom found in the sense of *come*†. But ἔρχεσθαι partakes almost equally of both meanings. In their *compounds* on the other hand, where the preposition generally defines the relation, all three themes have no distinction of meaning‡.

'Εσθημένος, *clad, clothed*, a defective part. perf, properly Ionic, occur-

* Instances of this meaning are the following; μὴ ἔλθῃς, *do not go* (away), Soph. Phil. 1182. εἰ ἔλθοι τις, Xen. Anab 7, 8, 9. although this may be interpreted as a *coming* to the distant place: συμβουλεύει ἐλθόντι εἰς Δελφοὺς ἀνακοινῶσαι, 3, 1, 5 that is ἰέναι εἰς Δ, καὶ ἐλθόντα ἀνακοινῶσαι

† They principally occur only where the immediate context expresses a *coming*, as ἆσσον ἴτε, or οὐκ ἦτε εἰς τήνδε τὴν χώραν, Xen. Anab 7, 7, 6 or in an antithesis as ἰόντες καὶ ἀπιόντες

‡ A more accurate examination will show that the distinction of the meanings *go* and *come* does not depend so much on the radical sense of the verb as on the ideas which we have of the time. The German and Latin with their cognate languages express, for instance, the going to the place where the speaker is or to which the thought is directed by the verb *to come*, venio. In Greek ἔρχεσθαι is both, as the particular relation *come* is announced by the context. The *Aorist* ἦλθον, as expressing the moment when the action is completed, looks to the point or place at which it is to arrive at last, for which we therefore can only use the word *come*, "when he came," be it thither or here. In the *Future, he will go*, and *he will come* give indeed two different ideas of time, in as much as the latter again looks only to the place where the arrival is to be. To express this two forms are therefore necessary; εἶσι means *he will go*, and for *he will come*, the Greek language has recourse to the verb ἥκω, *I come*, (i. e. I am arrived, I am there), therefore ἥξει, *he will come*. In the compounds these distinctions generally disappear, because the point or place of arrival is expressed by the preposition; προσέρχεσθαι in all its tenses gives the idea of *coming* to us; its contrary ἀπέρχεσθαι never has that sense· ἀπῆλθον expresses a point of time quite as well as ἦλθον, but it is always the moment of departure, consequently never a coming or arrival. What I have said may suffice to give a general idea of this subject, particulars and exceptions will be seen by individual observation.

ring in Herodot. 6, 112., but found also, and with the augm. ἠσθημένος, in Eurip., Hel. 1555. We meet with ἤσθητο also in the sense of *was clad in, had on,* in Ælian. V.H. 12, 32. 13, 1. For some other instances from the later writers see Stephan. Thesaur.

Ἐσθίω, *I eat,* has from the old ἔδω a fut. ἔδομαι or ἐδοῦμαι and less frequently ἐδέσω; perf. 2. ἐδήδοκα; perf. pass. ἐδήδεσμαι; aor. pass. ἠδέσθην; verbal adj. ἐδεστός, ἐδεστέον, Plat. Crito p. 47. b. Aor. act. ἔφαγον, infin. φαγεῖν.

The poets had also a shorter form ἔσθω; whence ἔσθουσι, Il. ω, 415. ἔσθων, 476. which was used on account of the metre even by Attic poets; see the passages quoted from some Comic writers in Athen. 7. p. 277. f., 13. p. 596. b., 14. p. 645. a. The radical form ἔδω was also frequently used by the Epics and even by Hippocrates De Vet. Med. 9. ἔδων τε καὶ πίνων. The infin. of this verb is by the Epics syncopated ἔδμεναι; and from an old perf. act. ἔδηδα they have the particip. ἐδηδώς; they use also an imperf. ἔδεσκον. The perf. 2. (with its change of vowel ε to ο) was ἐδήδοκα, which change was by the Epics transferred to the perf. pass., consequently instead of the usual ἐδήδεσμαι they have ἐδήδομαι, ἐδήδοται, Od. χ, 56. See Buttm. Lexil. pp. 137–140.

From ΦΑΓΩ, which is not in use, the LXX frequently formed a fut. φάγομαι, 2. pers. φάγεσαι, analogous to ἔδομαι*.

Ἔσπετε, ἔσπον, ἐσπόμην. See Εἰπεῖν and Ἕπω.

Ἑστιάω, *I receive as a guest, entertain at my table.* The augm. is ει. [Pass. with fut. midd. (Plato de Repub. 1. p. 345. c.), *I am a guest, feast upon* (anything, τινί), Lycophr. 1411. Casaub. Athen. 7. 1.—Passow.]

Εὔαδε. See Ἁνδάνω.

Εὕδω, καθεύδω, *I sleep*: fut. εὑδήσω, καθευδήσω; imperf. with augm. εὗδον, καθεῦδον, but also ηὗδον, καθηῦδον, and ἐκάθευδον. Generally the compound is more used in prose than the simple.

The forms with ηυ are more properly Attic; ηὗδεν, Plat. Symp. p.

* We can scarcely reckon as belonging to the Greek language solitary forms from the root ΦΑΓ-, which are occasionally found in the later writers, as φάγουσι in the paraphrast of Dionys. de Aucupio (Schneid. Oppian. p. 179.) and φαγέοις in the false Phocylides 145.

203. b. καθηῦδον, p. 217. e. 219. c.: καθεῦδον is found in Aristoph. Eccl. 479. Av. 495.: ἐκάθευδον is used by Xenoph. and most good writers.

Εὑρίσκω, *I find*: fut. εὑρήσω; perf. εὕρηκα; aor. 2. εὗρον, imperat. εὑρέ*, infin. εὑρεῖν; aor. 2. midd. εὑρόμην; perf. pass. εὕρημαι; aor. 1. pass. εὑρέθην; verb. adj. εὑρετός. In verbs beginning with ευ the augm. ηυ is generally rather Attic: but in this verb ηὕρισκον, ηὑρέθην are seldom found even in the Attics; the common way of writing them is εὕρισκον, εὗρον, εὑρέθην, and the perf. is always εὕρηκα.—Midd.

Non-Attic writers, as the Alexandrine and others of a later period, form the aor. 2. midd. as an aor. 1., εὑράμην for εὑρόμην: see the last paragraph under αἱρέω. Wolf. Lept. p. 216., Jacob. Anth. Poet. p. 880., Lobeck ad Phryn. p. 139.

Εὔχομαι, *I pray*, depon. midd.: fut. εὔξομαι; aor. 1. ηὐξάμην. The augment follows the general analogy of verbs beginning with ευ; compare εὑρίσκω.

The 3. sing. syncop. aor. εὖκτο for ηὔξατο occurs in an Epic fragment in Schol. Soph. Œd. C. 1375. The pluperf. ηὔγμην is in Soph. Tr. 610.

Εὔω, *I singe, roast*: fut. εὔσω, Ion. εὕω†; aor. 1. εὗσα, Hom. In prose generally ἀφεύω, ἀφεῦσα, and ἠφευμένος, Æschyl. ap. Athen. 9. p. 375. e.

In the dialects we find also ἀφαύω. In Aristophanes the reading is uncertain, but the better authorities are in favour of ἀφεύειν. So we have ἀφεῦσα in Simon. Fr. 136. and ἀφεύσαις in Nicand. ap. Athen. 2. p. 61. a. The pronunciation with the lenis εὔω and αὔω is known from single forms and derivations, among which are ἀπευήκασιν (Hesych.) in the sense of *I dry up*, αὑαίνω, *I dry*, &c. But the forms which belong here must not be confounded with αὔω, *I kindle* (see that verb), as the radical idea is essentially different.

Ἔχθω, *I hate*, used only in pres. and by the poets‡; hence ἀπεχθάνομαι, *I am hateful*; fut. ἀπεχθήσομαι. The aor. ἠχθό-

* For the accentuation of this imperat. see the second note under Ἔρχομαι.

† See the last note under Ἐρύω.

‡ [The active voice is found in Æschyl Fr. 296. Soph. Aj 459. Phil. 510. Eurip. Med. 118. Androm. 212 but the pass. ἔχθομαι is more common.—Passow.]

μην is Poet., but ἀπηχθόμην is more generally used. Perf. ἀπήχθημαι, *I am hated.* We find also a perf. ἤχθημαι, part. ἠχθημένος in Lycophr. 827.

Some have wished to reject the above relation, which has always been supposed by grammarians to exist between the forms of this middle verb, and they adopt, beside ἀπεχθάνομαι, a present, answering to the active, ἔχθομαι, ἀπέχθομαι, of which ἠχθόμην, ἀπηχθόμην would be imperfect. Now the true relation of which we are in search must be grounded on the usage of the older writers. And first then ἀπηχθόμην, when standing in immediate connexion with the present, cannot be an imperfect; it can only be an aorist. Thus in Od. ξ, 366. οἶδα ὅτ' ἤχθετο πᾶσι θεοῖσιν, "that he has been hated," consequently "is hated:" the same of ἀπήχθετο, Il. ι, 300.: again, θαυμάζω ὅτι, εἰ μέν τινι ὑμῶν ἀπηχθόμην, μέμνητε.... εἰ δέ τῳ ἐπεκούρησα, &c. Xen. Anab. 5, 8, 25. In the same way the conj. is plainly an aorist in Il. δ, 53: Τὰς διαπέρσαι, ὅταν τοι ἀπέχθωνται περὶ κηρί, "destroy them, as soon as they have become hateful to thee." Compare also the following passages in Plato's Apologia: and first the present, p. 24. "I tell you everything without concealment, καίτοι οἶδα σχεδὸν ὅτι τοῖς αὐτοῖς ἀπεχθάνομαι, that I make myself hateful to you by these very things." Again p. 21.; Socrates relates his going round to those who appeared to be wise, and his endeavouring to convince one of them that he was not so, and then he adds, ἐντεῦθεν οὖν τούτῳ τε ἀπηχθόμην καὶ πολλοῖς τῶν παρόντων; and immediately afterwards καὶ ἐνταῦθα κἀκείνῳ καὶ ἄλλοις πολλοῖς ἀπηχθόμην. μετὰ ταῦτ' οὖν ἤδη ἐφεξῆς ᾖα, αἰσθανόμενος μὲν...ὅτι ἀπηχθανόμην, where the relative meaning of the imperfect and aorists is most evident. In Demosth. Olynth. 3, p. 34. "I say it not, ἵν' ἀπέχθωμαί τισιν ὑμῶν," it evidently refers to the immediate consequences of the sentence; and just afterwards in a general sense, "for I am not so silly, ὥστε ἀπεχθάνεσθαι βούλεσθαι μηδὲν ὠφελεῖν νομίζων." But the passages where ἤχθετο, ἀπήχθετο have been translated as imperfects, *was hated*, may very well be understood, like other aorists, in the sense of the pluperf. *had made himself hateful, had been hated*, as Il. γ, 454. Eurip. Hipp. 1402. Compare particularly Il. ζ, 200. Notwithstanding this however we see the infin. ἀπέχθεσθαι, not only in every instance as a proparoxytone, but we find expressly in Lex. Seg. 6, p. 423. 25. the gloss 'Απέχθεσθαι· λέγουσι δέ ποτε καὶ ἀπεχθάνεσθαι. Nor do I feel sufficient confidence to recommend the aoristic accentuation for Il. φ, 83. Eurip. Med. 290. Thucyd. 1, 136. Plat. Rep. 1, p. 343. e. Lys. c. Andoc. p. 108, 2.; not so much because the sense is indecisive in favour of aorist or present (it generally is so in the infinitive), but because

I am waiting for manuscript examples of this accentuation*. Notwithstanding what has been said we need not be surprised at finding the indic. pres. ἀπέχθομαι in Eurip. Hipp. 1260. ; (compare αἴσθομαι) for it is ascertained to be a false reading for ἐπάχθομαι : and the usage of Theocritus (ἀπέχθεται, 7. 45.) is not of sufficient authority.

Ἔχω†, *I have, hold* : fut. ἕξω with the aspirate ; imperf. εἶχον‡ ; aor. (as from ΣΧΩ) ἔσχον, imperat. σχές (comp. παράσχες), optat. σχοίην, conj. σχῶ, σχῇς, &c., (comp. παράσχω, παράσχῃς &c.), infin. σχεῖν, part. σχών. Pass. and midd. ἔχομαι ; imperf. εἰχόμην ; fut. midd. ἕξομαι ; aor. midd. ἐσχόμην§ (παράσχου, παρασχέσθαι). From the aor. σχεῖν comes a new fut. act. σχήσω‖, and fut. midd. σχήσομαι, whence perf. act. ἔσχηκα, perf. pass. ἔσχημαι, aor. pass. ἐσχέθην, verbal adj. ἑκτός and σχετός.

From the aor. ἔσχον comes also a new pres. ἴσχω, which with its future σχήσω is principally used when the more definite ideas of *to hold firm, stop, seize on* (which are contained in the less expressive ἔχειν), require force and elevation. The aor. ἔσχον also (as the duration naturally implied in the idea of *to have* little suits the aorist,) belongs rather to these more definite meanings, when they are supposed to be transitory, as *seized, held on*, &c. In its compounds ἔχω has generally one of these more definite senses, whence also the aor. πάρεσχον &c. is found much more commonly in these than any other meanings.

Notwithstanding that the great difference of formation in the passive and middle aorist contributed necessarily to keep up a distinction between their respective meanings, we still find cases of the aor. midd. used instead of the passive ; the most common are σχέσθαι in the sense of *to*

* Bekker has never yet found it in any manuscript. The quotation of the above-mentioned verse of Eurip. in Plutarch with ἀπεχθεῖσθαι, contains a trace of it ; see Elmsley, who has written it ἀπεχθέσθαι.

† [Theognis has for the 2. sing. ἔχεισθα, 1316. like σχήσεισθα below.—Passow.]

‡ [Homer has the imperf. also without the augm. ἔχον.—Passow.]

§ [This aor. sometimes loses the augm. in Hom. in its 3. sing. σχέτο, Il. η, 248. φ, 345. We find also its imperat. σχοῦ, infin. σχέσθαι, part. σχόμενος.—Passow.]

‖ [We find a rare form of the 2. sing. fut. σχήσεισθα, Francke Hymn. Cer. 366. like ἔχεισθα mentioned above.—Passow.]

be seized, held, Od., ἔσχοντο Herodot. 1, 31., κατέσχετο Od. γ, 284. Eurip. Hipp. 27., κατασχόμενος Pind. Pyth. 1, 16. Plat. Phædr. p. 244; συσχόμενος Plat. Theæt. p. 165. b.

The way in which ἔσχον comes from ἔχω may be seen by comparing it with ἔσπον from ἕπω. In ἴσχω the ι supplies the place of a reduplication, as we see fully exemplified in μίμνω, γίγνομαι &c., where μν, γν are the syncopated stem of those verbs as σχ is of the one before us. This ι would have the aspirate, as in ἵστημι; but here again, as in ἔχω itself, it passed on account of the χ into the lenis, a change more frequent in the older times of the language: compare ἐσθής from ἕννυμι, ἕστο, *vestis*; ἀθρόος and ἁθρόος; ἀθύρω, Att. ἀθύρω.

We find also the analogous imperat. σχέ, and that in its simple form, in an oracle in Schol. Eurip. Phœn. 641. where however the reading is not certain. It is more frequent as a compound, πάρασχε; see Porson ad Eur. Hec. 836. Orest. 1330. Plat. Protag. p. 348. a.

The language of poetry has from a theme ΣΧΕΘΩ the forms ἔσχεθον, σχεθέειν, σχέθων, on which see ἀμύνω.

On εἴχεε, Herodot. 1, 118. for εἶχε, see ἕψεε under ἕψω, and compare ἐώθεε under ἔθω —From the part. perf. συνοχωκότε, Il. β, 218. we may conclude that there was an old Epic part. ὄχωκα, of which the following seems to be a satisfactory explanation. The simple perfect of ἔχω, with the usual change of vowel, would be ὄχα (compare the subst. ὀχή); which reduplicated becomes, according to the common analogy, ὄκωχα. But since of two aspirates the second may be changed, it is very possible that this became ὄχωκα, particularly as such a change made the derivation from ἔχω more sensible to the ear. And it is clear from the Hesychian gloss συνοκώχοτε, either that the old Grammarians explained the Homeric form in this way, or that both stood side by side as old various readings. That a reduplicated form of this kind did exist is certain at all events by the subst. ὀκωχή, as all similar verbal substantives (ὀπωπή, ὀδωδή, ἐδωδή, ἀγωγή, ἀκωκή) are connected with really reduplicated forms of their respective verbs. Compare also the exactly similar formation of οἴχωκα under οἴχω.

In the passage of Il. μ, 340. the reading πᾶσαι γὰρ ἐπώχατο (i. e. πύλαι) with the explanation "were shut" has very much in its favour, both from the sense and construction as well as from the antithesis at θ, 58. πᾶσαι δ' ὠΐγνυντο πύλαι. If with Wolf we adopt it, the only way of analogous explanation is this: Ὀχεύς, *a bolt*, has its meaning from the verb ἔχω; and the supposition that ἐπέχω τὰς πύλας meant *to hold together, shut*, is grounded on analogy, like ἐπέχειν τὰ ὦτα, τὴν γλῶσσαν &c. But as we have shown above that ὄκωχα was the perf. act, so is ὦγμαι formed as correctly as ἦγμαι with ἀγήοχα, and with the change of vowel continuing into the passive like ἄωρτο. According to this ἐπώχατο is the Ion. 3. plur. of the pluperf. pass. from ἐπέχω*.

The following compounds of ἔχω have other peculiarities:

ἀνέχω. When ἀνέχεσθαι in the midd. has the sense of *to bear*, its imperf. and aor. have a double augm., ἠνειχόμην, ἠνεσχόμην (ἀνασχέσθαι).

The simple augm. does however occur in this meaning of the verb, sometimes in the middle, as in ἀνεσχόμην (Aristoph. Pac. 347.), sometimes at the beginning, as in ἠνεχόμεσθα, which excellent emendation of Kuster for the unmetrical ἠνεσχόμεσθα (Aristoph. Lys. 507.) has been rejected through a mistake of Porson and others as not Greek.

ἀμπέχω, *I envelope*: imperf. ἀμπεῖχον; fut. ἀμφέξω; aor. ἤμπισχον, ἀμπισχεῖν. MIDD. ἀμπέχομαι or ἀμπισχνοῦμαι, *I have round me, have on me*; fut. ἀμφέξομαι; aor. ἠμπισχόμην.

Here too we find the double augment. In Aristoph. Thesm. 165. indeed, where ἠμπέσχετο stands, the aor. is embarrassing, and probably the true reading was ἠμπείχετο, which form of the imperf. has been restored from the manuscripts to Plat. Phædo. p. 87. b, and occurs also in Lucian. Peregr. 15.

A present ἀμπίσχω has also been adopted, which considered in itself, like ἴσχω and ἔχω, is not only admissible, but actually does occur (see Elmsl. ad Eurip. Med. 277.). Still however ἤμπισχον, which appears so frequently in the common language, is not the imperfect of it, as ἀμπισχεῖν alone would suffice to inform us. But instead of this another pres. ἀμπισχέω has been supposed, and supported not only by the gloss ἀμπισχούμενον in Hesychius, but also by the similar various reading in Aristoph. Av. 1090. That a form ἰσχέω, ἀμπισχέω should have existed in the Attic dialect, and that ἀμπίσχω and ἀμπισχοῦμαι should have become completely confounded together, is most improbable. But in the passage of Aristophanes there is an old reading ἀμπισχνούμενον, which is at once placed beyond a doubt by the parallel ὑπισχνοῦμαι: it is therefore evident that ἀμπισχοῦμαι, from a mere misunderstanding of the aor. ἀμπισχεῖν, crept not only into some of the manuscripts of Aristophanes, but into Hesychius also, where the gloss ἀμπισχεῖν occurs just

* The reading ἐπῴχατο, from a supposed pres. ἐποίγνυμι, is quite untenable; for as the simple οἰγνύναι means *to open*, this compound of it cannot mean *to shut*. Derived from οἴχομαι it might be in itself defensible, but in the passage in question it gives no idea recommended by its combining easily with the context.

before*. Now that ἤμπισχον, ἀμπισχεῖν, is really an aorist, we learn from the passages of Aristoph. and the following glosses of Hesych: Ἀμπισχεῖν, περιβαλεῖν. Ἠμπίσχετο (l. ἤμπισχε), περιέσχε, περιέβαλεν. Ἠμπίσχετο, ἐνεδύσατο, ἐφόρησε, περιεβάλλετο (l. περιεβάλετο). And therefore it is clear that this form is not resolvable into ἤμπ–ισχον, ἀμπ–ισχεῖν, but into ἤμπι–σχον, ἀμπι–σχεῖν; because instead of ἄμπ–εσχον the augm. passed over to the preposition, ἤμπι–σχον.

ὑπισχνέομαι, *I promise*, Ion. (Hom. and Herod.) ὑπίσχομαι: fut. ὑποσχήσομαι; aor. ὑπεσχόμην, imperat. ὑπόσχου†; perf. ὑπέσχημαι.

Ἕψω, *I cook*: fut. ἑψήσω, &c. Verbal adj. ἑφθός, or ἑψητός, ἑψητέος. A remarkable form of the aor. is συνῆψας in the comic writer Timocles ap. Athen. 9. p. 407. e.

We find in Herodotus (1, 48. 1, 118. 8, 26.) a resolution of εε for ε in the 3. sing. imperfect of three verbs, ἕψεε, ἐνείχεε, ὤφλεε, from ἕψω, ἐνέχω and ὦφλον, which reciprocally confirm each other‡. Some suppose a pres. ἑψέω from which they may be formed, but except in ἑψήσω, ὀφλήσω, there are no traces whatever of such a theme, unless we imagine something in ἑψεῖν, Hippocr. de Steril. 17. which to me seems to mean nothing of the kind; and in an aor. 2. (as we shall see ὦφλον is) a form in εον would be quite remote from all analogy. Compare the perf. ἐώθεε under Ἔθω.

The formation of the verbal adj. ἑφθός dates from a time when the double letters ξ and ψ were not yet introduced into the Attic writing; consequently the root of ἕψω was then ΕΦΣ–: when to this root the termination τος was added, the σ necessarily dropped out, as three consonants could not stand together, leaving ἑφ–τός, which by a change of the second consonant to make the root somewhat more visible, became ἑφθός.

ἝΩ, ἘΩ, ἽΩ. The first ἝΩ has three leading senses, which form so many verbs: 1. *I send*; 2. *I seat*; 3. *I clothe*. The second ἘΩ is the

* The critic must not be misled by finding the reading ἀμπισχούμενον in Aristoph. in so excellent a manuscript as the Cod. Ravenn., when the internal analogy is so decisive. Besides it is clear that a form so strange to the common grammarian as ἀμπισχνοῦμαι, and which is verified by such pure analogy, cannot have come into the manuscripts by chance or mistake; consequently that the worst which has it, is in such a case of more weight than the best which has it not.

† An imperat. pass. ὑποσχέθητι has been hitherto the reading in Plat. Phædr. p. 235. d., but there are only weak grounds for it in the manuscripts. See Bekker.

‡ The unanimity of the reading sometimes of all, at other times of the majority, of the manuscripts as to these three forms is so convincing, that I am not only unwilling to meddle with them, but I even suspect that ἐπεῖχέ τε in Herodot. 1, 153. where τε is injurious to the context, is a corruption of ἐπεῖχεε.

root of εἰμί, *I am.* The third, ἼΩ is the root of εἶμι, *I go.* As these two last will be found in their alphabetical places, we have here to treat only of the three derivates of ἝΩ.

1. ἵημι, *I send, throw.*

The conjugation of this verb scarcely differs from that of τίθημι; whatever tenses the one forms from ΤΙΘΕΩ, the other borrows from ἙΩ. The ι stands, for instance, instead of the reduplication; in the Attic language it is long*, in the Epic generally short. When the short radical vowel ε begins the word, it is capable of receiving the augment by changing to ει. The simple verb is not of frequent occurrence, and a large proportion of the undermentioned forms occur only in the compounds.

Active.

Pres. ἵημι, ἵης, ἵησι,—3. pl. (ἱέᾱσι) ἱᾶσι or ἱεῖσι. Imper. ἵει. Opt. ἱείην. Conj. ἱῶ. Infin. ἱέναι†. Part. ἱείς.

Imperf. ἵην and (from ἽΕΩ) ἵουν. Comp. ἀφίουν or ἠφίουν; 3. pl. ἠφίεσαν.

Fut. ἥσω.

Perf. εἶκα‡ (like τέθεικα). Pluperf. εἵκειν.

Aor. 1. ἧκα, Ion. ἕηκα.

Aor. 2. ἧν, &c. (not used in sing. but its place supplied by aor. 1.), pl. ἕμεν, ἕτε, ἕσαν, generally with augm. εἷμεν, εἷτε, εἷσαν (καθεῖμεν, ἀνεῖτε, ἀφεῖσαν §). Imper. ἕς. Opt. εἵην; pl. εἷμεν, εἷτε, εἷεν for εἵημεν, &c. Conj. ὧ. Infin. εἷναι. Part. εἵς. The compounds follow the simple, e. g. ἀφεῖναι, ἀφῶ, ἄφες, &c. Opt. pl. ἀνεῖμεν for ἀνείημεν, &c.

Pass. and Midd. (compare Τίθημι.)

Pres. ἵεμαι.

Perf. εἷμαι (as μεθεῖμαι, μεθεῖσθαι, μεθείσθω), &c. Διαειμένος, Apoll. Rh. 2, 372. belongs to the middle of εἶμι, ἵεμαι.

Aor. 1. pass. ἕθην, generally with the augm. εἵθην (ἀφείθην, part. ἀφεθείς, &c.; ἠφείθη, Plut. Sylla 28.).

* It may however be shortened in Att. poetry; see Lex. Seg. 6. p. 471, 10. Dobr. ad Aristoph. Plut. 75.

† [Instead of ἱέναι Homer has ἱέμεναι, Hesiod ἱέμεν: and in the imperf. Homer has ἵεν 3. plur. for ἵεσαν, Il. μ, 33.—Passow.]

‡ For ἕωκα, ἀφέωκα, and the pass. ἀφέωνται in N. T. see the note on ἀγήοχα under ἄγω. I will mention here a trace of the same form in Herodot. 2, 165. where the text has ἀνέονται ἐς τὸ μάχιμον, but the sense requires a perfect ἀνεῖνται, *they are given to, devoted to, vacant.* What therefore was a mere conjecture of Stephanus, ἀνέωνται, now deserves our highest consideration, as the valuable Florentine Codex of Schweighæuser actually has this reading.

§ In these forms of the aor. 2. act. and those of the aor. 2. pass. ἐφεῖντο, &c. the accent is not thrown back to the beginning of the word because the ει arises from the augment.

Aor. 1. midd. ἡκάμην, which in the indicative is used even in prose*; the other moods do not occur.

Aor. 2. midd. ἕμην, generally with the augm. εἵμην, εἶσο, εἶτο (ἀφεῖτο, ἐφεῖντο)†. Imper. οὗ (ἀφοῦ, προοῦ, πρόεσθε, &c.). Opt. εἵμην, εἶο, εἶτο, &c. Conj. ὧμαι. Infin. ἕσθαι (προέσθαι). Part. ἕμενος (ἀφέμενος).

Verbal adj. ἑτός, ἑτέος (ἄφετος, &c.).

Instances of the imperf. sing. in -ην are rare, and those which do occur are suspicious; in the 2. and 3. sing. we generally find ἵεις, ἵει (contracted like ἐτίθεις), and in the 1. sing. was formed, at least in the Ion. and Att. dialect, an anomalous form in -ειν, as προΐειν, Od. ι, 88. κ, 100. μ, 9. (Wolf's ed.); ἠφίειν, Plat. Euthyd. p. 293. a. Libanius 1, p. 793.; ἀνίειν, Lucian. Catapl. 4.

On the *Attic* conj. and optat., which imitate the regular conjugation of the barytone verbs in accent if not in form, as πρόωμαι, πρόηται, ἵοιτο, πρόοισθε, &c., see the second paragraph of Δύναμαι. We find in the active voice of this verb corresponding forms, but only in the present, e. g. ἀφίοιτε, Plat. Apol. p. 29. d.; ἀφίῃ, Xen. Cyr. 8, 1, 2. (6.); but the genuineness of these two is doubtful‡. The other dialectic forms of both moods correspond exactly with those of τίθημι, as ἀφέω, ἀφείω for conj. ἀφῶ; ἧσι for 3. sing. conj. ᾗ, &c.

From the ι of the pres. ἱέναι arose a new theme, 'ΙΩ, of which we find many forms, but always in the Ion. dialect, as ἀνίει for ἀνίησι, Herodot. 3, 109. ξύνιον frequently for ξυνίεσαν, Il. α, 273. ξύνιε, imperat. Theogn. 1240. Bekk. μετίετο or ἐμετίετο for μεθίετο, Herodot. 1, 12. and the augm. perf. μεμετιμένος frequently used for μεθειμένος; see also 3. pres. μετιεῖ in Schweigh. Lex. Herodot. There are many other such forms which vary only in the accent, and consequently are not to be depended on§.

Lastly we have some Epic forms compounded with ἀνά, which ac-

* Examples may be found in Fisch. ad Well. 2. p. 484. where we must restore προήκασθε.

† Xenoph. Hier. 7, 11. Eurip. Suppl. 1199.

‡ Yet we find in the Attics instances of the regular form, as παριῶμεν Plat. Phæd. p. 90., ἀφιῆτε Xen. Hell. 2, 4, 10. (16.), ἀφιεῖεν ib. 6, 4, 2. and 3., still with the various reading ἀφίοιεν in both passages.

§ For instance ἀνιεῖ is from 'ΙΕΩ, but ἀνίει pres. of 'ΙΩ. Compare Il. α, 326. with 336., β, 752. with γ, 118. where προΐει is sometimes pres. sometimes imperfect. See Brunck on Sophocl. Œd. T. 628. and Heyne on Il. ζ, 523. The imperat. ξύνιε in Theognis becomes suspicious when compared with the Homeric ξυνίει, Od. α, 271. and elsewhere; while the 3. plur. ξύνιον is rendered doubtful by the various reading ξύνιεν for ξυνίεσαν (see Heyne on Il. α, 273.). We have quoted these points to show the great uncertainty of the readings, not to recommend an uniformity, which is impossible if we pay any regard to manuscripts.

cording to meaning can only belong here, and which have this peculiarity, that they take ε instead of η in the future, and have the regular formation of the aor. 1. in σα instead of κα, as ἀνέσει, ἄνεσαν, ἀνέσαιμι, Il. ξ, 209. φ, 537. Od. σ, 265. But this form appears to be used only where the preposition gives the idea of *again, back*: compare Il. β, 276. ξ, 362, where ἀνήσει, ἀνῆκεν have merely the sense of *to stimulate.*

2. εἶσα, *I seated, placed*; ἧμαι, *I sit.*

Εἶσα is a defective verb, of which the following forms are found with the meaning of *to seat* or *place*:

Aor. εἶσα, ας, εν, &c. Imper. εἶσον. Infin. ἕσαι, ἕσσαι (ἐφέσσαι).
Part. ἕσας, εἴσας.—Midd. εἰσάμην. Imper. ἕσαι, ἕσσαι (ἔφεσσαι).
Part. ἑσάμενος (ἐφεσσάμενος, Od. π, 442.), εἰσάμενος:

some of which are liable to be confounded with similar forms of ἕννυμι.

Fut. midd. ἕσομαι, ἕσσομαι (ἐφέσσομαι).

Perf. pass. ἧμαι, &c. which see below.

Of these forms εἰσάμην only occurs in Attic prose in the sense of *to lay the foundation of, found, erect*; the others belong to the dialects and to poetry, particularly to the Epic. The defective parts of this verb are supplied by ἱδρύω (which is complete in all its moods and tenses), and by καθίζω, a word of still more general occurrence. The indisputable connection of this verb with ἵζω and ἕζεσθαι has induced many grammarians to place the above forms under ἕζω, the pres. act. of which however is nowhere found. But in that case the augm. ει, which does not occur in ἑζόμην, would form in Attic prose a deviation for which there are no grounds. Now as ἧμαι seems to presuppose a radical form ἝΩ, it is more natural to leave all the above forms in this their simplest formation, distinguish them from ἕζεσθαι, (which we shall see presently to be a word in very limited use), and class this latter as a form belonging to ἵζω, ἵζεσθαι*.

The ει in εἶσα, εἰσάμην, is indisputably the augment, for we see it dropped in the other moods ἕσαι, &c. which double the σ on account of the metre in Epic poetry; hence the imperat. εἶσον which occurs but once (Od. η, 163.) is very remarkable. In a later period however the ει of the augment certainly does become, and that too in prose, an integral part of the word, in order to strengthen the syllable; whence

* It might appear as if the fut. ἐφέσσεσθαι (Il. ι, 455.) could not be separated from ἕζεσθαι, as the curse of Amyntor, Μήποτε γούνασιν οἷσιν ἐφέσσεσθαι φίλον υἱὸν Ἐξ ἐμέθεν γεγαῶτα is understood by all commentators thus, "that a son born of me may never sit on his knees," and in this sense we find ἐφέζετο at Il. φ, 506. But a much more evident comparison is furnished by Od. π, 443. ἐμὲ... Ὀδυσσεὺς Πολλάκι γούνασιν οἷσιν ἐφεσσάμενος. The meaning of ἐφέσσεσθαι therefore in the above passage of the Iliad is "he will never seat," consequently it must not be separated from ἕσασθαι, ἕσαι.

εἰσάμενος not only in Herodot. 1, 66. but also in Plut. Thes. c. 17. and many other passages. In Thucyd. 3, 58. ἑσσάμενος is scarcely genuine, and the various reading ἑσάμενος is undoubtedly the true reading. Lastly we find in Od. ξ, 295. ἐέσσατο with the syllabic augment*, like ἔειπε, ἐείλεον, ἐελμένος, ἐερμένος, &c.

In Athen. 4, p. 142. is quoted from Phylarchus, a prose writer of the time of the Ptolemies, a fut. εἴσεται, *he will seat himself*, in which meaning none of the forms belonging to this verb are found elsewhere. It is probably an Alexandrian provincialism, written in the N. T. καθίζεσθε and καθήσεσθε.

The following forms are in use with the meaning of *to sit*:

Pres. ἧμαι†, ἧσαι, ἧσται, &c. 3. pl. ἧνται.

Imperf. ἥμην, ἧσο, ἧστο, &c. 3. pl. ἧντο. Imperat. ἧσο, ἥσθω, &c. Infin. ἧσθαι. Part. ἥμενος.

In prose however the compound κάθημαι with the same meaning is much more used, which takes no σ in the 3. sing. except when in the imperf. it has no augm., as—

κάθημαι, 3. sing. κάθηται,

ἐκαθήμην or καθήμην, 3. sing. ἐκάθητο or καθῆστο.

Imper. κάθησο. Opt. καθοίμην, 3. sing. κάθοιτο‡. Conj. κάθωμαι, -ῃ, -ηται. Infin. καθῆσθαι§. Part. καθήμενος.

The defective tenses are supplied by ἕζεσθαι or ἵζεσθαι with their compound.

Instead of the 2. sing. in -σαι and -σο we find also the shortened forms of the compounds, viz. pres. κάθῃ for κάθησαι and imperat. κάθου for κάθησο, which however are not so good Attic as the others.

Instead of ἧνται, ἧντο, the Ion. have ἕαται, ἕατο (the ending of the Ion. perf. pass.), and the Epics εἵαται, εἵατο. In the compound the Ion. use, according to their general analogy, κάτημαι, κατέαται, for καθ-.

The same form ἧμαι is also the true perf. of εἷσα, as used in the sense of ἵδρυμαι of inanimate objects, e. g. Herodot. 9, 57., Callim. Fr. 122.: these passages, with the Ion. 3. pl. εἵαται, Lucian. De Dea Syr. 31. prove decidedly that the reading of Od. υ, 106. is εἵατο with the

* This writing ἐέσσατο, with the lenis, to distinguish it from ἑέσσατο the aor. of ἕννυμι, is an arbitrary proceeding of the Grammarians, and scarcely correct, as the syllab. augm. takes the aspirate before aspirated vowels, as in ἑώρων, ἕηκα.

† This form may be considered either as a perf. pass. (*I have been seated*, or *I have seated myself*, consequently *I sit*), or as a separate formation in μι, like δίζημαι: the former appears to me the more probable. Compare Κεῖμαι.

‡ The accentuation of the opt. and conj. moods, from the rarity of their occurrence, is not to be depended on; I have accented these according to the general analogy of barytone verbs.

§ We must not overlook the difference of the accent in κάθημαι, καθῆσθαι, but compare the same appearance with the observations made on it under Κεῖμαι.

aspirate, not (as it is sometimes written) εἷατο the midd. of εἰμί. See also Ἵζω.

3. ἕννυμι, *to put on*, which see in its place.

Ἑῶμεν or ἑῶμεν. See Ἄω, 3.

Z.

Ζάω, *I live*, is contracted in η, like διψάω, πεινάω, χράω; it is used by old writers principally in the pres. and imperf., as βιόω is in the remaining tenses: thus pres. ζῶ, ζῇς, ζῇ; imperat. ζῆ (Herm. Soph. Ant. 1154.), or ζῆθι; opt. ζῴην; infin. ζῆν. Imperf. ἔζων, ἔζης, ἔζη, &c.

The forms with the η, particularly the imperf. ἔζης, ἔζη, soon drew the usage aside to the formation in μι, so that ἔζην as well as ἔζων was used in the imperf., and ζῆθι in the imperative. Herodian attempted indeed to defend the former against the latter (see Fr. 42. Herm. or p. 460. Piers.), but he unwisely drew his proofs from ἔζης, ἔζη. He quotes however ἔζων as the usage of Aristophanes, while Euripides, Plato, Xenophon, &c. have no other form; and the question is decided by the 3. plur. which never occurs otherwise than ἔζων*. Hence it is remarkable that the same Herodian (Fr. 43.), immediately after having pronounced the above opinion, rejects ζῆθι, which is necessarily connected with ἔζην. This imperat. occurs in the LXX. and sometimes in the Anthologia†; but ζῆ is found in Eurip. Iph. T. 699. and Fr. Phrixi, and in Soph. Fr. Danaës.

Beside the pres. and imperf. there was in common use among the older writers a future, as ζήσειν (Aristoph. Plut. 263.), ζήσουσι (Plat. Rep. 5.

* It is singular that Pierson (ad Moer. p. 148.) was so far misled by Herodian's authority as to reject contemptuously the very intelligible opinion of the grammarian in the Etym. M. p. 413, 8. (to which we may add Ib. p. 410, 49. &c. and Tho. M. v. ἔζων), and to defend ἔζην, which is there much censured, as the true reading of Eurip. Alc. 651. where some Codd. certainly have it. It is anything but probable that transcribers should have introduced into so many passages of the old writers ἔζων, which sounds so differently from ἔζη, nay the contrary is the more probable. See Fischer, 1. p. 125. In Demosth. Timocr. 702, 2. we certainly find ἔζην without any known various reading. All things considered I very much doubt whether Herodian ever gave it as his opinion that ἔζην was used for ἔζων. Pierson first took it from a manuscript (see his note p. 460. and Lob. post Phryn. p. 457.); but there is another manuscript in which ἔζων is by no means rejected, and nothing more is stated than that ἔζην, which belongs to ἔζης, ἔζη, is used by Demosthenes.

† That is to say, in the Epig. Incert. 242. where the first six hours of the day are allotted to labour, and then the seventh, eighth, ninth, tenth (ΖΗΘΙ) are said, by a play on the letters, to bid us enjoy life.

p. 465. d.), ζήσει (ib. 9. p. 591. c.), and ζήσεται (which is the common form in use among the later writers) in Dem. c. Aristog. I. p. 794, 19. In these last we find also the aor. 1. ἔζησα and the perf. ἔζηκα.

The Ion. and Dor. formed this verb with the vowel ω, and that not merely as a lengthening of the theme in ζώω, ζώοντες, ἔζωον, but throughout the persons, thus ζώεις, ζώειν, ζώετε, ζώουσιν, and also shortened to ζόειν, see Simonid. Gaisford. 231, 17. Herodot. 7, 46. Theodorid. Epig 8, 7. Hence also a future tense, ἐπέζωσε, which is now restored from the manuscripts to the text of Herodot. 1, 120.*.

Ζέω, *I seeth, boil*, retains the ε in the inflexion. From the examples given by Stephens it appears that ζέω, generally speaking at least, has an intransitive, and ζέννυμι a transitive sense; the other tenses have both meanings in common. The pass. takes σ, e. g ἀπεζεσμένος, ἀποζεσθείς.

Ζεύγνυμι, *I join*: fut. ζεύξω, &c.; aor. 2. pass. ἐζύγην.

Ζώννυμι, *I gird*: fut. ζώσω, &c.; perf. pass. ἔζωσμαι.—MIDD. ζώννυμαι, &c.

According to Suidas (v. σέσωσται) the older Attics had no σ in the perfect. This he proves by the authority of Thucyd. 1, 6. διεζωμένοι, where however all the Codd. have διεζωσμένοι. Compare Σώζω.

Ζώω. See Ζάω.

H.

Ἡβάω, *I am in the bloom and vigour of manhood, pubeo*; ἡβάσκω, *I am coming to manhood, pubesco*. The aor. ἥβησα, *I have arrived at manhood*, belongs to the second form.

See Moeris p. 180. with Pierson's note. In the compound however the form in άω has the sense of *to become*, ἀνηβᾶν *to become young again*.

When the ω is followed by a syllable naturally long it is lengthened by the Epics to ωο, and when it has the ι subscript it becomes ωοι; thus ἡβώοντες for ἡβῶντες, ἡβώοιμι for ἡβῷμι.

Ἡγέομαι, *I lead; I consider as such*: depon. midd. [The

* This formation may be supposed to arise from the mere lengthening of ζάω, ζῶ, making ζώω; but when I compare βώσεσθε (see Βιόω) and βέομαι with ζώειν and ζῆν, and the well-known forms ἐπεζάρει for ἐπεβάρει, ζέρεθρον for βέρεθρον, it seems to point out to me a radical identity in the verbs ζῆν and βιῶναι, which accounts for their being so mixed up together in usage.

act. ἡγέω is found only in its compounds, as περιηγέω, Schæf. Mel. p. 114., but it is better to derive these from the adj. περιηγής, &c.; I doubt therefore whether ἡγέω was ever really in use.—Passow.]

The Ion. and Dor. use, principally in the sense of *to consider in a certain light*, the perf. ἥγημαι instead of the pres.; it is common for instance in Herodotus, see Schweigh. Lex. Herod. v. ἡγέεσθαι; Fragm. Pythag. Gale p. 711. (ἄγηνται); whence it came into the language of poetry, e. g. μέγ' ἥγησαι τόδε, Eurip. Phœ. 553. In prose it does not appear frequent until the later writers*. In the sense of *to precede* ἄγημαι is found in Pind. Pyth. 4, 442. In a passive sense τὰ ἁγημένα is the same as τὰ νενομισμένα, *that which is usual*, Orac. ap. Demosth. adv. Macart. p. 1072, 25. In two of the passages of Herodot. there is a remarkable various reading ἄγημαι (see Schweigh. ib. v. ἀγέεσθαι); and it is very possible that this form had the Ion. short α for η with a different breathing.

Ἥδω, *I delight*: but little used in the active. Pass. *I am delighted*: fut. ἡσθήσομαι; aor. 1. ἥσθην. Compare Ἁνδάνω.

Homer has once the midd. ἥσατο for ἥσθη, Od. ι, 353.

Ἠθέω, *I strain, filter*: fut. in general use ἠθήσω, &c. But Galen quotes from Hippocrates ἦσαι from ΗΘΩ.

Ἥκω, *I come, am arrived* (see Ἱκνέομαι), has (in the older writers) only the present, the imperfect ἧκον, and the future ἥξω.

The form διῆξα belongs to διάττω; but later writers have also from ἥκω not only the aor. 1. ἧξα but a perf. ἧκα. See Lobeck ad Phryn. pp. 743. 744.

Ἧμαι. See ἙΩ, 2.

Ἠμί, ἦν. See Φημί.

Ἠμύω, *I sink*: fut. ἠμύσω, &c. The regular perf. of this verb was ἤμυκα; to this was prefixed the reduplic. with the shortened ε in order to preserve the relation between the first and second syllable: but on account of the verse the first syllable was to be again made long, for

* Schneider's remark in his Lexicon must be taken in this limited sense. See the word in Lucian Piscat. 14. Paus. 10, 6, 32. Some older examples would be desirable. I find it also in Hipp. Min. p. 374. d. (ἥγησαι for ἡγεῖ), and in Clitophon 407. c. (ἡγήσθε). Better examples perhaps may be found in Plat. Tim. p. 19. e. Legg. 8. p. 837. c.

which purpose μν was taken instead of μμ, as in the instances of ἀπάλαμνος from παλαμή, νώνυμνος for νώνυμος; thus was formed an Epic perf. ἐμνήμυκα, and its comp. ὑπεμνήμυκα, Il. χ. 491.

Ἡσσάομαι, ἡττάομαι, *I am inferior, am overcome*, used in the pure language only in the passive form. Fut. ἡσσηθήσομαι, occasionally ἡττήσομαι; Lys. c. Ergocl. 9., pro Polycr. 32. Verbal adj. ἡττητέον.

The Ion. formed from -όω a pass. ἑσσέομαι, ἑσσοῦμαι, ἑσσώθην, &c. Herodot. The later writers thought they might also form an active (*to overcome*), which Diodorus has occasionally (see Schæfer on Aristoph. Plut. p. 525.). The only passage in which it occurs in any of the older writers (Isæus 11, 31. p. 86, 3.) has been corrected by the Breslau manuscript from τὸν μὲν ἡττᾶν, τὸν δὲ νικᾶσθαι to ἡττᾶσθαι... νικᾶν*.

Θ.

Θάλλω, *I germinate*: fut. θαλῶ, also θαλλήσομαι; perf. 2. τέθηλα, Dor. τέθαλα.

Hom. has not the pres. θάλλω, but in its stead uses θηλέω; the Epic formation therefore is, θηλέω, -ήσω (Il. α, 236.) &c.; perf. τέθηλα, part. τεθαλυῖα; with a rare aor. 2. θάλε, Hymn. Pan. 33. The form θαλλέω, wherever it occurs, is only a corruption of the Doric θαλέω. The later Epics, as Quint Sm. 11, 96., have θαλέω. The pass. τεθηλημένος in Hippocr. Insomn. 5. is remarkable.

ΘΑΝ—. See Θνήσκω.

Θάπτω, *I bury*: fut. θάψω; perf. τέταφα; aor. 2. pass. ἐτάφην (but Herodotus has the aor. 1. ἐθάφθην); perf. pass. τεθάμμαι, τεθάφθαι. The root of this verb was therefore

* The conclusion that because we have ἡττᾶσθαι we must necessarily have ἡττᾶν is false: ἡττᾶσθαι is a neuter idea, ἥττων εἰμί τινος, whence it can be joined only with the gen. ἡττᾶσθαί τινος. The passive form, as in many other verbs, took this meaning, ἡττήθην like ἐφοβήθην, ἐπλάγχθην, &c. and *might* therefore have an active voice in a causative sense, but not necessarily. The common reading in Isæus condemns itself If the orator had wished merely to contrast the active and passive, he must have said τὸν μὲν νικᾶσθαι τὸν δὲ νικᾶν, and it would have been a most unnatural mode of speaking to have brought in the verb ἡττᾶν, even if it had been in use. The neuter ideas "to get the better, to win," are here contrasted with "to be worsted, to lose," and it was therefore necessary to say τὸν μὲν ἡττᾶσθαι, τὸν δὲ νικᾶν, exactly as had been said a little before ἂν ἡ ἑτέρα νικᾷ μετεῖναί τι καὶ τῇ ἡττηθείσῃ; where νικᾶν is taken in a judicial sense and stands absolutely, not having the opponent following it in the accusative case, as when it means to conquer any one in battle.

ΘΑΦ, as we see one or both of the aspirated letters in all the above forms. See below ΘΑΦ.

Thus we have *τεθάφθω* in Lucian Dial. Mar. 9, 1. *τεθάφαται* in Herodot. 6, 103. Compare Τρέφω, with note.

ΘΑΦ–. Perf. used as a pres. *τέθηπα*, *I am astonished*, where the second aspirated letter of the root is changed into the *tenuis*; on the contrary in the aor. *ἔταφον* the first undergoes that change*. Compare Θάπτω.

ΘΑΩ, an Epic defective verb, of which the act. has the causative sense *to give suck to*, the midd. the immediate sense *to suck*. Of the former we know nothing more than the aor. *θῆσαι*, and that only from Hesychius. Of the latter Hom. has the infin. pres. *θῆσθαι*† with the collateral meaning of *to milk* (Od. δ, 89.), and the aor. 1. midd. *ἐθήσατο*, *he sucked* (Il. ω, 58.). [So *ἐθήσαο*, Callim. Jov. 48. and *θησάμενος*, Hymn. Cer. 236. But in Hymn. Apoll. 123. *θήσατο* has the causative sense *she gave suck to*.—Passow.]

See another *θάομαι* in the following Θεάομαι.

Θεάομαι, *I look at attentively, consider.* Depon. Midd.

The following different formations from this stem or root have been preserved in the dialects:

1.) *θάομαι* in the following Doric forms; *θᾱμεθα*‡, Sophron ap. Apollon. de Pron. p. 359. a. Imperat. *θάεο*, Nossidis Epigr. 8., Anytes Epigr. 10. *θᾶσθε*, the Megarean in Aristoph. Ach. 770. Fut. and aor. *θασσόμεναι*, Theocr. 15, 23. *θάσασθαι*, 2, 72. *θᾶσαι* (imperat.) 1, 149. And the Epic *θησαίατο*, Od. σ, 191.

2.) *θαέομαι* Doric, Pind. Pyth. 8, 64. *θηέομαι* Ion. whence *ἐθηεῖτο*, *ἐθηεῦντο*, *θηεύμενοι*, aor. *ἐθηήσατο* &c. Hom. Herodot.

3.) *θεάομαι* Attic and common dialect.

Of these three formations the first and second have in Homer always the sense of being astonished and admiring. The simple *θά-ομαι* appears to be the oldest, whence *θαῦμα*; and the second merely the common lengthening of it, *θα-έομαι*, Ion. *θη-έομαι*. From the oldest form arose the simple verbal subst., properly *θάα*, but soon changed into *θέα*, like *μνάα* into *μνέα*; and hence first came the form *θεάομαι*, which

* A perfect *τέθαφα* with a causative meaning, *I astonish*, in Schweighæuser's Athen. 6. p. 258. c. is suspected, because the manuscript has (contrary to the metre it is true) *τέθαιφε*. Now the aor. p. *ἐθάμβη* in Hesych. supposes a theme *θάμβω*; perhaps therefore it ought to be, ἢ τοῦ βίου Ὑγρότης μέ σου τέθαμφε,... instead of *με τοῦ σοῦ*.

† This verb is contracted in *η* instead of *α*. See Ζάω.

‡ This is more of an Æolic than a Doric contraction: here the *ο* is swallowed up by the *α* preceding it, which consequently becomes long; thus the part. *γελᾶν* for *γελάων*, *φυσᾶντες* for *φυσάοντες*, *γελαῖσα* for *γελάοισα*, &c.

does not occur in Homer. In Herodotus we find indeed both forms, e. g. θηήσασθαι and θεήσασθαι (Ion. for θεάσασθαι), but this uncertainty would seem to arise more from traditionary corruptions of the text. He has also constantly recurring as various readings ἐθηεῖτο and ἐθηῆτο, of which the latter is perhaps according to the analogy of some verbs in άω contracted by the Epics in η instead of α, as ὁρῆαι 2. sing. pres. and ὁρῆτο 3. sing. imperf. of ὁράω, ὁμαρτήτην dual of ὁμαρτέω: verbal adj. θαητός, θηητός, θεατός. Compare Ζάω and ΘΑΩ.

Θείνω, *I beat*. This pres. is constantly used by the Epic poets and tragedians in both the act. and pass. voice. Beside this the Attic poets have a form θένειν, θένων, imper. θένε, conj. θένω, frequent for instance in Aristophanes, and consequently belonging to the common language of the time. But there is no instance of a pres. indic.; for in Acharn. 564. the manuscripts give, and the context requires, the fut. θενεῖς. Hence our latest critics have shown that those forms are aorists, (excepting occasionally that the fut. θενῶ, θενῶν ought to be restored,) and therefore that the infin. and part. must undoubtedly be accented θενεῖν, θενών*. All those passages certainly express a momentary beating, θείνειν on the contrary (e. g. θείνεται, Æschyl. Pers. 301. ἔθεινον, ib. 416. ἔθεινε, Eurip. Herc. 949. θεινόμενος, Hom.) continued blows, or the proper imperfect. Of the indic. of this aor. ἔθενον no instance has yet been found. The Epic language has the aor. 1. ἔθεινα, part. θείνας, Il. υ, 481. Hence we can point to ἔθεινε as evidently an imperf. at Il. π, 339., and as an aor. at φ, 491. The perfects and the aor. pass. are wanting.

Θέλω. See Ἐθέλω.

Θέρομαι, *I warm myself*: used in prose in the present and imperfect only.

Homer has, beside the above, a fut. θέρσομαι and an aor. pass. (ἐθέρην) conj. θερέω. The act. θέρω, *I warm*, stands in the lexicons without any good authority.

Quite as defective is the derivative form of which we find in Homer only θέρμετε and θέρμετο. See Buttm. Lexil. p. 546. note.

Θέσσασθαι, *to beseech*; a defective aor. of which we find only θέσσαντο (Pind. N. 5, 18.), and part. θεσσάμενος, Hes. Fr. 23.: see Schæf. Schol. Par. Apollon. Rh. 1, 824. The verbal adj. would be θεστός, from which come ἀπόθεστος and πολύθεστος, Hom.

* Blomfield on Æschyl. Sept. 378. (he has made some mistakes) and Elmsley on Eurip. Heracl. 272. We must not be surprised at the ε in an aor. 2. any more than in ἔτεμον: it was necessary on account of ἔθανον.

Θέω, *I run*: fut. midd. θεύσομαι* Hom., or θευσοῦμαί Dor. The other tenses are defective. Compare Τρέχω.

For the imperf. ἔθεον Hom. has θέεσκον. We find also an act. fut. θεύσω in Lycophr. 119. There are some forms from θέω, the root of τίθημι, which we must take care not to confound with those of θέω *I run*: e.g. προθέουσι (Il. α, 291.), the Ion. optat. θέοιτο for the aor. 2. midd. θεῖτο, and ποτίθει for ποτίθες, Theocr. 14, 45.

Θηέομαι. See Θεάομαι.

Θηλέω. See Θάλλω.

ΘΗΠ–. See ΘΑΦ–.

Θῆσθαι. See ΘΑΩ.

Θιγγάνω, *I touch*: fut. θίξομαι†; aor. 2. ἔθιγον. See note under Αἰσθάνομαι.

Beside θιγγάνω a pres. θίγω is generally adopted, of which ἔθιγον would be at the same time imperf. and aor., and θίγειν would be different from θιγεῖν (compare κλύω). But there are not sufficient proofs of the indic. θίγω or of ἔθιγον as a decided imperfect. The accentuation of θίγειν θιγεῖν, and θίγων θιγών, is indeed generally confounded in the manuscripts; but when for instance we read in Hesychius Θίγειν· ψαῦσαι, ἅψασθαι, ἅπτεσθαι, we see how little dependence is to be placed on these accents. If we were to accent in every passage of our text θιγεῖν, θιγών, as aorists, we should not find the sense disturbed in any one instance‡.

Θλάω, *I contuse, bruise, crush*: fut. θλάσω, &c. It has α short in the inflexion, and in the pass. takes the σ.

The part. perf. pass. is τεθλαγμένος, Theocr. 22, 45.; as in the Doric dialect all verbs ending in ζω and some in άω, which have α short in

* Six verbs in έω take ευ in the fut. or in some derivative, viz. θέω, νέω, πλέω, πνέω, ῥέω, χέω; thus πλεύσομαι, ἔπνευσα, χεῦμα, &c. And two in αίω take αυ, viz. καίω, κλαίω (Att κάω, κλάω), fut καύσω, κλαύσομαι.

† In Eurip. Heracl 652. the reading of the text was προσθίξεις, but it is now amended from the manuscripts to -ει. [Passow has a fut act. θίξω, but without example or remark, further than that θίξομαι is more general.]

‡ Schneider in his Lexicon quotes ἔθιγεν from Apollon. Rh 4, 1013. as an imperf. and θίγων from Æschyl Prom. 855. as a present but the immediate context does not agree with this statement. If we look at the passages, we shall see a plain difference between these aorists and the sense of μειλίσσετο in the former and ἐπαφῶν in the latter, which express a duration of the thought; nay in the passage of Æschylus we shall find them contrasted, Ἐπαφῶν ἀταρβεῖ χειρὶ καὶ θιγὼν μόνον [There are a few other instances in the Tragedians, but none to be depended on e. g. in Soph. Phil. 9 the Ald ed has προσθιγεῖν. compare also Æschyl. Agam. 1049. Soph. Aj. 1410. Elmsl and Herm. Œd C. 470. Schæf. Eurip Or. p. 12. Greg. Cor. p. 990. Monk Eurip. Alc. 1136. Elmsl. Eurip. Bacch. 304. Wunderl. Obs. Critt p. 151.—Passow.]

the inflexion, change to the other formation with the ξ; as κομίζω; Dor. fut. κομίξω· γελάω, ἐγέλασα, Dor. ἐγέλαξα, &c.

Θλίβω, *I press, squeeze*: fut. θλίψω; aor. 2. pass. ἐθλίβην (like τρίβω).

In Homer we find the fut. midd. θλίψεται, Od ρ, 221. The pass. part. pres. θλιβόμενος is in Dioscor. Epig. 37., and the part. perf. pass. ἐθλιμμένη in Leon. Tar. Epig. 70.

Θνήσκω, *I die*: fut. θανοῦμαι; aor. 2. ἔθανον; perf. τέθνηκα: compare βέβληκα and note under Βάλλω. Of this perf. the following syncopated forms are in common use: τέθνᾰμεν, τέθνᾰτε, τεθνᾶσι, and 3. plur. pluperf. ἐτέθνᾰσαν; imp. τέθνᾰθι, opt. τεθναίην, infin. τεθνάναι, part. τεθνεώς, gen. -ῶτος, fem. τεθνεῶσα, neut. τεθνεώς, but in Herodot. I, 112. τεθνεός, which is perhaps preferable. From τέθνηκα arose also an Attic fut. τεθνήξω or τεθνήξομαι (like ἑστήξω or ἑστήξομαι), the latter of which is not to be considered in the light of a passive, but as a fut. midd. with an active sense. Verbal adj. θνητός.

That the α in the infin. τεθνάναι was short in the common language is evident from Aristoph. Ran. 1012: but we find in Æschyl. Agam. 550. τεθνᾶναι which was perhaps a contraction of τεθναέναι. The Epics have also τεθνάμεν, and Homer τεθνάμεναι. The Ion. and Hom. language has a perf. part. τεθνηώς, -ῶτος, (comp. βεβαώς under βαίνω, and ἑστηώς under Ἵστημι,) for which Homer has sometimes τεθνηότος, and once, τεθνεῶτι, as a trisyllable, Od. τ, 331. For τεθνηῶτος there is also a frequent various reading τεθνειῶτος, and for τεθνηότος sometimes τεθνειότος. To preserve Homeric uniformity Heyne wrote all the above with ει, whilst Wolf for the same purpose preferred η: of the two the latter seems to have made the better choice; but after maturely examining every part of the question, I think there are the strongest grounds both internal and external for the following as the Epic usage; τεθνηώς, τεθνηυῖα, τεθνηότος and τεθνειῶτος.

In usage this verb is so mixed up with its compound ἀποθνήσκω, that the simple forms ἔθανον, θανεῖν, θανοῦμαι are entirely poetical, while on the contrary the perf. τέθνηκα with its derivative forms scarcely ever occurs compounded with ἀπό. Moreover of the perfect we find hardly any but syncopated forms: the part. τεθνηκώς is indeed interchanged with τεθνεώς, yet so that of the latter the masculine only occurs in prose. The usage of prose is therefore the following:

θνήσκω and ἀποθνήσκω; ἀπέθανον, ἀποθανεῖν, &c.; ἀποθανοῦμαι· τέθνηκα, ἐτεθνήκειν· τέθναμεν, τεθνάναι, &c.; τεθνηκώς and τεθνεώς, τεθνηκυῖα, τεθνηκός.

The part. θανών, οἱ θανόντες, is however common in prose as an adj. in the sense of *dead*.

The infin. perf. τεθνάναι is used generally in its natural meaning: but not unfrequently it stands also for the aor. θανεῖν, e. g. in Plat. Crito (at the beginning), ἢ τὸ πλοῖον ἀφῖκται οὗ δεῖ ἀφικομένου τεθνάναι με; and such is its meaning in the familiar hyperbolical expression πολλάκις, μυριάκις τεθνάναι: whence it is clear that in some other passages we must not force it to mean *to be dead*, as Plat. Crito 14. εἰ δέοι τεθνάναι σε. A wish to add force to the expression introduced the perfect, as a form of a more decided and more certain sound, in the place of the present.

The same was the case with the fut. τεθνήξω or τεθνήξομαι, of which we may first observe that the active form appears to be the older Attic: see Dawes p. 96., Buttm. notes on Plat. Gorg. p. 469. d., and Elmsl. ad Aristoph. Ach. 597. This fut. has evidently the meaning of the *futurum exactum* in the above passage of Plato, where τεθνήξεται (τεθνήξει) "he will be dead immediately" is a parallel case to such perfects as that mentioned above. But like the common fut. 3. of the passive (paulo-post fut.) this also passes over into a simple fut. with the idea of *immediately* or *certainly*. See Thom. Mag. in v. and the passages in Brunck ad Aristoph. Ach. 590., Fisch. ad Well. 3. p. 106.*.

The compound with κατά is likewise synonymous with the simple verb, but occurs only in the poets. and the forms of the aor. are never found but with the syncope, as κατθανεῖν, κατθανών, &c.: hence in the Attic poets, who do not willingly omit the augment, the indic. (κάτθανε) seldom occurs (Æsch. Agam. 1553.), while the other moods are frequent in Euripides and others.

Θορέω, θόρνυμαι. See Θρώσκω.

Θράσσω. See Ταράσσω.

Θραύω, *I break in pieces*. The passive takes σ. The old perf. pass. τέθραυμαι has been restored by Bekker to Plat. Legg. 6. p. 757. e. (425, 7.).

* An unwillingness to recognize the idea of a perfect in τεθνήξομαι arises partly from the custom of our language, particularly from such expressions as βιώσεται ἢ τεθνήξεται, where we always contrast *to live* with *to die*, whereas the true contrast is between *to live* and *to be dead*.

Θρύπτω, *I break in pieces*: fut. θρύψω; aor. 2. pass. ἐτρύφην. Compare Θάπτω and Τρέφω with note.

[This verb seems to have been scarcely used in its simple form and literal meaning by any good writers, but in a metaphorical sense it is very common, particularly in the passive, as μαλακίᾳ θρύπτεσθαι, Xenoph.—Passow.]

Θρώσκω, *I leap*: fut. θοροῦμαι, Ion. θορέομαι; aor. 2. ἔθορον, conj. θορῶ, infin. θορεῖν. See βέβληκα and note under Βάλλω.

The pres. θορέω, which is in all the lexicons, is scarcely to be found even in the later writers; and where we do find it, ἀποθοροῦντες is a false reading for ἀποθορόντες or something similar: see Stephan. Thesaurus*. That θρώσκω and θορεῖν are connected in usage was allowed by the old Grammarians: see Eustath. ad Il. β, 702. p. 246, 47. Basil. οὐ γὰρ εἶπεν ἐκθορόντα ἀλλ' ἔτι ἀποθρώσκοντα. Compare also Herodot. 6, 134., where the aorists ὑπερθορέειν, ὑπερθορόντα are used of leaping over a wall, and then follows the present; καταθρώσκοντα δὲ (*by leaping down*) τὸν μηρὸν σπασθῆναι.

Among the forms of this verb we may with safety class the perf. τέθορα, as it would not be easy to find an emendation more certain than this of Canter in a verse of Antimachus in Poll. 2, 4. 178. "Ὡς εἴτε κλόνιος τεθορυίης σφονδυλίων ἐξ," "as if either the spine were dislocated...", instead of θουρίης...ἐξ.

In the collateral sense of copulating (see θρώσκω and θορεῖν in Hesych.) the depon. θόρνυμαι is more common.

ΘΥΦ–. See Τύφω.

Θύω, *I sacrifice*: fut. θύσω; aor. 1. ἔθυσα; perf. τέθυκα†, Chœrobosc. p. 1286., Draco pp. 45, 26. and 87, 25.; aor. 1. pass. ἐτύθην, part. τυθείς.—Midd.

Θύω, and a sister-form θύνω, have also the sense of *I rage*; and with this meaning we find a syncop. part. aor. midd. θύμενος in Pratinas ap. Athen. 14, p. 617. d. according to the reading as now corrected.

I.

Ἰάομαι, *I heal*, depon. midd.: fut. ἰάσομαι, Ion. and Ep.

* Even in Quint. Sm. 1, 542. θορεῖ should be amended to the far more suitable poetical aor. θόρεν.

† On this perf. compare Δέω with note, and Δύω with second note.

ἰήσομαι; aor. 1. ἰασάμην. Pass. *I am healed*, used only in pres. imperf. and aor. 1. ἰάθην, Ion. ἰήθην, Hippocr. De Arte 20. In the older writers from Homer's time the ι and α are long through all the moods and tenses: in the later authors, particularly in the Anthologia, ι became common.

Ἱδρόω, *I sweat*; fut. ἱδρώσω, &c. This verb, like its contrary ῥιγόω, is contracted irregularly in ω and ῳ, instead of ου and οι; thus ἱδρῶσα, Il. δ, 27., ἱδρῴην, ἱδρῶσι, ἱδρῶντες, Hippocr. This however seems to hold good of the Ionic dialect only, as in Xen. Hell. 4, 5, 7. the best editions now read ἱδροῦντι, not ἱδρῶντι.

Ἱδρύω, *I place, build*: fut. ἱδρύσω, &c.—Midd.

The aor. 1. pass. ἱδρύθην, regular with υ long, is recommended as exclusively the Attic form; on the other hand ἱδρύνθην* (which supposes a theme in -ύνω, which occurs in Homer, and came into use again in a later period,) is rejected by the Atticists: see Thom. M. in voc. It is found however, and sometimes even without a various reading, in the best writers. See Lobeck ad Phryn. in voc. p. 37. note. Oudend. ad Thom. M. Fisch. 3. p. 108.

Ἵζω, more generally καθίζω, has in the active voice both the causative meaning *to seat, place*, and the immediate or neuter *to sit*. The simple verb appears to occur only in the pres. and imperf.† (Hom. and Herodot. 8, 52. 71.); but of καθίζω we find a fut. καθιῶ, an aor. 1. ἐκάθισα, and perf. κεκάθικα. The Middle has the sense of *to sit*, and its future is generally καθιζήσομαι.

With regard to the accentuation of this verb, we know that the vowels ι and υ when short can be augmented only by being made long, as ἱκετεύω, aor. ἱκέτευσα; but where they are already long by position, the augment can be marked only by the difference of pronunciation and accent; thus in ἵζω the imperat. pres. is ἵζε, the imperf. is ἷζε; though from errors of transcription this rule is very frequently broken in the manuscripts, and consequently in the text of all writers. The older

* Instances occur where there is no ν in the pres. of a verb, and yet it is found in the aor. 1. pass., as ἱδρύνθην, ἀμπνύνθη under Ἱδρύω and Πνέω. In such cases it is not necessary to suppose an actual theme in -ύνω. Compare ἰθύντατα for ἰθύτατα. See also Τείνω.

† [Passow has also a fut. ἱζήσω, Att. ἱῶ; and in the compound he has fut. καθιζήσω, Dor. καθίξω, Att. καθιῶ; aor. 1. ἐκάθισα, also καθῖσα, Thuc. 6, 66. 7, 82. Aristoph. Ran. 911. The Epic part. καθίσσας is used by Homer.]

Attics augmented καθίζω in the middle also, κάθιζε, καθίσεν*. See Buttm. Lexil. p. 122. Dindorf. ad Aristoph. Ran. 921. Bekk. Thucyd. 6, 66. 7, 82. with the various readings.

The later writers, from the time of Aristotle, have also a pres. ἱζάνω, καθιζάνω.

With this verb is intimately connected the verb ἕζεσθαι, καθέζεσθαι, which never occurs in the older writers except in the aorist ἑζόμην, ἐκαθεζόμην, *I sat, I have sat down*, καθεζόμενος, &c., and of which the fut. 2. is καθεδοῦμαι† (like μαχοῦμαι and πιοῦμαι). The defective tenses are supplied by εἷσα, ἵζω, and ἱδρύω, with the comp. καθεῖσα, &c.

The general supposition is, that there are two synonymous verbal forms ἵζεσθαι and ἕζεσθαι. In that case ἑζόμην must be an imperf. as well as ἱζόμην; whereas we can prove, not from the Homeric language, which is in this respect uncertain, but from Attic prose, that it is invariably a pure aorist. Plat. Meno. 26. p. 89. καὶ δὴ καὶ νῦν εἰς καλὸν ἡμῖν παρεκαθέζετο, ᾧ μεταδῶμεν τῆς ζητήσεως: in this construction the imperf. is not to be thought of, and the sense runs plainly thus, "he sat himself down by us," &c. Again in Xen. Anab. 5, 8, 14. (6.) καὶ αὐτός ποτε καθεζόμενος συχνὸν χρόνον κατέμαθον ἀναστὰς μόγις, not "while I was seating myself," nor "while I was sitting," but "after having sat a considerable time," &c. And in confirmation of this comes the strong inductive conclusion, which every one will draw for himself, that ἕζετο in the poets, and ἐκαθέζετο in all writers, are regularly used in the narrative of the momentary action of sitting down, as is also καθέζωμαι, &c.: those passages, therefore, where the context does not necessarily show this, must be understood in the same sense. And thus the few instances where the pres. καθέζομαι is found become very suspicious‡.

* [Wolf always accents the imperf. κάθιζον, not καθῖζον, and his is indisputably the more correct way if we suppose the original form to be ἐκάθιζον: but Buttmann does not allow this to hold good in all cases.—Passow.]

† [Diogen. Laert. has also a fut. καθεδήσομαι.—Passow.]

‡ In Lucian Solœc. 11. τό γε μὴν καθέζεσθαι τοῦ καθίζειν διενήνοχεν. Here is a various reading καθίζεσθαι. Now when we find further on, τὸ δὲ καθίζω τοῦ καθέζομαι ἆρά σοι δοκεῖ μικρῷ τινὶ διαφέρειν; εἴπερ τὸ μὲν ἕτερον δρῶμεν (*we do that to another*), τὸ καθίζειν λέγω, τὸ δὲ μόνους ἡμᾶς αὐτοὺς, τὸ καθέζεσθαι,—we must undoubtedly read here also καθίζομαι and καθίζεσθαι; for it is clear that the point in discussion is the difference between the midd. and act. voices, in the same way as καταδουλοῦσθαι and καταδουλοῦν are spoken of just afterwards. But in the direction given by Thom. M. (p. 489.) λέγε οὖν καθέζομαι, ἐκαθεζόμην, &c., καθέζομαι is evidently an interpolation, for among the preceding forms which are rejected there is no present: and in Lucian Philopseud. 27. the reading καθέζεται is uncertain. In Eurip. Heracl. 33. Ἱκέται καθεζόμεσθα the augment is in the synalœpha, and the context requires either *we are sitting* (καθήμεθα)

We can now then join together as the usage of common prose all the forms of this family of verbs which belong to the meanings *to sit* and *to seat*, together with εἶσα and ἧμαι, whose immediate connection with ἵζω and ἕζεσθαι is shown in the note below: thus, καθίζω, *I seat, place*, ἐκάθισα, καθιῶ. Midd. καθίζομαι, *I seat myself, sit*, fut. καθεδοῦμαι and καθιζήσομαι, aor. ἐκαθεζόμην. In the more remote meaning of the middle voice, *I seat* or *place* (*for myself*), *cause to be placed*, are used εἰσάμην and καθεισάμην, whence ἐγκαθείσατο, Eurip. Hipp. 31.: perf. κάθημαι, properly *I have seated myself*, whence pres. *I sit*. Nor must we forget to mention with the above the usage of καθίζω, *I seat* or *place for myself*; as well as the general remark that the meanings *I sit* and *I seat myself* play into each other in many ways, and therefore the distinction between them is not to be observed too strictly: compare a similar case in κρεμάννυμι.

The meaning of *I seat* or *place myself* may also be understood passively; and so arose (ἑσθην) ἐκαθέσθην, καθεσθήσομαι, forms which are frequent in the later writers but banished from the pure language*.

On the Homeric ἐφέσσεσθαι see note on εἶσα 2. under 'ΕΩ.

Ἵημι, *I send*. See under 'ΕΩ 1.

Ἰθύνω, *I go straight on*: fut. ἰθύσω; aor. 1. ἴθυσα, &c., to which be-

or *we seated ourselves*, consequently ἐκαθεζόμεθα.' Again in Phœn. 73. and Helen. 1587. καθέζετ' is ἐκαθέζετο. Whether in a later period a usage was formed from this, according to which καθέζομαι, as a present, was the same as κάθημαι, *I sit*, I will not take upon myself to determine. We certainly find in Pausan. 10, 5. init., in speaking of the official sitting of a board or council, καθέζονται; and again the same expression, which I own surprises me, in a work probably of antiquity, the dialogue of Axiochus, p. 371. c., where the various reading καθίζονται is of no assistance, the context requiring κάθηνται. However the language of this dialogue, in which we find ἦς for ἦσθα, περιέστακας (see ἵστημι) p. 570. d., and διψῷ p. 366. a., with many other unusual words and phrases, gives ample scope for critical examination.

I explain the point thus: The radical form of all these verbs was evidently 'ΕΔΩ, as proved by ἐδοῦμαι, ἕδος and *sedeo*. Now as ἑσπόμην and ἑσχόμην come from ἕπω and 'ΕΧΩ, so ἑσδόμην comes from 'ΕΔΩ: and here even better than in ἑσπέσθαι we can see the augment which in the common language had become equally fixed throughout all the moods, ἕσδωμαι, ἑζώμαι, ἑζόμενος. To the above we may add the pres. ἵσδω, ἵζω, exactly like ἴσχω to ἔσχον. In καθίζω, καθέζετο this origin naturally enough ceased to be heard any longer, and then were formed ἐκάθισα, καθιῶ: καθέζετο received a new augment at the beginning: and as to the aoristic accentuation of the infin., there is still less reason for insisting on it in the case of καθέζεσθαι than in that of other aorists, which we have seen mistaken in a similar manner. But it is now clear also that εἶσα and ἧμαι, whose connection with ἕζεσθαι we acknowledged (see p. 117.), and yet separated them from it on practical grounds, do not come from 'ΕΩ, but from this same 'ΕΔΩ; that is to say ἧμαι was softened down from ἧσμαι, of which latter there are still remains in ἧσται and in εἶσα, εἰσάμην, both formed with that oldest of augments ει, which being misunderstood in this case also was carried on to some forms to which it did not belong.

* See Lobeck ad Phryn. p. 269. The reading προσκαθιζήσει there proposed for Æschin. c. Ctes. p. 77, 33. has been now adopted by Bekker from evident traces in the Codd. The conj. ἐσθῶ in Soph. Œd. C. 195. was indeed still more improbable: see Brunck and Reisig.

longs also in Homer and others ἐπιθύω, with the ι long. But ἰθύνω is Ionic and Epic for εὐθύνω, *I direct* or *guide straight forward*: aor. 1. ἴθυνα; also in the midd. ἰθύνετο in the act. sense, Od. χ, 8.

Ἱκνέομαι, more generally ἀφικνέομαι, *I come*, depon. midd.: fut. ἵξομαι; aor. ἱκόμην; perf. ἷγμαι, ἀφῖγμαι, ἀφῖχθαι.

The Ion. 3. plur. perf. pass. ἀπίκαται in Herodotus is remarkable as the only known instance of the *tenuis* in the stem being retained. But ἷκτο in Hes. θ, 481. is a syncopated aorist: and to this belongs also ἵκμενος for ἱκόμενος in Soph. Phil. 494.: see note in Buttm. edit.

The Epic language has the pres. and imperf. of the active, ἵκω, ἷκον, with the aor. ἷξον; on which last, as a mixture of the aor. 1. and 2. see ἐδύσετο, p. 73., and οἶσε under Φέρω.

In the pres. ἵκω the ι is long throughout, while in the aor. ἱκόμην it is, according to the root, short, but becomes long by the augment; consequently in ἱκόμην, ἀφῑκόμην it is long; in ἱκέσθαι, ἵκωμαι, &c. short: and accordingly in the Epic language the indicative ἱκόμην, from the augment being moveable, is both long and short. The form ἱκνοῦμαι (Eurip. Or. 670. 679. &c.) has the ι short. Another poetical present is ἱκάνω, with ι short and α long.

The pres. ἱκνοῦμαι occurs in its simple form in particular senses only; in Hom. *to go through, travel from one place to another*, Od. ι, 128. ω, 338.; in the Attics, *to go to as a suppliant* (ἱκέτης), *implore*, and *to be suitable to*. The true pres. as to meaning is in the Epic language ἵκω and ἱκάνω, in the Tragic principally ἱκάνω, in prose ἀφικνοῦμαι. The aor. ἷξον is solely Epic; but ἱκόμην and ἵξομαι are common to all the poets.

To these we may add ἥκω, which is to be found in its alphabetical place, and which we there see is used by good writers in the pres. imperf. and fut. only. This verb is connected with the above as one of its presents, but with this limitation, that it is used only in the sense of being *already come* to a place, but *not long arrived* there, with some other collateral meanings to be found in the lexicons. In a very early period however this form appears to have been confounded with ἵκω; whence, as Eustathius (ad Il. α, p. 82, 33.) expressly informs us, the Grammarians agreed that ἵκω was the only form used in Homer, and ἥκω the only one in succeeding writers. But the more critical way of understanding it is that ἵκω and ἥκω are properly but one word in different dialects, like σκίπων and σκήπων*. The older poets (for this relates

* That is to say, that in this verb the short syllable of the stem or root, as seen in the aorist (ἱκεῖν) ἱκέσθαι, instead of being strengthened in the present by changing it to ει, as in πείθω πιθεῖν, passed over into ῑ or η; making therefore ἵκω or ἥκω instead of εἵκω.

principally to them, including Pindar; see Bœckh ad Pind. Ol. 4, 11.) had the dialectic form *ἵκω*, which, like our *come*, was used of being already arrived at a place, e. g. in Il. *σ*, 406.; but the language of the succeeding period, i. e. the Ionic and Attic prose with Attic poetry, in which *ἥκω* had become established, limited the usage of the latter verb to that particular meaning, while the lengthened forms *ἱκάνω*, *ἀφικνοῦμαι*, retained the more general sense of *to come to, arrive at a place.* In the future also the difference is pretty much the same: *ἥξω*, 'I shall come (to you) and be with you'; *ἀφίξομαι*, 'I shall set out from hence and come to you.'

Ἱλάσκομαι, *I appease*, midd.: fut. *ἱλάσομαι* (Ep. *ἱλάσσομαι*, Dor. *ἱλάξομαι*); aor. 1. *ἱλασάμην* with *α* short.

The Epics have also *ἱλάομαι*, (Il. *β*, 550.) and *ἵλαμαι* (Hom. Hymn. 20. Orph. Arg. 942.); while Æschylus has *ἱλέομαι*, Suppl. 123. 134. The *ι* of the radical syllable is long, but it is also shortened by the Epics.

In the old language the active voice had the sense of *to be gracious, kind*, whence the Epics took an imperat. *ἵληθι* (Od. *γ*, 380. *π*, 184. *ἵλᾰθι*, Theocr. 15, 143.) from *ἵλημι*, and a conj. and opt. from *ἱλήκω**.

Ἱμάσσω†, *I whip*: fut. *ἱμάσω* (ᾰ); aor. 1. *ἵμασα*. On the formation of this fut. see Ἁρμόττω.

Ἱμάω, *I draw up* (a rope or water): fut. *ἱμήσω*, &c. The Att. infin. pres. is *ἱμῆν*: compare *ζάω*, *θάω*.—Midd.

Ἱμείρω and *ἱμείρομαι*, *I desire, wish for*. The aor. opt. midd. is *ἱμείραιτο* (Il. *ξ*, 163.); and the aor. 1. pass. *ἱμέρθη* (Herodot. 7, 44.). The *ι* is always long.

Ἵπταμαι. See Πέτομαι.

Ἴσημι, *I know*. [Of this verb we find only the Dor. pres. *ἴσᾱμι* in Pind. and Theocr., the 2. sing. *ἴσης*, 3. sing. *ἴσᾱτι*, and 1. plur. *ἴσᾰμεν*, Pind. N. 7, 21., and the part. *ἴσας*, Pind. P. 3, 52. The forms which *only appear* to belong to this verb, such as *ἴσμεν*, *ἴδμεν*, *ἴσασι*, *ἴσθι*, *ἴσαν*, will be found under Εἴδω.—Passow.]

Ἴσκω. Ἴσκεν, *he spoke*, is a defective imperf. (Od. *χ*, 31.), differing essentially from *ἴσκω* or *ἐΐσκω*, *I make or think like* (which occurs only

* We must compare these imperatives with *στῆθι*, *ἕστηκα*, &c., and suppose that the pres. and aor. 1. took the causative sense *to make gracious*; of which *ἱλάομαι*, *ἱλᾰσάμην*, would then be the middle, *I make gracious to me, appease.*

† The characteristic *σσ* of this verb may be doubted, for *ἱμάσσω* (Il. *ο*, 17.) may be the conj. aor., as it is in Hesychius; nor do I know other authority for the pres. than *ἱμασσόμενοι* in Archiæ Epig. 22. which was perhaps first made from the passage of Homer.

in the pres. and imperf., Il. λ, 798. ε, 181. Od. δ, 279. ν, 313.), and arising from the insertion of the σ in IK– the root of εἴκω, like λάσκω from λακεῖν, πιτύσκω from τεύχω, &c. With respect to ἐ-ίσκω see note on Ἔλδομαι, ἐέλδομαι.

Ἵστημι: imperf. ἵστην; fut. στήσω; aor. 1. ἔστησα; perf. ἕστηκα; pluperf. ἑστήκειν, Att. εἱστήκειν. The aor. 2. indic., ἔστην is seldom used before the time of Polybius; its other moods are found in Homer. Pass. ἵσταμαι; imperf. ἱστάμην; fut. σταθήσομαι; aor. 1. ἐστάθην (ᾰ); perf. ἕσταμαι; pluperf. ἑστάμην. Fut. midd. στήσομαι; aor. 1. ἐστησάμην; fut. 3. (paulo-post) ἑστήξω old Att., and ἑστήξομαι later, Elmsl. Aristoph. Ach. 597., like τεθνήξω, τεθνήξομαι, from θνήσκω. Verbal adj. στατός, στατέος.

The 2. and 3. sing. of the indic. pres. in -ᾷς and -ᾷ are found only in the later writers. The 3. plur. ἱστᾶσι is the Attic form, ἱστέασι the Ionic, ἱστάντι the Doric. In the optat. is an abridged form of the dual and plural by dropping the η, and in the 3. plur. changing -ησαν into -εν, thus returning to the regular optat. of the barytone verbs; as dual, ἱσταῖτον, ἱσταίτην, plur. ἱσταῖμεν, ἱσταῖτε, ἱσταῖεν: the same is found in the optat. of the aor. 2. as σταῖτε for σταίητε; but here the abridged form is not so usual as the other, while in the imperf. it is preferred by the Attics, who sometimes use it in the 3. plur. pres. In the imperf. we find an Epic 3. sing. ἵστασκε (Od. τ, 574.) with a sister-form in -ων, -ας, -α, peculiar to the Ionic dialect and the later writers: Homer has also an aor. 2. στάσκον. In the aor. 2. imperat. instead of στῆθι we have in the compounds παράστα, ἀπόστα*, as from a theme ΣΤΑΩ. In the infin. pres. are ἱστάμεν, ἱστάμεναι, with α short, for ἱστάναι, but in the aor. 2. the long vowel remains, as στῆμεν, στήμεναι, Od. ε, 414. Il. ρ, 167. In the middle the fut. and aor. 1. are Homeric; the latter is also in common use: but an aor. 2. ἐστάμην is nowhere found in any of its moods or tenses. In the passive the Ion. 3. plur. is ἱστέαται for ἵσταντι.

In the conjunct. we find in the later writers the 2. and 3. sing ἱστᾷς, -ᾷ, instead of ἱστῇς, -ῇ, in which case they belong to the inferior form ἱστάω. The Epics for the 3. sing. ἱστῇ have ἱστῇσι. And as the conj. is a contracted form the Ionics resolve it, using for ἱστῶ and στῶ, -ῇς, &c. ἱστέω, ἱστέῃς, &c., στέω, στέῃς, στέωμεν, &c. This resolution again the

* The length of the α is sufficiently evident from two passages in Menand. ap. Suid. v. ἀπόστα. We see in Lex. Seguer. p. 81. that some Atticists considered this form inferior to the other.

Epics vary to suit the metre, using *στείω, στήῃς, στήῃ, στήητον*, &c., and *στείομεν* for *στέωμεν*, *στήετον* for *στήητον*: but it is very difficult indeed to distinguish some of the above forms from those of the optative. In the conjunct. and optat. of the passive voice of all verbs in *μι* a formation has been introduced into the common language, by which they assimilate, sometimes in sound but always in accent, to the regular conjugation (compare *δύναμαι*): thus we find in all writers *ἵσταιο, ἵσταιτο, ἵσταισθε, ἵσταιντο*; but in the conjunct. always *ἱστῶμαι, συνιστῆται*, &c. See Δύναμαι and Ἐπίσταμαι.

The tenses of this verb, like those of *δύω, φύω*, and many others, are divided between the causative meaning of *to place*, and the immediate one of *to stand*. In the active voice we find, with the meaning of *to place*, the pres. and imperf. *ἵστημι, ἵστην*; fut. *στήσω*; aor. 1. *ἔστησα*: whence therefore the whole of the passive voice has the sense of *to be placed*; and a middle (*ἵσταμαι, στήσομαι, ἐστησάμην*), answering to the above tenses of the active, has the meaning of *to place for oneself, cause to be placed* or *erected*.

But the middle has also the pure reflective meaning of *to place oneself*, which however was felt more as an intransitive, or as the inchoative belonging to the sense of *to stand*, like the Latin *consistere, to stop*. Considered in this light the relation between *ἵστημι* and *ἵσταμαι* is that of causative and immediate. Now as the aor. 2. act. and the perf. of many verbs take the immediate sense (see note under Τεύχω), we have the meaning of the

aor. 2. *ἔστην*, *constiti* as aorist, *I placed myself, stopped*;

perf. *ἕστηκα*, properly *constiti* as perfect, *I have placed myself, stopped*, and thence *I stand*;

so that this perf. in Greek supplies the place of the Latin *stare, to stand*, and the pluperf. *ἑστήκειν* or *εἱστήκειν* the imperf. of the same*.

To suit this present meaning of the perfect was formed

* In the later and corrupted state of the language a pres. was formed from ἕστηκα, viz. στήκω, whence στήκετε, 1 Cor. 16, 13. and στήκοντες, Alex. Aphrod. Probl. 1, 49. And again another pres. ἑστήκω, Posidippi Epigr. 15.

also a proper future ἑστήξω or ἑστήξομαι, *I shall stand*, which, though a passive form, is not to be regarded as properly such (for in meaning it corresponds with the active), but as a fut. midd. with an active sense, like θανοῦμαι, λήψομαι, &c.

We see from the examples given by Elmsley, ad Acharn. 590, that the active form of this future is the older Attic. And in the compound (e. g. ἀφεστήξει, Xen. Anab. 2, 4, 5.) we may observe the same change which occurs in τεθνήξω to the future meaning belonging to the pres. in -αμαι.

Of all the syncopated forms of this perfect the infin. ἑστάναι* is most used, and ἑστηκέναι perhaps not at all. Of the others are found principally ἕσταμεν, -ατε†, -ᾶσιν: ἕστασαν: ἑστώς, -ῶσα, gen. -ῶτος.

In this abridged form the pluperf. has never its proper augment ει, but remains ἕστασαν: hence the two first persons, as being similar to the perfect, seldom occur in prose‡. Beside these syncopated forms the complete forms of ἕστηκα are also in general use: ἑσταίην, ἕσταθι are perhaps exclusively poetical: while of the conj. are found only those persons which have an ω, e. g. ἑστῶμεν, Plat. Gorg. 52. p. 468. b. ἐφεστῶσιν, Eurip. Bacch. 319.

Instead of the regular perf. part. ἑστηκώς, -υῖα, -ός, gen. -ότος, is used a syncopated form ἑστώς, ἑστῶσα, ἑστώς and ἑστός (of the last we shall speak hereafter), gen. ἑστῶτος. There is also an Ionic form ἑστεώς, -ῶσα, -ώς, gen. -ῶτος, like τεθνεώς, &c. (see under Θνήσκω); and Homer has frequently a gen. ἑστἄότος, an accus. ἑστἄότα, and a nom. plur. ἑστἄότες, as from ἑσταώς; while another form ἑστηώς§, from ἑστηκώς by dropping the κ (like τετληώς and others; see under Βαίνω), is found in Hes. θ, 519., and a gen. ἑστηῶτος, with a fem. ἑστηυῖα in Apollon. Rhod. Again, like ἑστήως for ἑστηκώς, we have a singular form in Hom. ἕστητε‖

* For which Homer has ἑστάμεν and ἑστάμεναι.

† For which Homer has also ἕστητε, Il. δ, 243. 246.

‡ In Andoc. 2, 8. καθέστατε is pluperf., and at 1, 112. παρέσταμεν according to Bekker is the same. [Homer has ἕστἄτον as dual of both perf. and pluperf.; and ἑστάτην, plur. ἕστἄμεν, ἕστἄτε, ἕστἄσαν as pluperfects.—Passow.]

§ We may gather from different parts of Buttmann's Grammar the following formation: the regular part. was ἑστηκώς, whence by dropping the κ came ἑστήως: the Ionics changed the η into short α (see under Βαίνω), whence ἑστάως; while again in ἑστήως the length of the η passed on into the following vowel, making ἑστεώς, though the origin of this change was not visible in the nom. as it is in the gen. ἑστηότος ἑστεῶτος, like μετήορος μετέωρος.—Ed.]

‖ This reading, according to the correct criticism of the grammarian in the scho-

for ἐστήκατε or ἔστατε, Il. δ, 243. 246. We find also for the syncopated 3. plur. ἑστᾶσι the Ion. resolved form ἑστέασι in Herodot. 1, 200. 3, 62.; and without doubt the 2. pl. ἑστέατε, προεστέατε, in Herodot. 5, 49. is genuine, notwithstanding the various reading προέστατε has crept in from the common language.

If we follow analogy the neut. part. of ἑστώς, contracted from ἑσταός, must be the same as the masc., and this is the reading of most of the manuscripts and editions wherever the word occurs. But the oldest and best manuscripts have generally the unanalogous ἑστός. Hence it is very probable that in this case the language of the Attics followed apparent analogy, and formed from ἑστώς the neuter ἑστός. Still the gen. and other cases are ἑστῶτος, &c.*

There is also a perf. for the transitive meaning ἕστακα, *I have placed*, which belongs however to a later æra†. The older Attics used instead of the perfect, whether in a transitive or intransitive sense, (for there is no proper form to express *I have stood*,) either the aorists or a circumlocution, turning the perf. act. for instance into the perf. passive, and instead of εὖ λέλεχας saying εὖ λέλεκταί σοι; because λέλεχα was not in common use.

In Homer we find εστασαν (for the accent and breathing must be determined by criticism) in both a transitive and intransitive sense: the plainest instance is in Il. μ, 55. and 56. where it has the two meanings in two succeeding verses. In the description there given of the ditch round the Grecian camp we read, κρημνοὶ...Εστασαν ἀμφοτέρωθεν, ὕπερθεν δὲ σκολόπεσσιν Ὀξέσιν ἠρήρει, τοὺς εστασαν υἷες Ἀχαιῶν. Here the first is beyond a doubt ἕστασαν: for there is no other form to express the imperf. *they stood* or *were standing*. It seemed therefore most natural to write the same in the second instance also, and to suppose that the old language used the perfect in both senses: and the context is much in favour of this, "which the Greeks had placed." But there are other instances of εστασαν in a transitive sense, as Il. β, 525. Od. γ, 182. σ, 306., in all which it is evidently an aorist; whereas the pluperf. (which necessarily is and remains ἕστασαν, if we deduce it in a transitive sense from the perfect *have placed*) cannot stand in these

lium, has been admitted by Wolf into the text instead of ἕστητε, which was directly contrary to the sense.

* See the unanimity of the best Codd., e. g. in Plat. Parmen. pp. 63, 15. 16. 64, 2. 12. Bekk. Compare also Plat. Tim. pp. 30, 7. 41, 6, &c. Thucyd. 3, 9. 4, 10. Hence Bekker always reads ἑστός, as does Hermann in Soph. Œd. T. 632. Compare Dind. Aristoph. Equ 567. The other reading is defended in Alb. Hesych. 1, p. 503.

† In Polyb. 10, 20. stands ἐφεστάκει, according to which therefore, if we find in the same writer ἐφέστηκε in a transitive sense, it must be altered. See Fisch. 2, p. 368. Schaef. ad Dionys. De Comp 22, p. 331, and compare Reisk. ad Dem. Phil. 3. p. 117, 26. (Reisk Appar. p. 251).

passages, particularly in Od. σ, 306, without the greatest violence. But if ἔστασαν be an aorist, it must be a shortened form of ἔστησαν: and this opinion of Aristarchus, which Wolf has followed in his last edition, appears to me undoubted, particularly when I compare it with a similar case in Hesiod, ἔπρεσε for ἔπρησε* (see Πίμπρημι).

Ἐπίσταμαι see in its alphabetical place.

Ἴσχω. See Ἔχω.

ΙΩ. See Εἶμι.

K.

ΚΑΔ–, κέκασμαι, κέκαδμαι. See Καίνυμαι.

Κεκαδεῖν, -ήσειν. See Κήδω and Χάζω.

Κᾰθαίρω, *I cleanse*: fut. κᾰθᾰρῶ; aor. 1. ἐκάθηρα (later ἐκάθᾱρα also), infin. καθᾶραι, Lobeck ad Phryn. p. 25.—MIDD. This verb is no compound; see Buttm. Lexil. p. 119.

Καθέζομαι. See Ἵζω.

Καθεύδω. Se Εὕδω.

Κάθημαι. See Ἧμαι.

Καθίζω. See Ἵζω.

Καίνυμαι, *I am distinguished, excel*: defective depon. without fut. or aor., and occurring only in pres. and imperf. There is however a synonymous perf. κέκασμαι, Dor. κέκαδμαι; pluperf. ἐκεκάσμην. That these forms are correctly classed under one verb both sense and construction plainly show. For as in Od. γ, 282. we read ἐκαίνυτο φῦλ' ἀνθρώπων Νῆα κυβερνῆσαι, so at β, 158. we find ὁμηλικίην ἐκέκαστο Ὄρνιθας γνῶναι: and as at θ, 219. Οἶος δή με Φιλοκτήτης ἀπεκαίνυτο τόξῳ, so at Il. ξ, 124. ὃς ἡλικίην ἐκέκαστο Ἔγχεϊ. But κέκασμαι occurs also without an accusative; therefore, as a necessary result of the above comparison, it stands absolutely in the sense of *to excel* or *be distinguished in anything*, as κεκάσθαι ἱπποσύνῃ, μύθοισι, ἀλκῇ· κακοῖσι δόλοισι κεκασμένε, &c. For these expressions a present κάζω has been supposed with the meaning of *to equip, adorn*; but the above comparison shows that καίνυμαι might have been used in that absolute sense quite as well

* An opposite case is found in Callim. L. P. 83. ἐστάθη with ᾰ long; if it is not a false reading for ἑστάκῃ (ἑστήκει); for it is translated *stabat*, and we shall find that the sense gains by this correction, particularly in comparison with the unsuitable passive. [In the above passage from Il. μ, 55, 56. Passow differs in one point only from Buttmann: he reads with him the 3. plur. aor. 1. ἔστᾰσαν for ἔστησαν in Il. β, 525. Od. γ, 182. and σ, 306., but he also reads it in *both* lines 55 and 56 of Il. μ., whereas Buttmann reads in the former of the two the pluperf. ἑστασαν with the force of an imperfect.]

as κέκασμαι, and no doubt would have been if it had occurred more frequently. It is found however only three times, and in its simple form but once through the whole of Homer. We must therefore join καίνυμαι with κέκασμαι, to which and to the Doric κέκαδμαι it bears exactly the same relation as ῥαίνω* does to ῥάσσατε and ἐῤῥάδαται. But compared with each other as pres. and perf. they are like our expressions *I distinguish myself* and *I am distinguished*: and the radical idea is undoubtedly that of *shining, glittering*†, as in the Pindaric passage ἐλέφαντι φαίδιμον ὦμον κεκαδμένος; for the shoulder was not adorned with ivory, but composed of it, of which therefore the poet could say, it shone with ivory, or in Latin *candebat*. To this verb, as to so many others in the middle voice, was joined the accusative of the person, or μετὰ τοῖς, ἐν τοῖς, together with the dative of the thing; and sometimes (as in Od. τ, 82. δ, 725. Il. ω, 546.‡) this dative stood alone.

Καίνω, *I kill*: fut. κᾰνῶ; aor. 2. ἔκᾰνον, infin. κᾰνεῖν. The perf. is wanting. In the passive the pres. and imperf. only are in use.

This verb is a sister-form of κτείνω, κτανεῖν, to which it bears the same relation as πτόλις to πόλις, or χθαμαλός to χαμαί. [It is very common both in the Poets and Tragedians and found also in the best Attic writers.—Passow.]

Καίω, *I burn* (transit.), Att. κάω with α long and without contraction: imperf. ἔκαιον, Att. ἔκᾱον; fut. καύσω (compare Θέω); aor. 1. pass. ἐκαύθην. Verbal adj. καυτός, καυστός, καυστέος.

In the passive voice the aor. 1. is the only tense in use by the Attics; see Thom. M. v. κατεκαύθη. Beside Homer and Herodotus none but the later writers have the aor 2. pass. ἐκάην (ᾰ).

The Epics have also an aor. 1. act. (without σ in the termination) ἔκηα§; many forms of which fluctuate between η and ει, while a third

* For the terminations -νω and -νυμι are essentially the same; as in τίνω τίνυμι, κτείνω κτίννυμι.

† [Passow supposes it to be *probably* from καίνω, κτείνω, consequently from a radical form ΚΕΝΩ in the sense of *to overpower, conquer.*]

‡ The above account does not agree with the usage of Eurip in Elect. 616., where the walls of the town Φρουραῖς κέκασται δεξιαῖς τε δορυφόρων Here κέκασται evidently means *are furnished, equipped,* a deviation in every respect from the usage of Homer, of which it is a partial imitation.

§ Some verbs form their aor. 1. in α instead of σα. In the common language there are only three, ἔχεα (Ep. ἔχευα) from χέω, εἶπα from εἰπεῖν, ἤνεγκα from φέρω. The poets have also ἔκηα from καίω and ἔσσευα from σεύω. As these aorists go over into the middle voice also (ἐχεάμην, ἐσσεύατο, &c.), the Epic forms ἀλέασθαι, ἀλεύασθαι, δατέασθαι may be considered as belonging to the same.

with ε has been retained by the Tragedians only, e. g. κέαντες Æschyl. Agam. 858., ἐκκέαντες Eurip. Rhes. 97.; but this last can scarcely be considered in any other light than as derived like the others from the old Epic language. The forms ἔκηα, ἔκηε, and the optat. 3. sing. κήαι, plur. κήαιεν, have no various reading with the ει, as all the others have: e. g. infin. aor. κεῖαι and κῆαι, Od. ο, 97: imperat. κεῖον and κῆον, Od. φ, 176: conj. κείομεν and κήομεν, Il. η, 333. and 337: indic. midd. 3. plur. κείαντο and κήαντο, Il. ι, 88., and the same in the participles κείαντες, Od. ι, 231. ν, 26., κειάμενος, Il. ι, 234. Od. π, 2. ψ, 51. If we compare with this the exactly similar appearance in the Epic conjunctives of the form in μι,—those for instance from ἔστην, ἔβην*,—it is evident that when the η before the other vowel had been shortened in the old language into ε, it was again lengthened by the Epics into ει, like βείω, στείομεν, &c. in the two verbs above mentioned. Now as in some of these forms the various reading does not appear, while in others it is supported by the greatest authority of the manuscripts (see Heyne on the passages of the Iliad quoted above), I have no doubt of the reading κείαντο, κείομεν, κεῖαι, &c. in all those passages being the genuine one, i. e. having the oldest tradition in its favour†. Compare a similar case of the text fluctuating between τεθνειῶτος and τεθνηῶτος.

Some have also supposed a present κέω and κήω, on account of κατακειέμεν (var. reading κατακηέμεν), Il. η, 408. and ἔκηον, Od. ι, 553. To place this κήω as an Ionicism by the side of the Attic κάω cannot be satisfactory, as καίω is the Ionicism like κλαίω, ἐλαία; nor is it easy to perceive what grounds there are for those forms, when we have καιέμεν, Il. ξ, 397. and ἔκαιον, Od. χ, 336. As therefore in the one passage ἔκηον has been already expelled from the text by the reading of the manuscripts ἔκαιον, so in the other κατακαιέμεν is undoubtedly the old reading, and the corruption was produced by confounding it with the forms of the aorist.

That the iota subscript with which κάω and ἔκηα are written in many editions, new as well as old, rests entirely on a false opinion, is evident without further investigation. See Piers. ad Moer. p. 231.

Καλέω, *I call*: fut. καλέσω, fut. midd. καλέσομαι (Ep. and Poet. καλέσσω, καλέσσομαι, Attic καλῶ‡, καλοῦμαι);

* As στείω for στέω, στῆῃς for στέῃς; again στείομεν for στέωμεν, στήετον for στήητον, &c. See Βαίνω and Ἵστημι.

† The form with ει is found once in Sophocl. El. 759. κείαντες with the various reading κήαντες, the alteration of which to κέαντες I cannot approve of. See Aristoph. Fr. 1133. and compare Piers. ad Moer. p. 321.

‡ The fut. καλέσω, or, as the Attics spoke it, καλῶ, is indisputably the fut. of the simple stem or root ΚΑΛΩ, and the common pres καλέω arose out of that fut. as the Ionic pres. μαχέομαι came from

aor. 1. ἐκάλεσα (Poet. καλέσσα); midd. ἐκαλεσάμην (Poet. καλεσσάμην); perf. κέκληκα; perf. pass. κέκλημαι (*I am called, named*), opt. κεκλῄμην, κέκλῃο, &c.; aor. 1. pass. ἐκλήθην; fut. pass. κληθήσομαι; fut. 3. (paulo-post) κεκλήσομαι, *I shall be called, named*. Ion. and Hom. imperf. καλέεσκον.

From this verb came also by metathesis an Ionic sister-form κικλήσκω, used by Homer in pres. and imperf. only; see note under Κέλομαι. On ἔκλεο or ἐκλέο see Κλέω. This verb is the old Latin *calo, calare*.

Κάμνω, *I am weary*: fut. κᾰμοῦμαι; aor. 2. ἔκᾰμον*, infin. καμεῖν; aor. 2. midd. ἐκαμόμην; perf. by metathesis κέκμηκα: on which see βέβληκα under Βάλλω, and κέκληκα under Καλέω, with the note underneath.

Sophocles (Trach. 1215.) has the 2. sing. fut. καμεῖ. In the Epic part. perf. the κ is dropped as in κεκαφηώς, τετληώς and others; thus κεκμηώς, gen. -ότος and -ῶτος†, as in Hom. κεκμηῶτι, -ῶτα, and in accus. plur. -ότας; see under Βαίνω and Ἵστημι; also γεγαώς under Γείνομαι. The Epics have also very frequently the aor. 2. act. and midd. with the reduplication, which then remains in all the moods; thus λέλαθον, λελαθών; κέκλυθι, πεπύθοιτο, &c., and in the verb before us Homer has the conj. κεκάμω, κεκάμῃσι, κεκάμωσι.

Κάμπτω, *I bend*: fut. κάμψω, &c. In the perf. pass. when the 1. pers. has μμ, one is naturally dropped, as κέκαμμαι, κέκαμψαι, &c.

Καταπροΐξεσθαι, Ion. (Archil. ap. Etym. M. v. προΐκτης), καταπροΐξεσθαι Att. (Aristoph. frequently); a defective verb found only in the fut.‡,

μαχέσομαι-οῦμαι. From ΚΑΛΩ was formed κέκληκα by metathesis like τέτμηκα from τέμνω, κέκμηκα from κάμνω: see also βέβληκα under Βάλλω. Instances of this fut. may be seen in καλεῖ, Xen. Symp. 1, 15. καλεῖσθε, Demosth. Lept. 5. παρακαλοῦντας, Xen. Hell. 6, 3, 2. See this formation also under Δέμω. Of the fut. καλέσω the only instances which we find in the older writers are in Æschin. c. Timarch. p. 10. and Lycurg. c. Leocr. p. 150. ἐπικαλέσεται. In Aristoph. Plut. 963. Brunck has mistaken the aorist for the future.

* See ἔδακον under Δάκνω, ἔταμον under Τέμνω.

† I cannot think there are any grounds for κεκμηῶτας in Thucyd. 3, 59. however supported it may be by the manuscripts against the various reading κεκμηκότας. It can hardly have been introduced by the antiquated meaning (the dead) or by the solemn tone of the oration, as κεκμηκότες is used even by Euripides in the same sense.

‡ Thus οὐ καταπροΐξεσθαι ἔφη, Herodot. 3, 36. καταπροΐξεται, ib. 3, 156. Archil. Fr. 23. Aristoph. Nub. 1240. Vesp. 1396. καπροΐξονται, Herodot. 5, 105. Aristoph. Vesp. 1366. Thesm. 566. Equ. 435.

and in such expressions as *οὐ καταπροίξει*, 'thou shalt not have done it for nothing' (i. e. not without being punished for it). A deviation to the aor. *καταπροίξασθαι* is very possible, but it occurs only in Themist. Or. 14. init.* In the Etym. M. we find also a verb *προΐσσομαι*, *I beg*, quoted from Archilochus, from which comes *προΐκτης* in Homer: but the etymological connection of the two is not clear †.

Κανάξαις. See Ἄγνυμι.

Καυχάομαι, *I talk big*. Dep. midd. Pindar uses it with infin. Herodotus 7, 39. has the aorist.

ΚΑΦ–; whence perf. part. *κεκαφηώς*, *-ότος*, breathing short and with difficulty, Il. ε, 698. Od. ε, 468. Of this root or stem we find no other trace except that Hesychius has *κέκηφε, τέθνηκε*: probably with the sense of *expirare*. [This perf. seems to be formed from an obsolete theme *καφέω*, akin to *κάπτω* and *καπύω*.—Passow.]

Κεῖμαι, *I lie*, belongs to the stem or root ΚΕΙΩ or ΚΕΩ, and has only a pres., imperf. and fut. Pres. *κεῖμαι, κεῖσαι* ‡, *κεῖται*, &c., 3. plur. *κεῖνται*: imperat. *κεῖσο, κείσθω*, &c.; optat. *κεοίμην*; conj. *κέωμαι* §, *κέῃ*, &c.; infin. *κεῖσθαι*; part. *κείμενος*. Imperf. *ἐκείμην, ἔκεισο, ἔκειτο*, &c. Fut. *κείσομαι*. Comp. *κατάκειμαι, κατάκεισαι*, &c.: but the infin. retains the accent on the syllable of the stem or root, *κατακεῖσθαι*. So also *ἐπίκειμαι*, &c.

The forms of the optative and conjunctive as well as the accent of the compound infinitive might possibly recommend ΚΕΩ as the radical form of *κεῖμαι*: but the whole formation of the verb, together with the derivatives *κοίτη, κοιμᾶν*, makes it far more probable that the ει is the radical syllable and the forms with the ε shortened from it. Κεῖμαι itself might certainly be considered as a syncopated form (like *οἶμαι*, *ῥῦσθαι*), by virtue of which it would agree with the formation in μι; but it is better to take it altogether as an old perfect (*I have laid my-*

* Brunck thought indeed that he had found in the Argument of the Antigone of Sophocles an aor. pass. *καταπροισθῆναι* in a different form and meaning; but it is a mere error of transcription for *καταπρησθῆναι*.

† That is to say, *προίξ* had the general sense of *a gift*, as originally *dos* had in Latin; thence *προῖκα*, like *δωρεάν*, *without pay or reward*, *gratis*. The verb from which this word is derived meant therefore *to make a present of*; and thus *καταπροίξει* is a neat sarcasm, "thou shalt not give me that for nothing," i. e. I will give thee something in return, I will pay thee for it. The connection is here plain and certain. Whereas *to beg* is, it is true, the correlative of *to make a present of*, but on that very account not fit to be joined in the same idea, because language rather strives to make the distinction between such words clearly perceptible. Otherwise it would be easy enough to have recourse to the idea of stretching out the hand as belonging to both actions.

‡ Homer always uses *κεῖσαι, κεῖσο*, but we find in the Hymn. Merc. 254. as 2. sing. *κατάκειαι*.

§ Whether *κέωμαι* was a genuine Attic form may be doubted. In an inscription in the Corp. Inscript. I. n. 102. p. 10. stands *κείωνται*.

self down, consequently *I lie*,) with the redupl. dropped, by which the accent in the compound κατάκειμαι, κατακεῖσθαι is accounted for in the most natural way, like κάθημαι, καθῆσθαι. From the shortening of ει to ε arose naturally the change to the form in -έω, whence in Homer κέονται, in Herodot. 1, 178. κέεται, and in Hippocr. de A. A. L. 9, p. 333. κέεσθαι.

Instead of the 3. sing. κεῖται Herodotus has κέεται, and later writers κέαται*: instead of the 3. plur. κεῖνται Homer has κέονται, and very frequently (according to Ionic analogy) κείαται and κέαται, the latter of which is found only in Homer and the later Ionics. In the 3. plur. imperf. Homer and the Ionics for ἔκειντο have κείατο and κέατο, with an iterative κέσκετο. Od. φ, 41. In the infin. pres. we find in Hippocr. κέεσθαι for κεῖσθαι.

In Il. τ, 32. Od. β, 102. Wolf has altered according to the Venet. manuscript the old reading of the text κεῖται (which as an indicat. would be certainly incorrect) to a conjunct. κῆται. But this was unnecessary, as by an old usage κεῖμαι, κεῖται served for both conjunct. and indicat. Thus in Plat. Phædo p. 84. e. μὴ διάκειμαι is conjunct.; and in p. 93. a. stands ἐξ ὧν ἂν συγκέηται with a various reading in the Ed. Bas. 2. συγκεῖται, which ought however to be accented σύγκειται: on the other hand, Bekker in Isocr. π. Ἀντιδ. 278. has corrected from a good codex ὅπως ἂν...διακεῖσθαι to διάκεισθε, but he supposes the true reading to be διακέησθε. Compare a similar case in δέῃ, δεῖ under Δέω†.

Homer has also an infin. κειέμεν and part. κείων, κέων (from ΚΕΙΩ) as future, Il. ξ, 340. Od. η, 342.; which undoubtedly come from the fut. κέεω contracted to κείω and again shortened to κέω. That this form should pass into a desiderative was very natural, Od. θ, 315. Compare a similar future in δήεις, δήομεν, δήετε from a fut. δαέω and a root ΔΑΩ.

Κείρω, *I shear*: fut. κερῶ; perf. pass. κέκαρμαι; aor. 2. pass. ἐκάρην.—Midd.

The Epic language forms the fut. κέρσω, aor. 1. ἔκερσα. Pindar (Pyth. 4, 146.) has the aor. 1. pass. ἐκέρθην.

Κείω. See δήω, p. 56.; also Καίω and Κεῖμαι.

* κέαται is properly the Ion. 3. plur. shortened from κείαται, but used as a 3. sing. by those later writers to whom the Ion. dialect was no longer natural. See Reitz ad Luc. de D. S. 6.

† See Herm. ad Vig. not. 526. and De Metr. 1. p. 86. where the very analogous form κέεται for κέηται, like φθίεται, ἱμείρεται, &c. is preferred for Homer; and it certainly appears to be an old reading; for at Il. τ, 32. the small Schol. have the gloss Κέεται ἀντὶ τοῦ κεῖται, which should be ἀντὶ τοῦ κέηται.

Κελαδέω, *I sound, roar,* is regular; but the Epic language has the participle as from a barytone verb, κελάδων, κελάδοντα: although it is used only as an adjective. [Passow has also κελάδω, which he calls the original form of κελαδέω, and from which he derives the above participle.]

Κέλλω, *I run in, land*: fut. κέλσω; aor. 1. ἔκελσα.

Κέλομαι, *I command,* exactly synonymous with κελεύω: fut. κελήσομαι; aor. 1. κελησάμην, Pind. O. 13, 113. The Homeric aor. ἐκεκλόμην, ἐκέκλετο, κεκλόμενος is most naturally considered as the aor. 2. of this verb with syncope and reduplication (according to the analogy mentioned under Κάμνω), and with the augm. like ἐπέφραδον: it has also exactly the same meaning at Il. π, 657. κέκλετο δ' ἄλλους φευγέμεναι, he bade them fly. In most other passages however it means merely *I call to,* although there is generally the collateral idea of *I exhort* and *command* implied in it*.

Ἔκλεο see under Κλέω.

Κεντέω, *I prick,* is regular. But Homer (Il. ψ, 337.) has the aor. 1. infin. κένσαι from the stem KENT– which shows itself in κοντός, *a pole.* The verbals κεστός, *pricked,* and κέντωρ, κέντρον are explained by the omission of ν before σ in the one case, and of σ between ν and τ in the others†.

Κεράννυμι, *I mix,* also κιρνάω‡, κίρνημι: fut. κεράσω, Att. κερῶ; aor. 1. ἐκέρᾰσα, aor. 1. midd. ἐκερᾰσάμην. The other forms are affected by syncope or rather by the metathesis (which we may see exemplified in βέβληκα under Βάλλω,) joined with a contraction into ᾱ: thus perf. κέκρᾱκα; perf. pass. κέκρᾱμαι; aor. 1. pass. ἐκρᾱθην; aor. 1. midd. ἐκρᾱσάμην; but there is also an aor. 1. pass. ἐκεράσθην.

In the perfect pass. is found also κεκέρασμαι, but only in a later period, to which belongs also Anacr. 29, 13. On the other hand, Homer

* It is generally acknowledged that κέλω, of which καλεῖν is properly the inf. aor. and καλῶ the fut., (compare κατακτανῶ), is the one original verbal stem, which afterwards branched off according to difference of meaning into three verbs, κέλομαι, καλέω and κλέω.

† If we examine this more closely we shall certainly find that the adopting a stem KENT- to unite the above-mentioned forms is the most suitable plan; better for instance than KENΩ, which does not explain κεστός satisfactorily, and than KEΩ through which we cannot immediately get to κέντωρ, &c. We must not however try to unite the ideas *to prick,* whence κεντεῖν, — *to cleave,* whence κεάζω,—and *to beat,* whence in all languages comes the idea of *to kill,* κτείνω, καίνω; nay we must rather endeavour to keep them separate.

‡ Κεράννυμι and its sister-form κε-

uses the shortened form in the infin. aor. 1. act. ἐπικρῆσαι, Od. η, 164. For the Ionians have the η in κέκρημαι, κρηθείς, &c. (ΚΕΡΑ, ΚΡΕΑ, ΚΡΗ), but in the Attic and common language the η is changed on account of the ρ into ᾱ in this and other similar cases.

The simple form κεράω is used by the poets: Homer has κερῶντας, κεράασθε, κερόωντο. Comicus ap. Athen. 2. p. 48. a. κέρα. Otherwise κερῶ is the Att. future: see Hesych.

[In the fut. and aor. Homer doubles the σ of the regular form, making κεράσσω, ἐκέρασσα.—Passow.]

The Homeric conj. κέρωνται, Il. δ, 260. is not to be traced back to a theme ΚΕΡΩ, but more analogically to κέραμαι, like δύνωμαι conj. of δύναμαι; compare also κρέμαμαι, conj. κρέμωμαι, under Κρεμάννυμι.

Lastly at Il. ι, 203. the text had until very lately the imperat. κέραιρε, but now has from better sources κέραιε: see under Δαίω.

Κερδαίνω, *I gain*, is regular in the Attic language, and in the aor. takes the α like κοιλᾶναι, λευκᾶναι, and others: thus fut. κερδᾰνῶ; aor. 1. infin. κερδᾶναι. But the Ionics and many of the later writers form κερδήσομαι, ἐκέρδησα.

This Ionic formation is undoubtedly the older, and -αίνω was originally nothing more than one mode of lengthening the present, as in ἀλιταίνω and similar verbs, so that the simple ΚΕΡΔΩ, -ήσω is the original stem, and τὸ κέρδος the verbal subst., as the analogy which it brings with it confirms. But in a very early period some imagined that κερδαίνω sounded like a derivation from κέρδος, like λευκαίνω from λευκός, &c., and they accordingly inflected all the tenses in the termination -αίνω. Herodotus has both inflexions; the older κερδήσεσθαι 3, 72., ἐκέρδησαν 4, 152., the other κερδανέομεν, 8, 60, 3. This latter has in the Ion. dialect the aor. ἐκέρδηνα, Hom. Epig. 14, 6.

In the Attic form the perf. has the unpleasant sound of κεκέρδαγκα; hence others formed κεκέρδακα (see Chœrob. Bekk. p. 1285. and compare Lobeck ad Phryn. p. 34.), while others again deduced from the Ionic formation κεκέρδηκα, and Bekker has now restored from the manuscripts προσκεκερδήκασι to Demosth. adv. Dionysod. (p. 1292. Reisk.).

Κεύθω, *I envelope, hide*: fut. κεύσω; perf. (synonymous with pres.) κέκευθα; pluperf. (synon. with imperf.) ἐκεκεύθειν, Od. ι, 348.; aor. 2.

-ραννύω are formed like other verbs in μι (see Ἄγω, ἄγνυμι) by changing the ω of the barytone form into -νυμι or -νύω, only that when ω is preceded by a vowel, the ν is doubled, thus κεράω, κεράννυμι.

Again κιρνάω, κίρνημι are formed from κεράω by changing -άω into -νάω, -νημι, and in some verbs changing the ε of the root into ι; thus κεράω, κιρνάω, κίρνημι: compare Δέμω, and Πίλνημι from πελάω.

ἔκυθον and 3. sing. without the augm. κύθε, Od. γ, 16.; aor. 2. conj. with the Ep. redupl. κεκύθω, Od. ζ, 303. Homer has also the aor. 1. conj. in the compound ἐπικεύσῃς, Od. ο, 263. Of the passive we find only the pres. and imperf. Sophocles repeatedly [and Æschylus once] use the active κεύθω, and κέκευθα, as intrans., *I am hidden**.

Κέω. See Κεῖμαι and Καίω; also Δήω under ΔΑ–.

Κήδομαι, *I feel care and anxiety*, occurs in prose merely in pres. and imperf.

The Epic language had at first an active in a causative sense, κήδω, *I fill with care*, fut. κηδήσω, Il. ω, 240.; afterwards a perf. κέκηδα, Tyrt. 3, 28. synonymous with the pres. κήδομαι.

The middle with a short vowel in the inflected syllable is found in Æschyl. Sept. 138. in the imperat. κήδεσαι: and the derivative verb ἀκηδέω has the same inflexion in Il. ξ, 427. ἀκήδεσεν as now corrected from ἀκήδησ': see Heyne.

In Il. θ, 353. we find κεκαδησόμεθα, which some commentators, looking only at its exterior, have classed with κέκαδον, κεκαδήσω (see Χάζομαι); but the sense when critically examined is opposed to that derivation†, and in favour of the old one from κήδομαι. And since the perf. κέκηδα is synonymous with the last-mentioned present, it is quite as agreeable to analogy to have a future formed from the one as from the other; and equally analogous is the shortening of the radical vowel required by the rhythm; and which takes place in the α, because, as we see from the Doric κάδομαι (Pind.), α is properly the vowel of the root: in this case therefore it is the Ionic ᾰ, as πάρη for πήρα, ἀμφισβᾰτέω for -ητέω, &c. See also ἀρᾰρυῖα under Ἀραρίσκω‡.

Κίδνημι. See Σκεδάννυμι.

ΚΙΚ–. See Κιχάνω.

Κικλήσκω. See Καλέω.

Κινέω, *I move*, is regular.

* [See Sophocl. Aj. 634. El. 868. Œd. T. 968. Ant. 911., Æschyl. Sept. 590. Ed.]

† In order to explain it in that way we must first understand χάζεσθαί τινος (which in its common acceptation means *to give way to any one*) in the sense of *to cease from pursuing any one*; and then suppose that the two goddesses blame themselves with a certain severity of expression, because, when their friends are pursued by the enemy, they do not assist them against the pursuit of the other gods; or we must take it without the interrogation (see Heyne), and understand οὐκέτι χάζεσθαί τινος in the sense of *not deserting*, and this said by those who, after having long deserted their friends, at last assist them.

‡ I adopt this mode that I may not take κέκαδον twice, once from χάζω and once from κήδω, but that I may ground my argument on two actually existing forms, κέκαδον for κεκαδήσω from χάζω, κέκηδα for κεκαδήσομαι from κήδω.

In the passive it has an Epic sister-form *κίνυμαι*, with ι long like the active. This form must not be classed with *κίω* (which will be found below), for that verb never gives the idea of continuous motion as *κινύμενον* most plainly does at Il. ξ, 173., where it is used of oil moved about or shaken: and in other places where *κίνυμαι* is used of a crowd of combatants pressing on to battle, it does not express their moving forward, but only the tumult and bustle of their motion; compare Il. δ, 281. 332. 427. with Od. κ, 556. I consider it therefore more correct to give it a root for itself, KIN-, *quatio**.

Κίρνυμι. See Κεράννυμι.

Κιχάνω and **Κιχάνομαι**, *I obtain, hit*: fut. *κιχήσομαι*; aor. 2. *ἔκιχον*, *κίχω*, &c. These are the only tenses found in the Attic poets; but the Epic language has (beside a new aor. midd. *ἐκιχησάμην*, *-σατο*) a very common preterite, which according to form is an imperf. of KIXEΩ, KIXHMI, without however this pres. ind. having been ever actually in use. Hence come *ἐκίχεις* (Od. ω, 283.), 2. sing. imperf. for *ἐκίχης*, like *ἐτίθουν*, *ἐτίθεις*, with the plur. *ἐκίχημεν* and dual *ἐκιχήτην*, for *ἐκίχεμεν* *-χέτην*; to which we must add the moods of the present, as the opt. *κιχείην*, conj. (*κιχῶ*) *κιχείω*, infin. *κιχῆναι*, part. *κιχείς*; and the midd. *κιχήμενος*; in which formation in *μι* therefore the *η* is retained quite as far as it is in *ἀῆναι* and *δίζημαι*. We find then (including the imperf. *ἐκίχανον*) four historic forms, which, from the momentary meaning that the verb has in itself, can with difficulty in the Epic language be divided according to the sense into aorist and imperfect, and which therefore in the narrative are interchanged with each other principally for no other reason than the metre. With this corresponds the circumstance, that the Epics have not the other moods of either *κιχάνω* or *ἔκιχον*, but only those above quoted; consequently beyond the indicative they have no distinction between present and aorist. The earliest occurrence of the conj. *κιχῶ*, *κίχῃς*, &c. is in the Tragedians (Soph. Aj. 657. Eurip. Suppl. 1069.).

In all the above forms the Epics have the ι short: and *ἔκιχον* has this quantity in all the poets†. But in *κιχάνω* both the principal syllables are different in the Epic and Attic poets, the former having the ι short and the α long, the latter the ι long and the α short. Now as Hesychius and other Glossographers have the glosses *κιγχάνειν*, *ἐκίγχανε*,

* Grammatical analogy also is in favour of it. For while *κυνέω*, from KY- *ἔκυσα*, retains the υ short, *κινέω* has the ι long: in the same way *κίνυμαι* is remote from the analogy of *ζώννυμι*, *ζέννυμι*, because it is written almost invariably with a single ν, and therefore (with *γάνυμαι*, *λάζυμαι*, &c.) comes under the analogy of those verbs which affix merely *-υμαι* to the stem or root.

† It was impossible therefore that Simonides could say *ἔκῖχε*, a reading which Brunck (in Gnomicis) in Sim. Fr. 7. preferred to *ἔφῖκε*.

some moderns have explained that to be the true Attic way of writing this verb, and even introduced it already into the latest editions of the Tragedians*.

The analogy of ἔτυχον τυγχάνω, or that of ἱκόμην ἱκάνω (with ι short), has been the cause of the general supposition that the stem of the verb is in ἔκιχον. Everything appears to me to lead to a form κίχημι (κι being a reduplication), with κιχάνω as a sister-form, which in the present prevailed over the former. Ἔκιχον arose from ἐκίχην by a shortening of the syllable, just as ξύνιον did from ξυνίην; and metrical causes confused the one with the other. According to this supposition the true stem or root is ΧΕ– or ΧΑ– (compare the note on πίμπλημι, πλείμην), from which came κιχᾱνω, like φθᾱνω from ΦΘΑ–.

There is a Doric aor. 1. ἔκιξα, *moved away, pushed away*, which Schneider in his Lexicon deduces from κίχω. There is certainly nothing to hinder this new aorist being formed from ἔκιχον; but the grounds which I have laid down in Schol. Od. λ, 579. make me think it more eligible to give it a stem or root of its own ΚΙΚΩ: and this last supposition is confirmed by a fragment of Simonides, although as it now stands unintelligible, ἐπικίκοι ἐρομέσι, Chœrobosc. ap. Bekk. p. 1185. and Herodian in Bandini Bibl. Laur. Med. (Græca) p. 146. See Blomf. ad Callim. pag ult.†

Κίχρημι. See Χράω.

Κίω, *I go*; used only in pres. and imperf.; indeed the indic. pres. seldom or ever‡ occurs (κίεις, Æschyl. Ch. 676.); the other moods of the present however, as the optat. κίοιμι, part. κιών, &c., together with the imperf., are in frequent use in Homer and the other poets. The part. pres. κιών has the accent on the last syllable, like ἰών, but is not therefore an aorist; and the verb itself is to be considered as a sister-form of ἼΩ, εἶμι, *I go*.

To be satisfied that ἔκιον is an imperf. we have only to look at Il. β,

* See Monk and Matthiæ on Eurip. Hipp. 1434. (1442.). Hitherto however this reading has not been introduced into any passage of the tragedians from manuscripts, except that Victorius has written it so on the margin of a copy in the Alcest. 480. (495.). These critics appear to me therefore to have been very premature: for Hesych. and the others quote peculiarities from all writers. Now that Photius and Suidas expressly quote κιγχάνειν from Solon; that Eustathius (on Od. p. 209, 32.) cites not merely κιγχάνω but also ἰγχάνω, and that as "more analogical"—these two things appear to me much more against than in favour of the introduction of it. The above supposition that κι- is a syllable of reduplication, agrees both with the fluctuation of the quantity, (as the Epics had both πῐφαύσκω and πῑφαύσκω,) and with the form κιγχάνω, which has its analogy in πίμπλημι. That πίμπλημι and κῑχάνω were preferred to πῖπλημι and κιγχάνω, (the two latter being also in use,) corresponds with other euphonic observances.

† [Passow mentions (from κίκω) a rare poet. aor. ἔκῐκον, infin. κικεῖν, and a Dor. aor. 1. ἔκιξα, midd. ἐκιξάμην.]

‡ [Passow says that the indic pres. is not used at all.]

588. ζ, 399.; and that κιών is not an aor. we may be convinced by such passages as ἄρχε λέχοσδε κιών, Il. γ, 447. see also π, 263. ω, 328.; while in such as κλισίηνδε κιών...θέτο, κ, 148. we must remember the usage of the participles ἰών, ἄγων; φέρων, stated in the construction of participles in the syntax; according to which therefore that sentence is to be construed in the same way as ἔστησε φέρων, Od. α, 127.

On μετεκίαθον see ἀμύναθον under Ἀμύνω and ἐδιώκαθον under Διώκω. The verb κίνυμαι see above under Κινέω.

Κλάζω, *I sound, scream*, &c.: fut. κλάγξω*; aor. 1. ἔκλαγξα; perf. κέκλαγγα synonymous with the present; whence the fut. κεκλάγξω and κεκλάγξομαι.

See κεκλαγγυῖαι, Xenoph. Ven. 3, 9. 6, 23. Conj. κεκλάγγω and fut. κεκλάγξομαι, Aristoph. Vesp. 929. 930. Both futures are quoted by Suidas. There are other presents formed from some tense of κλάζω; for instance κλαγγέω whence κλαγγεῦντι, Theocr. Epigr. 6. and κλαγγάνω, which however is doubtful†; see Schneid. ad Xen. Ven. 4, 5.

In the Epic language this verb is also inflected with one γ. In the oldest poets however this is found only in the perf. κέκληγα, used as a present, of which the part. masc. κεκληγώς changes in its oblique cases to κεκλήγοντος, as though formed from a new present κεκλήγω (Hom.), like ἐρρίγοντι in Hes. α, 228: see πεφρίκοντας under Φρίσσω. An aor. 2. ἔκλαγον is found in Hymn. Pan. 14. and Eurip. Iph. A. 1062. in the chorus. But the aor. 1. ἔκλαξα‡ belongs merely to the Doric inflexion of κλείω. [The regular aor. 1. ἔκλαγξα is used in a transit. sense in Pind. Pyth. 4, 40. Compare Æschyl. Sept. 388. Agam. 48. The presents κλάγω or κλάγγω never occur.—Passow.]

Κλαίω, *I weep*, Att. κλάω with α long and without contraction: fut. κλαύσομαι§ (κλαυσοῦμαι, Aristoph. Pac. 1081.); aor. 1. ἔκλαυσα. The fut. κλαιήσω, κλαήσω is less frequent. Verbal adj. κλαυστός and κλαυτός, κλαυστέος.—Midd. [Passow remarks that the middle voice is used by Æschylus Sept. 903. but otherwise seldom found in the older writers.]

The fut. active is used by the Dorics, as Theocr. 23, 24. An aor.

* Some verbs in ζ have γγ for their characteristic, as for instance κλάζω, πλάζω, σαλπίζω.

† [Passow however makes no mention of κλαγγάνω being a suspected form, and quotes it from Æschyl. Eum. 126. and Xen. Ven. 6, 23. He has also κλαγγαίνω.]

‡ This aor. was formerly quoted from Archiæ Epigr. 28., but the true reading ἀποκλάγξασα is now adopted by Jacobs.

§ On the formation of this future see Θέω.

ἔκλαεν standing in the text of Theocr. 14, 32. but occurring nowhere else, has been altered by Hermann to ἔκλαι'; and no doubt correctly, for that imperf. exactly suits the passage, as it does also 23, 17. in both which the description is that of a continuous weeping.

Κλάω, *I break*: fut. κλάσω (with α short); aor. 1. ἔκλασα; aor. 1. pass. ἐκλάσθην; perf. pass. κέκλασμαι. Thus the α is short in the inflexion; and the passive takes σ.

In Anacr. Fr. 16. we find a syncopated aor. 2. part. ἀποκλάς as from ἀπόκλημι, on which see ἔγνων, &c. under Γιγνώσκω.

Κλείω, *I shut*, is regular: thus fut. κλείσω, &c. But the perf. pass. is both κέκλεισμαι and κέκλειμαι; while the aor. 1. pass. is ἐκλείσθην only.

The Ionians pronounced this verb κληΐω, and formed it ἐκλήϊσα, κληῖσαι, κεκλήϊμαι without the σ, but always ἐκληΐσθην. These forms had therefore, like the corresponding ones from τίω, μηνίω, &c., the ι according to the rules of formation long; consequently those editions of Homer which have ἐκλήϊσσε, κληΐσσαι are so far incorrect, and these forms, from being written thus, are erroneously given to κληΐζω, which verb has, it is true, in the lexicons, the meaning of *to shut*, but improperly so; for the old writers know κληΐζω ἐκλήϊσα in no other sense than that of *celebro*, and κληΐω ἐκλήϊσα in that of *claudo*. Hence arose again an Attic form κλῄω, ἔκλῃσα, which occurs frequently in the text, and still more frequently as a various reading in the manuscripts. Valckenaer's (ad Phœniss. 268.) opinion, that κλείω must be older than κλῄω because in the earlier times the η was not yet come into use at Athens, is nothing to the point; for the question here is, not how it was written, but how it was spoken: now as κλείω was the general form in use at a later period, κλῄω certainly appears to me, wherever it is found, to have great authority as a critical form of the oldest grammarians, who knew that the earlier Attics spoke it so. This decision is however very difficult to be supported through all writers. And equally difficult is it in the case of κέκλεισμαι, κέκλειμαι, κέκλῃμαι. See Thom. Mag. in voc. Theodosii Canones p. 1020, 25. Chœrob. in Ind. Bekk. v. κέκλειμαι: and among the moderns Elmsl. ad Eurip. Heracl. 729. Matth. ad Hecub. 482. Androm. 495. Schneid. v. κλείω*.

* [The article in Schneider runs thus: Κλείω, -είσω, whence perf. pass. κεκλεισμένος. According to the Etym. Mag. κέκλειμαι was used for κέκλεισμαι.' In Demosth. Philipp. p. 22. Bekker reads κεκλῃμένων τῶν ἐμπορίων. In Eurip. Hel. 983. stands κεκλῄμεθα: and in Æschyl. Suppl. 957. κεκλειμένος for κεκλεισμένος.—Ed.]

The Ionic 3. plur. κεκλέαται (for κεκλήαται from κεκλῄμαι) belongs to this verb quite as much as it does to καλέω when put for κεκλήαται from κέκλημαι: (see ἀποκεκλέατο, Herodot. 9, 50. and κεκλέαται (from καλέω); 2, 164.

The Dorians had a fut. κλαξῶ and an aor. ἔκλαξα formed from κλάζω Dor. for κλῄζω: compare Γελάω and Θλάω.

There is one instance of a fut. 2. κλιῶ as used by the Comic poet Eupolis according to a remarkable observation of Chœroboscus (F. 279. v.) in Bekker's Excerpta. "Herodian," it is there said, "tells us that there is no fut. 2. act. in use. Apollonius quotes some, but they are either invented by him, like φυγῶν, δραμῶν, or they are presents." And then is added, "solitary exceptions there are in ἐγχεῶ and in κατακλιεῖ from κατακλείω in Eupolis ἐν Χρυσῷ γένει. Εἰ μή τις αὐτὴν κατακλιεῖ."

Κλέπτω, *I steal*: fut. κλέψομαι; perf. κέκλοφα*; perf. pass. κέκλεμμαι, Att. κέκλαμμαι: [aor. 1. pass. ἐκλέφθην;] aor. 2. pass. ἐκλάπην.

Κλέω†, κλείω, *I celebrate*; pass. κλέομαι, *I am celebrated.* In Il. ω, 202. ἔκλεο is the 2. sing. imperf. for ἐκλέεο, like φοβέο, αἰτέο, ἐξηγέο. In Callim. Del. 40. ἔκλεο Δῆλος must at all events be accented like the above, ἐκλέο, in as much as either *celebrabaris* is poet. for *vocabaris*, or the poet thought himself at liberty to use the syncope thus, ἐκαλέεο, ἐκαλέο, ἐκλέο.

Κλῑνω‡, *I bend*: fut. κλῐνῶ; aor. 1. ἔκλῑνα; aor. 1. midd. ἐκλῑνάμην; aor. 1. pass. ἐκλίνθην and ἐκλίθην (ῐ), both forms in Homer, but ἐκλίνθην§ exclusively Ep. and Poet.: much less frequent is the aor. 2. pass. and perhaps used only in the compounds as κατακλῐνῆναι, Plato and Aristoph. ξυγκατακλῐνείς, Aristoph. Ach. 981. Perf. pass. κέκλῐμαι, part. κεκλῐμένος.—Midd.

Κλύω, *I hear*, a poetical verb, whose imperf. ἔκλυον is used as an

* It is certain that in the older language the ο, which is supposed to be peculiar to the perf. 2. (perf. midd.), belonged to the perf. 1. act.; but as it is not generally so in the language as now grammatically formed, we put down as deviations from the established analogy three perfects, viz., πέμπω—πέπομφα, κλέπτω—κέκλοφα, τρέπω—τέτροφα. But this ο never goes into the perf. passive.

† This form, which does not appear to have been ever in use, but which I have placed here merely on account of κλέομαι, some have wished to bring back to the text of Eurip. Alc. 449. (461.) and Iph. A. 1047. (1035.). See Matthiæ on the former passage.

‡ On the formation of the perf. and aor. 1. pass., see Τείνω.

§ Examples however of κλινθῆναι may be found in Plutarch (see Stephan. Thesaur.); and in Æsop. Fab. 143. Heusing., but in this latter the reading is uncertain.

aorist, and also in the *present* sense of *to be in the habit of hearing*; see above in Ἔννεπον. Imperat. κλύε, κλύετε, more commonly κλῦθι, κλῦτε, like βῆθι, γνῶθι, &c. and with Homeric reduplication κέκλυθι, κέκλυτε; see Κάμνω. To this syncopated aorist belongs the adjectival part. pass κλύμενος synonymous with the verbal adj. κλυτός, *celebrated*.

With regard to the aoristic usage of ἔκλυον it is to be observed that the pres. indic. κλύω never occurs in Homer. Hesiod has it once, ε, 724., the Tragedians frequently.

ΚΜΑ–. See Κάμνω.

Κνάω, *I scrape, scratch*, infin. κνᾶν, but in the more accurate Att. writers κνῆν, like σμῆν and ψῆν*, Pollux, 7, 196.; fut. κνήσω; aor. 1. ἔκνησα; of an aor. 2. ἔκνην, as formed from κνῆμι, is found only a 3. sing. κνῆ, and that but once, Il. λ, 639. compare Herodot. 7, 139.—Midd. κνᾶσθαι, Att. κνῆσθαι, Plat. Gorg. p. 494. c. Xen. Mem. 1, 2, 30. (Schneid. 3.)

Κνώσσω, *I sleep*: fut. κνώσω, &c. See Ἁρμόττω: but examples of this verb are so rare that we cannot settle its inflexion with any grammatical certainty. In Apollon. 3, 690. the aor. 1. κατακνώσασα is found in many of the manuscripts, but the old reading κατακνώσσουσα is likewise in the best manuscripts (see Brunck), so that nothing can be decided in favour of either.

Κοιμάω, Ion. κοιμέω, Herodot., 2, 95. *I cause to sleep, put to rest*: fut. κοιμήσω, &c. Pass. (and in the Epics midd. also) *I sleep*. [Homer has the pass. κοιμάομαι with fut. κοιμήσομαι, and the aor. κοιμήσασθαι as well as κοιμηθῆναι; the former is used by the poets only.—Passow.]

Κολάζω, *I punish*: fut. κολάσω (Xen. Athen. 1, 9.), and more frequently κολάσομαι (Xen. Anab. 2, 5, 13.); the apparently Attic forms of the fut. κολῶ, midd. κολῶμαι†, are used by Aristophanes, (Equ. 459.) merely as a play on the word; the participle of the fut. midd. κολώμενος (not κολούμενος) is the true reading of Aristoph. Vesp. 244. as we gather from Hesych. in voc. and from the explanation of

* See also ζῆν from Ζάω, χρῆσθαι from Χράω, διψῆν, πεινῆν, &c.

† Most of the polysyllabic verbs in -ίζω prefer the Attic fut to the other; but of those in -άζω nothing like a decided analogy can be laid down: for while in βιβάζω the Attic fut. is very common, in ἀγοράζω and others it is a barbarism: see Lex. Seg p 331. and Maitt. pp. 47. 48.

the Scholiast. [This form is the more usual one in prose, instead of the poetical κολούω. In the present the Attics sometimes use the middle instead of the active; see Schneid. and Heind. Xen. Cyrop. 1, 2, 7. Plat. Menex. p. 240. d. Stallb. Protag. p. 324. c. But in the fut. they never use the active κολάσω, Xen. Anab. 2, 5, 13. Hellen. 1, 7, 20. Porson post Hemsterh. Plut. p. 575.—Passow.]

Κολούω, *I mutilate*: fut. κολούσω, &c. The pass. is formed both with and without σ; thus perf. pass. κεκόλουμαι and κεκόλουσμαι; aor. 1. pass. ἐκολούθην and ἐκολούσθην.

Schneider in Theophr. caus. plant. 2, 20. (15.) invariably reads κολουσθεῖσα, κολουσθῇ on very slight authority: but the form without the σ does occur in other writers (see Stephan. Thesaur.), and κεκολουμένος in Philippi Epigr. 25. is undisputed.

Κομίζω, *I bring*: fut. κομίσω, Att. -ιῶ, &c.—Midd. κομίζομαι, *I get*: fut. κομιοῦμαι, &c. See Aristoph. Av. 552.

Κονίω, *I cover with dust*: fut. κονίσω. This is the old and genuine form of the verb; whence the perf. pass. κεκόνιμαι; and hence in the poets the only way of writing the aorist is ἐκόνισε. The Attic form κονίζω, fut. κονιῶ and κονίσω, perf. pass. κεκόνισμαι, did not come into use until later*.

Κόπτω, *I hew, cut down*: fut. κόψω; perf. κέκοφα; aor. 2. pass. ἐκόπην.—Midd.

Homer has the perf. 2. in the sense of the present, κεκοπώς, Il. ν, 60. Od. σ, 334.

Κορέννυμι, *I satiate*: fut. κορέσω; aor. 1. ἐκόρεσα. The

* See the examples in Stephens, and compare the various readings. Brunck was therefore quite right in Theocr. 1, 30. in preferring the reading of the majority of the manuscripts; as was Jacobs in Hegesippi Epigr. 3. (Anth. Vat. p. 164.) in suspecting the reading of the Vatican manuscript κεκονημένα to be, what is much more probable, and must at all events be preferred in the hexameter, -ιμένα. The assertion of Hemsterhuys (on Lucian Timon. 45.), that κεκονιμένος and κεκονισμένος are both equally good, cannot, as applied there, be satisfactory: compare μηνίω. Whether, as some critics contend (see Valck. ad Theocr. l. c.), we ought in Thom. Mag. instead of Καὶ κεκονιαμένος καὶ κεκονιμένος to read Καὶ κεκονισμένος κ. κ., and whether there be sufficient grounds for the rejection of κονιᾶν in the sense of *to cover with dust*, requires perhaps a closer investigation.

pass. takes σ; thus perf. κεκόρεσμαι; aor. 1. ἐκορέσθην.—MIDD.

The Att. fut. must have been κορῶ, for the Epic one is κορέω, Il. θ, 379, ν, 831. The Ionic dialect takes the η in the perf., as act. κεκόρηκα, pass. κεκόρημαι; and the Epic language has also a perf. part. with act. form and pass. meaning, κεκορηώς, Od. σ, 372. See τετμηώς in note under Τέμνω.

Κορύσσω, *I arm* (with a helmet): fut. κορύξω; aor. 1. midd. ἐκορυσσάμην (in Hippocr. ἐκορυξάμην), part. κορυσσάμενος, Il. τ, 397; perf. pass. κεκόρυθμαι, part. κεκορυθμένος.

Κοτέω, and more frequently in midd. κοτέομαι, *I feel enmity against*: Ep. fut. κοτέσσομαι; Ep. aor. 1. midd. κοτέσσατο, part. κοτεσσάμενος. This verb retains ε in the formation, except in the Ep. perf. part. κεκοτηώς, with the meaning of the pres. increased in force; thus κεκοτηότι θυμῷ, Hom. The part. of the aor. 1. act. κοτέσασα occurs in Hymn. Cer. 254. The word is entirely poetical.

Κράζω, *I scream, croak*: fut. κεκράξομαι; aor. 2. ἔκρᾰγον, Lobeck ad Phryn. p. 337. But instead of this present the perf. κέκρᾱγα (with the force of a pres.) is generally used, whence by syncope 1. plur. κέκραγμεν (pluperf. ἐκέκραγμεν), imperat. κέκραχθι, infin. κεκρᾱγέναι, part. κεκρᾱγώς. The 2. plur. imperat. of the perf. κεκράγετε without syncope in Aristoph. Vesp. 415. is a very rare case; for we find scarcely any instance of the imperative of a perf. unless where that perf. is used as a present like the one before us, and even then in most cases a syncopated form is preferred. Compare γέγωνε, and κεχήνετε under Χάσκω.

Κραίνω, *I complete*: fut. κρᾰνῶ; aor. 1. ἔκρηνα, imperat. κρῆνον, infin. κρῆναι, Od.; aor. 1. pass. ἐκράνθην, Pind. The Epic infin. fut. midd. in a pass. sense is κρανέεσθαι, Il. ι, 622. In Eurip. Hippol. 1255. κέκρανται is 3. plur. perf.; nor do I find any instance of it as 3. sing. also. In the Epic language this verb is capable of being produced in all its tenses, as imperf. ἐκραίαινεν, aor. 1. infin. κρηῆναι, perf. pass. κεκράανται*.

* As the Epic aor. of φαίνω is ἐφαάνθην because that verb is contracted from φαείνω, so is the remarkable production of the tenses of κραίνω the result of contraction, and most probably of κραίνω from κρεαίνω: in which this striking peculiarity is to be observed; that it is not the resolution of a contracted syllable, but a production by repeating the vowel or syllable, as φῶς is contracted from φάος and again produced to the Ep. φόως: compare also θῶκος, θόωκος and θαάσσω in Buttm. Lexil.

Κρεμάννῡμι, *I hang* (anything); pass. *I am hanged*; midd. *I hang myself*: in addition to which comes a particular form for the intransit., κρέμαμαι, *I am hanging*. This last is conjugated like δύναμαι with conj. κρέμωμαι, opt. κρεμαίμην*, κρέμαιτο. In the inflexion α is short, as in the fut. κρεμάσω and aor. 1. ἐκρέμασα, and the pass. takes σ. The Att. fut. is κρεμῶ, -ᾷς, -ᾷ, &c. The aor. 1. pass. ἐκρεμάσθην is common to the passive (with a passive and middle sense) and to the intransitive; but the fut. κρεμασθήσομαι belongs wholly to κρεμάννυμι, as the intransit. sense has its own future κρεμήσομαι, *I shall hang, be in a state of suspension.*

This distinction of forms and meanings is, generally speaking, observed by the Attic writers, although it must not be expected that they had analogy so constantly before their eyes, as never to deviate from it. Forms of the middle are found both in Homer and Hesiod, as ἐκρέμω, 2. sing. aor. 1. for ἐκρέμασο, Il. υ, 18. 21. and the aor. 1. infin. κρεμάσασθαι (with an accus.) *to hang anything on*, Hes. ε, 627. The pres. κρεμάω is used by the later writers†. In the pure Attic language the only future is κρεμῶ, -ᾷς, &c. Epic κρεμόω.

In Aristoph. Vesp. 298. all the manuscripts have the optat. κρέμοισθε from κρέμαμαι, except the Venetian, which has κρέμεσθε, naturally leading us to κρέμαισθε. The other reading however is not to be rejected too hastily: compare μαρνοίμην, μεμνοίμην with the accentuation of the optat. and conjunct. under Δύναμαι. There must however have been a uniformity in Aristophanes, and we find in Nub. 868. Acharn. 944, at least as the text now stands, κρέμαιο, κρέμαιτο.

An Attic sister-form of this verb in the pres. and imperf. is κρήμνημι, κρήμναμαι (the latter for κρέμαμαι), which deviates from analogy by the η in the radical syllable‡. Hence this way of writing it may well appear doubtful, particularly as κρεμν- and κριμν- are found occasionally in the manuscripts§. On the whole however they are in favour of the η; and we find κρημνάμεναι (without any known various reading) in Æschyl. Sept. 231. κατακρημνάμεναι, Aristoph. Nub. 377. κρημνάντων, Pind.

* On the accentuation of these forms see Δύναμαι.

† Stephens quotes it from two works falsely attributed to Aristotle; Hist. Mirab. c. 6. and Œc. 2.

‡ This verb is the only instance of the change of ε to η, κρεμάω and κρεμάννυμι to κρήμνημι: see note under Κεράννυμι.

§ See Müncker ad Ant. Lib. 13. extr. Var. Lect. ad Eurip. El. 1217. Barnes. et Musgr. ad Eurip. Herc. 520. Piers. ad Mœr. v. Ἐκρεμάννυεν.

Pyth. 4, 43. the imperat. *κρήμνη*. Etym. M. in voc. and in fragments of Euripides there quoted (see Piers. ad Moer. v. *κίρνη*). Eustathius also on Il. θ, 19. (if any reliance is to be placed on it) expressly mentions the change of ε to η. And lastly in the subst. *κρημνός* (*an overhanging precipice*), which is of the same family, the η is undoubted.

Κρῖνω*, *I separate, judge*: fut. κρῐνῶ; aor. ἔκρῑνα; perf. κέκρῐκα; perf. pass. κέκρῐμαι; aor. 1. midd. ἐκρινάμην; aor. 1. pass. ἐκρίθην (ῐ). In Homer is also a poet. part. aor. pass. κρινθείς, Il. ν, 129. Od. θ, 48. This verb has a middle voice, but only in the Epic language (κρίνασθαι ὀνείρους, *to interpret*, Il. ε, 150.): it has however two compounds, depon. midd.,

ἀποκρίνομαι, *I answer*; ὑποκρίνομαι, *I explain, represent.*

Hence in good writers the passive form ἀποκριθῆναι is nothing more than a real passive of *ἀποκρίνω, I separate*: but later writers used it for ἀποκρίνασθαι: see Lobeck ad Phryn. p. 108. The perf. 2. κέκρινα belongs to the later writers.

Κρούω, *I knock, push*: perf. pass. κέκρουμαι†, and κέκρουσμαι; aor. 1. pass. ἐκρούσθην.—MIDD.

Κρύπτω, *I conceal*: fut. κρύψω. The characteristic is β. Pass. aor. 1. ἐκρύφθην; aor. 2. ἐκρύβην (ῠ).—MIDD.

The aor. 2. act. ἔκρῠβον and the forms with the simple characteristic φ, as ἔκρυφον, are found only in the later writers, Quintus, Nonnus, &c. See also Lobeck ad Phryn. p. 318. The Ep. imperf. κρύπτασκον (see ῥίπτασκον) is in Il. θ, 272. The perf. pass. κέκρυμμαι in Od.

Κτάομαι, Ion. κτέομαι, Herodot., *I get possession of, obtain*: fut. κτήσομαι; aor. 1. ἐκτησάμην; perf. κέκτημαι‡, *I possess*; Hes. ε, 439. Ion. ἔκτημαι, Il. ι, 402. perf. conj. κέκτωμαι, ῃ, ηται, &c., perf. opt. κεκτῄμην, κέκτῃο, κέκτῃτο, &c. There is also another form of the perf. opt. κεκτῴμην§

* On the formation of the two perfects and the aor. 1. pass., see Τείνω.

† Aristoph. Ach. 459. according to the manuscripts.

‡ The perf. *κέκτημαι*, like *μέμνημαι* from *μνάω*, is formed with the regular reduplication; but ἔκτημαι follows the analogy of verbs beginning with two consonants (not mutes before liquids), which take ε instead of the reduplication. This latter is properly Ionic, but used occasionally by the Attics, as Plat. Menop. 97. e. et sæpe. See Heindorf. ad Plat. Protag. 75.

§ The ω in this form may be thus accounted for. As the perfects with the sense of a present borrow more or less

(like μεμνῴμην from μέμνημαι), of which we find κεκτῴμεθα, Eurip. Heracl. 283. Compare Il. ψ, 361. Xen. Cyr. 1, 6, 3.

In a somewhat later period we find the passive τὰ κτηθέντα. [Indeed κτάομαι as a passive is rare, and generally confined to the very late writers, Schæf. Schol. Par. Apollon. Rhod. 1, 695. Gnom. Græc. p. 145. sqq. Still however the aor. 1. pass. ἐκτήθη occurs in a passive sense in Thucyd. 1, 123., the fem. part. aor. κτηθεῖσα in Eurip. Hec. 453. and the perf. part. κεκτημένος in Thucyd. 7, 70. An active κτάω is never found —Passow]

Κτείνω, *I kill*: fut. κτενῶ, Ion. κτανῶ; aor. 1. ἔκτεινα; aor. 2. ἔκτανον; perf. 2. ἔκτονα. We have only to observe here that the aor. 1. is more common in prose than the aor. 2., and that the only perf. in use by the older writers is ἔκτονα. The perf. pass. and aor. pass. were not used in the common language, but in their places the verb θνήσκω in a passive combination, τέθνηκεν or ἀπέθανεν ὑπ' αὐτοῦ.

From the opinions of the Grammarians which have come down to us confused and corrupted (Thom. Mag in ἀπέκτονα, Mœr. in ἀπέκτονεν) we can extract nothing certain on the various forms of the perfect. The aor. 2. occurs in Xenophon more frequently, where however we must not forget the possible exchange of this verb with καίνειν, κανεῖν. See Sturz. in κατακτείνειν. The perf. ἔκτακα, ἀπέκτακα, always however accompanied with the various reading ἔκταγκα, was likewise in the written language from the time of Menander: see Meineke ad Men. p. 120. Schæf. ad Schol. Apollon. p. 147.*

from that tense, the termination of the opt. pres. οίμην was affixed to κεκτη-, which contained the stem of the verb, making κεκτηοίμην This was changed according to Ionic custom (like νηός to νεώς) to κεκτεῴμην, and again contracted by the Attics to κεκτῴμην. The form in -ήμην appears to have been preferred by the older Attics, that of -ῴμην to be peculiar to Euripides and Xenophon.

* Of the two non-Attic forms ἔκταγκα was undoubtedly the more disagreeable to the ear, while the better-sounding ἔκτακα was recommended by the analogy of τέτακα I would therefore, contrary to the opinion of the above-mentioned philologists, acquit the language of Menander at least of having used that form, and in a fragment of him preserved by Suidas defend the old reading (which is also that of the Ed Mediol.) ἀπεκτάκασι The direction in Thom. Mag 'Απέκτονα κάλλιον ἢ ἀπέκτεινα. ἀπέκτανον δὲ ἀδόκιμον πάντη is nonsense arising from repeated mistakes In that passage three perfects must have been mentioned, and nothing can be more suited to the point in question than, 'Απέκτονα κάλλιον ἢ ἀπέκτακα. ἀπέκταγκα δὲ ἀδόκιμον πάντη. That is to say, the strict Atticist preferred the old Attic perfect to all others, even to the well-formed one of the later Attics, but against the form which he saw and heard everywhere around him he cautioned his readers in the strongest language. Mœris, whom we may with the

There existed also a perf. ἐκτόνηκα, formed like δεδοκημένος from δέχομαι or μεμόρηται from μείρομαι*. Wherever this form occurs in the older Attics it is corrupted; as in Plat. Apol. p. 38. c. the present reading taken from the best Codd. is ἀπεκτόνατε, and of Xen. Hier. 3, 7., the various reading ἀπεκτονότας is in Stobæus: but we must allow that it is used by the later writers, for we find it in Plut. Timol. 16. p. 137. in Parthen. 24. and in all three manuscripts of Aristot. Elench. 33, 2.

The Epic language had the aor. 1. pass. both with and without the ν (see Κλίνω and Τείνω), ἐκτάθην and ἐκτάνθην, of which the latter was used again in the later prose, as κτανθῆναι in Dio Cassius (see Lobeck ad Phryn. p. 36.), and κτανθείς, Brunck Anal. Ænigm. 34. Ἔκτᾰθεν is Æol. 3. plur. for ἐκτάθησαν, Il. λ, 691. Od. δ, 537.

Homer has the syncopated aorist, corresponding with the aor. 2., like ἔβην, ἔγνων, &c. (see under Γιγνώσκω); thus, ἔκτᾰν, -ας, -α, plur. ἔκτᾰμεν, &c. and 3. plur. ἔκτᾰν for -ασαν; opt. κταίην; infin. κτάμεν, κτάμεναι for κτάναι; part. κτάς. The Homeric conj. is κτέω for κτῶ (like ἱστέω for ἱστῶ; see Ἵστημι), whence κτέωμεν, Od. χ, 216. To this we must add a corresponding aorist midd. with passive meaning, ἐκτάμην†, -σό, -το (like ἐβλήμην from βάλλω), infin. κτᾰσθαι, part. κτάμενος; all formed as from κτάω. Homer has also an Epic conj. pres. κτείνωμι, Od. τ, 490.

The fut. in Hom. is the common one κτενῶ, but always in a resolved form κτενέω, -έεις, -έει, in which the manuscripts agree in almost every instance: only the compound with κατά takes, as universally, the change of vowel to α, as κατακτανέουσιν, Il. ζ, 409. κατακτανέεσθε, ξ, 481. consequently they are fut. midd. with a *passive sense.* To these we must add the simple form καί τε κτανέοντα κατέκτα, Il. σ, 309., where however as regards the sense a doubt still prevails. Both old and modern commentators agree indeed that it is a future, translating it "and he who *wishes to slay* is himself slain" (for the aor. κατέκτα is here used in the sense of *to be accustomed to slay*). But the context immediately preceding, ξυνὸς Ἄρης, requires much rather this sense, "they slay and are slain"‡; which leads us to conjecture that from κτανεῖν arose a new

greatest certainty restore from the manuscripts thus, Ἀπέκτονεν Ἀττικῶς, ἀπέκταγκεν Ἑλληνικῶς, speaks more concisely to the same point. And lastly, Sextus, who (Adv. Gramm. 10.) says, κτείνεται μὲν λέγεται, ἔκταγκα δὲ οὐ λέγεται, speaks not of the language of common life, but of that taught scientifically by the Grammarians. The only thing therefore which we learn from this passage also is, that ἔκταγκα was rejected.

* From κτείνω we suppose a form κτονέω, like φέρω and φορέω (see Δέμω), from which comes regularly ἐκτόνηκα.

† In all verbs which have in the perf. the augment instead of the reduplication, the indicative of this pass. aor. cannot be distinguished from the pluperf.: ὤρμην, ἐκτάμην, ἐφθίμην, ἐσσύμην.

‡ [Or still more literally, "war is accustomed to slay the slayer."—Ed.]

present κταὐέω, by which the continuation of the action appears to have been expressed, just as it is by ἐπιτραπέουσι in κ, 421.

An Attic sister-form of this verb for the pres. and imperf. in prose is κτίννυμι; for so this form is generally written in the text; but the manuscripts fluctuate between ι and ει, ν and νν*.

Κτίζω, *I found, build*: fut. ίσω, &c. The part. pass. κτίμενος (like πτάμενος under πετάννυμι, θύμενος, ἁρπάμενος; see ἐκτάμην under Κτείνω), and the verb adj. κτιτός, which occur in the compounds ἐϋκτίμενος, ἐΰκτιτος, come from the older form in ίω, whence also περικτίονες.

Κτυπέω, *I resound*: fut. κτυπήσω, &c. is regular: but the Epics have the aor. 2. ἔκτυπον (like ἔπιτνον under πιτνέω), in which indeed lies the true primitive form or stem of the verb, and the subst. κτύπος as well as κτυπέω are derivatives from it.

Κυλίνδω and κυλίω, *I roll* (anything). The only formation which occurs from these two verbs is fut. κυλῑσω; aor. 1. ἐκύλῑσα, infin. κυλῖσαι; aor. 1. pass. ἐκυλίσθην; perf. pass. κεκύλισμαι.—Midd. To these we must add a lengthened present κυλινδέω†, which, in its present tense only, is the prevailing form in Attic prose.

The two fuller forms of the present are used in preference to the other, when it is wished to express certain modifications of the sense implying a continuation of motion (see the lexicons); yet no fixed distinction can be laid down, and all three occur in the simple sense of *to roll, push*. Homer has exclusively the form κυλίνδω (of which he uses only pres. and imperf.) with the aor. ἐκυλίσθην. It is also probable that κυλίνδω, fut. κυλῑσω, was the original form of this verb, and that κυλίω, which is found in the later poets, arose merely from the fut. κυλίσω.

With the midd. κυλινδεῖσθαι, *to roll* (neut.), correspond three other forms,

ἀλινδεῖσθαι, καλινδεῖσθαι, εἰλινδεῖσθαι,

* Phrynichus in Lex. Seguer. 1. p. 29, 7. prefers writing κτίνυμι and rejects the νν; but he has no grounds for doing so. If we suppose that this form came from a root without any ν, there is nothing to lead us to a stem κτι- or κτει- only to κτα- (ἔκταν, ἔκτα); and analogy would therefore require κτάννυμι. But if it is formed from κτειν- as a stem, we have (like δείκνυμι) the completely analogous word κτείν-νυμι: and as a diphthong before νν is something unusual, it was to be expected that the pronunciation would either drop one ν or shorten the ει to ι. The latter is the most current tradition; but κτείνυμι is found in the best manuscripts, as for instance almost invariably in the Cod. Clark. of Plato. Hence I conjecture that this is also the opinion of Phrynichus, and that ἀποκτιννύναι, which is now the reading there, is owing to the common corruption of ι for ει.

† Of this form we find only the present, but it is probable that the formation in -ήσω, which we see just below in the verbs similarly formed, was borrowed from this.

all used in the intransitive sense of *to roll, turn*, or *drive round*; and these we find inflected according to the form in *έω*; thus *εἰλινδημένῳ* or *ἠλινδημένῳ*, Plut. Agis 3., and in a passage quoted by Stephens *ἐγκεκαλινδημένη*. The form ἀλινδεῖσθαι is pre-eminently the Attic, and of this alone we find an active voice with the meaning of *to make* (a horse) *roll*, lead him out to roll on the exercise-ground,

(ἀλῖσαι) ἐξαλῖσαι, ἐξήλικα,

for these are the only forms which occur (see Piers. ad Mœr. p. 51.), and they are evidently from ἀλίνδω, ἀλίσω. See all these forms detailed fully in Buttm. Lexil. p. 396., &c.

Κῠνέω, *I kiss*: (fut. κύσω*;) aor. 1. ἔκῠσα, like βυνέω, ἔβυσα†. The comp. προσκυνέω, *I salute, worship*, is regular; but in verse it has also the aor. infin. προσκύσαι, e. g. in Soph. Phil. 657. Aristoph. Equ. 156. See Κύω.

Κύπτω, *I bow, bend forward*, is regular: fut. κύψω; perf. κέκῡφα.

The length of the υ is not merely in the perfect (see for instance Epig. incert. 125.), but in the stem or root itself, as is plain from words of the same family, like κύφος; it must therefore remain long in syllables long by position, and consequently be written κῦψαι, like πέπρᾱγα, πρᾶξαι and the like.

Κῠρέω, *I meet with*, an Ionic verb, used by the Attics for τυγχάνω in poetry only‡, is regular. But the poets made use also of the older barytone form with υ long, κύρω, which however is not very frequent. Thus we find the imperf. ἐκύρουν, and in Soph. Œd. C. 1159. ἐκῦρον, whence 3. sing. κῦρε, Il. ψ, 821.§. Fut. κῡρήσω and κύρσω; aor. ἐκύρησα, infin. κῠρῆσαι, Hom. Epigr. 6, 6., part. κῠρήσας, Hes. ε, 757.; and (from κύρω) ἔκυρσα, infin. κύρσαι or κῦρσαι, Hes. ε, 693., part. κύρσας, Il γ, 23. The formation from κύρω is more usual in all the poets than that from κυρέω. The midd. κύρομαι is used as a deponent in Il. ω, 530.

* The fut. κυνήσομαι depends entirely on the corrupted passage of Eurip. Cycl 171.. the comp. προσκυνήσω (Plat. Rep. p. 469. a.) is no argument in favour of the simple form, for in the comp. we find προσεκύνησα as well as προσέκυσα, in the simple ἔκυσα only. In Aristoph. Thesm. 915 κύσω is conjunctive.

† The midd κυσάμεναι, *kissing* or *caressing each other*, is in Athen. 9. p. 394 d.

‡ Κεκυρηκότα in the Second Alcibiades 6. belongs to the orthography of Plato, which it would be so desirable to ascertain.

§ The pres. act. κύρω has been also restored to some passages by criticism on which we may depend: see Herm. ad Soph. Aj. 307. Matth. ad Eurip. Hipp. 741. with which I may reckon the passage in Aj. (314. Br.), where Hermann has left κυρεῖ, but the reading of the Scholiast, κύροι, is more agreeable. Nor would I reject his historical information that the Attics used in the optat. κύροι rather than κυροίη (or κυροῖ).

Κύω and κυέω, *I am pregnant.* The formation through all the moods and tenses is κυήσω, &c. To these we may add an inchoative form κυΐσκω, and κυΐσκομαι, *I conceive*

To fix the usage between κύω and κυέω is difficult, because the forms which occur most frequently vary only in the accent, as κύει κυεῖ, κύουσα κυοῦσα, &c. In Plato however (where in all other instances of this kind the accent fluctuates in the manuscripts, and in Theæt. p. 151. b. we find both κύοντα and κυοῦντα,) *all* the manuscripts have in the following passages, κυοῦμεν, Theæt. p. 210. κυοῦντι, Symp. 206. e. ἐκύει, 209. c.; which seems to me to settle the question as far as regards this writer*. In the authors of a later period the only decisive forms which I have found are in favour of κύω†; for instance, κύοντα, Aristot. H. A. 7, 5. τὰ κυόμενα παιδία, id. Probl. (see Stephens): τὸ δὲ κύεται, *is in the womb*, Poll. 5. 12. p. 73. ἔκυε, Æl. V. H. 5, 18.; while the accent in Aristotle and the later writers is pretty decisive in favour of this same form. Now as Homer has κυέουσαν, Il. ψ, 266. and ἐκύει, τ, 117. perhaps we may be safest in attributing κυεῖν to the older, and κύειν to the later writers. That is to say, the stem or root KY– with the meaning of *to have in itself*, is indisputably the old foundation of the verb, which in a very early period took the lengthened form of a present, κυέω, like στυγέω, κτυπέω, &c. To the simple stem belonged also, as in other verbs, an aor. 1. ἔκῦσα with a *causative* meaning, *to fructify*, ὄμβρος… ἔκῦσε γαῖαν, Æschyl. Fr. Danaid. ap. Athen. 13. p. 600.: and with this is connected the Epic. midd. κυσαμένη, ὑποκυσαμένη, literally "suffering herself to be impregnated", *conceiving*, which form, on account of its apparent affinity with κύσαι (see Κυνέω), is erroneously written with double σ. To express the same meaning was afterwards formed a present κυΐσκομαι (Aristot.); with which the active κυΐσκω as *inchoative* from κυέω was synonymous‡.

* In Hippocr. I find more than once κυέουσα (e. g. in De Superfetat.), which I think may be reconciled with κύει occurring frequently in the same writer.

† Macrob. De Verbo Græco cap. 5. acknowledges both forms; but they are not easy to be recognised there on account of an error of transcription in ι for υ.

‡ Schneider in the Supplement to his Lexicon [and Passow follows him,] takes κυΐσκω to be the causative of κυΐσκομαι, consequently in the sense of *to impregnate*; but all the passages in which the word occurs lead to the conclusion that the active voice is synonymous with the passive. See Poll. 4. extr. Schol. Theocr. 2, 66. Stephan. Thesaur. Hippocr. De Steril.

Λ.

Λαγχάνω, *I receive by lot or fate*: fut. λήξομαι; aor. 2. ἔλαχον, see note under Αἰσθάνομαι; perf. εἴληχα (like εἴληφα from λαμβάνω), or Λέλογχα*, which the Atticists rejected: see Lucian Solœc. 7.

The fut. λήξομαι appears to have been rare: I find it in Plat. Repub. 10. p. 617. e. For λήξομαι the Ionics have λάξομαι, Herodot. 7, 144. with α short according to the Ion. analogy of changing η into short α.

In this verb the aor. with reduplication, λελάχωσι, λελάχητε, Hom., is not the same as the common aor. 2. but has the causative sense *to make a person partaker of*, as in Il. η, 80.

Λάζυμαι and λάζομαι, *I lay hold on, take*, an Ionic (Hom., Hippocr.) and poetic (Eurip.) defective deponent, used only in pres. and imperfect.

ΛΑΚ–. See Λάσκω.

Λαμβάνω, *I take*: fut. λήψομαι; aor. 2. ἔλαβον†, imperat. λάβε and λαβέ (see Ἔρχομαι), infin. λαβεῖν, part. λαβών; perf. εἴληφα with ει prefixed instead of reduplication, like εἴληχα, εἴρηκα.—Midd. aor. 2. ἐλαβόμην, &c.

The regular augment of the perf. occurs however sometimes in the dramatic writers: in the perf. pass. for instance instead of εἴλημμαι, we find λέλημμαι, Æschyl. Agam. 885. Eurip. Ion. 1113. Aristoph. Eccl. 1090.

The Ionics have in the perf. act. λελάβηκα, Herodot. 3, 42. 4, 79. 8, 122. and (retaining the μ of the pres.) a fut. λάμψομαι; perf. pass. λέλαμμαι, λελάμφθαι; aor. 1. pass. ἐλάμφθην (instead of ἐλήφθην), Herodot. and a verbal adj. λαμπτέος‡. The Dorics likewise have λελάβηκα, and in pass. λέλαμμαι, λελάφθαι with α long for η. In the fut. they have also λαψοῦμαι and λαψεῦμαι. The Epics and Ionics have the aor. 2. λάβεσκον, Hes. Fr. 61. and Herodot.

* In order to bring this change of vowel into an acknowledged analogy, it is perfectly allowable to suppose a change of the stem to ΛΕΓΧ– on account of πένθος, παθεῖν, πέπονθα.

† Compare Βλαστάνω ἔβλαστον, Λαγχάνω ἔλαχον, and see note under Αἰσθάνομαι.

‡ The infin. ἀναλελάμφθαι stands in the text of Hippocr. Offic. Med. 7. The gloss ἀναλελάφθαι in Erotian and Hesychius refers without doubt to it; but although this latter way of writing the perf. corresponds with the Ionicism (λέλαμμαι, -άφθαι with short α for λέλημμαι, as in λέλασμαι, λάζομαι, &c.), yet the former way agrees too well with the other forms, and (to mention one,) with λαμπτέος, Herodot. 3, 127. extr., for us to hesitate a moment in retaining it.

Λάμπω and λάμπομαι, *I shine*: fut. λάμψω and λάμψομαι, whence in comp. ἐλλάμψεσθαι, Herodot. 1, 80. 8, 74.; perf. λέλαμπα, Eurip. Androm. 1025. Tro. 1295.

Λανθάνω, less frequently λήθω*, (Xenoph.), *I lie hid, am concealed*: fut. λήσω; aor. 2. ἔλᾰθον, infin. λαθεῖν; perf. λέληθα, synonymous with the present. Midd. λανθάνομαι, less frequently λήθομαι, *I forget*; fut. λήσομαι; aor. 2. ἐλαθόμην; perf. λέλησμαι.

Λήσομαι occurs in the sense of *to be concealed*, in Aristot. Analyt. Prior. 2, 21. Apollon. 3, 737. The passive λησόμενος (*obliviscendus*) in Soph. El. 1248. is a lyric licence. The aor. 1. midd. ἐλησάμην is frequently used by the later poets; see Mosch. 3, 63. Lobeck ad Phryn. p. 719. Theocritus has the aor. 1. pass. ἐλήσθην; he has also made a depon. pass. from the midd. in the infin. aor. λασθῆμεν for λησθῆναι, 2, 46. The Dorics have also λᾱσῶ for λήσω, and in the midd. λᾱσεῦμαι for λήσομαι.

For λέλησμαι the Epics have λέλασμαι with short Ionic α. Pindar Ol. 10, 4. uses the perf. act. ἐπιλέλᾱθα for the perf. pass. with the sense of *I have forgotten*.

The Epic λελαθέσθαι is the same as λαθέσθαι according to the analogy of κεκάμω, &c. (see Κάμνω), Il. μ, 235. compared with τ, 136.†. But the *active* form λελαθεῖν is distinguished in usage from λαθεῖν, in as much as it is the exact causative of λελαθέσθαι, in the sense of *to make to forget*, Il. ο, 60. β, 600. Hymn. Ven. 40. Theocritus, in order to express this meaning in the present tense, merely changed the accent, and retained the reduplication, using τὸν ἐκλελάθοντα as a fixed epithet for Hades‡.

This same sense of *causing to forget* is expressed by the aor. 1. (which does not occur elsewhere) in Od. υ, 85. ἐπέλησεν ἁπάντων: and undoubtedly that meaning belonged also to the pres. ἐπιλήθω, of which we find in Od. δ, 221. the neut. part. ἐπιλῆθον, if we follow some of

* [The old pres. λήθω, midd. λήθομαι, is seldom used by the Attics, frequently by Homer, who on the other hand never uses λανθάνω, though he has the imperf. of it three times and the imperf. midd. once.—Passow.]

† In Hes. θ, 471. ὅπως λελάθοιτο τεκοῦσα, for λάθοι, is an Epic inaccuracy.

‡ It is quite a mistake to compare this form with those presents of Theocritus formed from perfects (such as δεδοίκω, 15, 58. &c.), not only because there is no perf. λέλᾰθα, but because λέληθα has not this meaning. We may be sure that Theocr. had merely the Homeric ἐκλέλαθον (Il. β, 600.) in his mind, and from it formed this part. pres., forsaking the proper analogy, as was frequently done by the later poets who imitated Homer.

the grammarians in accenting it thus instead of ἐπίληθον as an adjective*. In another passage Homer has for this sense a particular present ληθάνω, ἐκληθάνει, Od. η, 221. Of rare occurrence is the form ἔκλασας in Alcæus ap. Hephæst. Gaisf. p. 16.

Λάσκω, I sound, speak: fut. λακήσω: fut. midd. λακήσομαι, Aristoph. Fr. 383.: aor. 1. ἐλάκησα; aor. 2. ἔλᾰκον, infin. λᾰκεῖν, Il.; aor. 2. midd. ἐλακόμην; perf. act. λέλᾱκα synonymous with the present.

That ΛΑΚ– is the stem of this verb is evident from the aor. 2.: the σ in the present is therefore inserted to strengthen it, as in ἴσκω from εἴκω, τιτύσκω from τεύχω. This however is only the Attic form; the Ionics use ληκέω and the Dorics λᾰκέω. But ἐλάκησα, λακήσομαι, which belong to the Attics, can according to analogy be formed only from the aor. 2. ἔλακον, λακεῖν, and have therefore the α short, as appears also from λακήσῃς, Aristoph. Pac. 382.†.

The Epics have the Ionic η in the perf. also, λέληκα, but shorten it in λελᾰκυῖα, like μεμακυῖα and others; see ἀραρυῖα under Ἀραρίσκω. They have likewise the aor. 2. midd. with redupl., λελάκοντο, Hymn. Merc. 145.

Λάω. See Λῶ.

ΛΕΓΧ–. See Λαγχάνω.

Λέγω, in the sense of *to say*, has no perf. act.‡, and in the pass. the perf. λέλεγμαι and aor. 1. ἐλέχθην. But in the compounds, which have the meaning of *to collect, to choose*, the perf. is (εἴλοχα) συνείλοχα, ἐξείλοχα, &c.; and this augment remains also most commonly in the passive, κα-

* Through Aristarchus this is now become the established reading. That this adj. occurs nowhere else would be no objection to it, but there is nothing in the passage to render its adoption necessary. The common meaning too of the simple λήθω may be considered as the causative of λήθομαι, *I forget*; in as much as *to forget* is "to lose the consideration of an object," but λήθειν τινά is "to withdraw oneself from the observation or consideration of another." This therefore has the causative idea from the object itself, but ἐπιλήθειν from a third object. It is however conceivable that usage adopted different forms to express that difference, and thus λελαθεῖν and the compound ἐπιλήθω, together with the particular form ληθάνω (see above), attached themselves to this particular meaning.

† We may well therefore be surprised at διαλᾰκήσασα in Nub. 410. of the same writer: unless perhaps we suppose that in this longer word the syllable was lengthened by a licence approaching nearly to the Epic.—[Passow has διαλᾰκέω from λακέω Dor. for ληκέω, and quotes as his authority the above passage.]

‡ The perf. act. was in less general use than the other tenses, and where really wanted its place was frequently supplied by the perf. pass., as εὖ λέλεκταί σοι for εὖ λέλεχας.

-τείλεγμαι*: with which is joined the aor. 2. pass. κατελέγην. The depon. διαλέγομαι, *I discourse*, has also διείλεγμαι; but in the aor. 1, διελέχθην, for which Aristotle has διελέγην, Top. 7, 4, 2. 8, 3, 7.

In the old poetry the aorists of this family of verbs have another and a very different meaning: ἔλεξα, *I laid* (any one) *down to sleep*, ἐλεξάμην, *I lay down to sleep* (myself); and in a similar sense to this aor. midd. is used also the syncopated aor. ἐλέγμην, ἔλεκτο, &c., with the imperat. λέξο or λέξεο. The pres. and imperf. never occur with this meaning. On λέξαι, λέξασθαι, *to lay, to lie*, see Buttm. Lexil. p. 403.

Beside the above, the syncop. aor. has also some of the meanings belonging to the ideas *to reckon, to collect together*, sometimes as a middle, in the sense of *to choose oneself, offer oneself as a companion to others*, πέμπτος ἐλέγμην, Od. ι, 335. sometimes quite as a depon. λέκτο δ' ἀριθμόν, *he counted the number*, δ, 451.

Λείπω, *I leave*, fut. λείψω, has in the active voice in general use the aor. 2. ἔλῐπον, infin. λῐπεῖν, and the perf. 2. λέλοιπα.—MIDD.

The aor. 2. midd. ἐλιπόμην, with a kind of passive meaning, *I was left, I remained behind*, is very common in the Epic poets, e. g. Od. δ, 710. ν, 286. and is found also in the later prose of Lucian; see Schæf. ad Greg. p. 463.

In the pure times of the language the aor. 1. ἔλειψα belonged solely to λείβω; it is occasionally however found as the aor. of λείπω in the older writers, as in Aristoph. ap. Antiatt. Bekk. p. 106, Pythag. Aur. Carm. 70., but in the later writers it is more common; see Schæf. Gnom. Græc. p. 148. Lobeck ad Phryn. p. 713. For the pluperf. ἐλειπτο see γεύμεθα under Γεύω. In the formation of the aor. 1. pass. the ευ of the present was shortened to υ, as τεύχω ἐτύχθην, and sometimes in the dialects a change took place of ει to ι, as ἔλιφθεν, Callim. Cer. 94. See Ernesti on this passage, and Brunck on Apollon. Rhod. 1, 1325.

Λείχω is regular. For λελειχμότες see Λιχμᾶσθαι.

Λέπω, *I shell, peel*, &c. This verb, like βλέπω, λέγω, πλέκω, φλέγω, ψέγω, does not change the radical ε in forming the aor. 2. pass., as, ἐφλέγην, βλεπείς, &c.

* There is also the regular augment with this meaning; e. g. ξυλλελεγμένος, Aristoph. Eccl. 58. and ἐπιλελεγμένος from ἐπιλέγω is very common; yet in Isocr. Paneg. p. 71. b. Bekker has adopted from the best manuscript ἐπειλεγμένους.

Λεύσσω*, *I see.* The fut. λεύσω and aor. 1. ἔλευσα are certainly not old forms, if indeed they are Greek, Reisig Comm. Critt. de Soph. Œd. C. 120. We find indeed ἔλευσας in Æschyl. Pers. 707., but the acknowledged reading is now the imperf. ἔλευσσες. Again in Soph. Œd. C. 1197. λεύσῃς is a very probable emendation for λύσῃς, but Tyrwhitt's reading λεύσσῃς is as good or better.

Λεύω, *I stone.* The pass. takes σ.

ΛΗΒ–. See Λαμβάνω.

Λήθω. See Λανθάνω.

Ληκέω. See Λάσκω.

ΛΗΧ–. See Λαγχάνω.

Λιάζω, *I bend* (anything). Pass. *I bend myself, turn aside*: see Buttm. Lexil. p. 404. But the perf. λελίημαι see in Λιλαίομαι.

Λίγξε βιός, *the bow twanged*, Il. δ, 125. For this form a pres. λίζω has been supposed, according to the analogy of πλάζω, κλάζω, σαλπίζω; but it nowhere occurs†.

Λιλαίομαι, *I desire, long for*; formed from λάω (see Λῶ) by reduplication. It is used only in pres. and imperfect. But from λιλάω or λιλέω (λιλεῖ· φθονεῖ, ἐπιθυμεῖ, Hesych.) comes the perf. λελίημαι, *I strive, hasten*, for λελίλημαι: see Buttm. Lexil. p. 406.

Λίσσομαι, *I beg*, less frequently λίτομαι: fut. λίσομαι; aor. 1. ἐλισάμην; aor. 2. ἐλιτόμην. Homer has the Ep. imperf. λισσέσκετο; of the aor. 1. the Ep. 1. pers. ἐλλισάμην and the Ep. imperat. λίσαι; and of the aor. 2. the infin. λιτέσθαι and optat. λιτοίμην. This is one of the few verbs whose pure theme (from which comes the aor. 2.) is used also as a present: e. g. λίτομαι, Hom. Hymn. 15. λιτόμεσθα, Aristoph. Thesm. 313.

Λιχμάομαι, *I protrude the tongue.* We mention this verb for the sake of observing that the Hesiodic participle λελειχμότες bears the same relation to it as μέμυκα does to μυκᾶσθαι; for the diphthong of the radical λείχω entering into the participle seems to be founded on the natural inclination of the perfect for a long vowel. This participial form and two others very similar,

πεφυζότες, Hom.,

μεμυζότε, Antim. ap. Eust. ad Od. ν, 401. p. 523, 46. Basil.,

λελειχμότες, Hes. θ, 826.,

* The difficulty of ascertaining whether the Greeks ever used a fut. λεύσω is greatly increased by our finding the present very commonly written in the manuscripts with a single σ.

† [Passow says that λίζω occurs only in the later authors, and in the sense of *to give a superficial wound, graze, scratch*, consequently akin to the Homeric λίγδην. He forms λίγξε from λίγγω, and connects it with λίγα, λιγύς.]

appear to be remains of the earlier periods of the language, when analogies formed subsequently were not yet in existence. In virtue of their characteristic letters (ζ and χμ) they are not analogous to the perf. 1. or perf. 2. (perf. midd.): and except in these participles the perfects themselves never occur: nor in the sentence does their connection with the context resemble that of a verb, but rather of an adjective descriptive of the situation or continuous motion of an object. I am therefore inclined to consider them as old verbal adjectives formed something like participles perfect, instances of which we find in German and other languages*. For a more particular account of this verb see Buttm. Lexil. p. 546. and note.

Λούω, *I wash*: fut. λούσω. The Attic and even the Ionic dialect shorten, in the imperf. of the active and in the pres. and imperf. of the passive voice, all the forms which have ε and ο in the termination, as in the imperf. ἔλου for ἔλουε, and ἐλοῦμεν for ἐλούομεν; in the pass. λοῦμαι for λούομαι, λοῦται for λούεται, λοῦσθαι for λούεσθαι, &c. See Lobeck ad Phryn. p. 189.

Homer has a 3. sing. aor. 2. λόε, Od. κ, 361.; and in Hymn. Ap. 120. is a 3. plur. λόον†: from λοέω he has an imperf. ἐλόευν, and an infin. aor. act. λοέσσαι, part. λοέσσας, an aor. midd. λοέσσατο, infin. λοέσσασθαι, part. λοεσσάμενος, and a fut. midd. λοέσσομαι, infin. λοέσσεσθαι; in addition to which he uses all the common as well as the abridged forms. The most natural way therefore of treating this verb is to suppose that from the simple stem λόω came the lengthened one λοέω (compare Κύω, κυέω), and from this by contraction the common λούω, ἔλουσα. Ἐλούεον, Hymn. Cer. 290. is a form of λούω again produced or resolved.

With regard to those *abridged* forms, the accentuation of ἐλοῦμεν, Aristoph. Plut. 657. of ἐλοῦτο, Herodot. 3, 125. and of ἐλοῦντο, Xen. Cyr. 4, 5. 4. lead us to suppose that they are contracted from λόω, ἐλόομεν, &c., which is confirmed by the infin. λοῦν as quoted from Hippocr. in Galeni Gloss.; although in the works of Hippocr. it is always written λούειν. Accordingly we do not with some of the older grammarians reckon λοῦμαι among the examples of the syncope like οἶμαι, but sup-

* The Germans say "the heavens are (gestirnt) *starred*," but they cannot say "God (stirnte) *starred* the heavens."—[So our word *frosted* is formed like a participle, without however the existence of a verb *to frost*.—Ed.]

† [In Hes. ε. 751. Schneider is correct in having accented it λοέσθαι as the infin. aor. midd.: and instead of λόει (Scol. 21, 4. Br.) the true accentuation is λοεῖ.—Passow]

pose the verb in common use to be a mixture of the contractions of the two old forms, λόω and λοέω*.

This statement is fully confirmed by a further piece of information from Bekker's labours on Aristophanes. In Nub. 838. the old reading is Ὥσπερ τεθνεῶτος καταλούει μου τὸν βίον, where the verb is the 2. sing. midd., "thou squanderest my property in bathing"; see the Scholia. Brunck assisted the metre by the reading of a Paris manuscript, μου καταλούει, by which truth as well as error was glossed over. We know now that the former reading is in all the other manuscripts, particularly in the two best (*Ravennas* and *Venetus*); and by this Bekker discovered a sure trace of the true reading, καταλόει. That is to say, in the indic. pass., the shorter form was the only current one in the old Attic dialect; hence in the 2. sing. they did not use λούει, which is the same as the 3. sing. indic. act., but preferred the shorter form; not however in the inharmonious contraction λοῖ, but without the contraction λόει†.

The 2. and 3. sing. of the pres. act. also might certainly have been λόεις, λόει; but these persons were undoubtedly occupied by λούω, which had already established itself in all the dialects in the 1. sing., as it

* The Scholiast on Aristoph. Plut. 657. has both opinions; Ἐλοῦμεν· ἀπὸ τοῦ λόω (the corrupted λύω of the first editions has been erroneously altered to λούω), ἢ ἀπὸ τοῦ ἐλούομεν κατὰ συγκοπήν. But Plutarch (De Poesi Hom.) quotes λοῦται and οἶμαι as instances of the Attic usage τοῦ ἐξαιρεῖν τὰ βραχέα.

† If those forms were abridged by syncope, then, according to general analogy, we should find between λοῦμαι—λοῦται and between ἐλούμην—ἐλοῦτο the second persons λοῦσαι and ἔλουσο, nor would the imperat. λοῦσο be defective. But these nowhere occur either in authors or grammarians: for λοῦσαι, which stands in some editions of Phrynichus, (see Ed. Pauw. p. 80.) is a mere corruption of λοῦται. Lobeck has extracted the whole article from the first edition, according to which the forms disapproved of by Phrynichus (and they are the common ones) are the following—ἐλουόμην, ἐλούου, ἐλούετο, λούομαι, λούεται, ἐλουόμεθα, ἐλούοντο, λούεσθαι; to which are opposed as pure Attic λοῦσθαι καὶ λοῦμαι, λοῦται, ἐλούμην, ἐλοῦτο, ἐλούμεθα, ἐλοῦντο. Here λούει is omitted in the first series between λούομαι and λούεται, and is therefore silently approved; of: while no notice is taken of λόει (which we have brought forward above), probably because it was strange to the grammarians, who rejected it wherever it occurred in the way that it does in the before-mentioned passage of Aristophanes. On the other hand ἐλούου is expressly objected to; consequently the form recommended in its stead, which is the very one we are in search of, whether it be ἔλουσο or ἐλοῦ (from ἐλόου), has been omitted by mistake. Now the gloss of Hesychius, Λοῦ, λοῦσαι, will assist us in discovering it. Here λοῦ cannot be the imperat. act., because it is impossible that in a verb whose active and middle voice are so essentially different, it could be explained by the imperat. of the aor. middle. It is therefore the imperative of the pres. midd. (contracted from λόου) which the grammarians did not hesitate to explain by the imperat. aor., because in the imperative the difference of these tenses is but trifling, and in other instances very commonly overlooked by the grammarians. This analogy shows us also with certainty the 2. sing. imperf. ἐλοῦ, which by a very conceivable oversight was omitted in Phrynichus before ἐλοῦτο. The abridged form in the passive voice is therefore, when completed, λοῦμαι, λόει, λοῦται &c., ἐλούμην, ἐλοῦ, ἐλοῦτο &c., infin. λοῦσθαι, imperat. λοῦ.

did also in the optat. λούοιμι, -οίμην, in the conj. λούω, -ῃς, &c., in the part. λούων, and probably also in the imperat. act. λοῦε. See note in the preceding page.

Λύω, *I loose*: fut. λύσω(ῡ); aor. 1. ἔλῡσα; perf. λέλῠκα; perf. pass. λέλῠμαι; pluperf. ἐλελύμην; aor. 1. pass. ἐλύθην (ῠ).

This verb together with δύω and θύω shortens the υ in the perf. act. and in the perf. and aor. pass.: see Chœroboscus p. 1286. Draco pp. 45, 26. 87, 25. Compare also Δύω and Θύω.

In Od. σ, 238. Homer has the 3. sing. optat. perf. pass. λέλῦτο for λελύοιτο; where the υ is lengthened by its absorbing the ι of the optative; and the accent on the antepenult., though not according to the directions of the Grammarians, is yet agreeable to analogy, and corresponds with δαίνυτο in Hom. and πήγνυτο in Plato, as they are found accented in the great majority of the manuscripts. Again from an Epic syncop. aor. pass. ἐλύμην (corresponding with the regular aor 2. midd.), Homer has a 1. and 3. sing. λύμην, λύτο, and 3. plur. λύντο. An imperat. syncop. aor. act. λῦθι (for λῦσον) in Pind. ap. Etym. M. v. διθύραμβος may perhaps have been formed merely on account of the play on etymology there mentioned; for which it was quite sufficient that the form, though not in use, should be strictly analogical.

Λῶ, *I wish, desire*, a Doric defective verb, the only remains of an old theme ΛΑΩ, used only in the three persons of the sing. λῶ, λῇς, λῇ, 3. plur. λῶντι, optat. λέωμι, Hesych. infin. λῆν; compare Markl. Eurip. Suppl. 221.

M.

Μαίνομαι, *I am mad*, has a fut. midd. and an aor. 2. pass. ἐμάνην, infin. μᾰνῆναι, part. μᾰνείς. The perf. μέμηνα has the meaning of the present. But the aor. 1. act. ἔμηνα, Aristoph. Thesm. 561. has the causative meaning *to make mad*, in which tense, and indeed in the present also, the compound ἐκμαίνω is more usual.

The fut. 2. pass. μᾰνήσομαι is not Attic*; see Mœr. and Thom. Mag. the perf. pass. μεμάνημαι is used in Theocrit. 10, 31. in the same sense as the pres. μαίνομαι.

* [Passow says that the Attics use μανήσομαι as a kind of exclamation, as we say "I shall go mad." He mentions also a fut. 2. μᾰνοῦμαι.]

Μαίομαι. See ΜΑΩ.

ΜΑΚ–. See Μηκάομαι.

Μαλκιῆν is an Attic infin. mentioned by Phrynichus (in Lex. Seg. p. 51.), Photius and Hesych. from μαλκιάω, *I am frost-bitten.* Perhaps the suspected form μαλκιεῖν in Æl. N. A. 9, 4. should be μαλκιῆν. See Lobeck ad Phryn. p. 82.

Μανθάνω, *I learn*: aor. 2. ἔμᾰθον; fut. μαθήσομαι; perf. μεμάθηκα. See notes under Λαμβάνω and Αἰσθάνομαι; also Ἀκαχίζω. The aor. pass. is wanting.

The Dor. fut. 2. μᾰθεῦμαι for μαθοῦμαι, Theocr. 2, 60. (like μαχοῦμαι, πιοῦμαι, &c.) supposes a root ΜΗΘΩ.

Μαπέειν. See Μάρπτω.

Μάρνᾰμαι, *I contend, fight*; used only in pres. and imperf. which follow ἵσταμαι or δύναμαι; thus infin. μάρνασθαι, part. μαρνάμενος, but the optat. is μαρνοίμην, Od. λ, 512. imperf. ἐμαρνάμην. [But ἐμαρνάσθην, Il. η, 301. is an aor.—Passow.]

Μάρπτω, *I seize*: fut. μάρψω; aor. 1. ἔμαρψα; part. perf. μεμαρπώς, Hes. ε, 206. To these must be added the Ep. aor. 2. with redupl. (ἔμαρπον) μέμαρπον, Hes. α, 245. or with ρ dropped (ἔμᾰπον), infin. μᾰπέειν, Hes. α, 231. 304. optat. with redupl. μεμάποιεν, Hes. α, 252.

Μαρτυρέω (υ short), *I bear witness* (for or against a person or of a thing). Μαρτύρομαι (υ long) depon. midd. *I call as a witness.*

In this case the active μαρτύρω, which is not in use, must be considered as the causative to μαρτυρέω, *I cause witness to be borne*; and μαρτύρομαι the midd. of it, *I cause witness to be borne for myself, call to witness.*

Μάσσω, Att. μάττω, *I knead*: fut. μάξω; perf. μέμᾰχα, Aristoph. Equ. 55; perf. pass. μέμαγμαι, ib. 57. Also aor. 2. pass.

See also in note to Μαίομαι, p. 172. another μάσσω which has been erroneously supposed to exist.

Μάχομαι, *I fight*: fut. μαχέσομαι and more generally μαχοῦμαι (compare καθεδοῦμαι under Ἵζω); aor. 1. ἐμαχεσάμην; perf. μεμάχημαι. Verbal adj. μαχετέος and μαχητέος.

The perf. μεμάχημαι is in Isocr. Archid. p. 127. b. Another form of the perf. μεμάχεσμαι, found in good manuscripts in Xenoph. Cyr. 7, 1,

14. would be recommended by analogy, but the context makes the common reading preferable, τῶν πρόσθεν ξυμμαχεσαμένων. The form μαχετέον in Plato Sophist. p. 249. c. Rep. 2. p. 380. b. is supported by the authority of good manuscripts.

When in Homer the metre requires a long syllable the reading fluctuates between εσσ and ησ, yet so that the text (at least as it is handed down to us) and a great majority of the manuscripts have in the fut. μαχήσομαι and in the aor. μαχέσσατο*.

The Ionics had also in the pres. μαχέομαι (μαχέοιτο, Il. α, 272. συμμαχέεται, Herodot. 7, 239.), which form therefore as to time is ambiguous, unless perhaps the Ionic prose used as a fut. μαχέσομαι only: see Fisch. 3. p. 131. Schweigh. Lex. Herodot., and compare Il. β, 366. not. Heyn. Homer has, on account of so many short syllables following each other, lengthened each of the vowels in the pres. part. μαχειόμενος and μαχεούμενος. Compare Ῥεούμενος.

MA–. To this stem or root belong three poetical verbs†:

1. μέμαα, *I strive after, am eager, desire*; a perf. with the force of a pres., of which however we find in use only the 3. plur. μεμάασι, and the syncopated 1. plur. μέμἄμεν, 2. plur. μέμἄτε, 2. dual μέμἄτον, the 3. sing. imperat. μεμάτω, 3. plur. pluperf. μέμἄσαν, and the part. μεμαώς of which the fem. is μεμἄυῖα, and the gen. μεμἄῶτος or μεμἄότος, Il. β, 818. Theocr. 25, 105. compare βεβαώς and γεγαώς.—The form μέμαεν in Theocr. 25, 64. is a false reading‡. That all these forms are connected immediately with μέμονα, will be shown under Μένω.

* See Heyne's critical notes on Il. α, 153. β, 801. γ, 137, 254. and on α, 304. β, 377. γ, 393. ο, 633. It would be a very hazardous step therefore to follow Aristarchus and Wolf in introducing the reading with the η in all the passages. Besides, if we wish to observe analogy, we should rather make the εσσ the universal reading, as some of the older critics have proposed: see Heyne on Il. α, 298. Compare the verb Αἴδομαι (for although αἰδέομαι became the common form in a later period, it is still to be looked upon like μαχέομαι), of which the fut. αἰδέσσομαι is the only defensible form in Il. χ, 419. while in Od. ξ, 388. it is opposed by αἰδήσομαι: on this passage see Porson. in Postscripto.

† The three verbs which we have here joined together on account of their having the same letters in the stem, are certainly so similar to each other in meaning also, that no one would take it on himself to separate them. The identity of the first verb with μέμονα, μένος, will be shown under Μένω; but then it does not unite so immediately with μαίεσθαι, ἐπιμάσασθαι, μάστιξ, (which evidently come from the physical idea of *feeling*,) as grammatical and exegetic etymology require. We therefore place together, in pursuance of our present object, three verbs only, leaving to the philosophical philologist to extend the inquiry.

‡ If μέμαεν be a true reading, it is one example among many of the later poets having misunderstood the older ones and attributed to them forms which they never used. At all events it cannot be a perf., but must be an imperf. or aor., like δέδαε which is an aor. with reduplication. Brunck has with some probability preferred μέμονε, but the context requires the imperf. (pluperf.) consequently μεμόνει δέ μιν αἰὲν ἐρέσθαι.

2. μῶμαι, *I desire, seek after*: part. μώμενος (Soph. Œd. C. 836.) contracted from μάομαι; but the ω generally prevails, as in the infin. μῶσθαι, Theogn. 769. the imperat. μώεο, Epicharm. ap. Xen. Mem. 2, 1, 20. formed as from μώομαι. Compare μνώεο from μνάομαι μνῶμαι under Μιμνήσκω, and Ζάω: see also Toup. ad Suid. v. ὠχρός.

3. μαίομαι, *I feel, touch; seek for, desire.* To this belong the fut. μάσομαι, aor. ἐμασάμην, with α short; but occurring principally in the compounds, as infin. aor. ἐπιμάσασθαι, Od. λ, 591. fut. ἐπιμάσσεται, Il. δ, 190. aor. ἐσεμάσσατο, Il. ρ, 564. For that the above present and this aor. answer exactly to each other, we may see by such passages as Od. ι, 441. and 446., confirmed by the analogy of δαίω δάσασθαι, ναίω νάσασθαι*.—Verb. adj. μαστός.

Μεθύω, *I am drunken*, used only in pres. and imperf., takes its other tenses from the pass., as, ἐμεθύσθην, &c.: for the other tenses of the active, as ἐμέθυσα, &c., belong to μεθύσκω, *I make drunken*†.

Μείρομαι, *I share, partake, obtain.* The older poets have (beside this present, Il. ι, 616. Theogn. 1228.) a 3. sing. ἔμμορε. This is plainly an aorist in Il. α, 278. οὔποθ' ὁμοίης ἔμμορε τιμῆς βασιλεύς, "never yet has a king received such honour." The later Epics use it in the same way, e. g. Apollon, 3, 4. ἔμμορες. And we might perhaps consider it as an aor. in all the Epic passages, even when by the context it has evidently the force of a present, "he has obtained, he obtained, i. e., he has." In other cases, however, it will be more natural to take it as a perf. (ἔμμορα for μέμορα), e. g. in Od. ε, 335. Νῦν δ' ἁλὸς ἐν πελάγεσσι θεῶν ἒξ ἔμμορε τιμῆς, "now is she a partaker of divine honours." And this is confirmed by the Doric Ἐμμόραντι· τετεύχασι, Hesych.‡.

This perf. 2. as well as the aor. 2. belong therefore, according to the analogy given in the note below§, to the immediate meaning, with which the midd. μείρομαι was used in the present. The act. μείρω (properly *to divide*, whence μέρος) had therefore the causative sense *to give out in*

* We find in the lexicons for μάσασθαι a present μάσσω, fut. μάσω; but there are no grounds for such a present, nor does any such exist. Μάσσω, μάξω, *I knead*, although perhaps akin to it, is a different verb.

† In the well-known Alcaic fragment, instead of Νῦν χρὴ μεθύσκειν we must read μεθύσθην, Æolic infin. for μεθυσθῆναι.

‡ [Thus Passow has μείρομαι; aor. ἔμμορον, perf. ἔμμορα.]

§ In many primitive verbs the fut. and aor. 1. act. give the preference to the *causative* meaning. the aor. 2. and perf. act, particularly the perf. 2., (perf. midd.) prefer the *immediate* and indeed principally the *intransitive*.

shares, to allot, whence comes the perf. pass., which occurs only in the third person:

εἵμαρμαι, 3. pers. εἵμαρται* (with the syllable ει instead of the reduplication like εἴληφα, εἴρηκα, &c.), *it is allotted by fate, it is fated*: part. εἱμαρμένος: ἡ εἱμαρμένη (scil. μοῖρα) *that which is allotted to any one; his fate, destiny.* Pluperf. εἵμαρτο. Compare πέπρωμαι in Πορεῖν.

In Apollonius 1, 646. 973. we find in a similar sense μεμόρηται, and in 3, 1130. μεμορμένος: the latter with the change of vowel to ο retained in the perf. pass. as in ἤορτο, ἄωρτο, the former according to the analogy of φέρω φορέω (see under Δέμω), or of δεδοκημένος and ἐκτόνηκα (see Κτείνω).

Μέλλω, *I am about to do a thing, intend to do it*: fut. μελλήσω; aor. 1. ἐμέλλησα, *I have delayed doing it.* The Attics add the temporal augment to the syllabic one of the imperfect, making ἤμελλον, like ἠδυνάμην, ἠβουλόμην: see Βούλομαι.

Μέλπω, midd. μέλπομαι, *I sing, play.* It has no perfect.

Μέλω, *I am an object of care or concern, I vex, go to the heart*, is used in the active voice principally in the third person; pres. μέλει, μέλουσι; impert. ἔμελε; fut. μελήσει; infin. pres. μέλειν, fut. μελήσειν, &c., *it is an object of care*, &c. Pass. μέλομαι, *I am careful of, anxious about*, more generally ἐπιμέλομαι, -ήσομαι, &c.

The personal use of the active is in its nature rare, according to which it means, for instance, *to be the object of care*, e. g. ἵνα νερτέροισι μέλω, Eurip. Andr. 851. Now as this is most commonly said of impersonal objects, the third persons are naturally the most familiar; and thus arose the impersonal usage. The compound μεταμέλει, *it repents*,

* The aspirate on this word may be compared with that on ἕστηκα, and on the presents ἵστημι and ἵπταμαι, whence we may conclude that it was intended as a substitute for the reduplication; but this principle, like many others, was observed only partially. We find however a trace of its having extended in the dialects further than might at first appear, by a frequently recurring form in the Milesian Inscription in Chishull, p. 67. ἀφέσταλκα, which supposes the existence of ἕσταλκα. On the other hand the instances of εἱμαρμένος with the lenis, which Schæfer (Melet. p. 22. and ad Soph. Œd. T. 1082.) has quoted from the later writers, are to be considered as mere sophistry of the later grammarians.

admits indeed of no other. The passive μέλομαι bears exactly the same relation to the imperf. μέλει, as δέομαι does to δεῖ.

The forms of the compound ἐπιμελήσομαι, &c., are generally placed with ἐπιμελεῖσθαι, which is an exactly synonymous sister-form of ἐπιμέλεσθαι; but this latter is declared by the Atticists (see Moer. and Thom. Mag.) to be less pure than the former. Both are, however, of such frequent occurrence in our editions, that no one can decide which was the original reading of any separate passage. Still there is no doubt of ἐπιμέλεσθαι being the older form, to which the inflexion of ἐπιμελήσομαι originally belonged.

The perf. μεμέληκέ μοι has generally the meaning of, *I have been considering about a thing, it has been an object of my care and thought*, e. g. Xen. Mem. 3, 6, 10. But the Epic language has a perf. 2. μέμηλε, Dor. μέμαλε, which has the same meaning as the present, *it lies at my heart, is a source of care and anxiety to me*: to which we must add the pluperf. μεμήλει for ἐμεμήλει with the force of an imperf., Il. β, 614. The same perf. has, however, sometimes the personal meaning of the pass. μέλομαι; in the first place as a real perfect, ταῦτα μέμηλας, *these things hast thou thought carefully about, invented*, Hymn. Merc. 437. and next equally as much like a present, μεμηλὼς τινός, *thinking carefully, anxiously about anything, intent upon it*, Il. ε, 708. ν, 297.

The pass. μέλομαι is also used poetically for μέλω, as μελέσθω σοι, Od. κ, 505. ᾧ μελόμεσθα, *cui curæ sumus*, Eurip. Hipp. 60. in which sense we find also the perf. as a pres. and consequently the pluperf. as imperf., σοὶ μεμέλητο, *tibi curæ erat*, Theocr. 17, 46. in which usage it has undergone also an Epic abridgement, as perf. μέμβλεται, pluperf. μέμβλετο, Il. τ, 343. φ, 516. Hes. θ, 61.* like μεσημβρία from ἡμέρα. —[The aor. 1. pass. μεληθῆναι is sometimes used actively, *to have taken care of*, τάφου, Soph. Aj. 1184. sometimes passively, *to be taken care of*, Epig. Ad. 112, 3.—Passow.]

Μέμφομαι, *I blame*: fut. μέμψομαι. Depon. midd. without a perfect.

[This verb occurs first in Hes. ε, 188. and Theogn. 795. 871.; but more frequently in Pindar and Herodotus: it is found also in the Attics, as Thucyd. 7, 77. Plato and Isocrates.—Passow.] The Ionics and Tragedians use in a similar deponent sense the aor. 1. pass. ἐμέμφθην also.

* As no other forms occur than the 3. sing. μέμβλεται, μέμβλετο, a first person μέμβλομαι has been supposed to exist as the present from which these might be formed. But it is far more correct to compare this with the similar perfects μέμνεο for μέμνησο, and ἀρήρεμαι.

Μένω, *I remain*: Epic fut. μενέω; Attic contracted μενῶ; aor. 1. ἔμεινα; perf. μεμένηκα*. Verbal adj. μενετέος, Plato Rep. 1. p. 328. b.

The Ionic and poet. perfect *μέμονα, I feel a strong desire, I am determined, I intend,* (Herodot. 6, 84. Il. ε, 482. ω, 657. &c.) belongs to a stem or family differing in meaning from the above μένω, as we see from its derivative τὸ μένος, from which again is derived another Epic verb, μενεαίνω, μενέηνα, having in its most common acceptation the same sense as μέμονα, e. g. Il. ν, 628. ο, 565. Od. δ, 282. At the same time the analogy of γέγονα γεγάασιν &c. leads to one evident remark, that the relation between those two perfects is the same as between μέμονα and μεμάασιν &c., which latter correspond also in meaning. All this must prevent us from placing μέμονα, which could not be done without violence, among the forms of μένειν, *to remain*; although Euripides, who uses μέμονε quite in the old sense at Iph. T. 656. δίδυμα μέμονε φρήν, has the same word in another passage (Iph. A. 1495.) for μένει; this latter is however merely an instance of Lyric caprice, without proving anything as to the language.

ΜΕΤΙΩ, or μετίημι, Ion. for μεθίημι; of which we find among others the 3. pres. μετίει, Herodot. 6, 37. 59.; the 3. sing. imperf. midd. μετίετο (or ἐμετίετο) for μεθίετο, Herodot. 1, 12.; the infin. fut. midd. μετήσεσθαι for μεθήσεσθαι, Herodot.; and μεμετιμένος part. perf. pass. for μεθειμένος, Herodot. According to the analogy of τίθημι the 3. sing. pres. should be accented μετιεῖ, and μετίει should be the imperf.; see Heyne on Il. ζ, 523, where Wolf now reads in his last edition μεθιεῖς. Compare the simple Ἵημι.

Μηκάομαι, *I bleat, cry out*: probably a depon. midd. like μυκάομαι.

This verb has some simpler Epic forms; e. g. μέμηκα with the force of a pres., whence part. μεμηκώς, Il. κ, 362. and fem. with the short Ion. α, μεμᾰκυῖα, Il. δ, 435. And as this perf. had the sense of a present, an imperf. ἐμέμηκον (Od. ι, 439.) was formed from it, like πέφυκα ἐπέφυκον, Hes. α, 76. θ, 673. To this we must add the aor. ἔμακον, of which however only the part. μακών remains, Il. π, 469. compare Od. κ, 163. Thus this verb is strictly analogous to the Epic forms of μυκάομαι.

* The verbs in μω (νέμω, δέμω, βρέμω, τρέμω) cannot follow the analogy of verbs which have λ, μ, ν, ρ as their characteristic, further than the fut. and aor.; hence in their other tenses they are sometimes defective, and sometimes form them as from a verb in -έω, in which latter case μένω may be joined with them, as μεμένηκα, νενέμηκα, δέδμηκα &c.

Μιαίνω, *I stain, defile*: fut. μιανῶ; aor. 1. ἐμίηνα, Att. also ἐμίᾱνα, Lobeck ad Phryn. p. 24.; aor. 1. pass. ἐμιάνθην; perf. pass. μεμίασμαι.

At Il. δ, 146. μιάνθην αἵματι μηροί, the verb is either the 3. dual or plural. The old grammarians explained it to be for μιανθήτην, but of such an abbreviation no other instance is to be found; the moderns have considered it to be for ἐμιάνθησαν, but the η is so unusual in the abridged 3 plur., that no example of it can be adduced even in the dialects*; compare ἔτυφθεν, ἔτυπεν for -ησαν, or ἔβᾰν, ἔδρᾰν, ἔδῠν &c. I consider therefore μιάνθην to be the dual of a syncop. aor. pass.: (3. sing. ἐμίαν-το) 3. dual (ἐμιάν-σθην) ἐμιάνθην, like δέχθαι, ὄρθαι, in both of which the σ is dropped before the θ.

Μίγνυμι, or μίσγω†, *I mix*: fut. μίξω, &c. Pass. aor. 1. ἐμίχθην; aor. 2. ἐμίγην; perf. μέμιγμαι, part. μεμιγμένος, Plat. Legg. 12. p. 951. d.

In the old-Attic inscriptions the derivatives of this verb are very often written with ει, as ξύμμεικτα, which shows that the ι (except in the aor. 2. pass.) is long. We must therefore write μῖξαι.

Μιμνήσκω, *I remind*, has from ΜΝΑΩ a fut. μνήσω and aor. 1. ἔμνησα, &c., Il. α, 407. Pass. μιμνήσκομαι, *I remember*, also *I mention*; aor. 1. ἐμνήσθην; fut. μνησθήσομαι; verbal adj. μνηστός. The perf. pass. μέμνημαι has the force of a present, *I remember*, whence imper. μέμνησο, optat. μεμνῄμην, Il. ω, 745. Att. μεμνοίμην and μεμνῴμην, Herm. Soph. Œd. T. 49. (whence μεμνῷτο, Xen. Cyr. 1, 6, 3. contracted from the Ion. μεμνεῴμην, μεμνέῳτο, Il. ψ, 361.), conj. μέμνωμαι, -η, -ηται, &c.‡. To this perf. belong the pluperf. ἐμεμνήμην (whence Ion. 3. plur. ἐμεμνέατο for ἐμέμνηντο, Herodot. 2, 104.), and the fut. 3. (paullo-post fut.) μεμνήσομαι, Herod. 8, 62.

* I must not conceal that in a Cretan inscription in Chishull, p. 111. διελεγην occurs as a plural; but as the other Cretan inscriptions in the same collection have διελεγεν, it naturally throws great suspicion on the former, which however, whether true or not, would be of very little authority in deciding on a Homeric form.

† [Μίσγω is used by Hom. and the Attics, and by Herodot. exclusively, particularly in the pass. voice. The common pres. μίγνυμι is never found in Hom. either act. or pass.: in the fut. he has the midd. μίξομαι, and the pass. μιγήσομαι, while Hes. has μεμίξομαι.—Passow.]

‡ See Κτάομαι with notes.

Ionic abbreviations are (μέμνεαι) μέμνῃ 2. sing. indicat. for μέμνησαι, Hom., and μέμνεο imperat. for μέμνησο, Herodot. 5, 105: compare μέμβλεται under Μέλω.

The radical form μνάομαι, μνῶμαι is in the above sense solely Ionic, in which dialect the α is changed into ε, consequently we have 3. sing. pres. μνέεται (like χρέεται from χράομαι), and by the similar Ionic change of αο to εω (like χράομαι to χρέωμαι), we have the part. μνεώμενος: again by the Ionic lengthening of ῶ to ώο (like γελώοντες, ἡβώοντες, ἡβοιμι ἡβώοιμι), we find the 3. plur. imperf. μνώοντο, Hom., the imperat. μνώεο, Apollon. Rh., and the part. μνωόμενος, Od. The fut. of μνάομαι is μνήσομαι, but we have also μεμνήσομαι, Herodot. 8, 62. and the aor. 1. midd. ἐμνησάμην, infin. μνήσασθαι with the sense of *to remember*, τινος, Hom. In the meaning of *to woo*, μνᾶσθαι is used not only in Homer but also in the common language.

Μολεῖν. See Βλώσκω.

ΜΥ–. We will here place the following verbs by the side of each other, that it may be at once seen in what they correspond and in what they differ:

Μυέω, *I initiate into the mysteries*, is regular.

Μύω, (whence also καταμύω, καμμύω) *I shut, close*, e.g. the lips, eyes, &c., and used both transit. and intransit. This verb is regular. Perf. μέμῡκα, *I am shut, I am silent.*

Μύζω, *I emit a sound by compressing the lips and breathing loud through the nose, I moan, grumble*; aor. 1. ἔμυσα, Hippocr. (of the rumbling of the intestines; see Foes. and Schneider): but ἔμυξα, ἐπέμυξαν are used by Homer as sounds of anger and reproach. This latter formation, with γ as its characteristic, is common to many verbs which express the uttering of some sound or exclamation, as κράζω, στενάζω, τρίζω, οἰμώζω, whence μυγμός, στεναγμός, οἰμωγμός, &c.

Μύζω, *I suck*: fut. μυζήσω, &c., from which inflexion first arose, it appears, in a later æra the pres. μυζάω and μυζέω*.

For the part. μεμυζότε see Αἰχμάομαι.

Μύσσω, μύττω, but more generally ἀπομύττω, *emungo*: fut. μύξω, &c.—Midd.

[The simple verb occurs only in the writings of the Grammarians and

* See Hemst. ad Lucian. Tim. 8. and Schneider's Lexicon. That μύζω is the older form appears certain not only from the glosses of Hesychius, who explains μύζει, ἔμυζεν, μύζουσι; but in Hippocr. π. ἀρχ. 8. we find μύζει and ἔμυζεν, and in Xen. Anab. 4, 5, 27., where the text now has εἰς τὸ στόμα ἀμύζειν, it is evident that this last form, which occurs nowhere else, is corrupted by the addition of a superfluous α.

as the root of *ἀπομύττω, ἐπιμύττω, προμύττω*, and of the Lat. *mungo, emungo*.—Passow.]

Μῡκάομαι, *I bellow, roar*: Dep. midd.

From the simple stem of this verb the Epics have formed a perf. with the force of a pres. *μέμῡκα*, part. *μεμυκώς*, and an aor. *ἔμῡκον*. Compare Μηκάομαι.

N.

Ναιετάω, *I dwell*. This Epic verb is never contracted, nor, except in one instance, produced, but is almost invariably found in a purely resolved form, as *ναιετάω*, Od. ι, 21. *ναιετάει*, Hes. θ, 775. *ναιετάουσι, ναιετάοντες*, Hom. Conj. *ναιετάωσι*, Hes. θ, 370. The only instance of the regular production is in the imperf. *ναιετάασκον*, and of an irregular one in the fem. part. *ναιετάωσα**.

Ναίω, *I dwell*, forms its tenses with simple ᾰ†. In the active, however, we find only the aor. 1. (*ἔνᾰσα*) *ἔνασσα* with a causative meaning, *to cause to inhabit, settle*, or *cause to be inhabited, colonize, found*. The midd. and pass. fut. *νάσσομαι* (Apoll. Rh. 2, 747.), the aor. 1. midd. *ἐνασσάμην* (*ἀπενάσσατο*, Hom.), and the aor. 1. pass. *ἐνάσθην* have the intransit. sense of *to settle in a place*. The post-Homeric poets, however, use the midd. *ἐνασσάμην* in the sense of *ἔνασσα* also: see Brunck. ad Apollon. 1, 1356. The perf. *νένασμαι* is not found before the later poets. See Schneider's Lexicon.

The syncop. aor. *κατένασθε*, *you have settled yourselves, you dwell*, (comp. Hesych. *νάσθαι—οἰκῆσαι*) in Aristoph. Vesp. 662. in the anapæsts would be remarkable, but both the best manuscripts have *κατένασθεν*, and the third person suits the passage very well.

See also Νάω, *I flow*.

Νάσσω, *I stop up, I fill in and beat close together* (as earth into a hole): fut. *νάξω*, aor. 1. *ἔναξα*: but the perf. pass. is *νένασμαι*, and the verbal adj. *ναστός*‡.

* That this was the old traditionary form is clear from the observations of the Grammarians in Schol. Il. γ, 387. in the Etym. M. in voc., and particularly from Aristarchus having written *ναιετόωσα* (Schol. Il. ζ, 415.). Uncritically enough. For if we suppose that Homer, having used *ναιετάουσι*, could not use *ναιετάωσα*, both analogy and the old way of writing lead us to *ναιετάουσα*, which the manuscripts have here and there, and which in Hymn. 17, 6., is the only reading. And if this be the traditionary form, there must have been some grounds for it. Compare the imperat. *σάω* under Σώζω.

† The termination *-αίω*, like *-άζω* and *-άννυμι*, serves to strengthen the pres. where the *α* is short in the other tenses.

‡ This verb, like *ἀφύσσω* and some others, follows therefore in its act. voice the general analogy of verbs in *-σσω*, with a palatic as its characteristic letter; but in the perf. pass. and verbal adj. its characteristic seems to have been a labial; compare Βαστάζω, Διστάζω. See also Ἁρμόττω.

The passive formation with the σ, as above given, is most indisputable in the verbal adj. ναστός. The perf. νένασται, too, is undoubted in Aristoph. Eccl. 840., on which and some other suspected passages see the note to Νέω 1. The only trace which I find of the regular form νένακται is in Suidas in voc., where it is quoted from Josephus.

Νάω, *I flow*, an old verb, found only in pres. and imperf.; written also ναίω. See Schol. Od. ι, 222. On νῶσιν, &c. see Νέω 2.

Νεικέω, *I rebuke, dispute*, retains ε in its inflexion, thus fut. νεικέσω, &c.

[Hom. and Hes. have also, when the metre requires it, an Ion. sister-form νεικείω, whence 3. conj. νεικείῃσι; imperf. νείκειον and νεικείεσκον; fut. νεικέσσω; aor. 1. νείκεσσα, &c.—Passow.]

Νείφω. See Νέφω.

Νέμω, *I distribute, allot*: fut. νεμῶ and νεμήσω; aor. 1. ἔνειμα; perf. νενέμηκα; aor. 1. pass. ἐνεμήθην and ἐνεμέθην*. Verbal adj. νεμητέος.—MIDD.

The fut. νεμήσω is mentioned by Herodian (post Mœr. et Phryn.) and Thom. Mag.; but I find it quoted only from the later writers; Longus p. 55. Schæf. Eurip. Epist. 5. On the other hand νεμεῖσθαι is in Demosth. Mid. p. 579. infra. [The later writers have also an aor. 1. midd. ἐνεμησάμην, Lobeck ad Phryn. p. 742.—Passow.]

Νέφω: 3. sing. νέφει, more generally συννέφει, *it is overcast with clouds*; or Ζεὺς συννέφει, *covers the sky with clouds*, Aristoph. Av. 1489. Perf. συννένοφεν.

See Aristoph. ap. Suid. v. ξυννένοφεν. The forms of the pres. are also written with the circumflex, as συννεφεῖ, -οῦσα: see Schneid. Lexicon. The pres. νείφω (with the explanation βρέχω) which the Grammarians connect with the above verb (see the Etymologica, and Eust. ad Il. α, 420.) is only another way of writing νίφω, *to snow*, which the later writers used also of rain: see Stephens in Νίφω†.

Νέω, 1. *I heap up*: aor. 1. ἔνησα, infin. νῆσαι, &c.; perf. pass. νένημαι or νένησμαι. Verbal adj. νητός.

The pres. νέω is found only in Herodotus, περινέειν, 6, 80; ἐπινέουσι, 4, 62.‡. Homer has a lengthened form which fluctuates between νηέω

* We find νεμηθῶσιν, Demosth. Neær. 1380. ult. and νεμεθείσης, id. Phorm. 956, 12.

† [Passow in his Lex. has the following article: Νέφω, fut. νέψω, perf. νένοφα, same as νίφω; a rare, nay a suspected form.]

‡ See, however, the following note.

and νηνέω. The inflexion follows the former, as the imperf. νήεον, Il. ψ, 139. aor. 1. νήησαν, Od. τ, 64. infin. νηῆσαι, ο, 321. Herodot. 2, 107. aor. 1. infin. midd. νηήσασθαι, Il. ι, 137.

The perf. pass. without σ see in Lex. Seguer. 1. p. 13, 24. Thucyd. 7, 87. Xen. Anab. 5, 4, 27. The other form νένησμαι seems to me to stand on good grounds in Aristoph. Nub. 1203, where with ἀμφορῆς νενησμένοι is the various reading νενασμένοι, which being untenable on account of the sense, could have arisen only from the true verb being written with the σ. Nor is the reading less sure in Aristoph. Eccles. 838., which I will quote at length: Ὡς αἱ τράπεζαί γ' εἰσὶν ἐπινενασμέναι Ἀγαθῶν ἁπάντων καὶ παρεσκευασμέναι, Κλῖναί τε σισυρῶν καὶ δαπίδων νενασμέναι. Now the reading of ἐπινενασμέναι is quite as untenable as that of νενασμέναι (looking at the sense) is certain; and Brunck's emendation ἐπινενησμέναι is now confirmed by the quotation in Phryn. Seguer. p. 13. Ἀγαθῶν πάντων ἐπινένηται ἡ τράπεζα: for the writing with the σ is supported here again by the false reading ἐπινενασμ- and by the similarity of this case to that quoted above from the Nubes. Lastly, we must examine the passage of Theocr. 9, 9. where νένασται is used of a heap of skins, which, it is true, the derivation from νάσσω appears to suit: but as the dialect of this poet requires νένακται, it would seem, according to the direction of the scholium σεσώρευται, that in the passage in question it should be pronounced νένᾱσται, i. e. νένησται.

2. *I spin*: fut. νήσω, &c.; in addition to which was formed, but at an early period, another pres. νήθω (like πλήθω from πίμπλημι, ΠΛΕΩ); and this became afterwards the common form.

It is difficult to decide anything on the usage of νεῖν and νήθειν in good writers, as the verb occurs so seldom in those which have come down to us. We must therefore content ourselves with the observation of the Antiatticist, Νήθειν, οὐ μόνον νεῖν, and with what we gather from the glosses of the Grammarians, that the simpler form was peculiar to the older Ionics and Attics. And herein we find an irregularity of contraction; for while the regular form is νεῖν, νεῖ, Hes. ε, 779. ἔνει, Hesych., the other contractions are invariably quoted by all the grammarians in ω instead of ου; as νῶσιν, Pollux 7, 32. 10, 125. νῶντα, Hesych. νώμενος, Phot.*. The contraction to ου was therefore studi-

* Photius has also Νῶντος, σωρεύοντος, belonging therefore to Νέω 1. This agrees also very well with the supposition, which indeed is pretty certain, that the meanings of *to heap up* (*glomerare*) and *to spin*, are properly the

ously avoided, and from *νῶ*, *νῶν* the *ω* was carried on through the tenses.

The passive forms I find quoted always with the *σ*; but it is possible that these came first into use with *νήθω*, and that the old form for the meaning of *to spin* was *νένημαι*, to which we are also led by the verbals *νητός*, *νῆμα*, &c.

3. *I swim.* None of the forms of the pres. are contracted by the Attics in this short verb except those in *ει* (compare Δέω, *I bind*); thus *νέω*, *νέων*, *νέομεν*, &c., but *νεῖ*, *νεῖν*, &c. Fut. *νεύσομαι* and *νευσοῦμαι* (like *πλέω*, *πλευσοῦμαι*); aor. 1. *ἔνευσα*, &c.

An Epic sister-form is *νήχω*, and the later prose writers use *νήχομαι*, a depon. midd.

4. The poetical verb *νέεσθαι*, *νεῖσθαι*, *to go*, more generally *to go away*, *return*, is used in present and imperfect only: the pres. indic. has the force of a future, as *νέομαι*, contr. *νεῦμαι*, Epic 2. sing. *νεῖαι* like *μυθεῖαι*, *νεῖται* like *μυθεῖται*.

Νίζω, *I wash*, takes its tenses from *νίπτω*, an unusual verb in the older writers: fut. *νίψω*; aor. 1. *ἔνιψα*, &c.; perf. pass. *νένιμμαι*.—Midd.

The pres. *νίζω* is found frequently in Homer, also in Herodot. 2, 172. Aristoph. Vesp. 608. Eurip. Iph. T. 1338. Plat. Symp. p. 175. a. All these writers form *νίψω*, &c.: while the pres. *νίπτω* occurs only in the later writers*, except in one single Homeric passage, Od. *σ*, 178.; and this is the more remarkable, as in ten others the reading is *νίζειν*. See Damm.

Νίσσομαι, *I go*, *return to*. Two questions have been started respecting this verb, one as to its orthography and another as to its inflexion. With regard to the first, we find *νίσομαι*, Il. *ψ*, 76. *νείσεσθε*, Eurip. Phœn. 1240. *ἀπονισόμεθα*, Apollon. Rh. 3, 899., and in each case the manuscripts fluctuate between *εις*, *εισσ*, *ισ*, *ισσ*. The form *νείσσομαι* is found in the best manuscripts, (whence we infer that the vowel is long independently

same. Nor is this at variance with the *ἐπινέουσι* of Herodot. quoted at the beginning of No. 1.; for the Ionics constantly use this form, like all those from verbs in *εω*, without contraction. On the other hand we are warranted in supposing that the Attics from *νεῖν to heap up*, *to spin*, formed *νῶσι*, from *νεῖν*, *to swim*—*νέουσιν*.

* Thom Mag. admits both forms, *καὶ ἔνιπτε καὶ ἔνιζεν*. for this is the reading of the manuscripts. The note of Hemsterhuys, which exactly reverses the usage, is incorrect.

of the σσ,) and its authenticity is further supported by the cognate forms *νέομαι*, *νείομαι*, as well as by its being actually found in inscriptions of the purest times, Bœckh Pind. Ol. 3, 10. On the other hand usage was in favour of *νίσσομαι* (see Etym. M. p. 606, 12.); and the Grammarians seem to have agreed in writing the pres. *νίσσομαι*, the fut. *νίσομαι*, Eustath. Il. ψ, 76. Heyne Il. ι, 381. There are other passages with the same doubtful orthography, as *νείσσονται*, Hes. Op. 235. *νεισσομένων*, Theog. 71. Gaisf., both with the various reading *νισσ*.; and *νίσσοντο*, Scut. 469. This uncertainty of the reading leaves the second question equally undecided: for in the three passages first mentioned the sense is that of a future; but then in the verbs which signify *to go*, the present has frequently the force of the future, as in *εἶμι* and *νέομαι*, Il. ν. 186. ο, 577.: thus in Il. ψ, 76. if we read *νίσομαι* we have the future, if *νίσσομαι* we have the present with the meaning of a future: compare also the scholium in the passage of Euripides. On the gloss of Hesychius *νείσαντο*, until we know to what it refers, nothing can be said.

Νίφω, *νείφω*. See **Νέφω**.

Νοέω, *I think*, has in the Ionic writers the same contraction and accentuation as *βοάω*; e. g. perf. *νένωμαι*; pluperf. *ἐνενώμην*, whence 3. sing. *ἐνένωτο* for *ἐνενόητο*, Herodot. 1, 77. and the compound aor. 1. part. *ἐννώσας* for *ἐννοήσας*, ib. 1, 86. See the note on **Βοάω**.

Νυστάζω, *I nod* (as being sleepy), *I sleep*: fut. *νυστάσω* and *νυστάξω**: but all the derivatives are formed with the palatic letter, as *νυστακτής*, &c.

Ξ.

Ξέω, *I shave, scrape*, retains ε in the inflexion, and takes σ in the passive: thus fut. *ξέσω*, Epic *ξέσσω*.

Ξυρέω, *I shave, shear*, has more commonly in the midd. *ξύρομαι*; aor. 1. *ἐξυράμην*; but the perfect is *ἐξύρημαι*.

The midd. form *ξυρέομαι* is Ionic; but it occurs in Attic writers, as *ξυρούμενον*, Alexis ap. Athen. 13. p. 565. b. In the later writers the pres. *ξυράω* was common, but the inflexion in -*άσω* is never found. See Lobeck ad Phryn. p. 205. Passow has also another later form *ξυρίζω*, *ξυρίζομαι*.

* See Stephan. Thesaur. in *καταννυστάζω*. Fisch. 2. p. 328. Asclep. Epig. 10. (*ἐνύσταζε*).

Ξύω, *I shave smooth, polish*: fut. ξύσω, &c. It takes σ in the passive: ξύσασθαι, aor. 1. midd. *to polish for one's self, for one's own use*, Xen. Cyr. 6, 2, 11.

O.

Ὀδύρομαι, *I lament, bewail*; depon. midd. with both trans. and intrans. sense. The act. appears to have never been in use.

Ὀδύσσομαι, *I am enraged with, I hate.* Neither this pres. nor ὀδύω, ὀδύζω, or ὀδύζομαι appear to have been ever in use; but we find in Hom. an aor. 1. midd. (ὠδυσάμην) -αο, -ατο and 3. plur. without the augm. ὀδύσαντο, part. ὀδυσσάμενος; also 3. sing. perf. pass. with the force of a pres. ὀδώδυσται for ὤδυσται, Od. ε, 423.

Ὄζω, *I send forth a* (good or bad) *smell*: fut. ὀζήσω; aor. 1. ὤζησα, Aristoph. Vesp. 1059.; perf. with the force of the pres. ὄδωδα. Generally with gen. of the thing or part from which the smell proceeds.

The inflexion ὀζέσω, ὤζεσα is found in the Ionic (Hippocr. De Steril. 10. De Superfet. 10.) and the later writers.

Οἴγω, or οἴγνυμι, *I open*: fut. οἴξω; aor. 1. ᾦξα, part. οἴξας: but the Epics generally separate the diphthong in the augmented forms, as in the aor. 1. ὤϊξεν, ὤϊξαν, and in the imperf. pass. ὠΐγνυντο. In prose the following compound is in use:

ἀνοίγω, ἀνοίγνυμι. In the augmented tenses the syllabic augment is added to the temporal as in the imperf. ἐῳνοχόει from οἰνοχοέω, ἑήνδανε from ἅνδανω; thus imperf. ἀνέῳγον; aor. 1. ἀνέῳξα (infin. ἀνοῖξαι), &c.; perf. 1. ἀνέῳχα; perf. 2. ἀνέῳγα. This last tense had from a very early period (Hippocr., &c.) an intransitive meaning, *I stand open*; which however was unknown to the Attics, who in this sense used the perf. pass. ἀνέῳγμαι. See Lobeck ad Phryn. pp. 157. 158.

In the dialects, as in Herodot., Theocr., &c., we find the aor. 1. with the regular augment ἀνῷξα; and in the later writers the act. ἤνοιξα, pass. ἠνοίγην, &c. Fisch. III. pp. 36. 37.

Οἰδέω, *I swell.* For this verb, with the forms οἰδάω, οἰδάνω, οἰδαίνω, we cannot lay down any fixed usage. We can only observe that the formation in -ήσω is the only one for all four forms; and that the two last are used also in a causative sense. See Stephens' Thesaur.

Οἰμώζω, *I bewail*: fut. οἰμώξω* and οἰμώξομαι; aor. 1. ᾤμωξα.

Οἴομαι, *I think*: imperf. ᾠόμην; fut. οἰήσομαι; aor. 1. ᾠήθην, infin. οἰηθῆναι, part. οἰηθείς. The 1. pers. sing. of both pres. and imperf. was also pronounced in a syncopated form, οἶμαι, ᾤμην. The 2. pers. sing. of the pres. οἴει, (like βούλει and ὄψει) was not only the Attic form, but almost the only one in use in the common language.

"The old grammarians (see Thom. Mag. in voc.) laid it down as a rule, that the form οἶμαι was used only of things *fixed and certain*, consequently merely a milder expression for "I am convinced, I know well." That is to say, οἶμαι, ᾤμην was a kind of interjectional phrase introduced into a sentence without much stress laid upon it, like our expression "I believe," which in different languages is used in courtesy to soften the harshness of a positive assertion; and which frequently arises from a slight irony incorporated, as it were, into the tone of polished conversation." We can readily imagine that this must have been particularly natural to the Attic language: and the necessary result therefore was, that as soon as it was wished to give the word its *proper* force, it was generally pronounced at full length. If now we read this οἴομαι, for example, in the two passages of Isæus (pp. 50, 22. 58, 14.) which are adduced in a note on Thom. Mag. as supposed instances of a contrary nature, we shall feel that the tone of the sentence loses by it. And the further we extend our observation the more we shall find the above rule verified. One thing however may fairly be presumed, that in order to follow it up in all cases, we ought to have the reading more certain than it can possibly be made where the difference in the forms is so slight.

The Epics make use also of the active οἴω, but only in the present; more frequently they separate the diphthong, ὀΐω, and in the middle always, ὀΐομαι, in which the ι is long; and in this form, which has the midd.

* [Passow says that the Attic fut. is οἰμώξομαι, not οἰμώξω, which last occurs only in the Orac. Sibyll.: see Jac. anim. in Athen. p. 170.]

as well as the pass. aorist, we find only the regular inflexion; e. g. pres. *οἴομαι, οἴεαι* &c., part. *οἰόμενος*; imperf. *ᾠόμην*; aor. 1. pass. *ᾠΐσθην*, part. *οἰσθεὶς*; aor. 1. midd. *ᾠϊσάμην*, whence in Hom. 3. sing. without the augment *ὀΐσατο*, and part. *οἰσάμενος*. This Epic form of the verb has the collateral meaning of *to conjecture, to foresee*; in which sense we find it in the Ionic prose of Arrian, *οἰσθῶσι* (Ind. 13, 5.), which however may also be written *ὀϊσθῶσι*. From *ᾠΐσθην* the later (not Attic) writers formed again an infin. aor. *οἰσθῆναι* with the part. *οἰσθείς*: and Aratus has with the common formation an aor. 1. infin. midd. *οἰήσασθαι*, used by still later writers in prose: (see Lobeck ad Phryn. p. 719.)

Οἴχομαι, *I go, I am gone*: imperf. (or aor.) *ᾠχόμην, I went away*; fut. *οἰχήσομαι*.

Although the radical meaning of this verb is, as we shall see in the next paragraph, simply *to go*, yet an established usage has existed in the common language from Homer's time, by which *οἴχομαι* never means *I am going*, but always *I am gone*. We will first prove this by a number of decisive passages. At Il. ο, 223. ἤδη Ἐννοσίγαιος Οἴχεται εἰς ἅλα δῖαν, after it had been before said δῦνε δὲ πόντον ἰών. At ε, 472. πῇ δή τοι μένος οἴχεται ὃ πρὶν ἔχεσκες; see also ξ, 11. Again ἐκπέφευγ', οἴχεται φροῦδος, Aristoph. Acharn. 208. Πόσον χρόνον δὲ μητρὸς οἴχονται πνοαί; *how long has thy mother's breath been gone?* Eurip. Or. 440. compare also 844. In Xenophon we find many instances; e. g. (addressing a dead body) οἴχῃ δὴ ἀπολιπὼν ἡμᾶς, Cyrop. 7, 3, 8. see also 5, 4, 11. 6, 1, 45. and Anab. 3, 1, 32. This usage is continued in the imperf. *ᾠχόμην, I was gone*; as Penelope says to her son, οὔ σ' ἔτ' ἔγωγε Ὄψεσθαι ἐφάμην, ἐπεὶ ᾤχεο νηὶ Πύλονδε, *when I heard that thou wert gone to Pylos*, Od. π, 24. See also Pind. P. 4, 145. and Xen. Cyr. 3, 2, 27. It may also be understood in the same sense when at the end of a spirited narrative a phrase is added with ᾤχετο; e. g. Οὕτω δὴ οὗτος μὲν ᾤχετο . . . . . οἱ δὲ Μῆδοι παρῆσαν . . . . . : *this man was now gone, when the Medes came* . . . . ., Xen. Cyr. 4, 6, 5. In the majority of passages however this imperfect cannot without force be made to signify more than simply *he went away*, e. g. Χωόμενος δ' ὁ γέρων πάλιν ᾤχετο, Il. α, 380. Ἀκούσαντες δὲ οἱ Χαλδαῖοι ταῦτα . . . . . ᾤχοντο οἴκαδε, Xen. Cyr. 3, 2, 14. compared with 8, 3, 28.

That the original meaning of *οἴχεσθαι* was simply *to go*, without the addition of *away*, is clear not only from the sister-form *οἰχνέω*, but from the compound *ἐποίχομαι, I go to* or *towards*, as well as from some passages of Homer, in which the simple verb, but never in the pres. conj. (*quære*, is this accidental?), is used in that original sense: e. g. κατὰ στρατὸν ᾤχετο πάντῃ Ὀτρύνων μαχέσασθαι, Il. ε, 495. and Ἐννῆμαρ μὲν ἀνὰ στρατὸν ᾤχετο κῆλα θεοῖο, α, 53. with some similar passages.

Now that particular use of the present mentioned in the last paragraph may be explained, like many others, from the oral language: for whoever goes, is gone: whence "he is going thither" is much the same as "he is gone hence." But all such original ideas lose by custom their exact meaning; and so, οἴχεται was used of one who had been gone a long time, who had been long arrived at some other place, or who had quite disappeared from the world. But as soon as the thing is no longer actually present, the difference between the person being then just *going away*, or being supposed to be *on the road* to his place of destination, is in most cases unimportant. Although therefore ᾤχετο, as imperf. of the common οἴχεται, meant, wherever it was necessary and the context showed it, *he was gone*; yet it generally signified, agreeably to its origin, *he went, went away*. And the future had the same meaning; e. g. ἐπειδὰν πίω τὸ φάρμακον . . . . . οἰχήσομαι ἀπιὼν εἰς μακάρων δή τινας εὐδαιμονίας, Plat. Phæd. 115. d.

From what has been said, a perf. of this verb is superfluous for general use; it does however sometimes occur (e. g. ᾤχημαι, Ion. οἴχημαι, Herodot. 4, 136.), but in the common language in the compounds only, in which therefore παροίχομαι and παρῴχημαι, παρῳχημένος are synonymous; see Stephan. Thesaur. and Sturz. Lex. Xen.: and so is the other compound in Herodot. 4, 136. αἱ ἡμέραι διοίχηνται, compared with Soph. Aj. 973. Αἴας διοίχεται. In the older language the perf. is found in an *active* form also (ᾤχηκα) which will therefore connect it with οἰχνέω: it is however rare, and in Homer occurs but once, viz. in παρώχηκεν, *is past*, Il. κ, 252.; of more frequent occurrence is the form οἴχωκα*, which has exactly the common meaning of οἴχομαι; e. g. οἴχωκ', ὄλωλα, Soph. Aj. 896. οἰχωκώς, Herodot. 8, 108. οἰκωχότας, 9, 98. In this last writer οἰχώκεε, 8, 126. and παροιχώκεε, 8, 72. are evidently pluperfects with the force of an imperfect; but at 1, 189. 4, 127. 165. οἰχώκεε is exactly the same as ᾤχετο in the common language, that is to say used as an aorist, probably because the expression, "he was gone," marked the momentary act of going away†. [An Ion. 3. plur. pluperf. ἐπῴχατο also occurs, but seldom. A regular fut. οἴξομαι is found in some manuscripts in Herodot. 2, 29.—The pres. οἰχέομαι, contracted by the Ionics to οἰχεῦμαι, is met with only in Leon. Tar.: for the act. οἴχω there is no authority.—Passow.]

* The formation of this perf. corresponds exactly with that of ὄχωκα from ἔχω; thus οἴχω, perf. οἶχα, with redupl. οἴκωχα (for the ι of the second syllable could be omitted for no other reason than because there was one in the first; compare δείδεκτο from δείκνυμαι), and thence, by transposition of the two palatic letters, οἴχωκα.

† It is certain that the common meaning of ᾤχετο may be explained in this same way, that is to say as a pluperf., οἴχεται having the force of a perf.: but the view which I have taken of it appears to me simpler.

Οἴω. See Οἴομαι and Φέρω.

Ὀκέλλω, *I land*, has (beside the pres. and imperf.) only the aor. ὤκειλα, infin. ὀκεῖλαι, &c.: τὰς νῆας ὤκελλον, *they stranded*, &c., Herodot. 8, 84.

Ὀλισθάνω, *I slip up* or *off from*: fut. ὀλισθήσω; aor. 2. ὤλισθον, infin. ὀλισθεῖν, part. ὀλισθών.

The form ὀλισθαίνω is not Attic: see Porson ad Phœniss. 1398. Bast. Ep. Cr. p. 248. Isolated instances of its occurrence in the older writers, (as in Plat. Lys. p. 216. c. compared with Cratyl. p. 427. b.), are but little to be depended on: in the later writers, as Lucian, &c., it is found very frequently*.—An aor. 1. ὠλίσθησα is also used by the later writers; see Lobeck ad Phryn. p. 742. Passow has also a perf. ὠλίσθηκα.

Ὄλλυμι†, *I destroy, annihilate*: fut. ὀλῶ; aor. 1. ὤλεσα; perf. ὀλώλεκα. Midd. *I perish, am undone*; fut. ὀλοῦμαι; aor. 2. ὠλόμην; to which belongs the perf. 2. (perf. midd.) ὄλωλα.

The intransitive forms ὠλόμην and ὄλωλα serve at the same time for passives (ἀπολωλέναι ὑπό τινος: compare Ἀποθανεῖν); whence the proper forms of the pass. are not used; none but writers of a very late period having ὠλέσθην, ὀλεσθῆναι, Lobeck ad Phryn. p. 732.

Of the same æra is also the fut. ὀλέσω‡, e. g. Long. 3, 17. ἀπολέσων, Lucian. Asin. 33. The examples quoted from Attic writers in Lobeck p. 746. are not critically examined.

From the perf. act. was formed an Epic sister-form of the present, ὀλέκω§, of which (both in the act. and midd.) Homer has only the pres. and imperf.; the latter without the augment, ὄλεκον, ὀλέκοντο. Compare ἐμέμηκον under Μηκάομαι.

In Il. τ, 135. stands the iterative imperf. ὀλέεσκεν, which supposes an imperf. ὤλεον not quite agreeable to analogy. Heyne has adopted the reading ὀλέσκεν, which would be the iterative aorist; but the itera-

* [According to Porson ὀλισθάνω is the only form used by good writers, but ὀλισθαίνω is found in Aristoph. Equ. 494. and is therefore as pure Attic as the other: ὀλισθέω on the contrary is not a genuine form.—Passow.]

† If we compare the analogy of ἄγνυμι, &c. with this verb, we shall see that the latter is an euphonic change for ὄλνυμι.

‡ [What can Buttmann mean by stating ὀλέσω to be the usage of the later writers only? We find it in Od. ν, 399. Hes. ε, 178. and ὀλέσσω, Il. μ, 250.—Ed.]

§ [Beside this Epic pres. we find ὄλλω, ὀλέω, ὀλέσκω, which are not Greek, ὀλλυνέω, which is suspected, and ὀλλύω in Hesych.—Passow.]

tive imperfect is the only tense to suit the passage, therefore the various reading ὀλέκεσκεν ought to have been adopted long ago.

The part. aor. midd. ὀλόμενος, beside its proper meaning (e. g. ὥς σ' ὀλόμενον στένω, Eurip. Or. 1384.), is used as an adjective with the *active* sense of *destructive*, ὀλομέναν Ἐρινύν, Phœn. 1030. In the Epic poets, who on account of the metre can have only οὐλόμενος, the adjectival usage is the only one, and generally in the active sense with μῆνις, Ἄτη, &c.: but it has also the strictly passive meaning *wretched, undone*, οὐλομένης ἐμέθεν, τῆς τε Ζεὺς ὄλβον ἀπηύρα, Od. σ, 273.

[At Il. θ, 449. ὀλλῦσαι is the regular pres. part. fem. Ὀλέσσαι is the Ep. aor. infin. in Hom. and Hes.—Passow.]

Ὄμνυμι, *I swear*: fut. ὀμοῦμαι, -εῖ, -εῖται, &c., infin. ὀμεῖσθαι*; the other tenses take an ο in the inflexion, as aor. 1. ὤμοσα; perf. ὀμώμοκα; perf. pass. ὀμώμοσμαι, part. ὀμωμοσμένος; but in the remaining forms and in the aorist the Attics generally drop the σ, as in 3. sing. perf. pass. ὀμώμοται, and aor. 1. pass. ὠμόθην.—The middle occurs in the compounds, e. g. ἐπωμοσάμην.

From the σ having been properly admitted into those forms only in which the three μ followed each other, we see that it was done for the sake of euphony; and consequently they never appear without it. But it was afterwards transferred to some of the other forms, perhaps however not in the pure Attic writers. Thus in Demosth. c. Olymp. p. 1174, 8. the reading has always been ὑπομοθέντος, and in Demosth. c. Leptin. p. 805. extr. ὀμώμοται has been restored from the best manuscript†.

[Homer generally uses the aor. 1. without the augment, and frequently with double σ, ὀμόσσαι, &c. In the simple verb he has the imperf. ὤμνυε as from ὀμνύω, but in the compound ἀπώμνυ, Od. β, 377. In Herodot. 1, 153. is the Ionic part. pres. ὀμοῦντες as from ὀμόω.—Passow.]

Ὀμόργνυμι, *I wipe off*: fut. ὀμόρξω; aor. 1. ὤμορξα; aor. 1. midd. ὠμορξάμην; infin. ὀμόρξασθαι, &c. This verb is inflected according to the analogy of ἄγνυμι, δείκνυμι, &c.—Midd.

* This verb is formed according to the analogy of ἄγνυμι: compare also Δείκνυμι, Ὄλλυμι.

† In Andoc. de Pace, p 27, 43. the text still has ὀμοσθήσεται; in Hyperides ap. Schol. Aristoph. Plut. 725. ὑπομοσθείσης; and in Eurip. Rhes. 816., without any necessity from the metre, ὀμώμοσται.

Ὀνίνημι, *I am of use to, I help*: (no imperf. act.*) fut. ὀνήσω; aor. 1. ὤνησα. Midd. ὀνίναμαι, *I derive assistance, advantage*; fut. ὀνήσομαι; aor. 2. ὠνήμην, -ησο, -ητο, &c., part. ὀνήμενος (Od. β, 33. ω, 30.); but the other moods of this aorist have the α, as optat. ὀναίμην, infin. ὄνασθαι; and the indicative also borrowed this formation, but not until a later period, ὠνάμην.

On this peculiarity of the aorist see Lobeck ad Phryn. pp. 12. 13. Hence ὤνασθε in Eurip. Herc. 1368. and occurring in that passage only, well deserves our consideration. For a further account of this aor. ὠνάμην and the similar one from ὄνομαι, see the latter verb. The aor. pass. ὠνήθην is also found (instead of ὠνήμην) in Xen. Anab. 5, 5, 2. Theocr. 15, 55.

This is one of those verbs formed by the reduplication of the first syllable like ἀραρίσκω, ἀκαχίζω; only that in this case the vowel of the reduplication is ι (as in γιγνώσκω, δίδωμι, &c.), and it is substituted for the vowel of the root, as the temp. augment η is in ἀκήκοα, &c.; thus ὀνάω (whence ὠνάμην) ὀνίνημι, like ἀτάλλω ἀτιτάλλω, and ὀπτεύω ὀπιπτεύω. There is however no instance of ὀνάω, ὀνέω or ὄνημι being used by any writer.

The 3. sing. pres. act. ὀνίνησι and the midd. ὀνίναμαι are found in Homer, Plato, and others: but those forms in which there was anything displeasing to the ear were not used, and their places were supplied by the synonymous ὠφελεῖν. This was the case for instance with the imperf. act.†; and for the same reason it might also seem very likely that the infin. act. ὀνῑνάναι would have been avoided. This however cannot be asserted positively; and there is even great probability in Matthiæ's suspicion that ὀνίναι in Plat. Rep. 10. p. 600. d. may be a corruption of this word‡.

Ὄνομαι, *I think lightly of, reject with disdain*, 2. sing. ὄνοσαι, 3. plur. ὄνονται, imper. ὄνοσο and ὄνοσσο§, opt. ὀνοίμην, ὄνοιτο (compare δύνωμαι, δύναιτο, &c. under Δύναμαι); fut. ὀνόσομαι, whence in Hom. the infin. with double σ, ὀνόσσεσθαι; aor. 1. pass. ὠνόσθην; aor. 1. midd.

* See Grammat. ap. Herm. de Em. Gr. Gr.

† [The imperf. midd. however occurs in Plato. The perf. ὤνημαι is also found, but rarely.—Passow.]

‡ The manuscripts fluctuate indeed between ὀνίναι, -ῖναι, -εῖναι, -ῆναι, and Bekker has thence adopted ὀνῆναι; but I cannot prefer that aor. 2. act. (unknown in any other instance, and used here for the common ὀνῆσαι,) to Matthiæ's correction, particularly as the imperf is the only tense naturally suited to that passage.

§ Τῶν μηδὲν κατόνοσσο, Arat. 1142. according to the Paris manuscript.

ὠνοσάμην, whence in Hom. the opt. *ὀνοσαίμην, -αιο, -αιτο*, and infin. with double *σ*, *ὀνόσσασθαι*.

From a comparison of the forms we see that this is exclusively an Ionic and Epic verb, a formation in *μι* from the root or stem ΟΝΟΩ. We must not therefore consider, as others frequently have done, *ὄνομαι, ὄνονται, ὤνοντο*, &c. as forms of the common barytone conjugation.

The inflexion of this verb however is certainly nothing more than a lengthening of the simple root ΟΝ– by the insertion of the vowel *ο*, to which we are led by two Homeric forms; viz.

1. Aor. *ὤνατο*, Il. *ρ*, 25. This Homeric form is separated from the *ὤνατο* of the later language belonging to *ὀνίνημι*, not merely by its meaning, but, if accurately examined, by its form also; only that this latter difference happens to be not marked by a difference of letters. That is to say, *ὀνίνημι, ὀνίναμαι* is a formation in *μι* with the radical vowel *α*, ΟΝΑ–: *ὠνάμην* therefore bears the same relation to it as *ἐστάμην*, if it were in use, would to *ἵσταμαι*, or as *ἐπτάμην* actually does to *ἵπταμαι*, and it is the aor. 2. midd. Whereas the formation of *ὄνομαι* from ΟΝΟ– is not to be unnecessarily confounded with the formation from ΟΝΑ–, but is to be traced back, as in other similar cases, to the simple stem or root ΟΝ–*. According to this *ὠνάμην* is the aor. 1. midd. of ΟΝΩ; or (which is the same thing) the aor. 2. *ὠνόμην, ὤνετο*, &c. took the Ionic *α*, making *ὤνατο*, like *εὔρατο*, &c.

2. Pres. *οὔνεσθε*, Il. *ω*, 241. Here the *ο* of the radical syllable is lengthened, as in *οὐλόμενος*. It stands therefore for *ὄνεσθε*, and this again for *ὄνοσθε*, which is singular; as there was no metrical reason for forming this particular present from the simple stem†.

ΟΠ–. See *Ὁράω*.

Ὀπυίω, *I marry, cohabit with*, loses in the inflexion the *ι*; thus fut. *ὀπύσω*, &c., Aristoph. Acharn. 255.

* [The radical idea of the old root ΟΝΩ was perhaps *to speak of a person in his absence, give him a good or bad character*; whence *ὄνομα* (by some incorrectly derived from *νέμω*), *a good or bad name*; and the same double meaning was originally in *ὄνειδος* (likewise a derivative from this word), as in the Lat. *honos*: *ὀνίνημι* on the other hand belongs to a different root, and has no connection with *ὄνομαι*.—Passow.]

† Both ancient and modern commentators, mistaking the Epic language, were led by the explanation *ὄνησιν ἔχετε* to place this form under *ὀνίνημι*. But grammatical analogy gains nothing by such an arrangement, for the pres. *ὄνεσθε* is as strange in connection with the root ΟΝΑ– as with ΟΝΟ–. Yet Hesychius has the glosses Οὐλιᾶσθε (corrupted from *οὔνασθε*), Οὔνεσθε and Οὔνοσθε, all three with that false explanation; for all evidently refer to the Homeric passage. From this and from Aristarchus writing *ὀνόσασθε* we see clearly how uncertain the reading was from the earliest times; and I have no doubt therefore that the old and genuine one was *οὔνοσθε*; nay, this becomes a certainty by the occurrence of the same phrase in the 2. sing. *ἦ ὄνοσαι* . . . ; Od. *ρ*, 378. therefore in plur. *ἦ* (*ὄνοσθε*) *οὔνοσθε* . . . ;

[According to Piers. ad Mœr. p. 278. and Porson on Od. δ. 798. the old and genuine form was ὀπτάω; compare Schæf. Schol. Par. Apoll. Rh. 1, 45.—Passow.]

Ὁράω, *I see*: imperf. with double augment ἑώρων (see ἀνοίγω under Οἴγω); perf. ἑώρᾱκα or ἑόρᾱκα*; from the verb εἴδω (which see) were borrowed the aor. 2. εἶδον, imper. ἴδε Att. ἰδέ (see ἐλθέ under Ἔρχομαι), opt. ἴδοιμι, infin. ἰδεῖν, part. ἰδών. Midd. aor. 2. εἰδόμην, imper. ἰδοῦ (as an interjection ἰδού, *ecce*), infin. ἰδέσθαι; and from an unusual stem ΟΠ . . . the fut. in the midd. form ὄψομαι (*I shall see*). The perf. pass. is either ἑώραμαι (ἑόραμαι), or ὦμμαι, ὦψαι, ὦπται, &c., infin. ὦφθαι; but in the aor. 1. pass. the Attics use only ὤφθην, while the later writers formed this tense from ὁράω, as infin. ὁραθῆναι. Verbal adj. ὁρᾱτός and ὁρᾱτέος, or ὀπτός† and ὀπτέος. The midd. ὁρᾶσθαι, ἰδέσθαι is in the simple verbs solely poetical.

The regular imperf. of ὁράω is ὥρων, Ion. ὥρεον from the Ion. pres. ὁρέω, Herodot. 2, 148.; compare ἤντεον from Ἀντάω, and μνέεται, χρέεται under Μιμνήσκω. We find also an Epic 2. sing. pres. midd. ὁρῆαι or ὅρηαι (for ὁράῃ or ὁράεαι), as from ὅρημαι, Od. ξ, 343. If we adopt the latter accentuation we must suppose it formed as from a verb in μι; if the former (which is expressly mentioned by Eustath. p. 548, 40. Basil.), we form ὁράεαι ὁρᾶαι like μυθέεαι μυθεῖαι, and we can

* The general form of this perfect as handed down to us in all the writers both of the Attic and common dialect is ἑώρακα. But as in Aristoph. Plut. 98. 1046. Av. 1572. and in Comic. ap. Athen. 1. p. 15. 7. p. 279. a trisyllable was required, Dawes (Misc. p. 202. and 313.) introduced as an Attic form the Ion. ὤρακα. There were however other passages where this did not suit; these he altered arbitrarily, substituting for instance in Aristoph. Thesm. 32. 33. ἑώρας: and he supported his general principle by the analogy of ἑάλων and ἥλωκα, both Attic forms. Tyrwhitt however (ad Dawes. p. 454.) quoted two passages of the Alexandrine comic poet Machon, from Athen. 6. p. 244. with ἑώρακα, as Μὴ παρεώρακεν Ἀρχεφῶν . . . and Πτολεμαῖ' ἑώρακα πρῶτος . . ., both of which verses require ἑόρακα. Now as all the passages where Dawes wrote ὤρακα (except two totally corrupted in Athen. 2. p. 49.) become quite regular by adopting Tyrwhitt's emendation, ἑόρακα has been considered an undoubted Attic form, and adopted in all the above-mentioned passages; see Porson ad Eurip. Phœn. 1367. Reisig ad Aristoph. p. 73. Meineke ad Menand. p. 119. And in support of this reading the ο is actually found in the Cod. Ravenn. of Aristoph. Plut. 1046. Thesm. 32. 33. At the same time it must be remembered that in other passages there is very strong traditionary authority in favour of the old reading ἑώρακα, which must then be pronounced occasionally as a trisyllable.

† This same ὀπτός is also formed from ὀπτάω, *I roast*, consequently for ὀπτητός, as in Lat. *assus* for *assatus*.

easily see why the η was preferred to the α, a change not uncommon in the Epic language, as in προσαυδήτην and the infinitives in -ήμεναι and -ῆναι. The 3. sing. imperf. midd. ὁρῆτο or ὅρητο, having come down to us only as a various reading of Zenodotus for ὁρᾶτο, cannot certainly with any propriety be admitted into Homer's text, as long as ὁρᾶται and ὁρᾶσθαι stand in other passages without a similar various reading. The other grammarians call this not an Ionic but a Doric form; which no doubt Zenodotus knew as well as they, otherwise he would have written ὁρῆν, ὁρῆ, κοιμῆτο, &c. Whatever it is, we may be sure that it was a reading founded on old copies, which Zenodotus was unwilling to erase. To account for it we have no occasion to have recourse to the formation in μι. We should rather say that the infin. in -έμεναι being a sister-form of that in -ειν may be supposed to exist in the contracted shape also, and as there is no other Epic sister-form for -ᾶν and -εῖν than that in -ήμεναι, the natural supposition is that this belongs to the same contraction. There are instances enough in the Epic language of η used for εε, which is still further supported by a remark of Heraclides in Eustath. ad Od. υ, 287. p. 735, 15. Basil., that "the Dorians, whose dialect is used by the old Attics, said ἔπλην, ἔῤῥην for ἔπλεεν, ἔῤῥεεν." At all events we must remember that a great portion of the Doric dialect is at the same time archaisms, and therefore not surprising in the Epic language. And the infin. in -ήμεναι is proved to be pure Doric by ἀριθμήμεναι in Tim. Locr.—The imperfect generally used by Homer is (always without the augment) the 3. sing. act. ὅρα, midd. ὁρᾶτο, and plur. ὁρῶντο.

[Homer has used this verb both in a contracted and resolved shape, as ὁρῶ, ὁρᾷς, ὁρᾷ, ὁρᾶν, ὁρῶν, ὁρῶσα, ὁρῶμαι, ὁρᾶται, ὁρᾶσθαι, ὁρώμενος, 3. sing. opt. ὁρῷτο, 3. plur. ὁρῴατο, Hom. Epig. 14, 20. again ὁρόω, ὁράᾳς, ὁρόων, ὁρόωσα, 2. plur. opt. ὁρόῳτε, for ὁράοιτε, ὁρῷτε (Il. δ, 347), ὁράασθαι, &c.—Passow.]

From the root ΟΠ– comes the Ion. perf. (2.) ὄπωπα, never used by the Attic prose writers; and thence in the Od. we find the 3. sing. pluperf. ὀπώπει, in Herodot. ὀπώπεε, 1, 68. 5, 92, 6. 7, 208. but at 3, 37. ὀπώπεε is a pure perfect: compare ἐώθεε under Ἔθω.

In the compounds ἐπόψομαι must be distinguished from ἐπιόψομαι. The former is the common fut. of ἐφορᾶν occurring in Il. ξ, 145. Od. η, 324.; the latter has the particular sense of *to select, choose*, Il. ι, 167. Od. β, 294. which ἐφορᾶν never has. And it is a singular fact that of both forms we find an aor. 1. midd. (the simple being never used*), as

* [Passow speaks of the aor. midd. ὠψάμην being merely a *rare* form, whence the 3. plur. opt. ὄψαιντο in Herm. Soph. Œd. T. 1271. See Lobeck ad Phryn. p. 734.]

for instance, ἐπόψατο, from ἐφορᾷν, in Pind. Fr. 58 Bœckh.; and ἐπιώψατο, *he chose*, in an old Attic expression, for which see Piers. ad Mœr. v. ἐῤῥηφόροι*.

Ὀρέγω, *I stretch out, reach out*: fut. ὀρέξω, &c. with accusative. Pass. and midd. *I desire*, with genitive; e. g. aor. 1. infin. midd. ὀρέξασθαι, Xen. Mem. 1, 2, 15. aor. 1. pass. ὠρέχθην, ibid. 16.

In the poets the midd. occurs also in its proper meaning, *I stretch myself out*, or with ποσσίν, χερσί, &c. *I stretch out my feet, hands*; in which sense is found also the perf. pass. ὀρώρεγμαι, 3. plur. ὀρωρέχαται, Il. π, 834. and 3. plur. pluperf. ὀρωρέχατο, Il. λ, 26.

Ὄρνυμι†, *I raise, excite, put in motion*: fut. ὄρσω; aor. 1. ὦρσα, part. ὄρσας, and frequently in Hom. the Ionic aor. ὄρσασκε for ὦρσε. Midd. ὄρνυμαι, *I raise myself, rise up*; imperf. ὠρνύμην; aor. 2. ὠρόμην, or more frequently by syncope (ὤρμην) 3. sing. ὦρτο, imper. ὄρσο, Epic ὄρσεο (like ἀείσεο, λέξεο‡), contracted ὄρσευ, Il., 3. sing. conj. ὄρηται, Od., infin. ὄρθαι§ for ὀρέσθαι, part. ὀρμένος for ὀρόμενος: for an account of these syncopated forms see ἔγεντο under Γείνομαι.

I know of no authority for the fut. midd. ὄρσομαι, instead of which Homer has (from a fut. 2. ὀροῦμαι) the 3. sing. ὀρεῖται (Il. υ, 140.); but the various reading ὄρηται as aor. 2. conj. may very well be preferred to the future.

With the above are joined two reduplicated forms:

1. ὄρωρα, a perf. belonging to the immediate meaning of the middle, *I am risen up*. Of this form Homer has only the 3. sing. ὄρωρε, conj. ὀρώρῃ; pluperf. ὀρώρει and ὠρώρει, Il. σ, 498.

2. (ὤρορον) ὤρορεν, aor. 2. with redupl. according to the analogy of ἤραρεν, ἤκαχεν, &c.; see note on ἀγαγεῖν under Ἄγω. Like ἤραρεν it has generally a causative meaning and is therefore the same as the aor. 1. ὦρσα: but like that perfect it has sometimes the immediate meaning; and this was the foundation of an earlier opinion, according to

* The same phrase ought undoubtedly to be restored to Plat. Legg. 12. p. 947. c. in the following passage, "a hundred youths from the Gymnasia οὓς ἂν οἱ προσήκοντες ἐπιόψωνται," where the common reading is ἐπόψονται, but the best manuscript has ἐπόψωνται, which is evidently a corruption of that old Attic and unusual form.

† [Homer forms his imper. from the verb in μι, ὄρνυθι, ὄρνυτε, but the rest of the pres. and the imperf. from ὀρνύω (-⏑-).—Passow.]

‡ See ἐδύσετο under Δύω and οἶσε under Φέρω.

§ This perfectly regular form was for a long time ejected from Il. θ, 474. by ὦρθαι, because ὄρθαι was considered to be the perfect (see Heyne), the cause of the abbreviation being unknown. But Homer never uses the perf. ὦρμαι, while he has the aor. ὦρτο, ὄρσο, ὄρμενος frequently. The true reading ὄρθαι is now restored to the text from the most undoubted sources.

which ὤρορε was supposed to be a perfect with the quantities transposed, which idea seemed also supported by Il. ν, 78. Οὕτω νῦν καὶ ἐμοὶ περὶ δούρατι χεῖρες ἄαπτοι Μαιμῶσιν, καί μοι μένος ὤρορε, νέρθε δὲ ποσσὶν Ἔσσυμαι. But as the aoristic meaning of this form is firmly established by analogy and usage, ὤρορε must be understood here as well as elsewhere to indicate the moment of his courage being first roused, and indeed in this passage ἠγέρθη might have been joined with the pres. and perf. quite as well as ὤρορε.

Beside the above Homer has from a perf. pass. ὀρώρεμαι the 3. sing. ὀρώρεται (Od. τ, 377. 524.) and the conj. ὀρώρηται (Il. ν, 271.). In the Epic language are three similar perfects ἀκήχεμαι, ἀρήρεμαι, ὀρώρεμαι: and as from ΑΧΩ, ἤκαχον came a perf. pass. ἤκαχμαι, so from ἄρηρα and ὄρωρα were formed ἀρήρμαι, ὀρώρμαι, and all three were smoothed off into their present shape according to the analogy of the formation in έω: thus the conj. ὀρώρηται is quite as agreeable to analogy as κέκτωμαι, &c. is from κέκτημαι.

Another Homeric form is ὀρέοντο (Il. β, 398. ψ, 212.), which is not quite according to analogy, particularly if supposed to be the same as ὤροντο. But according to form it can be only an imperfect; and if we examine the passages more closely we shall see that it belongs to a peculiar meaning. It is said of the Greeks, that Ἀνστάντες ὀρέοντο κεδασθέντες κατὰ νῆας: here ὀρέοντο being joined with the aor. κεδασθέντες must mean *they hastened, rushed*; and the same of the winds, τοὶ δ' ὀρέοντο ἠχῇ θεσπεσίῃ νέφεα κλονέοντε πάροιθεν: see Hesych. &c. This is never the meaning of ὤρνυντο, &c. We must therefore suppose a separate verb ὀρέομαι* derived from ΟΡΩ: and we find the pres. of such a verb in the epitaph on Hesiod given by Pausanias (9, 38.) Ἡσιόδου, τοῦ πλεῖστον ἐν Ἑλλάδι κῦδος ὀρεῖται, which must mean not *arises*, still less *will arise*, but *rushes in every direction, is spread far and wide.*

Lastly, there is a difficult form ὄρονται in Od. ξ, 104. ἐπὶ δ' ἀνέρες ἐσθλοὶ ὄρονται, *the herdsmen* ...... *over the herds.* Here the old grammarians, as the meaning of the verb is not clear, supposed a separate verb ὄρομαι with the meaning *I take care of*; of which ὄροντο, at Od. γ, 471. (where the same phrase recurs) would be imperfect†. But at Il. ψ, 112. we find in the same sense of an overlooker or superintending servant, ἐπὶ δ' ἀνὴρ ἐσθλὸς ὀρώρει. I know of no other way to

* [Passow has given this verb a place in his Lexicon, and supposes it to be synonymous with ὄρνυμαι.]

† [Passow has the following article: Ὄρομαι (from οὖρος, ὁράω) *I watch, keep watch*, Od. ξ, 104. Others place the verb in this passage under ΟΡΩ, ὄρνυμι; but neither ὄρω nor ὄρομαι is ever found in actual usage, and the sense of the passage is contrary to it.]

reconcile these passages, but to suppose a separate verb ὄρομαι synonymous with ὀρέομαι; then ἐπόρομαι will mean, *I bestir* or *busy myself about anything*: while in the third passage, where the metre would not admit of the same form, the pluperf. ἐπὶ . . . . ὀρώρει was substituted for it with the sense of, *he had bestirred himself, had risen up* (to accompany them.). Thus in both passages the preposition ἐπὶ gives of itself the idea of *guard* or *protection*.

Ὀρύσσω, -ττω, *I dig*: fut. ὀρύξω, &c.; perf. (with Attic reduplication) ὀρώρυχα; pluperf. ὀρωρύχειν; perf. pass. ὀρώρυγμαι, Xen. Cyr. 7, 5, 7. Midd. e. g. aor. 1. infin. ὀρύξασθαι, Herodot. 1, 186.

In the later writers the reduplication of the perfect was dropped and the temporal augment substituted for it, particularly in the pass. ὤρυγμαι, of which we may see instances from the time of Polybius in Lobeck ad Phryn. p. 33. Whether we ought to suffer ὤρυκτο, 1, 186. and ὤρυκται, 2, 158. to remain in the text of Herodotus, when we find ὀρώρυκτο only a few lines afterwards in the former passage, I will not venture to decide.

Ὀσφραίνομαι, *I smell* (something): fut. ὀσφρήσομαι; aor. ὠσφρόμην: see note under Αἰσθάνομαι. [It is joined with accus. in Herodot. 1, 80.; in the later writers as Ælian, Lucian, &c. with genitive.—Passow.]

The pres. ὀσφρᾶσθαι was also an Attic form, Antiphanes ap. Athen. p. 299. e. ὀσφρᾶται, Lucian Piscat. 48.

Instead of ὠσφρόμην we find, but less frequently, ὠσφράμην, whence ὄσφραντο, Herodot. 1, 80, 26. see εἱλάμην under Αἱρέω and εὑράμην from Εὑρίσκω. The aor. 1. midd. ὠσφρησάμην came also into use among the later writers (Arat. Dios. 223. see Lobeck ad Phryn. p. 741.), as did also from the regular inflexion other forms, e. g. aor. 1. pass. ὀσφρανθῆναι, verbal adj. ὀσφραντός, &c., and that in Aristotle.

[This verb was used also as a passive with the meaning of *to be smelt*, but only by the later medical writers, who have likewise the active ὀσφραίνω τινά τινι, *I give a person something to smell at*, Lobeck ad Phryn. p. 468. But the presents, which have been erroneously derived from aorists, as ὄσφρω, ὄσφρομαι, ὀσφράω, ὀσφρέω and the like, are not Greek.—Passow.]

Οὐλόμενος. See Ὄλλυμι.

Οὔνεσθε. See Ὄνομαι.

Οὐρέω, *mingo*: imperf. (with syllab. augm.) ἐούρουν*; fut. midd. οὐρήσομαι; perf. act. ἐούρηκα. Beside the regular infin. οὐρεῖν, Hes. ε, 760. the common language used οὐρῆν, like ζῆν†.

Οὐτάω, *I wound*: fut. οὐτήσω; aor. 1. οὔτησα; aor. 1. pass. οὐτήθην. The following Epic forms belong to a syncopated aorist with ă short (like ἔκταν, ἔκτα; see ἔγνων under Γιγνώσκω:), as 3. pers. sing. οὖτᾰ, infin. οὐτάμεναι and οὐτάμεν, part. pass. οὐτάμενος. Beside the above Homer has the pres. οὐτάζω, with its aor. 1. οὔτᾰσα, and perf. pass. οὔτασμαι; also the imperf. οὔτασκε and οὐτήσασκε.

Ὀφείλω, *I owe, I ought, I must*: fut. ὀφειλήσω, &c. The aor. 2. ὤφελον is used only as a wish, as ὤφελον ποιῆσαι, *oh that I had done it!* also with εἴθε and ὡς: so ὤφελες . . . ., ὤφελε . . . . *oh that thou hadst* . . . ., *that he had* . . . ., &c.

There are some Ionic forms of the present which come immediately from ὀφειλέω, as ὀφειλεούσῃ, ὀφειλεύμενος, Euseb. Philos. ap. Stob. S. 44. p. 309.

Homer uses ὀφέλλω sometimes as a separate verb with the sense of *I increase, enlarge*, sometimes as synonymous with ὀφείλω‡.

The form ὤφελον, -ες, -ε (the 1. and 2. pers. plur. were not in use) had no augment either in the Ion. dialect, in the whole range of Greek poetry (except what was strictly Attic), or in the later prose, e. g. ὄφελον, -ες, -ε; and in this form as well as in the other the Epics doubled the λ whenever the metre required it, as ὤφελλον, ὤφελλε, ὄφελλον, &c. But Hesiod has in a similar case ὤφειλον; Μηκέτ' ἔπειτ' ὤφειλον ἐγὼ πέμπτοισι μετεῖναι, ε, 172. Εἴθε μοι . . . . ὤφειλες δοῦναι, Fragm. Melamp. ap. Tzetz. ad Lycophr. 682. And there is no doubt that the imperfect, however it may have been written, was the true old form of

* This verb, like ὠθέω and ὠνέομαι, took the syllabic augment instead of the temporal; thus, προσεούρουν, Demosth. c. Conon. init. ἐνεουρηκότας, Aristoph. Lys. ἐούρει, Lucian. Conviv. 35. Compare ἔοικα under Εἴκω.

† Οὐρῆν is joined by the Grammarians Gaza and Chrysoloras (see Fisch. 1. p. 127.) with πεινῆν and διψῆν as an acknowledged form; we may therefore be sure that they had precedents for it from the older Grammarians.

‡ That this verb is sometimes written in Homer ὀφείλω (Il. λ, 686. 688. 698.), and sometimes ὀφέλλω (Il. τ, 200. Od. γ, 367. θ, 332. 462.), is an old mistake naturally arising from tradition. Without wishing to prove the affinity of the two meanings, I have still no doubt of the Homeric form for both being ὀφέλλω; consequently the three verses in Il. λ. ought properly to be written the same as the others.

this wish, "it was my duty to have been there, I ought to have been there." The common ὤφελον arose therefore entirely from a quick pronunciation of the above formula, and has the appearance only of an aor. 2.

Of ὀφέλλω, *I increase*, there is in Homer an anomalous 3. sing. opt. ὀφέλλειεν, Il. π, 651. Od. β, 334. If we call this word a present, its irregularity will be quite unexampled. But by a closer examination of the verse in the former of the two passages we shall see that the subject of it is not Hector but Jupiter, who was then in the act of making his decision. In this case then the aor. is the proper form, and it is the more natural one in the other passage. But the aor. of ὀφέλλω can be no other than ὤφειλα, opt. ὀφείλειεν; and it is not at all improbable that the Rhapsodists, who had but an obscure feeling of analogy, being reminded by this form of the meaning of ὀφείλω, might have altered it to the clearer but less analogous ὀφέλλειεν*.

Ὀφλισκάνω, *I am guilty* (of a crime), *incur* (as a punishment): fut. ὀφλήσω; perf. ὤφληκα; aor. ὦφλον, infin. ὀφλεῖν, part. ὀφλών, Elmsl. Aristoph. Ach. 689. and Eurip. Heracl. 985.

A pres. ὄφλω is nowhere found, and wherever ὦφλον occurs, it presupposes a juridical decision or something equivalent to have already taken place; while ὀφλισκάνω†, ὠφλίσκανον represents the investigation as still continuing, and in a metaphor borrowed from common life describes the situation of one who is constantly exposing himself to something unpleasant, as ὀφλισκάνει γέλωτα, *he incurs laughter, makes himself ridiculous*, and the like. Bekker was therefore quite right in accenting ὀφλεῖν for ὄφλειν according to the reading of the best manuscripts in Plat. Alcib. I. 35. (p. 121. b.): but with regard to ὀφλών for ὄφλων we must not decide too hastily: compare Πέφνων. The aor. 1. προσοφλῆσαι (Alciphr. 3, 26.) belongs therefore to the later forms enumerated in Lobeck's Parerg. c. 5.

Among the Ionic resolutions in Herodotus, one of the most remarkable is that of the 3. pers. of the imperf. εε for ε in three verbs, ἔψεε, ἐνείχεε, ὤφλεε, Herodot. 1, 48. 1, 118. 8, 26. See also ἐώθεε under Ἔθω.

It is clear that ὦφλον is properly the aor. of ὀφείλω according to the

* If all the above suppositions are correct, it will follow that there was an old verb ὀφέλλω, imperf. ὤφελλον, aor. 1. ὤφειλα with a twofold meaning; 1. *I increase*. 2. *I owe*: of which the former became obsolete, and the latter took in the present the form of ὀφείλω.

† Some verbs have a pres both in -σκω and -άνω, as ἀμβλίσκω, ἀμβλισκάνω: see ἀλύσκανε under Ἀλύσκω. but in ὀφλισκάνω no other present is in use than the one thus doubly strengthened by combining both terminations.

analogy of ἤγρετο and ἦλθον; and that the other forms for this particular meaning were framed after it.

Π.

Παίζω, *I sport, joke*: fut. παίξομαι and παιξοῦμαι; whence the later writers formed an aor. 1. ἔπαιξα, perf. pass. πέπαιγμαι, &c.; but in the Ionic and pure Attic dialect the aor. 1. is always ἔπαισα and the perf. pass. πέπαισμαι*, notwithstanding their similarity to the same tenses in παίω.

[This verb does not occur at all in the Iliad; but in the Odyssey we find (beside the pres. and imperf.) the imperat. aor. παίσατε, Od. θ, 251. On the other hand the later writers, as Plutarch, &c., have the regular Dor. aor. infin. παῖξαι; the aor. 1. pass. ἐπαίχθην; perf. act. πέπαιχα, perf. pass. πέπαῖγμαι, Lobeck ad Phryn. p. 240.—Passow.]

Παίω, *I strike*, is regular. The pass. takes σ.—Midd. as aor. 1. ἐπαίσατο, Xen.

The Attics have another fut. παιήσω, which is more in use than the regular one, Aristoph. Nub. 1125. Lys. 459.

Παλαίω, *I wrestle, struggle*: fut. παλαίσω; aor. 1. ἐπάλησα, whence 3. sing. opt. παλήσειε, Herodot. 8, 21. where however one manuscript has παλαίσειεν. The pass. takes σ.

Πάλλω, *I shake, swing*: aor. 1. ἔπηλα, Soph. El. 710. Pass. aor. 2.

Homer has also the aor. 2. act. with the reduplication in the compound part. ἀμπεπαλών: and the syncop. aor. 2. midd. πάλτο, Il. ο, 645. In Callimachus 1. 64. we find the aor. 1. midd. infin. πήλασθαι.

Πάομαι, *I acquire*, occurs only in its aor. 1., ἐπᾱσάμην, infin. πάσασθαι; and perf. πέπᾱμαι†, 3. sing. pluperf. πέπᾱτο. This verb was used exactly like κτάομαι, κέκτημαι. The aorist is found only in the poets; the perfect and pluperfect in prose also, e. g. in Xenophon.

The aorist of this verb is sufficiently distinguished from the aorist of πατέομαι, *I eat*, (although they are written the same,) by the α of the former being long while that of the latter is short. The perfect of the latter differs by having the σ‡.

* See Πιέζω.

† A false reading πέπαμμαι, as also πολυπάμμων, is now banished from the printed text. Compare the subst. πᾶμα, κτῆμα.

‡ Schneider in his Lexicon attempts to unite these two verbs, but he does it by etymological art, which ought to have no influence on grammatical treatment.

Πάσσω, Att. πάττω, *I strew, sprinkle, besprinkle*: fut. πάσω (⏑ -); perf. pass. πέπασμαι.—Midd. See Πλάσσω and Ἁρμόττω.

Some of the forms of this verb are written the same as those of πατέομαι.

Πάσχω*, *I suffer*: fut. πείσομαι as the fut. midd. of πείθω; perf. 2. πέπονθα (from the stem ΠΕΝΘ– as seen in the subst. πένθος); aor. 2. ἔπαθον. Verbal adj. παθητός†.

Beside the above, we find the following old sister-forms; in Od. ρ, 555. a fem. perf. part. πεπᾰθυῖα, which supposes a perf. πέπηθα according to the analogy of ἀραρυῖα and others under Ἀραρίσκω: and in Æschyl. Agam. 1635. in the Iambics the aor. 1. part. πήσας (from an aor. ἔπησα). The fut. πήσομαι is uncertain‡.

We find also in Homer a syncopated perf. πέποσθε for πεπόνθατε, like ἐγρήγορθε for ἐγρηγόρατε, by an imitation of the passive termination: that is to say, as soon as in πεπόνθατε the θ preceded the τ, it was changed to σ (as ἴδμεν, ἴστε) and the ν was dropped, making πέποστε; a transition was then made to a passive form πέποσθε.

Πατάσσω, *I strike*, is regular: it was used by the Attics in the *active* voice only. See Πλήσσω.

Πατέω, *I tread*, is regular. The pres. pass. accidentally coincides with the following verb.

Πατέομαι, *I taste, eat*; an Ion. depon. midd.: aor. 1. ἐπᾰσάμην, infin. πάσασθαι; perf. πέπασμαι. That these forms belong to each other is proved by identity of usage (e.g. Herodot. 1, 73. and 2, 47 ἐπάσαντο and πατέονται τῶν κρεῶν:), as well as by the exact analogy of δατεῖσθαι, δάσασθαι.

Παύω, *I cause to cease, stop*: fut. παύσω; aor. 1. ἔπαυσα, &c.: there are no traces of a perfect. Midd. παύομαι, *I cease*: fut. πεπαύσομαι§; perf. pass. πέπαυμαι, *I have ceased*, i. e. *I no longer continue to do so*; aor. 1. midd. ἐπαυσάμην; aor. 1. pass. ἐπαύθην and ἐπαύσθην‖; the former, Ionic and

* Dœderlein has a very good remark, that while from ΠΑΘ– is formed πά-σκω by affixing the termination -σκω, the aspiration of the θ, which disappears, is thrown on the κ, making πάσχω.

† The fut. παθήσω, which is quoted by the old Grammarians, rests on a false separation of εὐπαθήσω.

‡ It occurs here and there as a various reading, e.g. in Herodot. 9, 37. Xen. Cyrop. 7, 3, 10. See also Schweigh. Index to Polybius.

§ [The regular fut. midd. is παύσομαι, but the purer Attic writers prefer πεπαύσομαι, Soph Ant. 91. Piers. ad Mœr p. 293.—Passow.]

‖ [There is said to have been also an aor. ἐπάην, Chœroboscus A B. 3. p. 1324.—Passow.]

perhaps old Attic, is found in Hes. θ, 533. Herodot. 1, 130.; while the latter is preferred by Thucydides and the Attics who followed him *.

The imperat. act. παῦε is very commonly used in the immediate sense for παύου: and there is one instance mentioned of the aor. ἔπαυσα in this same sense, viz. Od. δ, 659. Μνηστῆρες δ' ἄμυδις κάθισαν καὶ παῦσαν ἀέθλων, but the excellent Cod. Vindob. 56. has Μνηστῆρας, according to which the subject of the verb is the two chief suitors mentioned in the verse before. By this emendation the connection of the whole sentence becomes so much more natural, that it helps to prove the truth of the reading. Compare also the Ambrosian Scholium.

Πείθω, *I persuade*: fut. πείσω; aor. 1. ἔπεισα †; perf. πέπεικα. Pass. πείθομαι, *I am persuaded, I believe, I obey*: fut. midd. πείσομαι; perf. pass. πέπεισμαι, *I have been convinced*, therefore *I believe firmly*; aor. 1. ἐπείσθην: to which we may add the perf. 2. πέποιθα, generally with the intransitive sense, *I trust*.

In Il β, 341. δ, 159. we find a syncop. 1. plur. pluperf. ἐπέπιθμεν for ἐπεπίθειμεν. In this form, as in ἐκέκραγμεν from κράζω, εἰλήλουθμεν from ἐλήλυθα under Ἔρχομαι, and several others, everything between the root and the termination is dropped: and as some of these perfects (κέκραγα, πέποιθα, &c.) have the force of a pres., they have also an imperative ending in θι, as κέκραχθι, πέπεισθι, Æschyl. Eum. 602. in which latter the diphthong of the root is retained.

Poetry has also (see the Indexes of Aristoph. and Eurip.) the aor. 2. act. ἔπιθον, πιθών for ἔπεισα, &c. and an aor. 2. midd. ἐπιθόμην, πίθου, πιθέσθαι for ἐπείσθην, &c. The Epic language never uses the act. aor. without the redupl., πέπιθον, πέπιθε, πεπίθοιμι, &c.; but in the midd. it has the usual πιθέσθαι. The reduplicated form of the midd. (at least in the only passage where it occurs) belongs as to meaning to πέποιθα, e.g. πεπίθοιθ' ἑῷ αὐτοῦ θυμῷ, Il. κ, 204.; as does the act. πεπιθών, Pind. Isth. 4, 122.‡

From this aor. 2. arose again other active forms, as fut. πεπιθήσω, and πιθήσω, aor. 1. ἐπίθησα, and part. πιθήσας: but with this difference,

* It must be observed, however, that even in Thucydides (2, 77. 5, 91. 100) the reading παυθῆναι has been restored from the best manuscripts.

† [Of this tense Homer has only the opt. πείσειε, Od. ξ, 123.—Passow.]

‡ Bœckh says the same of the simple aor. part. πιθών, Pyth. 3, 28. (50.), but I cannot subscribe to his opinion.

that πεπιθήσω has the meaning of *to persuade*, but πιθήσω, πιθῆσαι the intransitive sense of πείθομαι and πέποιθα, *to obey* or *follow*; *to trust to*.

Such is the distinction which must be observed, if we follow our present Homeric text. But here our attention is at once arrested by the circumstance, that according to this rule πεποιθώς and πιθήσας would be used in many passages indifferently, without distinction of sense or metre. Now it should be observed, that πεποιθώς, of which the established meaning has always been, *trusting to, relying on, fretus*, never occurs in any other sense; as γηυσὶ, λαοῖς, χείρεσσι, ἀλκὶ, ποδωκείῃσι, πεποιθώς, &c.: while we cannot but feel, that in opposition to these the following two passages, φρεσὶ λευγαλέῃσι πιθήσας, Il. ι, 119. and ἀναιδείῃφι πιθήσας, Hes. ε, 357. express a very different idea, viz. *obeying* or *yielding to*; which sense the future of the same verb has also in the only passage where any part of it occurs beside the participle; e. g. πιθήσεις, *thou wilt obey*, Od. φ, 369. In the same way when at Il. δ, 398. Tydeus, having slain all the Thebans, (who lay in wait for him,) excepting Mæon, spares him alone, θεῶν τεράεσσι πιθήσας, it is quite clear that he does it "*in obedience to* the signs of the gods." When, however, at ζ, 183. Bellerophon attacks and kills the terrible Chimæra, and the same expression is used, θεῶν τεράεσσι πιθήσας, the word can mean nothing more than *trusting to, confiding in*. But we find in the same sense at Il. μ, 256 speaking of the Trojans attacking the Grecian walls, Τοῦπερ δὴ (i. e. of Jupiter,) τεράεσσι πεποιθότες: which passage alone makes it very probable that πεποιθώς was also the original reading in the other, viz. ζ, 183. And this supposition is strengthened by Il. ν, 369. Od. φ, 315. where our text reads πιθήσας in the same sense of *trusting to*, but the manuscripts actually have the various reading πεποιθώς. It is therefore very probable that through the affinity of the two readings, and the similarity of the expressions, both verbs were very early confounded together; and that πεποιθώς was also the original reading in Il. λ, 235. ρ, 48. χ, 107. and Hes. ε, 669.

Πείκω, *I shear, comb*: fut. πέξω, &c. Compare the Ion. δέξω from δείκνυμι.—MIDD. In the Attic language the pres. πεκτέω was in use*.

* As the verb occurs but seldom, (in the former sense κείρειν is more usual, in the latter κτενίζειν, ξαίνειν) little can be said with any certainty on the use of its forms. Whether πέκω is ever found I know not. Stephens has πεκόμενον δέρμα, but without giving the passage from which he has taken it. The Epics have πείκω, πέξω, &c.; and this is the only formation which occurs That the old Grammarians also considered πείκω as the pres. of πέξω, is clear from Schol Theocr. 5, 98. Etym. M. vv. πέσκος and πείκω (p 667, 40.) Etym. Gud v. πείκω (p. 456.). Aristophanes has πεκτεῖν and πεκτούμενον but whether πέκτειν or πεκτεῖν is doubtful. In Pollux 7. c. 33, 1. we find πέκτειν as a pres. of πέξατο, but through a misunderstanding the text of our editions has πέκειν. See Jungermann's note. Thus we see that the simple stem πέκω was strengthened by the Attics to πέκτω, which again was changed to πεκτῶ, like ῥίπτω to ῥιπτῶ.

Πεινάω, *I hunger*: fut. πεινήσω, &c. This verb, like διψάω, ζάω, &c., has both in the Attic and common dialect an η, as infin. πεινῆν, διψῆν, &c. We find also ζῇς, ζῇ, ἔζη, πεινῇς, χρῆται, δίψητε, so that in these forms the indic. and conj. are the same.

Πειράω, *I try*, is regular, with α long, Ion. η, in the inflexion. The passive as a deponent, with fut. middle, has the same sense; but it means also *to experience*.

The Epics use the aor. of the midd. as well as of the pass. in the sense of a deponent. The same poets have a form πειράζω with a frequentative meaning, *to try, to prove*, which again became common in the language of the later writers, while the Attics always used πειρᾷν only. The passive with the σ belongs entirely to this later πειράζω. The form πεπείρανται may come also from περαίνω. See Περάω.

Πέκω, πεκτέω. See Πείκω.

Πελάζω, *I approach*, is regular. The Attic fut. πελᾷν occurs sometimes in the poets.

In the older language this verb has the *causative* meaning *to bring near, carry* or *place near*; whence the pass. πελάζομαι, ἐπελάσθην takes the *immediate* sense, which the active has in the common language. Homer has πελάζω in the older meaning only, succeeding poets in both. The sister-form πελάω* occurs as a present in Hymn. Bacch. 44. πελάᾳν. The poetical aor. ἐπλάθην used by the Attics, and the verbal adj. ἄπλᾱτος which comes from it and is found both in the Attics and the Epic poets, are supposed to be formed by syncope: but the α is always long; whence it is clear that this is rather a transposition of sounds together with a contraction, like κέκρᾱκα from κεράω, πέπρᾱκα from περάω, &c. And in the same way we must explain in the Epics, 1. the perf. pass. πέπλημαι, πεπλημένος Od. μ, 108. and 2. the aor. ἐπλήμην, πλῆτο†; that is to say, as syncopated forms from πεπέλαμαι, ἐπελάμην, like ἐκτάμην under Κτείνω. Here therefore a contraction takes place, as it does in the similar case of κέκρᾱκα (under Κεράννυμι), Ion. into η, Att. in ᾱ‡. We find also frequently ἐπλάσθην, but this is indisputably through the common fault of corrupting the θ

* Wherever we find in the common language a verb in -άζω, which is not admissible in the hexameter, the Epics generally use a sister-form in -άω

† This aor. must not be confounded with ἐπλήμην under Πίμπλημι.

‡ According to general analogy, this contraction should take place in both dialects in η; for the α in κέκρᾱκα arises from the influence of the ρ. Perhaps, therefore, the Atticism in this verb was only to avoid a similarity with πλήθω, particularly in πλάθω mentioned at the top of the next page.

of the aor. 1. pass. into σθ; for it cannot be supposed that beside ἐπλάθην and ἐπελάσθην a third form not required by any metre could have been also in use. See Brunck on Eurip. Hec. 880.

The Tragedians have also a sister-form πελάθω, by adding -θω to the vowel of the stem or root, and this they again contract in the present (as in the last paragraph) into πλάθω with long α.

A pres. πλάζω (for πελάζω) is also supposed, on account of προσέπλαζε, Od. λ, 583. and the particip. προσπλάζον, Il. μ, 285. And the Epic language furnishes sufficient grounds arising from metrical difficulty, to account for the syncope in these forms. But there are other points to be considered: particularly that these two would then be the only Homeric passages among a very large number, in which the active voice would have the later immediate meaning of *to approach*. Besides in these two passages the water and the waves are the subject, and the case is the same in a third passage, Il. φ, 269. where the wave that is approaching Achilles πλάζ' ὤμους καθύπερθεν. Hence some of the commentators understand this last also to be for πέλαζε, although here the context makes it far less probable. In addition to this we must observe that the common πλάζω, -άγξω occurs very frequently in Homer, and is used also of waves, in as much as they *beat* and *drive* ships *from their course*. It is therefore pretty certain that πλάζω is the proper expression for the *beating of the waves*, and was used intransitively as well as transitively, in as much as an object is met and moved by them, consequently moved from its place, or *beaten and driven away*; whence therefore the common metaphorical sense of πλάζεσθαι, *to wander about*.

Another Epic sister-form is made by changing -αω into -νάω, -νημι, and the ε of the root into ι, as πελάω, πίλνημι, πίλναμαι: see κίρνημι from κεράω in note under Κεράννυμι.

Πέλω and more frequently πέλομαι, *I am*; an old verb which remained in use among the Dorics (πέλει, πέλη, Fragm. Pythagg. Gale, p. 749. 750.) and the poets. It has only pres. and imperf., which latter, when it retains the augment, suffers syncope; e. g. 3. sing. imperf. act. ἔπλε; 2. sing. imperf. midd. ἔπλεο, contr. ἔπλευ, 3. sing. ἔπλετο*. And here we find this peculiarity, that the imperfect passive has very commonly the meaning of the present, as Il. α, 418. ζ, 434.

To the above verb belong the Epic participles ἐπιπλόμενος, περιπλόμενος† in what appears to be the original meaning, *I am employed about; prevail amongst, versor*; and with the same syncope: as in Od. ν, 60. (*old age and death*,) ἐπ' ἀνθρώποισι πέλονται (ἐπιπέλονται,) *pre-*

* [Homer has also a 2d sing. imperf. midd πελέσκεο, Il χ, 433. and in Hes. Fr. 22, 4. is the 3. sing. πελέσκετο.—Passow.]

† Euphorion indeed (ap. Tzetz. ad Lycophr. 494) has the simple πλόμενος.

vail among men, frequentant, versantur; in which sense Homer elsewhere uses πωλέομαι, ἐπιπωλέομαι, which is therefore the only instance of the termination -έω having the change of vowel to ω.

Πέμπω, *I send*: fut. πέμψω; aor. 1. ἔπεμψα; perf. πέπομφα*. In the passive Pindar and Herodotus have the aor. 1. part. πεμφθείς, and Photius the part. perf. πεπεμμένος. The other tenses are generally supplied by ἀποστέλλω.

ΠΕΝΘ–. See Πάσχω.

Πένομαι, *I am poor*: in Hom. *I labour*, and transit. *I prepare by labour*, δαῖτα, &c. It is used only in pres. and imperf.

Πεπαρεῖν or Πεπορεῖν—and Πέπρωμαι. See Πορεῖν.

Πέποσθε. See Πάσχω.

Πέπρωμαι, &c. See Πορεῖν.

Πέπτω. See Πέσσω.

Περάω, *I go over, pass over* or *through*: fut. περάσω, Ion. περήσω; aor. 1. ἐπέρᾱσα, Ion. ἐπέρησα. This verb is regular, with α long, Ion. η.

Different from the above is an inflexion with α short, περάσω, ἐπέρᾰσα, and in the sense of *to sell*; but found only in the Epic poets, and without any trace of a present with the same meaning having been in use; for περῶ, infin. περᾷν is in this sense a future. Hence comes the verb in common use πιπράσκω with the subst. πρᾶσις. For further particulars we refer to that verb, only remarking here that the original identity of the two is undoubted. That is to say, the common meaning of περᾷν is *to go over*, and it governs as a transitive the accusative of the space to be passed, as περᾷν τὴν θάλασσαν; but it may also be taken causatively, *to carry over*†; whence arose the meaning of *to sell*, i. e. *to carry over the sea* or *into another country for sale*. And usage separated the formation, so that περάσω and its derivatives meant only *to sell*, while περᾱσω, περήσω retained only the sense of *to pass over*, with the single exception of πεπερημένος in Homer, for which see Πιπράσκω.

With these verbs we must compare a third, περαίνω, from πέρας *an end*, (consequently with the meaning of *to complete*,) which is regular

* Like κέκλοφα from κλέπτω, and τέτροφα from τρέπω: see note under Κλέπτω.

† I have not yet found any certain instances of this meaning in its strict and proper sense; for in the Hymn. Merc. 133. (see Hermann) the reading is not sure; and περᾷν πόδα, Eurip. Hec. 53. is like βαίνειν πόδα, for which see Βαίνω.

and takes α long in the aor., ἐπέρᾱνα, Ion. ἐπέρηνα, Perf. pass. πεπέρασμαι; 3. sing. πεπέρανται, and on account of the metre πειραίνω, πεπείρανται, Od. μ, 37. Soph. Trach. 581.*

Πέρδω, more generally πέρδομαι, *pedo*: aor. 2. ἔπαρδον; fut. παρδήσομαι; perf. πέπορδα.

In Aristoph. Vesp. 394. ἀποπαρδῶ is accented falsely. It must be ἀποπάρδω as aor. 2. conj.; for this conjunctive, after the particles οὐ μή, has the force of a future, even when it is joined in a sentence with real futures.

Πέρθω, *I lay waste*: fut. πέρσω; aor. 1. ἔπερσα; aor. 2. ἔπρᾰθον†, infin. πρᾰθεῖν, poet. πρᾰθέειν. Homer has also a fut. pass. πέρσομαι, Il. ω, 729. and a syncopated aor. (but only in the infin.) πέρθαι, which is to be explained by ἐπέρθμην, infin. πέρθ–θαι, and dropping the θ πέρθαι, like δέχθαι. The perf. act. πέπορθα is post-Homeric.

Πεσεῖν. See Πίπτω.

Πέσσω, πέττω, *I cook*: fut. πέψω, &c.; perf. pass. πέπεμμαι, infin. πεπέφθαι. The pres. πέπτω which corresponds with this formation, is found in the later writers.

That ΠΕΠ– is the simple stem or root is clear from some of the derivatives, as πέπων, ἀρτοπόπος: and the change from π to σσ or ττ is found also in ἐνίσσω for ἐνίπτω: compare φάσσα the fem. of φάψ, &c., as well as Kœn. ad Greg. Æol. 42., and Buttm. Lexilog. p. 126.

Πετάννυμι, or πεταννύω, *I spread wide, open*: fut. πετάσω (ᾰ); aor. 1. ἐπέτᾰσα, Ep. πέτασσα, &c. Perf. pass. by syncope πέπτᾰμαι; but aor. 1. pass. ἐπετάσθην.

The Att. fut. πετῶ, &c., was generally preferred to πετάσω: see Thom. Mag. p. 61. and Meineke Menand. Incert. 190. The later writers took the liberty of using this form or the simple theme as a present, e. g. ἀναπετῶσαι (for ἀναπεταννῦσαι), Lucian de Calumn. 21. The perf. pass. πεπέτασμαι occurs in its compound ἐκπεπέτασται in an oracle of Herodot. I, 62. and in ἀναπεπέτασται, Lucian. Somn. 29. Out of the Attic dialect this verb was very naturally confounded with the following one, which is so nearly akin to it: see, for instance, ἐπετάσθην under that verb; Parmenides (Fragm. v. 18.) had a part. aor. ἀναπτάμενος in an active sense, *having opened*; and Zenodotus read at Il. α, 351. χεῖρας ἀναπτάς.

* [Hermann doubts the admissibility of this Epic form in an Attic poet, and prefers reading πεπείραται.—Passow.]

† In this aor as in ἔδρακον from δέρκω, the natural length of the middle syllable is removed by transposing the letters.

For the form πίτνημι, πιτνάω, see κεράω in note under Κεράννυμι, and the end of the article on Πελάζω. Schneider in his Lexicon quotes the following authorities for it; viz. πίτνα for ἐπίτνα, imperf. of πιτνάω, Il. φ, 7., πιτνάς, part. pres. of πίτνημι, Od. λ, 392. πίτναν 3. plur. for ἐπίτνησαν, Pind. Nem. 5, 20. In Hes. Scut. 291. the reading of ἔπιτνον from πίτνω is doubtful, and Gaisford reads ἔπιπλων. Schneider improperly confounds this verb with πιτνέω, πιτνεῖν, a sister-form of πίπτω: see the latter.

Πέτομαι, *I fly*, depon. midd.: fut. πετήσομαι, Hom. and Aristoph. Pac. 77. 1126., but in Attic prose generally πτήσομαι; syncop. aor. 2. ἐπτόμην, infin. πτέσθαι*.

In addition to the above, which according to the Atticists are the only legitimate forms in Attic prose, we find also frequently a pres. ἵπταμαι with the aor. 1. ἐπτάμην, infin. πτάσθαι; and in an active form the aor. ἔπτην, infin. πτῆναι, part. πτάς.

See Lobeck ad Phryn. p. 325. Lucian. Lexiph. extr. By these and other testimonies the pres. ἵπταμαι, which is the common one in use among the later writers, becomes very suspicious as a form of the older language, although still found in some passages without any various reading: see Porson. ad Medeam. 1. Lobeck ad Phryn. l. c.† The aor. ἐπτάμην in the Ionic writers and old poets is unobjectionable and of frequent occurrence: see Porson on the passages quoted, and Hermann on Soph. Aj. 275.‡: but in the prose of the older time it is very doubtful, as in many passages where it is the common reading, the manuscripts have πτέσθαι, πτόμενος, &c. The form ἔπτην is old and genuine in the poets, although not so frequent; but in the later language it is very common.

Beside the above we find πέταμαι and πετάομαι used in the later prose; in which they are free from all suspicion, as even the pass. aor. ἐπετάσθην (for ἐπτόμην), notwithstanding its identity with the aor.

* [Passow adds the perf. act. πέπτηκα: on which see however the end of this article.]

† Porson did not venture to reject the imperfect which occurs in Euripides, although he remarks that in both the passages where it is found (Iph. A. 1608. and Fragm. Polyidi 1.) the aorist would be more accurate. Doubtless he was deterred by the somewhat bold alteration of ἀπέπτατο for ἀφίπτατο in the former of the two passages. But as Lucian will not once allow the form ἵπτατο to be μετοικικόν, this emendation does not appear to me too bold.

‡ Hermann's opinion on Soph. Œd. T. 17., that πτέσθαι is an imperf., still wants the necessary proofs: in the passage itself the sense of the imperfect is by no means decisive.

pass. of πετάννυμι, occurs in it, e. g. Aristot. H. A. 9, 40. (9, 27, 5. Schneid.) and in Lucian. Rhet. Præcept. 6. For the form πέταμαι there is older authority in the poets; for πέταται is found not only in Pindar, but also in the chorus and the anapæsts of the dramatic poets*; and Anacreon has the infin. πέτασθαι and the 2. sing. πέτασσαι†.

Lastly come the forms with the change of vowel to ο or ω according to the analogy of φέρω and φορέω, τρέμω and τρομέω, or στρέφω and στρώφαω, τρέχω and τρωχάω, and others mentioned under Δέμω; in which however it must be observed that this is the only verb with the formation in -άω which changes the vowel to ο: for the principal form, used also by the Attic poets, is ποτάομαι (ποτᾶται, ποτῶνται), which in the Epics takes the formation in -έω, but only in a resolved shape, as ποτέονται; and when the metre requires, it has an ω in the stem or root, as πωτῶντο. Of the further formation of this verb we find the Doric forms πεπόταμαι, Eurip. Hippol. 564. and ἐποτάθην, Aristoph. Av. 1338. Aristophanes has however the perfect πεπότημαι not only in the Anapæsts (Nub. 319.) but also in the Iambics (Av. 1445.); whence Bekker's opinion is very probable that this was the usual perfect of πέτομαι in the Attic dialect: for I know of no authority for the active πέπτηκα‡ beyond grammatical tradition. If this supposition be correct, the Attic prose usage of the above verb will be as follows:

Πέτομαι, πτήσομαι, ἐπτόμην, πεπότημαι.

ΠΕΤ–. See Πίπτω.

Πεύθομαι. See Πυνθάνομαι.

Πέφνον, ἔπεφνον, *I slew*, the reduplicated and at the same time syncopated aorist of ΦΕΝΩ (whence φόνος), like ἐκεκλόμην from κέλομαι. The participle is accented contrary to analogy πέφνων (Il. π, 827. ρ, 539.); and this is expressly mentioned by the grammarians as a peculiarity; see Etym. Mag. vv. ἔπεφνον, βαλών, ἐών§. Of the aoristic meaning in all the Homeric forms belonging to ἔπεφνον there can be

* e. g. in Eurip. Ion. 90. and Aristoph. Av. 573. 574. where Brunck, contrary to all the manuscripts, reads as Attic πέτεται.

† Whatever may be our opinion of the odes of Anacreon, the 9th is clearly of too pure a period for us to endure such a barbarism as πετᾶσαι. Compare ἔρασσαι from ἔραμαι, and ὄνοσσο from ὄνομαι.

‡ The perfects πέπταμαι, πέπτηκα, πέπτωκα, πεπτηώς (see Πετάννυμι, Πέτομαι, Πίπτω and Πτήσσω), formed from verbs coming from the root ΠΕΤΩ, are to be explained by syncope as for πεπέταμαι, &c. These perfects, like κέκτημαι and μέμνημαι, are exceptions to the general rule of verbs, beginning with two consonants, and forming their perfect with ε instead of the reduplication. See note under Κτάομαι

§ I see clearly however that we cannot build much on this grammatical tradition. It is possible that the aoristic force of this participle, which is not evident at first sight even in the passages where it occurs, was not observed until its accentuation as a present had become firmly established.

no doubt; and the supposition of a pres. πέφνω, as shown also by the analogy of ἐκέκλετο and ἐπέφραδον, is perfectly untenable*.

With this we must join the perf. pass. πέφᾰμαι, of which Homer has the 3. sing. πέφαται, 3. plur. πέφανται, infin. πεφάσθαι, and the 3. fut. (paulo-post fut.) πεφήσομαι, πεφήσεαι, Il. ν, 829. ο, 140. Od. χ, 217. This πέφαμαι bears exactly the same relation to the root ΦΕΝ– as τέταμαι does to TEN– in τείνω; while πεφήσομαι is formed from πέφαμαι like δεδήσομαι from δέδεμαι, λελύσομαι from λέλῠμαι. The same future form comes also from the root ΦΑ– in φαίνω; and Lycophron has allowed himself to use, in the sense of *killed*, the perf. part. πεφασμένος, which belongs also to φαίνω and φημί.

Πήγνῡμι and πηγνύω, *I fix*: and in the later writers πήσσω, Att. πήττω; fut. πήξω†; aor. 1. ἔπηξα; aor. 1. pass. ἐπήχθην; but more generally aor. 2. ἐπάγην (ᾰ); aor. 1. midd. ἐπηξάμην: the perf. 2. πέπηγα has the sense of the pass., πήγνυμαι, *I am fixed, I stick firm*‡; pluperf. ἐπεπήγειν: an aor. 2. midd. ἐπηγόμην occurs in Æsop. Fab. 146. Ern.—MIDD.

Πηδάω, *I leap*: fut. midd. πηδήσομαι.

Πιέζω, *I press*: fut. πιέσω; aor. 1. ἐπίεσα, Herodot. 9, 63.; aor. 1. pass. ἐπιέσθην, infin. πιεσθῆναι, but in Hippocr. πιεχθῆναι; perf. pass. πεπίεσμαι, but in Hippocr. πεπίεγμαι, infin. πεπιέχθαι. This verb therefore, like ἁρπάζω, παίζω and others, partakes of two formations, the one with a lingual as its characteristic letter, the other with a palatic.

There are some traces of a sister-form πιεζέω, as we find in Homer πιέζευν 3. plur. imperf. for ἐπίεζον, in Herodotus πιεζεύμενος, and in Plut. Thes. 6. πιεζοῦντος.

Πίμπλημι, *I fill*, infin. πιμπλάναι, follows ἵστημι in its pres. and imperf., imitating it even in the admission or rejection of the forms in -αω: fut. πλήσω; aor. 1. ἔπλησα;

* [The earliest occurrence of the pres. πέφνω seems to be in Oppian. Hal. 2, 133.—Passow.]

† See Ἄγνυμι, Ἄξω.

‡ See ἔαγα under Ἄγνυμι.

aor. 1. midd. ἐπλησάμην; perf. pass. πέπλησμαι; aor. 1. pass. ἐπλήσθην.

In the compounds of this and the following verb πίμπρημι, whenever a μ precedes the first π, it is dropped before the second, as ἐμπίπληθι, Il. φ, 311.; but resumed when the augment intervenes, as ἐνεπίμπλασαν.

The poets observe or disregard the above rule according to the metre; but the deviations from it which occur in prose, at least in the older writers, may be ascribed to the negligence of transcribers. See Lobeck ad Phryn. p. 95.

The syncopated pass. aor. ἐπλήμην, imper. πλῆσο, opt. πλείμην (like βλείμην), &c., is one of the few aorists of this kind which are found also in Attic prose; e. g. in Aristoph. ἐμπλήμενος, ἐμπλείμην*. In this last the diphthong of the optative ει is remarkable, as the formation πιμπλάναι, πίμπλαμαι, &c. supposes a stem or root ΠΛΑ–. But in the same way χρή, which comes from χράω, has in the opt. χρείη†. The supposition most agreeable to analogy is, that ΠΛΑΩ was changed after the Iono-Doric manner to ΠΛΕΩ, whence therefore the Lat. *pleo*. To this we must add the Hesiodic (θ, 880.) πιμπλεῦσαι for -ῶσαι; for as in the Epic Ionicism, unlike to the later, αου in those verbal forms is changed to ευ, the above participle supposes a present πιμπλέω.

The immediate sense *to be full* belongs to πλήθω. This verb, beside the pres. and imperf., has no other tense than the perf. πέπληθα synonymous with the present, Pherecr. in Lex. Seguer. 6. p. 330, 23. Antim. Theb. Fr. 12. Arat. 774.‡

* An aor. 2. act. of this form, ἔπλην like ἔστην, appears also in the later language, but contrary to general analogy it has the same causative sense as πίμπλημι, ἔπλησα; if indeed the reading ἀνέπλημεν in Alciphron 3, 46. be genuine.

† We have shown in the note on βλεῖο under Βάλλω, that there are no grounds in the analogy of this optative for anything but the pure diphthong αι or ει. I cannot therefore adopt πλῄμην as proposed by Dawes, although in Aristoph. Ach. 236. the reading ἐμπλῄμην is supported by the Cod. Rav. instead of the common ἐμπλείμην; and in Lysistr. 235., where the opt. is required, the emendation first suggested by the common corrupted reading ἐμπλήσθη is that judiciously adopted by Dawes, ἐμπλῇθ' ἡ. In this case then, as in βλεῖο, βλῷο, I recognise a twofold decision of the old grammarians, and declaring myself in favour of the former, I would leave the old reading untouched in the passage of Ach. 236., but in Lys. 235. I would complete the emendation by reading ἐμπλεῖθ' ἡ κύλιξ.

‡ This πλήθω is very commonly supposed to be the radical form, principally on account of ἐπλήσθην; but the supposition is erroneous, as we may learn from comparing it with ἐχρήσθην and others. We should much rather say that πλήθω and πρήθω may be quite as well deduced immediately from a radical form in -άω, as σήθω and νήθω are from similar forms in -άω and -έω. For the actual usage of the pres. πλήθω in the causative sense of πίμπλημι we have but a bad authority in Pseudo-Phocyl. 154. On the other hand we find a striking instance of

Πίμπρημι, *I burn* (transit.), infin. πιμπράναι, follows in the common language the analogy of πίμπλημι in every part of its formation, even to the dropping or retaining of the μ before the π.

Photius in his Lex. v. σέσωται quotes as one of the older Atticisms πεπρημένος.

The shortening of ἔπρησε to ἔπρεσε in Hes. θ, 856. is remarkable. Compare the forms under Πίμπλημι which lead to a formation in -έω*.

In this verb the form πρήθω is synonymous with πίμπρημι, but found only in Il. ι, 589. ἐνέπρηθον.

Πίνω, *I drink*: fut. πίομαι (like ἔδομαι); aor. 2. ἔπιον, infin. πιεῖν, &c., imper. πίε (Od. ι, 347. Eurip. Cycl. 560.) solely poetical, the common term being πῖθι (like κλῦθι, βῆθι, γνῶθι, &c.), Athen. 10. p. 446. B. The other tenses come from the root ΠΟ–, with variable quantity, as perf. πέπωκα†; perf. pass. πέπομαι; aor. 1. pass. ἐπόθην; verbal adj. ποτός, ποτέος, whence the Lat. *poto*.

The Ion. particip. πινεύμενος (like πιεζεύμενος) for πινόμενος, is found in Hippocr. de A. A. L. 22.

A future in the shape of the fut. 2. πιοῦμαι is of frequent occurrence from the time of Aristotle. We find indeed πιεῖσθε in Xen. Symp. 4, 7. but probably the old reading πίεσθε ought to be restored: see also Schweigh. Athen. 5. p. 497. Lobeck ad Phryn. p. 31.—The ι in πίομαι is long in Aristophanes, e. g. Equ. 1289. 1401. but in the other comedians it is short: see Athen. 10. p. 446. e. 11. 783. e. (p. 221. Schweigh.) p. 471. a. 13. p. 570. d.—A solitary instance of πίομαι (with ι long) as a present for πίνω is found in Pind. Ol. 6, 147.

The syncop. infin. πῖν or πεῖν, accented also πίν, πείν, occurs in Lucill. Epig. 28, 3. Meineke Euphor. Fr. 105. See Mus. Antiqu. Stud. p. 247. sqq. Herodian. Hermanni § 47.

the aor. ἀποπλῆσαι in a neuter sense in Herodot. 8, 96. ὥστε ἀποπλῆσαι τὸν χρησμόν: for nothing but a very improbable degree of violence can supply a subject to the verb, so as to give it the sense of *to fulfil*. So decisive however is the usage of the same aorist in its common sense in all the other passages of Herodotus (see Schweigh. Lex. Herod. for the simple verb and all its compounds), that this reading cannot but be looked on with the greatest suspicion. And may not the syncop. aor. πλῆσθαι, which we have seen above in the Attic usage, have belonged to Ionic prose also?

* The various reading ἐμπιπρεῖς in Herodot. 8, 159. deserves also in this respect our attention. It may be an ancient form and grounded perhaps on some old uncertainty in the actual usage. Compare Γηράω.

† Compare βώσεσθε under Βιόω.

Πιπίσκω, *I give to drink*: fut. πίσω (Pind. Isthm. 6, 108. with ι long); aor. 1. ἔπισα. Compare Μεθύω and Μεθύσκω.

Πιπράσκω, *I sell*, Ion. πιπρήσκω, Herodot. It has in the common language neither fut. nor aor. active: the other forms are, perf. πέπρᾱκα; perf. pass. πέπρᾱμαι, infin. πεπρᾶσθαι; aor. 1. pass. ἐπράθην (ᾱ), Ion. ἐπρήθην, Herodot. In all these forms the Ionics changed the long α to η.

In the common language the defective tenses were made up by ἀποδώσομαι, ἀπεδόμην. The forms properly belonging to this verb are in the old and Epic language, fut. περάσω (with α short), Att. περῶ, infin. περᾶν, περάᾳν; aor. ἐπέρασα; of which the pres. περάω, as we have seen above, is nowhere found with this meaning, but occurs only in the cognate sense of *to go over*, in which however it is inflected with -ᾱσω, Ion. -ήσω. The above πέπρᾱκα with the other forms came from the formation περᾰσω (πεπέρᾰκα) by the same metathesis, which we have frequently seen, for instance in κεράννυμι, κερᾰσω, (κεκέρᾰκα) κέκρᾱκα, Ion. κέκρηκα.

The Homeric πεπερημένος, Il. φ, 58., formed from περάω, -ήσω, and referring to ἐπέρασσεν at *v.* 40., would therefore be a particular deviation from the above; according to which it would stand for πεπερᾰμένος with the α lengthened on account of the metre: but this metrical necessity was much more likely to have suggested, according to the above analogy, and with the Ionic η, the form πεπρημένος; which without doubt is the true reading of the passage*.

The pres. πιπρήσκω does not occur in the Epic language, but in its stead is found πέρνημι (compare δαμνάω, δάμνημι under Δέμω). In the old language, therefore, the following is the established usage; πέρνημι, περᾰσω (περῶ), ἐπέρᾰσα, πέπρᾱκα, &c.

The Atticists lay it down as a rule that πεπράσομαι, not πραθήσομαι, is used as the common future: and in reading the Attic writers we shall find that this rule holds good, in as much as the text has πεπράσεται where there is not the slightest expression of certainty or quickness. And what is particularly confirmed by the rule is this, that although ἐπράθην is good Attic, yet πεπρᾶσθαι is very frequently found, without any of the force of a perfect, instead of the mere aorist, e. g. ἐκήρυξε πεπρᾶσθαι, "*he proclaimed that . . . should be sold*," Xen.

* It is true that in Heyne I find no variety of reading mentioned; but in Seber's Index this verse is quoted under πεπερημένος, and under πεπρημένος, and in each case the other form is expressly referred to as a various reading.

Hell. 6, 2, 15. *Τούτοις ἡ μὲν ἔκτισις ἦν ἐπὶ τῆς ἐννάτης πρυτανείας· εἰ δὲ μή, διπλάσιον ὀφείλειν καὶ τὰ κτήματα αὐτῶν πεπρᾶσθαι*, Andoc. de Myst. p. 10, 18. These forms therefore bear the same relation to each other as *τεθνάναι* does to *τεθνήξεσθαι*. See Θνήσκω.

Πίπτω, *I fall*, with *ι* naturally long*, consequently the imperat. is accented *πῖπτε*: the formation is from ΠΕΤΩ; e. g. fut. *πεσοῦμαι*, Ion. *πεσέομαι*; aor. 2. *ἔπεσον*†, infin. *πεσεῖν*; perf. *πέπτωκα*, Attic part. *πεπτώς*, *ῶτος*.

The part. perf. is shortened by the Epic poets to *πεπτεώς*, by the Attic to *πεπτώς*. The latter carries us back to the regular *πεπτωκώς*, as the *βεβρῶτες* of Sophocles comes from *βεβρωκώς*; but *πεπτεώς* points to *πέπτηκα* (compare *τεθνεώς*). And this is without doubt the original form (ΠΕΤΩ *πέπτηκα*, like *δέμω δέδμηκα*), from which by the change of vowel came *πέπτωκα*: see Buttm. Lexil. p. 137.

We find also both aorists regularly formed from the simple stem or root ΠΕΤΩ: viz.

1. *ἔπετον*, aor. 2. in Pindar and other Doric writers.

2. *ἔπεσα*, the regular aor. 1. As we shall see hereafter that in *χέζω* a verb of the common popular dialect, the two aorists *ἔχεσα* and *ἔχεσον* have been confounded together in daily usage; so in the verb before us the aor. 1. was not found, indeed, in the current language of the day, yet it appears to have remained always in the dialects; hence it occurs among others in the Alexandrine and occasionally in the later ones; see Lobeck ad Phryn. p. 724. Orph. Arg. 519. Among the older writers Euripides has it twice in the Chorus, *προσέπεσα*, Tro. 291. *πέσειε*, Alc. 471. in both which passages these forms have been rejected in the latest editions by a precipitate criticism‡.

* [See Draco, p. 73, 18. 79, 21. Hermann ad Eurip. Herc. F. 1371.—Passow.]

† Compare *ἐδύσετο*, p. 73. and *οἶσε* under Φέρω.

‡ That the common form should be found in both passages even in the best manuscripts as a various reading, is natural; but this can be no reason why any one should reject here, more than in other similar cases, the less usual form selected by the poet, unless it be from having fallen into the error (certainly a very pardonable one) of condemning it at once as a barbarism because it is found in the Alexandrine dialect: in which, to mention particulars, it appears to belong to the class of aorists ending in *α* instead of *ον*, as *εἶδα*, *εἶλα*, *ἔλαβαν*, and acknowledged to be barbarous. But they who classed it thus, did not at the same time consider, that while these latter forms have very little in the pure language harmonizing with them, like *εἶπα*, *ἤνεγκα*, the form *ἔπεσα* on the other hand is the regular aor. 1., and with its future *πεσοῦμαι* answers to *ἔπλευσα*, *πλευσοῦμαι* and many others, in short to half the language. In this case therefore, where the anomalous *ἔπεσον* was in current use, the analogous but unusual *ἔπεσα* (*οὐκ ἐν χρήσει τὸ ἔπεσα*, Schol. Aristoph. Av. 840.) might very well remain as a not-discordant dialect in the Lyric poetry of the Iono-Attics, with quite as much reason as

Πιτνέω, *I fall*; aor. ἔπιτνον, infin. πιτνεῖν, part. πιτνών. Such appears to be the established formation of this verb by a comparison of some of the passages where it occurs; and thus it comes under the analogy of στυγέω, ἔστυγον and similar verbs, from the aorist of which arises a pres. in -έω: see κτυπέω. The accentuation however of πίτνω for πιτνῶ, of πίτνοντες, &c. not only occurs very frequently in the manuscripts and in the Grammarians, but sense and metre are by no means generally decisive between them. See Hermann on Eurip. Med. 53. (Ed. Elmsl. Lips. p. 340. sqq.) and Reisig on Soph. Œd. Col. 1754. (Enarr. p. CCXI.) The only cases where the aorist appears to me evident, are those where we find ἔπιτνον, ἔπιτνε. Since however this aorist does not contain the simple root, which is much more conspicuous in the Pindaric ἔπετον (see πίπτω); the formation of the aor. ἔπετον, pres. πίτνω has in its favour the analogy of the aor. ἔδακον, pres. δάκνω. I do not therefore by any means reject the supposition that πίτνω and πιτνέω might have existed together (like βυνέω and βύνω, δυνέω and δύνω), without ἔπιτνον being therefore necessarily an imperfect; for ἔκλυον from κλύω is used by the same Tragedians as an aorist. And here in particular, where from πίτνω arose a lengthened present πιτνῶ, it ap-

the similarly analogous and equally unusual ἔπετον remained in the Æolo-Doric dialect. Now it is at least worthy of remark, that this is the only one of all those Alexandrine aorists which tradition attributes to Euripides; and with regard to the correctness of the readings, if we had nothing else in support of them, we have this consideration, that while it was very conceivable and indeed almost unavoidable for ἔπεσον, πέσοι to have intruded themselves as various readings, it was quite inconceivable that transcribers or correctors of the metre should have interpolated ἔπεσα and πέσειε. For who has ever seen an instance of Christian transcribers having introduced into the tragedians or any of the Attic writers those other forms εἶδα, ἔλαβαν, which are so common in the LXX.? And this leads me back to the examination of another passage, which grammatical criticism has long lost sight of. In the well-known passage of Herodotus 6, 21. the text formerly had ἐς δάκρυα ἔπεσαν τὸ θέητρον. I much fear, that when ἔπεσε was adopted from some of the manuscripts, the historian was deprived of an intended grammatical figure as well as of his dialect. Longinus (24, 1.) quotes this passage as an instance of a collective singular used instead of a plural to elevate the diction. And certainly the expression, as it now stands in Herodotus, fully answers that purpose, as does also a passage quoted just before from Demosthenes, ἡ Πελοπόννησος ἅπασα διειστήκει. But the passage of Herodotus is so corrupted in Longinus that it contradicts the reason for its being quoted: the manuscripts have ἔπεσαν or ἔπεσον οἱ θεώμενοι. It will perhaps be said that the whole sentence has been corrupted, by the attempts made to explain it, from ἔπεσε τὸ θέητρον, which is now adopted as the text in Longinus also: this would be possible, if the reading had been only ἔπεσον; but how came the commentator or his corrupter by ἔπεσαν? Let us now suppose that the old reading both in Herodotus and Longinus was ἔπεσαν τὸ θέητρον, and we then discover the corruption in each writer; in the former ἔπεσε, in the latter οἱ θεώμενοι. If aught were wanting to complete the proof of ἔπεσα being a genuine form, it would be found, I think, in the comparison with the aorists ἔχεσα and ἔχεσον, the confusion between which was not remarked until very lately.

pears very natural that a distinction should have been made between the aor. ἔπιτνον, and the imperf. ἐπίτνουν*.

Πίτνημι, Πιτνάω. See Πετάννυμι.

ΠΛ–. See Πέλω.

ΠΛΑ–. See Πολάζω and Πίμπλημι.

Πλάζω, *I cause to wander, turn from its course*: fut. πλάγξω; aor. 1. ἔπλαγξα. Pass. πλάζομαι, *I am driven from my course, I wander about*: fut. πλάγξομαι; aor. 1. ἐπλάγχθην. See also Πελάζω.

These tenses are formed as from a pres. ΠΛΑΓΧΩ; or, which comes to the same, πλάζω has γγ for its characteristic letter, like κλάζω and σαλπίζω.

Πλάσσω, *I form*; fut. πλάσω, &c. This verb, like πάσσω, πτίσσω, ἐρέσσω, βράσσω and βλίττω, has for its characteristic letter a lingual instead of a palatic, which is generally seen by a σ in the inflexion instead of ξ, γ, κ, or χ: see Ἁρμόττω. From the compounds ἱπποπλάθος, κοροπλάθος the characteristic letter would seem to be θ.

Πλέκω, *I plat, weave*: fut. πλέξω; aor. 1. midd. ἐπλεξάμην; perf. pass. πέπλεγμαι. The aor. 2. pass. is generally ἐπλάκην, but Bekker has always found in the best manuscripts of Plato ἐπλέκην: see Βλέπω.

Πλέω, *I sail*: fut. πλεύσομαι, or more generally πλευσοῦμαι; aor. 1. ἔπλευσα; perf. πέπλευκα. The pass. takes σ; thus, perf. pass. πέπλευσμαι; aor. 1. pass. ἐπλεύσθην.

This verb was still found in the older Attic writers in a resolved form: at least the instance of ἔπλεεν (not ἔπλεε), in Xen. Hell. 6, 2, 27. has great weight; and in Thucyd. 4, 28. Bekker has followed the majority of the Codd. in retaining πλέει. See note to Δέω, *I want*.

There is an Ionic form of this verb πλώω†, infin. πλώειν; fut. πλώσω; aor. 1. ἔπλωσα; perf. πέπλωκα. Euripides, who introduced this

* In the passage of Soph. Œd. Col. 1732. I consider the sense of ἔπιτνε to be evidently that of an aorist, though Reisig doubts it; for the imperfect can hardly be compatible with the meaning of ἄταφος (*cadebat insepultus*). On the other hand he appears to me to be perfectly right in his opinion that πιτνόντων in Eurip. Supp. 691. is a present. But then Hermann can read only πιτνούντων, of which he avails himself also in (προσπίτνοντες) Æschyl. Pers. 461. If my view of the subject be adopted, no change is necessary.

† [Homer seems to have used πλώω with its derivatives more in the sense of *to swim*, and πλέω with the meaning of *to sail*.—Passow.]

perfect on the Attic stage (Hel. 539.), appears to have been ridiculed by Aristophanes (Thesm. 878.) for so doing. To this verb belongs also an Epic aor. 2. ἔπλων, -ως, -ω, -ωμεν, &c.; part. πλώς, πλῶντος; and its compounds ἀπέπλων, ἐπέπλων, παρέπλων with their participles ἐπιπλώς, &c., Il. ζ, 191. See ἔγνων, &c. under Γιγνώσκω.

Πλήθω. See Πίμπλημι.

Πλήσσω, Att. πλήττω, *I strike*: fut. πλήξω; perf. 2. (sometimes in a pass. sense) πέπληγα; perf. pass. πέπληγμαι; aor. 2. pass. ἐπλήγην.

Beside the active and passive of this verb we find in Homer the middle also (μηρὸν πληξάμενος); so that it is used in all its voices by the Epics and by them only. In the Attic dialect the place of the active was supplied by πατάσσω, which again was not used by the older Attics in the passive.

All this holds good of the simple verb only and of its proper meaning, in which however there is no compound in regular use. On the other hand ἐκπλήττω and καταπλήττω, which mean in the active *to strike with fear*, in the passive *to be struck with fear*, are used in both those voices and have in the aor. 2. pass. the ᾰ; as, ἐξεπλάγην, καταπλαγῆναι.

On the relative usage of πλήσσω and πατάσσω as laid down above, see Valcken. ad Act. Apost. 12, 7. and the passage of Lysias there quoted, πότερον πρότερον ἐπλήγην ἢ ἐπάταξα, 4, p. 102, 9.

The *perfect* however appears to have been an exception, which, as it could not be formed from πατάσσω so as to please the ear, was taken probably from the old Ionic dialect, and continued in constant use among the Attic writers with an active meaning in the form πέπληγα: as in Aristoph. Av. 1350. ὃς ἂν πεπλήγῃ τὸν πατέρα νεοττὸς ὤν*. In the later language the perf. πέπληγα was used in a *passive* sense; see

* See also Xen. Anab. 5, 9, 5. This passage alone would however leave the point still problematical. The old reading is τὸν ἄνθρωπον πεπληχέναι, a form for which there are nowhere any grounds; with a various reading πεπληγέναι. But from the context it would be much more natural to understand the accusative as the subject of the passive, a construction in which we cannot well use πεπληγέναι in Xenophon. I conjecture therefore that under πεπληχέναι is concealed the true reading πεπλῆχθαι.

ἑάλωκα under Ἁλίσκομαι; Stephan. Thes. *in v.*; and Oudend. ad Thom. Mag. *v.* πεπληγώς, p. 703.

On ἐπλήγην and ἐπλάγην compare what has been said on Ἄγνυμι, ἐάγην. We have only further to observe that Homer uses on account of the metre κατεπλήγην, Il. γ, 31.

The Epics have also an aor. 2. act. and midd. but only with the reduplication, as πέπληγον, infin. πεπληγέμεν, and πεπλήγετο, in the same sense as ἔπληξαν, ἐπλήξατο.

From a rare sister-form πλήγνυμι Thucydides 4, 25. has ἐκπλήγνυσθαι.

Πλύνω (ῡ), *I wash*: fut. πλῠνέω, contracted πλῠνῶ; aor. 1. ἔπλυνα; perf. πέπλῠκα; perf. pass. πέπλῠμαι; aor. 1. pass. ἐπλύθην (ῠ)*. This verb is generally poetical.

Πνέω, poet. πνείω, *I blow*: fut. πνεύσω, later πνεύσομαι, more generally πνευσοῦμαι; aor. 1. ἔπνευσα, &c.; aor. 1. pass. ἐπνεύσθην.

There is no instance of a perf. pass. formed according to the above formation; the only one in use is the poetical πέπνῡμαι, with the force of a present and the particular meaning of *to be inspired with wisdom, be wise, intelligent*: hence perf. infin. πεπνῦσθαι, and 2. sing. pluperf. (with the force of an imperf.) πέπνυσο, Od. ψ, 210. By the same formation come the Epic syncopated aor. 2. ἄμπνῡτο for ἀνέπνυτο; the aor. 1. pass. ἀμπνύνθη for ἀμπνῡθη (like ἱδρύνθην); and the imper. aor. 2. act. ἄμπνυε for ἀνάπνυε, consequently from an aorist ἄμπνυον used by the later Epics, as Quintus, &c.† On the aor. 1. pass. ἐπνύνθην see Τείνω.

Πνίγω, *I choke*: fut. midd. (with transit. meaning) πνίξομαι‡ or πνιξοῦμαι, and in Lucian πνίξω; aor. 1. ἔπνιξα, infin. πνῖξαι. Passive, *I am being choked*: fut. πνιγήσομαι;

* On the formation of the two perfects and the aor. 1. pass. see Τείνω

† A more strict analogy would have given ἔπνῡν, ἄμπνῡθι, to which ἄμπνυε bears the same relation as πίε does to πῖθι, only that ἔπιον is actually in use.

‡ It has been stated rather hastily that the Doric πνιξοῦμαι is the only acknowledged future of this active verb. I find but one instance of it, viz. in Stephan Thesaur. h. v., but the passage is useless as a proof on account of its being in the Doric dialect and from the uncertainty of the reading: οἷον αἱ μύκαι ἄρ' ἐπεσκληκότες πνιξεῖσθε, Epicharm. ap. Athen. p. 60. Without attempting to restore the whole of this tetrameter, I shall content myself with amending what the language and sense require, οἱ μύκαι and ὠπεσκληκότες (οἱ ἀπεσκλ.): and I therefore understand it as Stephens does, "you will poison (people) like dried mushrooms": which passage is at least an authority for the fut. middle; the probability of the *Doric* future πνιξοῦμαι having been used in the Attic dialect is strengthened by φευξοῦμαι, παιξοῦμαι. Lucian however (Contempl. 23.) has ἀποπνίξεις.

aor. 2. ἐπνίγην. The ι is long except in the aor. 2. pass.; Lobeck ad Phryn. p. 107.

ΠΟ–. See Πίνω.

Ποθέω, *I long for, regret*: Ionic and old Attic fut. ποθέσω, more generally ποθήσω, Xen. Mem. 3, 11, 3., also ποθέσομαι not only Ionic in Herodotus, but in Plato, e.g. Heind. Phædo, p. 98. a.; aor. 1. act. ἐπόθεσα, whence 3. plur. πόθεσαν, infin. ποθέσαι, Hom., and ἐπόθησα, Xen. and Isocr.; both forms of the aor. 1. are found in Herodot. 3, 36. 9, 22.; perf. πεπόθηκα; perf. pass. πεπόθημαι; aor. 1. pass. ἐποθέσθην.

Πονέω, *I labour, suffer*, is inflected regularly; thus, fut. πονήσω, &c.: but when it signifies physical pain or suffering, it makes πονέσω.

Such is the statement of the grammarians; see Chœrob. in Bekk. Anecd. in Ind.; where we find also quoted as an exception, πεπόνηκα τὼ σκέλη, Aristoph. Pac. 820.: but the probability is that the perfect is always formed with the η (whatever be its meaning) as in ποθέω. The formation of πονέσω, &c. is found in Hippocr. de Morb. 1, 15. 16. and three times in Lucian. Asin. 9.

[In the oldest language we find only the depon. midd. πονέομαι, -ήσομαι in an absolute sense: see Homer passim.—Passow.]

Πορεῖν, *to give*, infin. of ἔπορον, a defective aorist used by the poets. [The indicative without the augment is found frequently in Homer;] the part. πορών in Æschyl. Prom. 954.; the infin. πορεῖν in Hesychius.

In Pind. Pyth. 2, 105. is an infin. πεπορεῖν, but the majority of the manuscripts have πεπαρεῖν. According to the former reading the word is an infinitive of the above verb with reduplication: but there is in Hesychius an old explanation of πεπαρεῖν—ἐνδεῖξαι, σημῆναι, which appears to me to suit the sense of Pindar better; *ostentare*. See Bœckh. In this latter case it is therefore a solitary form of some lost verb*.

By the principle of the metathesis, as shown under Βάλλω and Καλέω, we find that to the stem or root of πορεῖν (with the sense of *to impart, allot*,) belongs the perf. pass. πέπρωμαι, *I am allotted by fate, fated*;

* Perhaps this verb might have arisen from the sense of the preposition παρά, as πάρα τι *is there*.

part. πεπρωμένος; whence 3. sing. pluperf. πέπρωτο, Hes. Th. 464. Compare Μείρομαι.

ΠΟ–. See Πίνω.

Πέποσθε. See Πάσχω.

ΠΡΑ–. See Πιπράσκω and Πίμπρημι.

Πράσσω, Ep. and Ion. πρήσσω, Att. πράττω*, transit. *I do*, intransit. *I am doing* (well or ill), *find myself in a certain state* or *situation*: fut. πράξω, Ion. πρήξω; perf. πέπρᾱχα; perf. 2. πέπρᾱγα; perf. pass. πέπραγμαι, &c. In the older writers πέπραγα was the only perfect; afterwards arose the custom of using πέπραγα in an intransitive sense only, πέπραχα in a transitive. The α is naturally long.

The above usage may be gathered from the direction of the Atticists, who merely tell us that πέπραγα is Attic, πέπραχα common Greek: see Piers. ad Mœr. p. 293. Phryn. App. Soph. p. 60. But the latter is found only in a transitive sense: e. g. in Xen. Cyr. 7, 5, 42. Hell. 5, 2, 32. Anab. 5, 7, 29. Menand. Incert. 75. (see Meineke, p. 221.), and as a rejected various reading in Aristoph. Equ. 683. Against this usage, therefore, the assertion of the Atticists is directed: and it is now uncertain in this as in many similar cases, with what writers the objectionable usage began, and when it is to be attributed to transcribers†.

Πρῆθω. See Πίμπρημι.

Πρίασθαι, *to buy*, infin. of επριάμην, a defective *aorist* (according to the analogy of επτάμην), used by the Attics instead of the obsolete aorist of ὠνέομαι‡; imperat. πρίασο

* [With the exception of the Tragedians, who always use πράσσω, Herm. ad Soph. Phil. 1435.—Passow.]

† That the perfect in -γα was the older form, is clear from the Epic poets generally using the perfect 2. But as the perfect active, particularly in transitive verbs, was not much wanted in Greek, it is conceivable that the ear might have become accustomed to what was of most frequent occurrence, κακῶς πέπραγα, εὖ πεπραγώς, &c.; so that when it was wished to express the transitive sense in the perfect, they endeavoured to represent it by the other form, which is also agreeable to analogy. I do not think the above decision of the Atticists sufficient to warrant our positively asserting that this form was not used by Xenophon.

‡ This is the meaning of the direction of Phrynichus, which is quite free from corruptions, though Lobeck (p. 137.) has misunderstood it. The grammarian directs that nothing of ὠνεῖσθαι should be used, as a form of πρίασθαι may stand in its place. At the time this was said, no one could misunderstand it, as a pres. πρίαμαι was unheard of in the whole range of Greek literature, and ἐπριάμην was equally unknown as an imperfect. The only thing intended was to guard against some forms of ὠνεῖσθαι. The grammarian excludes therefore from

(Aristoph. Ach. 870.), or πρίω (id. Nub. 614.); opt. πριαίμην; conj. πρίωμαι; infin. πρίασθαι; part. πριάμενος. See Lobeck ad Phryn. pp. 137. 360.

Πρίω, *I saw, gnash* (the teeth); imperat. πρῖε, Aristoph. Ran. 927. The passive takes σ; as, aor. 1. ἐπρίσθην; perf. πέπρισμαι.

The ι is undoubtedly long throughout all the inflexions of πρίω; and with this the σ in the passive agrees, according to the rule mentioned under ἀρόω*; so that it is not necessary on that account to have recourse to a present πρίζω, which, it appears, became very common at a later period†. See also Buttm. Lexil. p. 485.

Προΐσσομαι. See Καταπρ.

Προσελεῖν, Προυσελεῖν. See under Εἴλω.

Πρῶσαι, an infin. aor. of rare occurrence and of a rather uncertain character, supposed to be a contraction from προῶσαι, and explained as an expression of the palæstra in Lucian. Asin. 10. where (ib. 9.) we find also the imperat. ἐπίπρωσον as an emendation of τρώσας, and again of Straton. Epigr. 48., where the text has the part. πρώσας. Both Schneider and Passow derive it from προωθέω; fut. προωθήσω or -ώσω; aor. 1. προέωσα or ἐπρόωσα, contracted ἔπρωσα, infin. πρῶσαι, &c.

Πταίω, *I stumble*: fut. πταίσω, &c. It takes σ in the passive, as perf. ἔπταισμαι, &c. See Ἀρόω and Πρίω.

ΠΤΑ–, ΠΤΕ–. See Πετάννυμι, Πέτομαι, Πίπτω and Πτήσσω.

Πτήσσω, *I duck* or *drop the head from fear*: fut. πτήξω, &c., is regular: perf. ἔπτηχα.

In Æschyl. Eum. 247. all the manuscripts have καταπτακών, which some have changed to κατεπτακώς, on account of the Hesychian gloss ἐπτακέναι, κεκρυφέναι. But the verse requires a short ᾰ; and an aor. 2. ἔπτακον is quite analogous, as the majority of the cognate words, πτάκες, πτῶκες, &c., show κ to be the characteristic letter of πτήσσω. If, therefore, the gloss of Hesychius be genuine, this is the Doric perf. 2. with

the Attic style the whole aorist ἐωνησάμην, and even the perfect ἐώνημαι in cases where the aorist ἐπριάμην would supply its place. Compare Herodian Ed. Piers. p. 453.

* To the verbs mentioned under ἀρόω, as taking the σ in the passive, may be added, ἀκούω, κελεύω, λεύω, θραύω, παλαίω, πταίω, πρίω, χρίω, βύω, ξύω, ὕω.

† See Pollux 7. c. 26. The instance in Plat. Theag. p. 124. a. is of sufficient antiquity, notwithstanding the spuriousness of the dialogue.

α long for ἔπτηκα. Consequently the inflexion will run thus, πτήσσω; fut. πτήξω; aor. 1. ἔπτηξα; aor. 2. ἔπτακον; perf. ἔπτηχα and ἔπτηκα.

We find in the poets other forms from a more simple stem or root ΠΤΑΩ; as in Il. θ, 136. καταπτήτην, 3. dual aor. 2. from ἔπτην (see ἔγνων under Γιγνώσκω), and a part. perf. πεπτηώς (see Βαίνω), which is not to be confounded with πεπτεώς under Πίπτω. All the above, and in particular this reduplication (πεπτ–) comes from the root ΠΕΤ–, as we have observed in a note at the end of Πέτομαι.

Πτίσσω, *I stamp* (grain): fut. πτίσω; perf. pass. ἔπτισμαι. See Ἁρμόττω and Πλάσσω.

ΠΤΟ–. See Πίπτω.

Πτύρω, *I make fearful*: fut. πτυρῶ. Pass. πτύρομαι, with aor. 2. ἐπτύρην, *I become fearful*, said particularly of horses; infin. πτυρῆναι τὸν θάνατον.

Πτύσσω, *I fold up*: fut. πτύξω, &c., is regular.—MIDD. [*I fold* or *wrap* (anything) *round me*, with accus. Aristoph. Nub. 267.—Passow.]

Πτύω, *I spit*: fut. πτύσω. The pass. takes σ, as perf. ἔπτυσμαι.

[It is written also ψύω, whence the Latin *spuo*. The υ is long in pres. and imperf., but short in fut., &c.: see Graefe Mel. 124, 7., yet in Theocr. 24, 19. and Apollon. Rhod. 2, 570. 4, 925. the υ is short in the imperf., when the syllable following is short also; this is frequently the case in Nonnus.—Passow.]

Πύθω, *I cause to rot*: fut. πύσω; aor. 1. ἔπυσα, &c. Pass. *I rot*. The υ is long throughout, yet Callimachus (Fr. 313.) has allowed himself to use πύσε for πῦσε with υ short. Compare ἔπρεσε and ἔστᾰσαν.

Πυνθάνομαι, *I inquire, learn by inquiry*, depon. midd., forms its tenses from πεύθομαι*, which is still used by the Epic and Tragic poets; thus, fut. πεύσομαι†; aor. ἐπυθόμην, [imper. πυθοῦ, but Ion. with change of accent πύθευ, Herodot. 3, 68., Epic opt. πεπύθοιτο, infin. πῠθέσθαι;] perf. πέπυσμαι‡, 2. sing. πέπῦσαι, Plat. Protag. p. 310.

* Like ἁνδάνω, λανθάνω, λαμβάνω, λαγχάνω, μανθάνω, and others: see note under Αἰσθάνομαι.

† Perhaps also πευσοῦμαι, see Brunck. ad Eurip. Hippol. 1104. Æschyl. Prom. 987.

‡ On the υ of this perf. see note under Χέω.

b., Epic. πέπυσσαι, Od. λ, 494.; pluperf. ἐπεπύσμην. Verbal adj. πευστός, πευστέος.

Πυρέσσω, Att. -ττω, *I am in a fever*: fut. πυρέξω; aor. 1. ἐπύρεξα, &c., although it is derived from πυρετός. Compare ἐρέσσω.

P.

Ῥαίνω, *I besprinkle*, forms the following tenses regularly: fut. ῥᾰνῶ; aor. 1. ἔρρᾱνα; perf. pass. ἔρρασμαι.

In the Epic language we observe two irregular forms; 1.) the aor. 1. imper. ῥάσσατε, Od. υ, 150. and 2.) the 3. plur. perf. pass. ἐρράδαται*, Od. υ, 354. pluperf. ἐρράδατο, Il. μ, 431. That is to say, from the simple stem or root PA– were formed one derivative with its full complement of tenses—ῥαίνω, and another very defective –PAZΩ†.

Ῥάπτω, *I sew*: fut. ῥάψω, aor. 1. ἔρραψα; aor. 2. pass. ἐρράφην.

[Nonnus has an irregular aor. ἔρρᾰφε, Lobeck ad Phryn. p. 318.—Passow.]

Ῥέζω, *I do*: fut. ῥέξω; aor. 1. ἔρρεξα or ἔρεξα. This word is the same as ἔρδω, from which it is formed by transposing the two first letters; ἔρδω, fut. ἔρξω, aor. 1. ἔρξα; perf. ἔοργα; pluperf. ἐώργειν. Of the passive we find only ῥεχθῆναι, as ἔρχθην and ἔεργμαι are formed only from ἔργω, εἴργω. Verbal adj. ῥεκτός, ῥεκτέος.

In order to form a correct judgment on the connection of these forms, we must first keep in view the mutual change, founded on general rules, of the *middle*‡ consonants γ and δ, with which is connected that of γ to ζ occurring in other verbs, e. g. κράζω, κραγεῖν. The next thing to be observed is, that the forms ἔρδω, ἔρξα, with the subst. ἔργον, have the digamma in the old language, and that the aspirate which is joined with the ρ was frequently in the dialects changed into the digamma, for instance in the Æolic βρόδον, i. e. *wrodon* for ῥόδον, *a rose*. We must therefore consider ἔρξαι as *werxai*, ῥέξαι as *wrexai*, ἔοργα as *weworga*;

* Though there is neither δ nor ζ in the present to account for the δ in this form, yet there are sufficient grounds for it in the σ of ἔρρασμαι; for this perf. may be considered as the connecting link with a form in -άζω, from which comes ῥάσσατε.

† According to Apollon. de Adv. p. 600, 28. the fut. ῥανῶ was used by the Attics with α long. on which see Φαίνω.

‡ [Consonants are divided into aspirated, as θ, φ, χ; smooth, as κ, π, τ; and middle, as β, γ, δ.]

in order to distinguish in them the same appearance as we find in δέρκω, δρακεῖν, δέδορκα*.

'PE–. See Εἰπεῖν.

'Ρέω, *I flow*: fut. ῥεύσομαι, Theogn. 448.; aor. 1. ἔρρευσα; but these two forms are seldom found in the Attics (see Lobeck ad Phryn. p. 739.), who generally use the fut. ῥυήσομαι, the aor. 2. pass. (with an active sense) ἐῤῥύην, and the perf. ἐῤῥύηκα. This fut. and perf. are formed from the aorist†.

We may easily conceive that a neuter idea like that of *to flow* may be understood in an active as well as passive sense, and it is therefore unnecessary to have recourse to a theme ΡΥΗΜΙ in order to form ἐῤῥύην.

The part. ῥεούμενος in an oracle in Herodot. 7, 140. ἱδρῶτι ῥεούμενος, *dropping with sweat*, is merely a lengthening of the ο in ῥεόμενος, like μαχεούμενος for μαχεόμενος; and the various reading ῥεεύμενος, introduced into the passage without the slightest authority, is therefore to be rejected.

'Ρήγνυμι, *I break*: fut. ῥήξω‡, fut. midd. ῥήξομαι; aor. 1. ἔῤῥηξα; aor. 1. midd. ἐῤῥηξάμην; aor. 2. pass. ἐῤῥάγην. All the above have a transitive meaning, in which, however, there occurs no perfect; but we find in an intransitive sense a perf. 2. ἔῤῥωγα, *I am broken*, with the change of vowel from η to ω: on which see note on ἀγήοχα under Ἄγω, and ἑάλωκα under Ἁλίσκομαι.

[In Homer we find an Epic imperf. ῥήγνυσκε for ἐῤῥήγνυ, Il. η, 141. and in Arat. Dios. 85. an Ion. 3. plur. pass. ῥηγνύατο. There is a sister-form of ῥήγνυμι in Il. σ, 571. ῥήσσω, Att. ῥάσσω: this last, however, is particularly used as an expression of the palæstra, *to throw to the ground*, Jac. Ach. Tat. p. 821.—Passow.]

'Ριγέω, *I shudder*: fut. ῥιγήσω; perf. with the force of a pres. ἔῤῥιγα. On the irregular Epic part. ἐῤῥίγοντι (Hes. Sc. 228), see κεκλήγοντας under Κλάζω, and πεφρίκοντας under Φρίσσω. [The word is solely poetical.—Passow.]

* Here the Teutonic languages offer us a comparison so palpable and unsought for, that we cannot but make use of it; namely, in the English verb *work*, whence the perf. *wrought*, and the subst. *wright*; in which the *w* before the *r* is not pronounced; therefore *wright* is ῥέκτης. Compare Buttm. Lexil. p. 376.

† [A pres. ῥέομαι occurs also in the poets.—Passow.]

‡ See Ἄγνυμι.

Ῥιγόω, *I freeze*: fut. ῥιγώσω, &c. This word, like ἱδρόω, is contracted into ω and ῳ instead of the regular ου and οι; e.g. infin. ῥιγῶν, Aristoph. Vesp. 446. Av. 935. (yet we find ῥιγοῦν, Nub. 442.); dat. part. ῥιγῶντι, Ach. 1145.; part. fem. ῥιγῶσα, Simonid. De Mul. 29.; opt. ῥιγῴην, Brunck. Aristoph. Ach. 1146. Av. 935. Lucian De Luct. 11. Plut. Apophth. Lac. p. 233. a. Hippocr. De Sal. Diæt. 1.; conj. ῥιγῷ, Plat. Gorg. p. 507. d. (p. 527. Heind.) with Buttm. notes. See also Piers. ad Mœr. pp. 336. 339. All these are Attic forms.

Ῥίπτω, *I throw*: fut. ῥίψω, &c.; aor. 2. pass. ἐῤῥίφην. There are also two sister-forms ῥιπτέω*, ῥιπτῶ, from the former of which comes the imperf. ἐῤῥίπτεον, Herod. 8, 53.; but the formation follows ῥίπτω. The ι is long by nature (whence ῥῖπτε, ῥῖψαι), except in ἐῤῥίφην.

In Homer we find an Epic imperf. ῥίπτασκον, -ες, -ε, like κρύπτασκον, the only two instances in Homer of α instead of ε, except perhaps the doubtful ἀγνώσσασκε, Od. ψ, 95. To these we must add ἀνάσσεσκε, Hymn. Apoll. 403. and ῥοίζασκε, Hes. θ, 835. [A reduplicated infin. perf. pass. ῥερῖφθαι is found in Pind. Fr. 281.—Passow.]

Ῥοίζασκε, Epic imperf., with the force of an aorist, from ῥοιζέω: see the preceding paragraph.

ῬΥ–. See Ῥέω.

Ῥύομαι. See Ἐρύω.

ῬΩΓ–. See Ῥήγνυμι.

Ῥώννυμι or ῥωννύω, *I strengthen*: fut. ῥώσω, &c. (compare Ἄγνυμι, Κεράννυμι, Ζώννυμι): perf. pass. ἔῤῥωμαι (with the force of a pres.), *I am strong*, *in health*, [whence the pluperf. ἐῤῥώμην has the sense of an imperf., e.g. ἔῤῥωντο, Thucyd. 2, 8.]; imperat. ἔῤῥωσο, like *vale*, farewell: part.

* [The form ῥιπτέω is found only in the pres. and imperf., and seems to bear the same relation to ῥίπτω as *jactare* does in Latin to *jacere*, i. e. it has the collateral idea of frequency, Herm. Soph. Aj. 235. Antig. 131. It occurs first in Herodot. 4, 94. 188. &c., afterwards in Xen. and other Attic writers. Elmsley excludes it from the Tragedians, but without grounds; while Buttmann confines the distinction between ῥιπτέω and ῥίπτω to the Attic writers.—Passow.]

ἐῤῥωμένος. The aor. 1. pass. is the only tense which takes the σ, as ἐῤῥώσθην.

Ῥώομαι, [an old Epic depon. midd.] *I move with rapidity, rush, wave,* Il. ψ, 367.: fut. ῥώσομαι; aor. 1. ἐῤῥωσάμην, Il. ω, 616. Od. ψ. 3. It is probably akin to ῥέω, as πλώω is to πλέω, χώομαι to χέω. [Some, however, connect it with ῥώννυμι, ῥώμη, ῥύομαι, ῥύμη and the Lat. *ruo*.—Passow.]

Σ.

Σαίρω, *I brush, sweep away*: fut. σαρῶ; aor. 1. ἔσηρα, part. σήρας, Soph. Ant. 409. No other tenses are in use.

Another form σαρόω, -ώσω was used in the active and passive, but not by the Attics: see Lobeck ad Phryn. p. 83. Whether perhaps the passive of it was used by the Attics to supply the defectiveness of σαίρω, I know not. Lycophron (389.) has σαρούμενος.

From the same stem or root, but with a different radical meaning, comes a perfect, with the force of a present, σέσηρα, *I grin*; part. σεσηρώς, -υῖα, -ός, Theocr. 7, 19. Epic fem. σεσᾰρυῖα, Hes. Sc. 268.

Σαλπίζω, *I blow the trumpet*: fut. σαλπίγξω; aor. 1. ἐσάλπιγξα, Il. φ, 388., but the later writers use σαλπίσω, ἐσάλπισα, Lobeck ad Phryn. p. 191. So also the old subst. was σαλπιγκτής, the later one σαλπιστής. Compare Πλάζω and Συρίζω.

Σαόω. See Σώζω.

Σάω, an old form for σήθω, *I sift*, whence 3. plur. σῶσι, Herodot. 1. 200.

Σβέννῡμι, or σβεννύω (Pind.), *I extinguish*: fut. σβέσω, less frequently σβήσομαι, Plat. Legg. 7. p. 805. c.; aor. 1. ἔσβεσα*; the perf. ἔσβηκα, and the syncopated aor. 2. ἔσβην, 1. plur. ἔσβημεν, opt. σβείην, infin. σβῆναι have the intrans. sense of the passive†. Pass. σβέννυμαι, *I am extin-*

* The direction in Phryn. Appar. p. 16. that the aor. 1. act should be written with an η, not with ε, appears to be an error. Aristophanes Plut. 668. has ἀποσβέσας. [Passow, however, advises us not to be too hasty in condemning it, on account of the fut σβήσομαι.]

† See note under Τεύχω.

guished, I die away, dry up; perf. ἔσβεσμαι; aor. 1. ἐσβέσθην. The passive therefore takes σ. On the formation of ἔσβην see ἔγνων under Γιγνώσκω: and on the intrans. sense of ἔσβην and ἔσβηκα see note under Τεύχω.

Strictly speaking, ἔσβεσμαι and ἐσβέσθην have only the passive sense, *to be extinguished*; but as in verbs of this kind the immediate sense comes so near to the passive, not only does σβέννυμαι serve for a pres. to ἔσβην, ἔσβηκα, but also ἐσβέσθην stands for ἔσβην, only that this latter, or rather its compound ἀπέσβην, is by far the more common of the two.

In the Doric dialect ἔσβην takes an α, ἔσβαν, Theocr. 4, 39.

Σέβω or σέβομαι, *I revere*, is found only in the present, and in the aor. 1. pass. ἐσέφθην, *I was filled with reverence*, Soph. ap. Hesych. whence part. fem. σεφθεῖσα, Plat. Phædr. p. 254. b.

[The act. σέβω, fut. σέψω, is post-Homeric.—Passow.]

Σείω, *I shake*: fut. σείσω; aor. 1. ἔσεισα, &c.; perf. pass. σέσεισμαι; aor. 1. pass. ἐσείσθην. For the Epic imperf. ἀνασσείασκε see ῥίπτασκον under Ῥίπτω.

Σεύω, *I drive*: pass. and midd. *I hasten*. This verb, like those beginning with ρ, doubles the first consonant in the augmented tenses, and retains it even in the perfect instead of the reduplication; e. g. imperf. ἔσσευον; imperf. pass. and midd. ἐσσευόμην; perf. pass. ἔσσυμαι*; aor. 1. pass. ἐσσύθην, Soph. Aj. 294. And having the σ thus doubled, it has none in the termination of the aor. 1. act. or midd., as ἔσσευα (see ἔκηα under καίω), ἐσσευάμην, part. σευάμενος, &c. The forms with one σ are of less frequent occurrence; ἐσύθην, Eurip. ἐξεσύθη, Hom. In this as in other cases, the Epic dialect rejects the augment entirely; as σεῦα, σεῦε, σεύατο.

The perf. pass. ἔσσυμαι, *I am put in motion*, has the meaning of, *I am restless, eager for*, as in Il. ν, 79. Od. κ, 484. in which sense the particip. ἐσσύμενος (see ἀκηχέμενος under Ἀκαχίζω) has the accentuation of a present, ἐσσύμενος πολέμου, Il. ω. 404. According to this the pluperf. ἐσσύμην would have the force of the imperfect; but it coincides in form with the syncop. aor. (see ἐκτάμην in note under Κτείνω) as in 2. sing. ἔσσυο for ἔσσυσο, in 3. sing. ἔσσυτο, Epic σύτο, part. σύμενος; and the sense is therefore always that of an aorist. In the second

* On the change from the diphthong to the υ of this perf. pass. see note under Χέω.

person of this pluperf. or aorist ἔσσυο (Il. π, 585.), the σ in the last syllable is rejected for the same euphonic reason as in ἔσσευα.

We find also syncopated forms of the present; as 3. sing. σεῦται, Soph. Trach. 645. but most commonly with a change of vowel, σοῦμαι, σοῦται, Æschyl. Ch. 636. σοῦνται, Pers. 25., whence the imperatives used in common life, σοῦ, *run*, *quick*, Aristoph. Vesp. 209. or σοῦσο, σούσθω, σοῦσθε, and infin. σοῦσθαι*. [These forms are used only by the Attic poets.—Passow.]

And lastly to this place belongs the well-known Laconian ἀπέσσουα, *he is gone*, from Xen. Hellen. 1, 1, 23. explained to be an aor. 2. pass. for ἀπεσσύη.

Σήπω, *I make rotten* or *putrid*. Pass. σήπομαι, *I rot*, *putrefy*, *mortify*; aor. 2. ἐσάπην; perf. act. (with the intrans. meaning of the pass.) σέσηπα.

Σίνομαι, Ion. σινέομαι, *I harm*, *injure*; a defective depon., used only in pres. and imperfect. The rare perf. σέσιμμαι is found in an inscription in a passive sense.

[We find, however, in Herodot. 8, 31. the aor. 1. midd. ἐσίναντο. The act. σίνω never occurs; and, except in the above-mentioned perfect and in Orph. Arg. 212., σίνομαι has never a passive sense.—Passow.]

Σκάπτω, *I dig*: fut. σκάψω; perf. pass. ἔσκαμμαι; aor. 2. pass. ἐσκάφην. The characteristic letter is therefore φ.

Σκεδάννυμι, or -ννύω, *I disperse*, *scatter*: fut. σκεδάσω, Att. σκεδῶ, -ᾷς, -ᾷ, Aristoph. Vesp. 229. but found also in Herodot. 8, 68. The passive takes σ, as perf. ἐσκέδασμαι; aor. 1. ἐσκεδάσθην.

Sister-forms of the above are σκίδνημι (compare κίρνημι from κεράννυμι), σκίδναμαι, and in the Epic poets, dropping the σ, κεδάννυμι, κίδνημι, like σμικρός, μικρός, &c. Apollonius and others have also κεδαίω: see δαίω. [Such a form as σκεδάζω appears to have never occurred.—Passow.]

* As σεῦται is indisputably a syncopated form, we class the others with it on account of the greater simplicity of the analogy; therefore σεύω, σούω· σεῦται, σοῦται. Otherwise we may suppose a theme ΣΟΩ, particularly on account of σοῦ; as then σοῦσο would be from σόομαι, contr. σοῦμαι, like ζεύγνυσο from ζεύγνυμαι. In case we adopt the syncope, σοῦσο will be quite regular, and σοῦ, which occurs only as a kind of interjection, (Aristoph. Vesp. 209.) will be a very natural abbreviation for such an usage. Compare a similar argument under Λούω.

Σκέλλω, or σκελέω, *I dry* anything. But more frequently used in the pass. σκέλλομαι or σκελοῦμαι, *I become dry*: fut. σκλήσομαι; to which we must add (with the same intransitive sense of the passive) the active forms, aor. 2. ἔσκλην, opt. σκλαίην, infin. σκλῆναι; and perf. ἔσκληκα. See note under Τεύχω.

The active of this verb scarcely ever occurs in a causative sense; nor do we find in the common language the aorist, which, according to analogy, would be ἔσκειλα. But in the Epic writers we find forms of an aorist ἔσκηλα, as opt. σκήλειε, Il. ψ, 191. conj., ἐνισκήλῃ, Nicand. Th. 694. These lead us to a theme σκάλλω, which also exists, but which in the common language is a completely different verb from the above, signifying *to scratch, scrape*. So common, however, is the mutual change of the vowels α and ε, that we may with full confidence suppose a theme σκάλλω to have existed in the old Ionic dialect with the former meaning, as we find the α in the optative σκλαίην (although known to us only from ἀποσκλαίη in Hesychius), and we have therefore here the metathesis ΣΚΑΛ–, ΣΚΛΑ–, according to the analogy of βάλλω βέβληκα, καλέω κέκληκα and many others.

Σκέπτομαι, *I look around me, consider*, (a depon. midd.) is inflected regularly. The Attics scarcely ever used the pres. and imperf., but generally σκοπῶ or σκοποῦμαι; on the contrary in the future always σκέψομαι, never σκοπήσω or σκοπήσομαι, as also in the aor. ἐσκεψάμην, and in the perf. ἔσκεμμαι, part. ἐσκεμμένος, Elmsl. Eurip. Heracl. 147. In this last-quoted passage it has its usual active signification, but in Demosth. Mid. p. 576, 27., and Erot. p. 1403, 21. it is used passively, although even in this writer its regular usage is active. Verbal adj. σκεπτέος.

The pres. and imperf. belong principally to the Epic language; e. g. σκέπτετο, Il. π, 361. imperat. σκέπτεο, Il. ρ, 652. Theogn. 1091. σκεπτόμενος, Apoll. Rhod. In the older Attics I have found σκεπτόμεθα in Plat. Lach. p. 185. and προυσκέπτετο in Thucyd. 8, 66. (see however the note below.) In the later writers these tenses are found more frequently, as in Lucian, &c.*

* The above account of the genuine Attic usage of this verb does not, it is true, rest on any statement of the old Grammarians; but that the great rarity of the pres. σκέπτεσθαι is not accidental, is proved by the very frequent occurrence

An aor. 2. pass. ἐσκέπην is found in the LXX, as in Numb. 1, 19. ἐπεσκέπησαν, *they were numbered.*

Σκοπέω, or σκοποῦμαι, *idem.* It is used only in the pres. and imperf.: all the other tenses are supplied by σκέπτομαι; which see.

Σκώπτω, *I joke, make a joke of*: fut. midd. σκώψομαι, Elmsl. Aristoph. Ach. 278. 844. [aor. 1. ἔσκωψα; and in Aristoph. Nub. 296. Reisig has restored to the text the act. fut. σκώψω. Compare Comm. Crit. de Soph. Œd. C. 398. —Passow.]

Σμάω, Ion. σμέω, *I smear, anoint*: fut. σμήσω, Dor. σμάσω; aor. 1. midd. ἐσμήσαμην; aor. 1. pass. ἐσμήχθην; verbal adj. σμηκτός. These two last are formed from a sister-form σμήχω, (fut. σμήξω, aor. 1. ἔσμηξα, &c.,) used by the Epics and in the later language: see Lobeck ad Phryn. p. 253. The present is contracted to σμῶ and inflected in η, as σμῇς, σμῇ, &c., infin. σμῆν; (see πεινάω) nor do σμᾷς, σμᾷν, &c., ever occur before the time of Lucian; Lobeck ad Phryn. p. 61.

Σοῦμαι. See Σεύω.

Σπάω, *I draw*: [fut. σπάσω; aor. 1. ἔσπασα; perf. ἔσπακα; perf. pass. ἔσπασμαι; aor. 1. midd. ἐσπασάμην; aor. 1. pass. ἐσπάσθην.] The α is short in all the tenses.

Σπεῖν, &c. See Ἕπω.

Σπείρω, *I sow*: [fut. σπερῶ; aor. 1. ἔσπειρα; perf. 2. ἔσπορα; perf. pass. ἔσπαρμαι;] aor. 2. pass. ἐσπάρην with α short.—Midd.

of ἐσκεψάμην, σκέψομαι, ἔσκεμμαι, σκοπῶ, σκοποῦμαι (compounds as well as simple), coupled with the decided defectiveness of the forms of σκοπεῖν in -ήσω, and -ῆσαι, of which I nowhere find any mention. Instances where σκέπτομαι formerly stood in the text may be seen in Sturz. Lex. Xenoph. in voc.; these require the particular examination of the critic. In the passage of Thucydides, all the manuscripts have τὰ ῥηθησόμενα πρότερον αὐτοῖς προυσκέπτετο. There is no objection here to the imperfect as a tense, but as the imperf. of a depon. in a pass. sense, it excites suspicion. If now we read προὔσκεπτο, the connection is as correct, and perhaps more suited to the context thus, "and they considered beforehand all that was to be brought forward:" and this sense Heilmannen gave it, although he did not contemplate any alteration in the reading.

Σπένδω, *I pour out*: fut. σπείσω; aor. 1. ἔσπεισα; perf. ἔσπεικα, Plut. Sertor. 14.; perf. pass. ἔσπεισμαι.

[Homer has the Ionic imperf. σπένδεσκε and the aor. σπείσασκε, as also the Ep. 2. sing. conj. pres. σπένδῃσθα, Od. δ, 591.—Passow.]

Στάζω, *I drop*: fut. στάξω, &c. Compare Βαστάζω, Διστάζω.

Στείβω, *I tread, tread upon*: [fut. στείψω; aor. 2. ἔστιβον;] aor. 2. pass. ἐστίβην, Soph. Aj. 883.

Στείχω, *I stride, march*: fut. στείξω; aor. 1. ἔστειξα; aor. 2. ἔστιχον. [The word is solely Poet. and Ion.]

Στέλλω, *I send*: [fut. στελῶ, Ep. στελέω; aor. 1. ἔστειλα; aor. 1. midd. ἐστειλάμην; perf. ἔσταλκα; perf. pass. ἔσταλμαι; pluperf. ἐστάλμην;] aor. 2. pass. ἐστάλην; and in the poets aor. 1. ἐστάλθην.

In Herodot. 7, 89. we find a 3. plur. pluperf. ἐσταλάδατο, which however is perhaps nothing more than an old error for ἐστάλατο, occurring in Hes. Scut. 288.

Στενάζω, *I groan*: fut. στενάξω, &c. Compare Στάζω, Βαστάζω, Διστάζω.

Στένω, *I sigh*, is used only in pres. and imperf.*.

The poets (Æschyl. and Eurip.) use also a pass. στένομαι, Epic στείνομαι, in the sense of *I am narrow, full.*

Στέργω, *I love, am contented with*: fut. στέρξω, &c.; perf. 2. ἔστοργα, Herodot. 7, 104.

Στερέω, *I deprive, bereave*: fut. στερήσω, but also στερέσω, Schæf. Schol. Par. Apollon. Rh. 1, 850. Jacob. Anthol. Poet. pp. 680. 711. whence the infin. aor. στερέσαι, Od. ν, 262. This verb is complete and regular in all its tenses in its compound ἀποστερέω, which, beside the more general idea of *to deprive*, has oftener the more immediate sense of *to take away*; e. g. fut. ἀποστερήσω; aor. 1. ἀπεστέρησα, &c.: pass. ἀποστεροῦμαι; aor. 1. ἀπε-

* [Reisig conjectures that we should read a fut. στενεῖ in Soph. Œd. Col. 1710.—Passow.]

στέρηθην; with the fut. midd. ἀποστερήσομαι. [In the simple verb the pres. in general use is στερίσκω, στερήσω, ἐστέρησα, &c.; and in the passive στεροῦμαι or στερίσκομαι, privor, I lose; fut. στερήσομαι; perf. ἐστέρημαι; aor. 1. ἐστερήθην.]

A particular form is στέρομαι with the meaning of *I am in the state of a person deprived of anything, I am without it.* [In prose this form is used only in pres. and imperf. —Passow.]

We must not confound, as is too commonly done, this στέρομαι with στεροῦμαι or στερίσκομαι. The meaning of στερόμενος is always *deprived*, that of στέρεσθαι *to be deprived*; so that these forms would be considered as an aorist of the principal verb, if the indic. pres. did not occur in the same full meaning in Xen. Symp. 4, 31. νῦν δ' ἐπειδὴ τῶν ὑπερορίων (of my foreign property) στέρομαι καὶ τὰ ἔγγεια οὐ καρποῦμαι: see also Anab. 3, 2, 2.

The poets have also from στέρομαι the part. aor. 2. pass. στερείς, synonymous with στερόμενος and στερηθείς.

Whether the simple verb στερῶ, στεροῦμαι occurs as a pres. in the old Attic writers I cannot venture to assert positively in the present imperfect state of our catalogues of Greek verbs. In Lucian and others it is, at least in the passive, not uncommon. But in Xen. Anab. 1, 9, 13. πολλάκις δ' ἦν ἰδεῖν καὶ ποδῶν καὶ χειρῶν καὶ ὀφθαλμῶν στερουμένους ἀνθρώπους, the sense requires στερομένους, deprived.

Homer seems to have inflected στερέω with the ε, for he has the aor. 1. infin. στερέσαι, Od. ν, 262. The fut. ἀποστερεῖσθε for ἀποστερήσεσθε, which occurs in the old Atticism, (Andocid. Myster. extr.) is to be explained by the same inflection.

Στεῦται, 3. sing. pres. and στεῦτο, 3. sing. imperf., Epic defective deponent. The above forms occur frequently in Homer in the sense of *he gives to understand, promises, threatens*: and we find the 3. plur. στεῦνται once in Æschyl. Pers. 49. in the same sense. At Od. λ, 584. στεῦτο δὲ διψάων, in a description of Tantalus, Passow derives it from ἵστημι, and translates it in its literal sense, *he stood*, but Voss renders it, *he strove, endeavoured*.

Στηρίζω, *I fix*: fut. στηρίσω; aor. 1. ἐστήριξα; aor. 1. midd. ἐστηριξάμην; perf. pass. ἐστήριγμαι; pluperf. ἐστηρίγμην. Compare Βαστάζω, Διστάζω.

Στίζω, *I prick*: fut. στίξω; aor. 1. ἔστιξα; perf. pass. ἔστιγμαι. See the preceding.

Στορέννυμι, *I spread, strew*, abbrev. στόρνυμι, and by metathesis στρώννυμι; so also in the formation*, fut. στορέσω or στρώσω (Att. παραστορῶ, Aristoph. Equ. 484.); aor. 1. ἐστόρεσα or ἔστρωσα; in the other tenses the usual forms are perf. pass. ἔστρωμαι; aor. 1. pass. ἐστρώθην; verbal adj. στρωτός.

Hippocrates uses καταστορεσθῆναι; see Foes. Œc. Hippocr.: and Hesychius explains ἐστορέσθη and ἐστορήθη by ἐστρώθη †.

Στρέφω, *I turn* (transit.); fut. στρέψω; perf. 2. ἔστροφα, Theognet. Conv. Athen. 3. p. 104. c. Lobeck ad Phryn. p. 578. perf. pass. ἔστραμμαι (like τέτραμμαι and τέθραμμαι, with α instead of ε‡); aor. 1. pass. ἐστρέφθην (compare Ἐτρέφθεν under Τρέπω); aor. 2. ἐστράφην.

The aor. 1. pass. ἐστράφθην occurs in the Doric dialect of Theocr. 7, 132. I know of no authority for a pres. στράφω; compare τράπω, τράφω. In Il. σ, 546. στρέψασκον is 3. plur. aor. for ἔστρεψαν.

Στυγέω, *I fear, hate*, is regular. The perf. ἀπεστύγηκα has the force of a present, Herodot. 2, 47.

From an obsolete stem ΣΤΥΓΩ or ΣΤΥΖΩ Homer has the aor. 2. ἔστυγον; and an aor. 1. ἔστυξα, opt. στύξαιμι, Od. λ, 502. with the causative meaning of *to make terrible*; which latter form is however again used by the later poets, e. g. by Apoll. Rh. 4, 512., in its original sense.

Συρίζω, Att. συρίττω, *I pipe*: fut. συρίξω, more frequently and purer Attic συρίξομαι, Non-Attic συρίσω, Dor. συρίσδω; see Hemsterh. Aristoph. Plut. p. 229. The aor. 1. infin. συρίσαι is found in Lucian. Harmon. 2. Compare Βαστάζω and Διστάζω.

Σύρω, *I draw, drag along*. Pass. σύρομαι; aor. 2. ἐσύρην.

* Compare Ἄγνυμι and Κεράννυμι.

† Stephens in his Thesaurus quotes κατεστόρηντο from Herodot. 8, 53., where however the text has κατάστρωντο without any various reading.

‡ See note on τέτραμμαι under Τρέπω.

Σφάζω, Att. σφάττω, [*I cut the throat*, *slaughter*, *offer up in sacrifice*: fut. σφάξω; aor. 1. ἔσφαξα; perf. pass. ἔσφαγμαι; aor. 1. pass. ἐσφάχθην, Herodot. 5, 5. and Pind.] but in the Attic writers generally aor. 2. ἐσφάγην, part. σφᾰγείς. Compare Βαστάζω, Διστάζω.

Σφάλλω, *I deceive*: [fut. σφᾰλῶ; aor. 1. ἔσφηλα, infin. σφῆλαι; aor. 2. ἔσφαλον, Pind.; perf. pass. ἔσφαλμαι;] aor. 2. pass. ἐσφάλην.

Σφίγγω, *I tie together*, *fasten together*: fut. σφίγξω; perf. pass. ἔσφιγμαι, (but 3. sing. ἔσφιγκται,) infin. ἐσφίγξαι, &c.

Σφύζω, *I beat* (as the pulse does), *palpito*: fut. σφύξω, &c. Compare Στάζω, Στίζω, &c.

Σχάζω, *I drop*, *open*: fut. σχάσω, &c. This verb has in the older language a pres. in -άω, as σχάω, infin. σχᾶν: imperf. ἔσχων; see Lobeck ad Phryn. p. 219.; but in the formation the α is always short.

[Both the act. and midd. voices of this verb have a transit. and intransit. meaning; in the former it seems connected with ἔχω, σχέθω, ἴσχω. An Alexandrian form ἐσχάζοσαν for ἔσχαζον is found in Lycophr. 21.—Passow.]

Σχεῖν, ἔσχον, ἐσχεθον. See Ἔχω.

Σώζω, *I save*: fut. σώσω, old Attic σώω; aor. 1. ἔσωσα; perf. pass. Att. σέσωμαι, otherwise generally σέσωσμαι; aor. 1. pass. ἐσώθην.—Midd.

The radical form is σαόω, σαώσω, coming regularly from σάος, *salvus*; and as from σάος came σῶς, so by contraction from σαόω was formed σώω, σώσω, σέσωμαι, ἐσώθην. The pres. σώω* σώει, &c. remained in the usage of the Epic poets; but σώζω, which sprung from it, was introduced into the common language, and gave rise afterwards to σέσωσμαι. The rarity of the older form σέσωμαι (on which see Suid. v. σέσωσται) arose from transcribers using the one then in common use†.

There is perhaps no instance whatever in the Epic writers of the pres. σώζω‡. In the other tenses they use the resolved form only, as fut.

* [Hence the part. σώοντες, Od. ι, 430. and the Ionic imperf. σώεσκον, Il. θ, 363. Apoll. Rhod. has also σώετε, and the midd. σώεσθαι.—Passow.]

† Bekker has in many cases restored the old form from the manuscripts.

‡ The single occurrence of σώζων in Od. ε, 490. is most likely a false reading for σώων, as we find at ι, 430. σώοντες: and in Hes. ε, 374. σώζοι is a rejected reading. Among the Alexandrine Epics Apollon. Rhod. has invariably σώω, &c.

σαώσω; aor. 1. ἐσάωσα; aor. 1. pass. ἐσαώθην; fut. midd. σαώσομαι; and in the present beside σώω, &c., a shortened form of it; as, conj. σόῃς, σόῃ, σόωσιν, Il. ι, 393. 424. 681. But the resolved form is seldom found in the present in the Epic writers; σαοῖ, Theogn. 868. Bekk. and Callim. Del. 22. σαοῦσι*, Tyrt. 2, 13. The imperative would therefore be σάου, and the imperf. (ἐσάουν) 3. sing. ἐσάου, σάου, and so the imperative is written in the manuscripts and in the text of the common editions in the following passages; Hom. Hymn. 12. (13.) Callim. Epigr. 35. Theodorid. Epigr. 4. Epigr. Adesp. 179. But Homer has ἐσάω, σάω, Il. φ, 238. π, 363. as the 3. sing. imperf., and σάω, Od. ν, 230. ρ, 595. as the imperat.; and so has Callimachus in his hymns: whence also the text of the first-quoted passages has been sometimes altered to σάω. Besides it has been already mentioned under ναιετάω, that this form is lengthened in the same anomalous manner as ναιετάωσα; that is to say from ἐσάου, σάου came ἐσῶ, σῶ; which contraction, instead of being resolved into -οω according to general analogy, was changed to -αω.

In an Attic inscription in Corp. Inscr. Gr. T. 1. p. 107. no. 71. stands legibly ΣΟΟ, while the context requires the fut. σώσω: that form must therefore be read σώω, which is the same old future as the Epic ἐρύουσι, τανύουσι, and which had therefore left its traces in the Attic language: see ἐκγεγάονται under Γένομαι, and the end of the article on Ἐρύω.

T.

ΤΑ–. We must suppose this stem or root on account of the old imperative τῆ, *take! here!* (in French *tiens!*) to which belonged also a plural τῆτε (Sophron. ap. Schol. Aristoph. Ach. 204.), formed according to the analogy of ζῆν, &c.

Akin to the above is another stem or root ΤΑΓ–,† from which Homer has a redupl. part. aor. 2. τεταγών, *seizing*.

That the supposition of a stem or root ΤΑ– for the formation of τέτακα, &c. from τείνω is grammatically unnecessary, although there may be etymological grounds for it, is shown under Τείνω. See also an account of all above-mentioned forms in Buttm. Lexil. Art. Τεταγών, p. 503. et sqq.

ΤΑΓ–. See ΤΑ– (ΤΑΩ).

Ταλάω. See Τλάω.

* The false reading σάουσι, and the similar error of σάοι (amended by Bekker in the above-quoted passage of Theognis) gave rise to the adoption of a form σάω.

† Compare ἐτμάγην under Τέμνω (τέτμηκα).

Τανύω, *I stretch out, strain*: fut. τανύσω; perf. pass. τετάνυσμαι; aor. 1. pass. ἐτανύσθην. The Epic fut. in -ύω*, τανύουσι occurs in Od. φ, 174. In Il. ρ, 393. we find a 3. sing. pres. τάνυται, as formed from τάνυμαι. The υ is short in all the tenses, so that Homer, in order to lengthen it, doubles the σ.

Ταράσσω, Att. ταράττω, *I disturb*: fut. ταράξω†, &c. Its inflexion is regular.

This verb has a sister-form of less frequent occurrence, 1.) in the Attics θράττω with long α, whence the neut. part. τὸ θρᾶττον: the pres. was used in prose, the aor. 1. ἔθραξα, infin. θρᾶξαι by the poets. 2.) in the Epic writers the perf., with an intransit. sense, τέτρηχα, *I am agitated, stormy.*

This θράττω was formed from ταράττω by transposing the first α with the ρ, and then contracting the two alphas into one long syllable: consequently the τ before the ρ became aspirated, like τέθριππον, θοιμάτιον, φροῦδος, &c. In τέτρηχα the τ was necessarily restored, and the η for ᾱ is a common Ionicism. From this perfect the later writers formed a pres. τρήχω. See the Art. on τέτρηχα in Buttm. Lexil. p. 506.

Τάσσω, Att. τάττω, *I set in order, arrange*: fut. τάξω; perf. pass. τέταγμαι; aor. 1. pass. ἐτάχθην; aor. 2. (less frequent) ἐτάγην. Midd. τάσσομαι, &c.; aor. 1. ἐταξάμην.

Ταφεῖν and ταφῆναι. See Θάπτω and ΘΑΦ–.

Τείνω, *I stretch out, extend* (anything): fut. τενῶ; aor. 1. ἔτεινα; perf. τέτᾰκα; perf. pass. τέταμαι; aor. 1. pass. ἐτάθην. See ΤΑ–, and Τανύω.

This verb with κλίνω, κρίνω, κτείνω, and πλύνω drop the ν in the perf. act., perf. pass., and aor. 1. pass., and take the short vowel of the future; the two verbs in -είνω changing also the ε to α. When we observe that ἔφθιμαι and δυθῆναι belong, both in form and meaning, to φθίω and δύω (not φθίνω, δύνω), that ἱδρύνθην, ἐπνύνθην must come from ἱδρύω, πνέω, there being no trace of a pres. in -νω for either, and that βαίνω comes from ΒΑΩ, φθάνω from ΦΘΑΩ, &c. &c., we may conclude that the above five verbs also (τείνω, &c.) came originally from roots which according to the more general analogy would be pure, and that another present was afterwards formed by the very common insertion of the ν. But as in these five verbs the ν is carried on to the future,

* See the end of the article on Σώζω, and the references there given.

† [Thucyd. 7, 36. has the fut. midd. ταράξομαι in a passive sense.—Passow.]

which is not the case with the other anomalous verbs in -γω, and there exists also a plain analogy between these and other verbs which have for their characteristic letter λ, μ, ν, or ρ, particularly in the change of the vowel ε to α; it seems to me a more grammatical and more practical arrangement to join them thus with each other and with the verbs in -νω, than to refer certain tenses to such themes as ΚΡΙΩ, ΤΑΩ, &c., by which the number of verbal anomalies would be unnecessarily increased.

Τείρω, *I rub out* (*attero*), *wear out, torment*, is used only in pres. and imperf. Τορεῖν and Τέρσομαι must be considered as distinct stems or roots, which, although akin to each other, have been separated by usage. See both in their places.

ΤΕΚ–. See Τίκτω.

Τελέω, *I finish, complete, fulfil*: fut. τελέσω*, τελέω (Il. θ, 415.), and Att. τελῶ, Plat. Protag. p. 311. b.; in the passive also τελεύμενα (Herodot. 3, 134.) is a future. See Δέμω and Καλέω. Pass. τελέομαι; fut. τελέσομαι; perf. τετέλεσμαι; aor. 1. pass. ἐτελέσθην.

[Homer has also the aor. 1. act. ἐτέλεσα, ἐτέλεσσα, of which Herodotus uses the infin. τελέσαι. We find also in Homer the Epic pres. τελείω, both in the act. and pass. voice.—Passow.]

Τέλλω, an old verb†, occurring only in its compounds, which may be found in the Lexicons; e. g. ἀνατέλλω, ἐπιτέλλω, &c. It is inflected regularly according to the analogy of verbs having as their characteristic letter λ, μ, ν, or ρ; and in the passive has only the aor. 1.—Midd.

[Passow gives the following inflection: τέλλω; fut. τελῶ, Æol. τέλσω; aor. 1. ἔτειλα, Æol. ἔτελσα; perf. pass. τέταλμαι; pluperf. ἐτετάλμην; aor. 1. ἐτάλθην. Midd. τέλλομαι; aor. 1. ἐτειλάμην.]

Τέμνω, *I cut*: fut. τεμῶ; aor. 2. ἔτεμον and ἔταμον; perf. τέτμηκα‡; perf. pass. τέτμημαι; aor. 1. pass. ἐτμήθην; 3. fut. τετμήσομαι, whence ἐκτετμήσεσθον, Plat. De Rep. 8. p. 564. c.—Midd.

In Il. ν, 707. τέμει is a solitary instance of a pres. τέμω; and so it is

* [In Homer, where the metre requires it, τελέσσω.—Passow.]

† See the note on Τλῆναι.

‡ The part. perf. τετμηώς is found in Apoll. Rhod. 4, 156. in a passive sense. See κεκορηώς under Κορέννυμι, and κεκμηώς under Κάμνω.

considered by Heyne: but Wolf and Passow read *τεμεῖ* as a future. The common form however in both Epic and Ionic writers is *τάμνω*: yet the aor. *ἔταμον* is found in the Attics, and was probably one of the older Atticisms, e. g. Thucyd. 1, 81. Eurip. Hel. 1240.

An Epic sister-form is *τμήγω*; aor. 1. *ἔτμηξα*; aor. 2. *ἔτμαγον*; aor. 2. pass. *ἐτμάγην*. See also Τέτμον.

Τέρπω, *I delight*: fut. τέρψω; aor. 1. ἔτερψα, &c. This verb is regular.

The pass. *τέρπομαι*, *I am delighted, satiated*, has in the Epic language three varieties of the aorist; viz. *ἐτέρφθην* (Od. θ, 131.); *ἐτάρπην* (Il. λ, 779. whence the infin. *ταρπῆναι*, *ταρπήμεναι*); and *ἐταρπόμην* (whence the conj. *ταρπώμεθα*, Il. ω, 636.) or with redupl. *τεταρπόμην*, *τετάρπετο*, *τεταρπώμεσθα*, *τεταρπόμενος*. But the aor. 1. pass. is found likewise in many passages of Homer with a change of vowel, e. g. *τάρφθη*, Od. τ, 213. *τάρφθεν*, ζ, 99.: for this however there are not sufficient analogical grounds; and as there is still less foundation for imagining that these two forms were used indifferently for each other in the same poem, it is possible that the one with the change of vowel might have been an impure dialect foisted into Homer's text at some very early period*.

Three times (Il. γ, 441. ξ, 314. Od. θ, 292.) Homer has *τραπείομεν*, which is aor. 2. conj. pass. for *τραπέωμεν*, *τραπῶμεν*, and formed according to the analogy of verbs in *μι*, that is like *θείομαι* for *θέωμαι* from *τίθημι*, or *στείομεν* for *στέωμεν* from *ἵστημι*. But in the above passages the verb comes from *τέρπω*, not from *τρέπω*, by the same metathesis as in *ἔπραθον*: see Πέρθω†.

Τέρσομαι, *I become dry*, depon. pass.; aor. 2. pass. (*ἐτέρσην*) infin. *τερσῆναι*, *τερσήμεναι*, Il. π, 519. Od. ζ, 98. The active voice does not occur in any ancient writer, but in its stead we find, in a causative sense, **Τερσαίνω**, *I make dry, dry up*, (regularly inflected) whence aor. 1. *ἐτέρσηνα* Il. π, 529.

At Il. π, 519. we find *τερσῆναι to become dry*, and at v. 529. *τέρσηνε*

* Indeed the use of the two forms *ἐτέρφθην* and *ἐτάρπην*, as there is no metrical cause for it, is very remarkable, and is perhaps one of the numerous traces of these poems having passed through a variety of mouths. Probably therefore *τάρφθη* (for which indeed at Od. τ, 213. some have read *τάρπη*,) is a mixture of the two genuine old readings above-mentioned.

† Heyne's objection to the derivation from *τρέπω*, grounded on grammatical construction, is correct. To which we may add that Homer in such a sense (*to turn oneself toward*) never uses *τραπῆναι* but *τραπέσθαι*; while on the other hand we meet with the same expression *τέρπεσθαι φιλότητι* at Od. ε, 227. In the passage of Od. θ, 292. we must join *εὐνηθέντε λέκτρονδε*, like *ἐς θρόνον ἷζε* and the like.

he made dry; hence the two forms, thus standing in evident relation to each other, have been generally considered as infinitive and indicative of the same verb, with no other difference than that of sense. Now as *τέρσηνε* can be nothing but an aor. 1. act., *τερσῆναι* would then be the infinitive of the same tense, with an immediate or neuter meaning. But *τερσήμεναι* (Od. ζ, 98.), which exactly corresponds with it, is clearly an aor. passive*.

Nicander (Ther. 96. 693. 709.) has some forms of an aor. *ἔτερσα* for *ἐτέρσηνα*; and again in Theocr. 22, 63. I would, rather on account of the context, consider *τέρσει* to be a future than a present. If this be so, and these forms of Nicander, like others of the same poet, were not made by himself, they come probably from *τέῤῥω, I dry up* (see the last note); fut. *τέρσω*; aor. 1. *ἔτερσα*.

Τεταγών. See ΤΑ–.

Τετευχῆσθαι, *to be armed*, Od. χ, 104. a perfect derived from the subst. *τεύχεα*. Compare Ἐσθημένος.

Τετίημαι. See ΤΙΕ–.

Τέτμον, ἔτετμον, *I found, hit upon, attained*: a defective aorist, of which we find no other tense than the conj. *τέτμῃς, ῃ*, Od. ο, 15. The analogy of *ἔπεφνον* and *ἐκεκλόμην* appears to lead us to a theme ΤΕΜΩ, which however being totally different in meaning from ΤΕΜΩ the stem or root of *τέμνω*, must be kept distinct from it, at least by the Grammarian.

[Of this latter root we find *ἐτέτμετο* in Orph. Arg. 366. which, as well as *ἔτετμον*, Passow forms from an obsolete pres. *τέτμω*.]

Τετραίνω. See Τιτράω.

Τεύχω. The two following cognate verbs must be kept distinct from each other.

1. **Τεύχω,** *I prepare*: a poetical word, regularly inflected, as fut.

* It is true that there is no other instance of an aor. 2. pass. in *σην*; but this arises only from there being in the common language no verb with *σ* as its characteristic. This aorist is therefore quite regular; and consequently to suppose an intransitive active ΤΕΡΣΕΩ, to which these infinitives might belong according to the analogy of *φορῆναι, φορήμεναι*, would be to increase unnecessarily the number of themes. Besides these forms must then be in the present, synonymous with *τέρσεσθαι*, the meaning of which is "*to continue* to get *drier*," whereas in both the above passages the idea is that of "being *completely* dry." And the plan of the older grammarians of joining *τέρσεσθαι* with *τείρειν* by means of a future and an aorist of this verb according to the analogy of *κείρω ἔκερσα* (compare Ἀλέξω), must be pronounced incorrect, because the *σ* in *τέρσεσθαι* is in the root through the Ionicism of *ρσ* for *ῤῥ*, as shown by the derivative subst. *ταῤῥός* and *ταρσός*, and the Lat. *torreo*. Nor is there so immediate an agreement between the meanings of (*τέῤῥω*) *τέρσω*, *I dry up*, and *τείρω*, *I rub off*, which latter may indeed have been pronounced in the Æolic dialect *τέῤῥω* also (see Greg. Cor. in Æol. ii.), as to justify the grammarian in joining both verbs under the same inflexion.

τεύξω; aor. 1. ἔτευξα; perf. τέτευχα; perf. pass. τέτυγμαι*; fut. 3. τετεύξομαι; aor. 1. pass. ἐτύχθην†. Verbal adj. τυκτός or τευκτός.

2. Τυγχάνω, *I happen, chance to be, hit upon*: fut. τεύξομαι; aor. 2. ἔτυχον; perf. τετύχηκα. On the formation of these tenses from τεύχω see notes under Πυνθάνομαι and Αἰσθάνομαι: and on the derivation of τετύχηκα from ἔτυχον (without having recourse to a new theme τυχέω) see Ἀκαχίζω and note.

The meaning of τυγχάνω, ἔτυχον is that of the passive of τεύχω with an intransitive immediate force. That is to say τετύχθαι very frequently means in the Epic poets *to be fated, destined, brought on by circumstances,* whence τετύκται is much the same as ἐστί, for which was afterwards used τυγχάνει ὤν or τυγχάνει; and ἐτύχθη in Il. β, 320. (θαυμάζομεν, οἷον ἐτύχθη) had precisely the same meaning as ἔτυχεν in prose. Thus ἔτυχέ μοι τοῦτο, *this happened to me,* was much the same as ἐτύχθη μοι: compare Il. λ, 683. οὕνεκά μοι τύχε πολλά, *because much had happened to me,* with ρ, 704. μεγάλη δὲ πόθη Πυλίοισιν ἐτύχθη, *was prepared for them, was their lot*: and sometimes in this as in other cases the relation is reversed, ἔτυχον τούτου, *I obtained that as my lot,* whence comes the meaning of *to obtain, light upon, find.* In a similar way it is easy to distinguish in the two aorists of the same theme, ἔτευξα and ἔτυχεν, the causative and the immediate meaning becoming active and passive, ("I caused, prepared," and "it was prepared, was my lot") a distinction which we see plainly in ἤρειψα and ἤριπον, in ἔφυσα and ἔφυν‡, and in others: e. g. θεοὶ κακὰ κήδεα ἔτευξάν μοι (Od. α, 244.) and κακὰ κήδεα ἔτυχέ μοι, like τύχε μοι πολλά.

With this aor. 2. is connected also, according to the analogy given in the last note, the perf. act. from the same simple form, τέτευχα. This was the true Ionic perfect of τυγχάνω, e. g. in Herodot. 3, 14. extr., which in a later period became frequent in the non-Attic writers, as in Aristot. Eth. 3, 14. Polyb. 1, 81: see Lobeck ad Phryn. p. 395. Nay, the part. of this perfect occurs in Homer in a completely passive sense

* On the change of the diphthong to υ, see note under Χέω.

† See the end of Art. on Λείπω.

‡ Wherever the causative and the immediate meaning are expressed by different active forms, the perf. (whether perf. 1. or 2.) and the aor. 2. belong always to the immediate sense, as,

φύω, φύσω, ἔφυσα, I produce,—ἔφυν, πέφυκα, I am produced, I grow.

The same may be observed of ἔστην and ἕστηκα, of ἔδυν and δέδυκα, of ἐσβην and ἔσβηκα, of ἐσκλην and ἔσκληκα (in σκέλλω), of ἤριπον and ἐρήριπα. Again by usage τέτευχα belongs not to τεύχω, but to τυγχάνω; and the Epics join τέτροφα with ἔτραφον.

in Od. μ, 423. βοὸς ῥινοῖο τετευχώς, "made of cow-hide:" of which similar instances may be seen in a note under Ἁλίσκομαι. For the perf. of τεύχω in an active sense, there is no genuine undisputed authority*.

From ἔτυχον, τυχεῖν were formed (according to the analogy of ἤκαχον, ἀκαχεῖν, ἀκαχήσω, ἠκάχησα: see Ἀκαχίζω and note) a new aorist and perfect, precisely synonymous with those above-mentioned, viz. ἐτύχησα and τετύχηκα, of which the aor. 1. remained in Epic usage, while the perfect became the Attic and common form.

In the Ionic 3. plur. of τέτυγμαι Homer has restored, on account of the metre, the diphthong of the present, making τετεύχαται, τετεύχατο; but we find also, at least in the later prose, τετεύγμαι (see Lobeck ad Phryn. p. 728.); whence ἀποτετευγμένος, of a thing which has not answered the expectation, Lucian. Alex. 28†. And lastly in Homer, the fut. 3. is not formed with υ, but written τετεύξομαι; which future is used at Il. μ, 345. φ, 585. in the neuter sense only of τέτυγμαι, and therefore cannot be mistaken at φ, 322.

The same uncertainty which is found in the vowel of τυκτός, τευκτός, appears to have existed also in the aor. 1. pass.; at least in Anacr. 10. τὸ τευχθὲν is the better accredited reading. Perhaps it was wished to distinguish ἐτεύχθην with the proper sense of τεύχω, from ἐτύχθην, which has in all other instances a neuter meaning.

The Epic language has another aorist, always found in a reduplicated shape, the aor. 2. τετυκεῖν, Midd. τετυκέσθαι, and corresponding in meaning with τεῦξαι, τεύξασθαι, *to prepare*: see Od. υ, 94. Il. α, 467. The κ comes from the Ionic dialect (see Δέκομαι), and is retained in this old form, which may be compared with κεκαδεῖν under Χάζω.

* In Il ν, 346. the reading of most of the manuscripts, and, until very lately, of the text also, was τετεύχατον in the sense of *to prepare*. But as the perfect cannot possibly stand in that passage, the other reading τετεύχετον, which the Scholiast also follows, has been adopted. This, however, is equally inadmissible. For whether it be considered as a present, (which is contrary to Homer's practice in the narrative,) or as an imperfect with the termination of -τον for -την, such a form as τετεύχω for τεύχω or τέτευχον for ἔτευχον is quite unheard of, and (which is decisive,) not required by the metre. There is no doubt, therefore, that the reading of the Schol. Ven., extracted from some old copies (ἐτεύχετον for ἐτευχέτην), is the only true one. That is to say, as the termination in -τον of this imperfect, though not without parallel cases (Il. κ, 364. σ, 583.) in the old Epic poetry, was yet contrary to the common rules of grammar established at a later period, the word was first altered to a supposed present τετεύχετον, and then to a perfect, which, as far as regarded formation, was a correct one. The present Scholium of this verse is most corrupt; that at Il. κ, 364. attributed to the Alexandrines, and containing the Scholiast's opinion of this dual in all three passages, reads indeed in the one before us τετεύχετον, but it can only be rendered consistent with itself by our reading there also ἡρώεσσιν ἐτεύχετον ἀντὶ τοῦ ἔτευχον.

† See also Stephan. Thesaur. in ἀποτυγχάνω, and Lex. Seguer. (Antiatt.), p 79., where the still more astonishing form ἀποτετύχηται is explained by ἀποτέτευκται.

With this *τετυκέσθαι* is joined in the same Epic language a new present *τιτύσκομαι*, like *λάσκω* from *λακεῖν*, *ἴσκω* from *εἴκω*. At Il. *φ*, 342. this form has plainly and without force the meaning of *τεύχειν*, *to prepare* (fire); and so it was understood by the ancients, as the usage of Apollonius proves, who uses it (4, 248.) in the sense of "*to prepare* the sacrifice." The active voice is found in the Alexandrine poets, as in Arat. 418. Antim. Fr. 26. Lycophr. 1403. Opp. Hal. 2, 99. Compare Ruhnk. Epist. Crit. p. 38. At the same time this form belongs also to the other meaning, that of *τυγχάνω*; for *τιτύσκεσθαί τινος* (Il. *ν*, 159.) *to aim at any one*, bears the same relation to *τυχεῖν τινος*, *to hit any one*, as *ἀποδιδράσκει*, *he runs away* (spoken of one who may still be caught), does to *ἀπέδρα*, *he escaped*, or as *captare* does to *capere*, and the like*.

Τόσσαι for *τυχεῖν*, see in its alphabetical place.

Τήκω, *I melt*, *soften*, (trans.): fut. *τήξω*, &c. Pass. *τήκομαι*, with aor. 2. *ἐτάκην* (ᾰ), and perf. *τέτηκα*, *I melt*, (intrans.): see *ἔαγα*, &c., under Ἄγνυμι, and note under Τεύχω.

TIE–, whence *τετίημαι*, *I am vexed*, of which we find only the 2. dual. *τετίησθον*, Il. *θ*, 447. and the part. *τετιημένος*, Il. *λ*, 555. In the same sense Homer uses also the active form *τετιηώς*, *-ότος*, Il. *ι*, 30. *λ*, 554. Compare *κεκαφηώς*, *κεκμηώς*, *βεβαρηώς*, &c.: see also *βεβαώς* under Βαίνω.

Τίκτω, *I bring forth*, *pario*†: fut. *τέξω*‡, more generally *τέξομαι*; aor. 2. *ἔτεκον*; perf. *τέτοκα*, part. *τετοκώς*, *-υῖα*, *-ός*, Hes. *ε*, 593.

* Modern critics have attempted to connect this verb with *τιταίνω*, by deducing the idea of *taking aim* from that of *drawing tight* the string of the bow, and because at Il. *θ*, 41. *ὑπ' ὄχεσφι τιτύσκετο* is used of *attaching* the horses to the chariot, i. e. *straining* or *drawing tight* the traces. But independently of the two verbs (*τιταίνω* and *τιτύσκω*,) being similar only in appearance, the similarity vanishes entirely between *τείνω* and *τιτύσκω*; nor can *τιτύσκεσθαι πῦρ* be explained by means of this deduction without very unusual force; and as for the idea of the horses *straining* or *stretching* the traces, it does not correspond with any Greek or Latin expression whatever, for Homer uses *τιταίνειν ἅρμα* in the sense of the horses *drawing along* the chariot. Τιτύσκεσθαι in the above passage is therefore only a slight deviation from *τεύχειν*, with the sense of *to set in order*, *make ready*, and hence the Greek commentators unanimously explain it by *ἑτοιμάζειν*.

† [Sometimes also, *I beget*, Eurip. Suppl. 1092. in which sense Homer very frequently uses the middle voice, Il. *β*, 742.—Ed.]

‡ Decisive authorities for this active form in the Iambic trimeter of the Attics will be found in Aristoph. Thesm. 509. Eurip. Tro. 742. Æschyl. Prom. 868.

The perf. pass. τέτεγμαι and aor. 1. pass. ἐτέχθην are found only in non-Attic writers, e. g. in Hippocr. De Superfet. 8. and Pausan. 3, 7. The same perfect, with change of vowel, τέτογμαι occurs in Synes. Epist. 141. The middle voice, with the same meaning as the active, is poetical only; τίκτεται, Æschyl. ap. Athen. p. 600. b. aor. 2. ἐτεκόμην, τέκετο, τεκέσθαι, Hom. [The aor. 1. τέξασθαι is found in some editions of Hes. θ, 889., but perhaps the better reading is τέξεσθαι. The aor. 1. act. ἔτεξα is very rare, Lobeck ad Phryn. p. 743.—Passow.]

A fut. infin. τεκεῖσθαι (as from τεκοῦμαι) is found in Hymn. Ven. 127., but I think τεκέσθαι would suit the syntax of the passage quite as well, in which case τεκεῖσθαι might be an old correction. The form τεξείεσθε, Arat. 124., which must be explained by supposing a fut. τεξοῦμαι, τεξείομαι, is very suspicious*.

Τίλλω, *I pluck, tear up*; fut. τιλῶ; aor. 1. ἔτιλα; perf. pass. τέτιλμαι.—Midd. This verb is inflected like κρίνω.

Τίνω, τίνυμι. See Τίω.

Τιτράω, *I perforate*: fut. τρήσω; aor. 1. ἔτρησα. We have also a sister-form Τετραίνω, fut. τετρανῶ; aor. 1. ἐτέτρηνα, Aristoph. Thesm. 18., but in Theophr. ἐτέτρανα†. This latter verb, which is properly nothing more than a strengthened form of the other, became the general one in Attic usage. The perfects are however always taken from the radical form, thus perf. act. τέτρηκα, perf. pass. τέτρημαι, Herodot. 4, 158.—Midd.

The aor. ἐτέτρηνα, formed contrary to the general rule of verbs in -αίνω (see Κερδαίνω), is an Ionicism which remained in the Attic language. Authorities from Theophrastus for ἐτέτρανα may be seen in Stephan. Thesaur. The form τιτραίνω, wherever found, is a corruption.

Τιτρώσκω, *I wound*: fut. τρώσω, &c. Perf. part. pass. τετρωμέναι νέες, *injured*, Herodot. 8, 18.

The stem or root of τιτρώσκω is in the verb τορεῖν, (as ΘΟΡ- is the root of θρώσκω, ΒΟΡ- of βιβρώσκω,) by the well-known metathesis detailed more at length under Βάλλω, Θνήσκω, and Καλέω. But as the

* [Passow is of opinion that Buttmann has not sufficient grounds for suspecting these two forms.]

† We find also in Hippocr. De Nat. Puer. c. 4. an Ionic form τετρήνω, which Passow pronounces to be a false reading for τετραίνω.

sense of the derivative verb has become more precise and limited than that of its original theme, they must be treated as two separate verbs. Homer has the present in a more simple shape, τρώω, τρώεις; but only once, and then in the general sense of *to hurt* or *injure*, Od. φ, 293.

Τιτύσκω. See Τεύχω.

Τίω. As usage has separated the two following verbs, it will be better to do the same.

Τίω, *I honour*, is solely poetical, and quite regular; e. g. fut. τίσω; aor. 1. ἔτισα, &c.; perf. pass. τέτιμαι, Il. ν, 426. Od. ν, 28., &c.

Τίνω, *I pay* or *suffer* (the penalty of an offence), forms, like the preceding, a fut. τίσω; aor. 1. ἔτισα, &c.; perf. τέτικα; but the Attics make the ι short in all the tenses, and the pass. takes σ, as perf. τέτισμαι; aor. 1. ἐτίσθην. Midd. τίνομαι, *I punish* (a person), *avenge* (a thing): fut. τίσομαι; aor. 1. ἐτισάμην.

According to the general analogy of verbs in -ίνω, the Epics have the ι long in τίνω and all its tenses. The Attics, on the contrary, generally use it short: see, as instances of τίνω, Æschyl. Prom. 112. Soph. Œd. Col. 1203. Eurip. Or. 7.; and of τίσαι, Aristoph. Eccl. 45. Vesp. 1424. The ι of the present is also short in the Doric dialect of Pindar (Pyth. 2, 44.); in the early time of Solon (5, 31.), as well as in that of the later Epigrammatists, Jac. Anthol. Poet. p. 823. On the other hand, the fut. and its derivative tenses have the ι long in Pind. Ol. 2, 106., in the Anapæsts of Aristoph. Eccl. 656. 663., in the Iambic Trimeter of Soph. Trach. 1113. Phil. 1041. and in a lyric passage of Aj. 182.; see Reisig. Comm. Crit. de Soph. Œd. Col. p. 220.

We find an Ionic sister-form of the pres. τίνω in τίννυμι, τίννυμαι, written in the Attic poetry τίνυμαι with ι short, Eurip. Or. 313*.

Τλῆναι, *to bear* or *suffer*, *bear up manfully*, *venture*, *dare*. Of this verb there is neither present nor imperfect: fut. τλήσομαι; perf. τέτληκα; aor. 2. ἔτλην, imper. τλῆθι, opt. τλαίην,† infin. τλῆναι, part. τλάς, τλᾶσα, τλάν. Compare ἔγνων, &c., under Γιγνώσκω.

These forms are used both in poetry and prose, while the defective tenses are supplied from the verbs of similar meaning ὑπομένω and

* [Passow objects to the writing of this form with νν, and prefers τίνυμι in all cases, with the ι long in the Epic, and short in the Attic writers, like τίνω.]

† The conjunctive is not in use.

ἀνέχομαι. Τέτληκα is a regular perfect, and used as such in Aristoph. Plut. 280., but the poets have formed from it (with the force of a present,) the following syncopated forms; perf. plur. τέτλαμεν, τέτλατε, τετλᾶσι, dual τέτλατον; imper. τέτλαθι, τετλάτω, &c.; opt. τετλαίην*; infin. τετλάναι (ᾰ), τετλάμεν and τετλάμεναι; part. τετληώς, -ότος; pluperf. plur. ἐτέτλαμεν, ἐτέτλατε, ἐτέτλασαν, dual ἐτέτλατον, ἐτετλάτην. The Epic language has also an unusual aor. 1. ἐτάλασα, ἐτάλασσα†, Il. ρ, 166., whence conj. ταλάσσω, -ῃς, -ῃ, Il. ν, 829. ο, 164., and in a later period we find a fut. ταλάσσω, Lycophr. 746.

TM–. See Τέμνω and Τέτμω.

Τμήγω. See Τέμνω.

Τορεῖν (Hesych.), *to pierce, stab*; aor. 2. ἔτορον, a defective aorist, Il. λ, 236., and (of less frequent occurrence,) aor. 1. ἐτόρησα, part. τορήσας, Hymn. Merc. 119. A pres. τορέω is nowhere found. [There are also traces in Hesych. of a reduplicated aor. τέτορον explained by τρῶσαι.—Passow.]

The same idea of *piercing* lies in τετορήσω, a future with the meaning of *to pierce* (the ears), *utter with a loud* or *shrill voice* in Aristophanes (Pac. 381.), who has also in the same sense a present τορεύω (Thesm. 986.)‡.

Τόσσας, Dor. τόσσαις, an aor. part. synonymous with τυχεῖν, Pind. Pyth. 3, 48., compare Bœckh. var. lect. p. 456. Beside the above we find only the compound ἐπέτοσσε, part. ἐπιτόσσαις, Pind. Pyth. 4, 43. 10, 52.

Τραπείω. See Τέρπω.

Τράπω. See Τρέπω.

Τρέμω, *I tremble*, is used only in the pres. and imperf.

Τρέπω, *I turn*: fut. τρέψω; aor. 1. ἔτρεψα; aor. 1. midd. ἐτρεψάμην; aor. 1. pass. ἐτρέφθην; aor. 2. ἔτραπον; aor. 2. pass. ἐτράπην; aor. 2. midd. ἐτραπόμην; perf. 2. τέτροφα§

* The conjunctive is not in use.

† There is no doubt of the verb τέλλω having had in the older language the meaning of *to bear*, traces of which we see in the Lat. *tollo* and *tuli*. Now τλῆναι, τλαίην have the same relation to τέλλω, as σκλῆναι, σκλαίην have to σκέλλω. In the course of time forms disappeared, and the meaning became modified, but was still quite perceptible in τλῆναι and *tollo*. The simple meaning of *to bear* remained only in *tuli*. The present τέλλω disappeared entirely as a simple verb; in its compounds, in which it has the aor. 1. ἔτειλα, the original sense is most evident in ἐπιτέλλειν.

‡ As ἔμμορον comes from μείρω, so is ἔτορον indisputably the aorist of a stem or root TEP–, which may be compared etymologically with τείρω, although this latter cannot in its precise meaning be joined grammatically with τορεῖν. Hesychius has preserved forms of the reduplicated aorist τέτορον (τέτορεν, τετόρῃ), but which are explained by τρῶσαι. See Τιτρώσκω.

§ See note under Κλέπτω. This τέτροφα is found in Aristoph. Nub. 858. in

and τέτρἄφα; perf. pass. τέτραμμαι*.—MIDD. Verbal adj. τρεπτός, and with the sense of the middle voice τραπητέος. With regard to the aorist, τρέπω is the only verb which prefers the aor. 2. to the aor. 1. in all three voices: still, however, the latter is used in each voice to express certain deviations of meaning; but this is a subject for the Lexicons.

A very singular instance of the aor. 2. midd. in a passive sense is found in Plat. Cratyl. p. 395. d. ἡ πατρὶς αὐτοῦ ὅλη ἀνετράπετο.

In this verb, as in στρέφω and τρέφω, the α of the perf. pass. is not carried on to the aor. 1. excepting in the Ionic and Doric dialects†: thus the Attics use ἐτρέφθην, τρεφθῆναι, τρεφθείς, Xen. Ven. 12, 5., but Herodotus (4, 12. 9, 56.) has ἐτράφθην, τραφθείς. At the same time it is difficult to form a decided judgement on this point, as Herodotus has not only a pres. τράπω, but also (3, 155.) επιτράψονται, and (4, 202.) ἐπέτραψε; though in all these instances the reading is uncertain‡. Compare στρέφω.

We find in a multiplicity of verbs, as in βλαστάνω, γίγνομαι, δαρθάνω, πέτομαι, &c. certain tenses formed from the aor. 2. (see ἀκαχήσω and note under Ἀκαχίζω): but in the verb before us, as well as in κτείνω, we have instances of a present so formed, e. g. ἐπιτραπέουσι, Il. κ, 421. We must here bear in mind that τραπέω, *I tread* (the grapes), is a very different verb. See τραπείομεν under Τέρπω. [We find also in Homer an imperat. perf. pass. τετράφθω, Il. μ, 273., an Epic 3. sing. of the pluperf. pass. τέτραπτο, and the Epic and Ionic 3. plur. of the perf. and pluperf. pass. τετράφαται, τετράφατο.—Passow.]

Andocid. Myster. p. 17, 13. Ald. and in Soph. Trach. 1009.; but it is probable that at a very early period, in order to avoid confusion with τέτροφα from τρέφω, it was changed to τέτραφα, although from the uncertainty of the readings it is difficult to ascertain with any degree of accuracy when this change took place. We find, for instance, in Demosth. Pro Cor. 324, 27., in the same passage quoted by Longin. 32., and in Æschin. c. Timarch. p. 179. Ctesiph. p. 545. ἀνατέτραφα always accompanied by the various reading ἀνατέτροφα, which latter Reiske has adopted in his text. Again in Dinarch. c. Demosth. pp. 23. 73. and c. Philocl. p. 93. we find τέτραφα, but without any various reading hitherto discovered.

* This α is peculiar to the three perfects passive of τρέπω, τρέφω and στρέφω: in κλέπτω also usage fluctuates between κέκλεμμαι and κέκλαμμαι. See Etym. M. voc. ἐπιτετράφαται, and Not. Crit. ad Aristoph. Vesp. 57. et ad Athen. 9. p. 409. c.

† [Passow adds the Epic language of Homer, and quotes ἐτράφθην from Od. ο, 80. but the reading seems to be uncertain.—Ed.]

‡ However singular it may appear that in the Ionic dialect the verb should be inflected τράπω, τρέψω, yet this is by far the most common mode of inflexion in our copies of Herodotus; see Schweigh. in ἐπιτρ.: nay, in the two passages quoted above we find ἐπιτρέψονται and ἐπέτρεψε in very excellent manuscripts.

Τρέφω, *I nourish*: fut. θρέψω*; aor. 1. ἔθρεψα; perf. 2. τέτροφα (see τέτροφα and note under Τρέπω); perf. pass. τέθραμμαι (see τέτραμμαι and note under Τρέπω), infin. τεθράφθαι†; aor. 2. pass. ἐτράφην: verbal adj. θρεπτός.

The stem or root of this verb had both the immediate sense *to become fat, large, strong*, and the causative one *to make fat*, &c. From this latter comes the common meaning; the former occurs in the Epic language, but only in the aor. 2. ἔτραφον and the perf. τέτροφα, according to the rule laid down in the note under Τεύχω: and undoubtedly these two forms had in that Epic language this intransitive meaning only, but in a later period the perfect took the causative sense also, as we see it in Soph. Œd. Col. 186. Alcæ. Messen. Epigr. 18. (Anal. 1. p. 490.), and Polyb. 5, 74., while the aor. 2. (ἔτραφε, Il. φ, 279. ἐτραφέτην, ε, 555. τραφέμεν for -εῖν, η, 199.) became obsolete‡. That is to say, when in this as in other similar verbs, that neuter meaning *to become large, grow up*, began to be expressed in the present by the passive voice (see Il. ι, 143.), it soon spread to the aor. and perf. passive: and thus we find, even as early as Homer, the forms ἐτράφη, ἐτράφημεν, and ἔτραφεν or τράφεν for ἐτράφησαν§.

* Among the laws which regulate the Greek aspirates, we may observe the following; that where two successive syllables begin each with an aspirate, one of the aspirates, generally the first, is changed to the tenuis of the same organ: and when by any formation the second disappears, the first is restored. Thus, the root of this verb is ΘΡΕΦ-, whence τρέφω, and again θρέψω.

† Not τέτραφθαι, which belongs to τρέπω, and which, though found in all the manuscripts in Xen. Hell. 2, 3, 24. (17.), must nevertheless be a corruption. Τέθραφθε in Plat. Legg. init. is the correct reading. Compare τεθάφθαι under Θάπτω.

‡ [Yet in Callim. Jov. 55. we find ἔτραφες for ἐτράφης.—Passow.]

§ Of the passages in which these passive forms are now found, we must first reject Il. β, 661. where the old reading Τληπόλεμος δ' ἐπεὶ οὖν τράφ' ἐνὶ μεγάροις εὐπήκτοις was first changed by Barnes to τράφη ἐν, to the injury of the rhythm, and at the same time in opposition to almost all the manuscripts; for not one has τράφη ἐν in regular order, nor is there the least trace of such a reading in any of the Grammarians. There was evidently, therefore, in the text of Homer, as handed down to us, a discrepancy between this passage and two others (γ, 201. Ὃς τράφη ἐν δήμῳ, and λ, 122. Ὃς τράφη ἐν Θρήκῃ), which those grammarians did not attempt to reconcile, and in which we ought to have followed their example. Nay, this discrepancy should have rather led us to conjecture that the passive forms had crept into Homer's text from the usage of a later period; that the 3. plur. τράφεν, for instance, had taken the place of τράφον, and that the original reading of the two passages quoted above was Ὃς τράφεν ἐν δήμῳ, and Ὃς τράφ' ἐνὶ Θρήκῃ. This conjecture is much strengthened by the circumstance, that the remaining passage, of which the emendation is not so easy, (Ἀλλ' ὁμοῦ ὡς ἐτράφημεν ἐν ὑμετέροισι δόμοισιν, Il. ψ, 84.), abounds in variety of readings. One, in particular, of great weight in criticising Homer's text as being a full quotation of the whole passage in Æschines (c. Timarch. p. 21.), has this striking difference, Ὡς ὁμοῦ ἐτράφεμέν περ ἐν ὑ. δ. Surprising as this latter form is, we see at once

The present with the radical vowel α, τράφω, is exclusively Doric, as in Pind. Pyth. 2, 82. 4, 205. Isthm. 8, 88. (7, 40. Bœckh.)*

Τρέχω, *I run*, forms its future like τρέφω (see note under that verb); thus fut. θρέξομαι; aor. 1. ἔθρεξα: but by far the more common future comes from a very different stem or root, fut. δραμοῦμαι†; aor. 2. ἔδραμον; perf. δεδράμηκα.

The forms ἔθρεξα, θρέξομαι were almost obsolete: Homer has the aorist (see Lobeck ad Phryn. p. 719.); and the future is still found as an old Atticism in Aristophanes, μεταθρέξομαι (see Fischer ad Well. 3. p. 182. Herm. ad Nub. 1005.) and περιθρέξαι, Thesm. 657., at which passage the Scholiast thinks it necessary (so little was the word in use,) to explain it.

The present of this verb is found in the Doric writers with the α, τράχω: see Bœckh on Pind. Pyth. 8, 34.

The perf. δεδράμηκα‡ is formed from the aor. 2. ἔδραμον according to the analogy described in note on ἀκαχήσω under Ἀκαχίζω. The fut.

that, with the mere additional insertion of δὲ after Ὡς required to connect it with the context, this was the old and genuine reading of the verse: instead of which some grammatical *Diaskeuastes* removed the ὡς from its natural place, where it answered to the corresponding Ὡς δὲ καὶ ὀστέα, and sacrificed the πέρ which served to exalt the comparison, merely to introduce into the verse the regular ἐτράφημεν, grating as this ἔτρ... must have been to an Ionic ear by the harshness which it gave the metre. Now as far as regards this ἐτράφεμεν, Bœckh (on Pind. Pyth. 4, 115.) is of opinion that the ancients saw in all these Homeric forms (τράφε, τραφέμεν, &c.) nothing more than a shortening of the η. I agree with him in this opinion: but a correct idea of the true relation of this verb in Homer's language can only be formed by our recollecting the mutual coincidence of meaning in ἔτραφε and τέτροφε, and the great leading analogy mentioned in a note under Μείρομαι, and again more fully illustrated in a note under Τεύχω. The form ἐτράφην is not Homeric, but ἔτραφον had the intransitive sense expressed afterwards by ἐτράφην only. Now, where the difference of form was so slight, it was very natural that any one, who did not carry in his mind the whole of Homer's usage, should suppose the forms τράφε, τραφέ-την, &c., to be merely a metrical shortening of the vowel, as in the conjunctives ἱμείρεται, ναυτίλλεται, &c.: and thus ἐτράφεμεν was introduced where the old Rhapsodist had used ἐ τ ρ ά φ ο μ ε ν, as also from the 3. plur. ἔτραφον was made ἔτραφεν. I have no doubt, therefore, that the old reading of the above verse was, Ὡς δ' ὁμοῦ ἐτράφομέν περ ἐν ὑμετέροισι δόμοισιν.

* In all three passages the forms in question are by some accented as aorists, τραφεῖν, τραφών: but we dare not so easily suppose ἔτραφον to be used for ἔθρεψα. In all three passages the present is correct, in the last it is indispensable.

† This future in an active form is found in the comic writer Philetærus ap. Athen. 10. p. 416. ὑπερδραμῶ: for such is the syntax of that whole passage that the Attic language does not allow it to be transferred altogether to the conjunctive (βάλω, δράμω) by a change of accent.

‡ Sufficient authority for this perfect is collected in Fischer vol. 3. p. 183. to which may be added ἐπιδεδράμηται, Xen. Œc. 15, 1. That the old Grammarians cite their proofs of δεδράμηκα from Menander or Philemon (see Lobeck ad Phryn. p. 619.), arose from the circumstance that this perfect active, like that of so many other verbs, is of very rare occurrence.

δραμοῦμαι cannot be formed from it in the same way, for then it would end in -ήσομαι like μαθήσομαι, γενήσομαι, &c. It must be derived, therefore, from the theme itself, which, on account of the old perf. δέδρομα (Od. ε, 412. ζ, 45.), is supposed to be ΔΡΕΜΩ; from which, it is true, that future cannot be formed in the usual Attic manner of verbs having λ, μ, ν, or ρ as their characteristic letter; but a fixed analogy in the change of the vowel is not to be expected in these primitive verbs, the present of which was probably never in actual existence. Compare what has been said on Βάλλω and Λαγχάνω.

The 3. sing. of a fut. ἀναδράμεται is found in Philipp. Thess. Epigr. 24, 4. for which it is probable the writer had some old Epic authority.

Τρέω, *I tremble*, retains ε in the inflexion: thus infin. τρεῖν: fut. τρέσω; aor. 1. ἔτρεσα. This verb keeps all its forms resolved, except where they can be contracted in ει: see Δέω, *I bind*.

[The Epic poets double the σ, making (with the omission of the augment) the aor. τρέσσε, τρέσσαι, &c. A poetical present is τρείω.—Passow.]

Τρίβω, *I rub*: fut. τρίψω; aor. 1. pass. ἐτρίφθην, Thuc. 2, 77. but more frequently is used the aor. 2: ἐτρίβην, (on which see Γράφω); perf. pass. τέτριμμαι.

[Homer has the aor. 1. act. of this verb in its compound διατρίψας, Il. λ, 846. The fut. midd. τρίψομαι is used in a passive sense in Thucyd. 6, 18.—Passow.]

Τρίζω, *I twitter, chirp*: fut. τρίσω and (Hemsterh. Aristoph. Plut. 1100.) τρίξω; perf. with force of a pres. τέτριγα, like κέκραγα, λέλακα, κέκλαγγα, &c. The pure characteristic letter of this verb is γ.

The Epics allowed themselves the liberty of pronouncing long the accented ι in the oblique cases of the part. perf., as τετριγῶτας for -γότας, Il. β, 314. Compare γεγαώς, -ῶτος, with note, p. 51.

ΤΡΥΦ–. See Θρύπτω.

Τρύχω, *I rub in pieces, wear out, consume*, forms from τρυχόω (a present of rare occurrence) an aor. 1. ἐτρύχωσα; aor. 1. pass. ἐτρυχώθην; part. perf. pass. τετρυχωμένος, &c. The pres. pass. τρύχονται is found in Mimnerm. Fr. 2.

Τρώγω, *I gnaw, eat*: fut. τρώξομαι; aor. 2. ἔτραγον; aor. 2. pass. ἐτράγην.

The α in this aorist would seem to lead us to a theme ΤΡΗΓΩ, a sister-form of τρώγω, like πτήσσω and πτώσσω. An aor. 1. in the compound καταρτρώξαντες is found in Timon Phlias. Fr. 7.

Τυγχάνω. See Τεύχω.

Τύπτω, *I beat*: fut. τύψω, &c.; aor. 2. pass. ἐτύπην.—MIDD.—Instead of the regular inflexions the Attics used a fut. τυπτήσω, a perf. pass. τετύπτημαι, and a verbal adj. τυπτητέος.

On the above deviation from the regular inflexion, see Thom. Mag. in voc. and Stephan. Thesaur. The fut. midd. τυπτήσομαι in Aristoph. Nub. 1382. with a passive sense, may possibly be a mistake for τυπήσομαι; as the old reading ὠθήσει in Eurip. Med. 336. is now proved by the Codd. to have been a corruption from ὠσθήσει. The aor. 1. ἔτυψα, τύψον, &c., appears to have been in constant use from Homer's time: the aor. 2. ἔτυπον is seldom found, but it does occur in Eurip. Ion. 766.

Τύφω, *I smoke, burn*: fut. θύψω*; aor. 1. ἔθυψα; perf. pass. τέθυμμαι or τέθῡμαι; aor. 2. pass. ἐτύφην.

Υ.

Ὑπισχνέομαι. See Ἔχω.

Ὑφαίνω, *I weave*; fut. ὑφᾰνῶ; aor. 1. ὕφηνα, Att. ὕφᾱνα; Lobeck ad Phryn. p. 26. perf. ὕφαγκα.

A very suspicious reduplicated perf. pass. ὑφήφασμαι is quoted by Suidas in voc. Phrynich. Seguer. p. 20, 3. Herodian π. μον. λέξ. 44, 25. The Grammarian in Suidas is puzzled how to account for the η in the second syllable, whence I conjecture it to be a corruption of ὑφύφασται, which is quoted in the Etym. M. in voc. as an old and rare form from Zenodotus. In all our Attic writers we find invariably ὕφασμαι. Homer has from the radical form ὑφάω a sister-form ὑφόω, whence the 3. plur. ὑφόωσι, Od. η, 105.

Ὕω, *I rain, make wet with rain*: fut. ὕσω; aor. 1. ὗσα. Pass. ὕομαι,

* On the formation of this future see Τρέφω, Θρέψω and note.

I am rained upon, made wet with rain; fut. midd. (in the same sense) ὕσομαι, Herodot. 2, 14. aor. 1. pass. ὕσθην, Herodot. 3, 10.

Φ.

ΦΑ–. See Φημί: also Φαίνω and Πέφνον.

ΦΑΓ–. See Ἐσθίω.

Φαίνω, *I bring to light, show*: intrans. *I shine.* Pass. *I am brought to light, I appear.* Act. φαίνω; fut. φᾰνῶ; aor. 1. ἔφηνα, infin. φῆναι; perf. πέφαγκα*; perf. 2. πέφηνα. Pass. φαίνομαι; fut. φανήσομαι; aor. 1. ἐφάνθην; aor. 2. ἐφάνην, infin. φανῆναι; perf. πέφασμαι. Midd. φαίνομαι; fut. φανοῦμαι; aor. 1. infin. φήνασθαι, Soph. The active voice has in the transitive sense the aor. 1.; in the intransitive the pres. the imperf. and the perf. 2. The passive has (beside the meaning attributed to it above) the strict passive sense of φαίνω as a transitive verb, and in this sense it employs the aor. 1.; e. g. τὰ φανθέντα, *the things announced* or *declared*, Demosth. c. Theocr. p. 1325., φρούρα ἐφάνθη, *was announced*, Xen. Hell. 6, 4, 11., ἀπεφάνθη, Lys. De Aristoph. Bon. p. 155, 28.; but in the sense of *to appear* the aor. 2. pass. is used. In this last sense we find a double future, viz. the fut. midd. which is the more common, and the fut. pass. which is of rarer occurrence: the latter is found more frequently in verse, but it is met with in prose also, e. g. φανήσοιντο, Isæ. De Philoct. p. 58, 33. ἀναφανήσονται, Xen. Hell. 3, 5, 11. The perf. 2. of the active serves as a perf. to φαίνομαι in this intransitive sense; while the perf. pass. (beside its proper passive meaning, *I have been announced*) has also the neuter sense of, *I have appeared.* And lastly we find a form of the middle voice (the aor. 1. infin. φήνασθαι, Soph. Phil. 944.) in the transitive sense of the active, which is particularly common in the compound ἀποφαίνω.

* Dinarchus has ἀποπέφαγκα twice.

This verb is contracted from the old *φαείνω* (Hom.), as *αἴρω* is from *ἀείρω*. Hence in the Epic writers the radical syllable admits of being lengthened, as *ἐφαάνθην** and the comparative *φαάντερος*, &c. This aor. 1. is used by Homer in the same sense as *ἐφάνην*.

By deriving the verb from this same radical form the Attics pronounced the future *φανῶ* with the α long, that is to say, they contracted it from *φαενῶ*. Apollonius (De Adv. p. 600, 28.) expressly mentions this quantity, and Bekker notices the same in Aristoph. Equ. 300. where the words *καί σε φανῶ* (- ◡ - -) have been arranged differently in opposition to all the Codd. The coincidence of this verb with the same appearance in *αἴρω* makes the thing certain: still however in both verbs the usual quantity is not altered in the Attic writers: e. g. *φᾰνῶ*, Soph. Aj. 1362. and *φᾰνοῦμαι* wherever it occurs †.

An aor. 2. act. and midd. of this verb is also quoted, but there is no certain authority for either. At Il. π, 299. the old editions certainly did read the 3. plur. *ἔφανον* ‡; but as many of the most undoubted forms of *φανῆναι* occur in Homer, it has been correctly altered to *ἔφανεν*, which is found in the best manuscripts. It is true that *φάνεσκεν* (Il. λ, 64.) appears to point to such an act. aorist; but this iterative may very well be formed from *ἐφάνην*, as *ἔσκε* was from *ἦν*, *στάσκε* from *ἔστην*, &c. The forms *προὔφανες* (Soph. Phil. 1191.) and *φάνῃς* (Philem. Fr. inc. 52. b.) are more than suspicious from their transitive meaning: see Buttmann's notes on Soph. Phil. And lastly in Xen. Cyr. 3, 1, 34. instead of *φανοίμην* the various reading *φαινοίμην* ought to have been long ago adopted. In Soph. Aj. 313. *φανοίην* is the Attic optat. fut. of the active voice.

At Od. ξ, 502. we find the stem of this verb in its most simple form, the 3. sing. *φάε* in the sense of the aorist, "the morning *broke*," which may be considered as the aor. 2. (*ἔφαον*, *φαεῖν*) from which came the pres. *φαείνω*. But Aratus has taken the liberty of using this simple form as a present, *λεπτὰ φάουσαι*, v. 607. where the sense of the aorist does not suit. And if we form from the same simple stem an analogous perf. act. and pass. we come to the Homeric fut. 3. *πεφήσομαι*, Il. ρ, 155, (*will have appeared, will have burst over*,) written precisely the same as the fut. of ΦΕΝΩ.

* See note under Κραίνω.

† It is singular that Apollonius does not, as might have been expected, quote *ἀρῶ* from *αἴρω* as similar in quantity to *φανῶ*, but *ῥανῶ*, of which the proofs are not so strong as they are of the two others. But perhaps the original word there was *κρανῶ*, which is very similar to *φαίνω* and *αἴρω*: or is *ῥανῶ* correct, and did the ρ produce the same effect here as in *κέρᾱτος*?

‡ [Passow unhesitatingly condemns this aorist as entirely obsolete; see Pors. Eurip. Or. 1266. Buttm. Soph. Phil. 1191. Meineke Menand. p. 416.—Ed.]

Φάσκω. See Φημί.

Φαύσκω or Φώσκω (compare τρῶσαι, τραῦμα), *I appear* or *break forth* as the morning does; a verb occurring only in its compounds with διά, ἐπί, and ὑπό (see the examples in Schneider's Lexicon *), of which the inflexion (fut. φαύσω, aor. ἔφαυσα) is known only from the Septuagint and New Testament, e. g. Sam. ii. 2, 32. Ephes. 5, 14., but it is supported by the subst. ὑπόφαυσις, Herodot. 7, 36.

The Epic verb πιφαύσκω, πιφαύσκομαι, *I show, give to understand*, of which we find only the pres. and imperf., is distinct from φαύσκω.

Φείδομαι, *I spare*, Depon. midd.; fut. φείσομαι; aor. 1. ἐφεισάμην, infin. φείσασθαι, Xen. Hell. 2, 3, 17.

The Epic poets have the aor. 2. with reduplication, e. g. infin. πεφιδέσθαι, opt. πεφιδοίμην, whence a fut. πεφιδήσομαι: compare πεπιθήσω from πεπιθεῖν under Πείθω, and ἀκαχήσω with note under Ἀκαχίζω. In Euseb. 10. p. 130. Valckenaer (ad Herodot. 8, 10.) has correctly amended φιλεύμενοι to φειδεύμενοι as from φειδέομαι, Ion. for φείδομαι, like ὀφειλεύμενος in Euseb and αἱρεύμενος in Hesiod.

ΦΕΝ–. See Πέφνον.

Φέρβω, *I feed, nourish*: perf. πέφορβα; pluperf. ἐπεφόρβειν, Hymn. Merc. 105. Pass. *I am nourished*, τινός, Hom. Hymn. 30, 4. The fut. and aor. are defective both in the act. and pass.

Φέρω, *I bring* or *carry*, forms its tenses from very different stems or roots; thus, fut. οἴσω, to which we must add from the common language an imperative (used also by the Epic and Attic writers) with the force of a pres. or aor. οἶσε, οἴσετε, οισέτω, οισόντων †, Od. χ. 106. 481. Aristoph. Bat. 482. Ach. 1099. 1101. 1122. Antim. Fr. 10.: see ἐδύσετο, p. 73. From the stem ΕΓΚΩ or ΕΝΕΓΚΩ come the aor. 1. ἤνεγκα, aor. 2. ἤνεγκον. In the first person of these two aorists and in the optative (ἐνέγκαιμι, ἐνέγκειε, and -οιμι, -οι) the usage is very fluctuating, as the Grammarians have observed‡. Of the remaining forms we find

* ["Αμ' ἡμέρῃ διαφαυσκούσῃ, Herodot. 3, 86. Διεπιφώσκω, Dionys. 9, 63. Ἐπιφώσκειν φέγγος ἐρυθρόν, Poet. Vet. De Herb. 25. Ὑποφώσκει ἡμέρα, Diod. Sic. 13, 18.]

† To these must be added the Epic infin. οισέμεν, οἰσέμεναι (which occurs as an aorist in Od. γ, 429. Il. γ, 120., but as a fut in Il. σ, 191.), and οἴσειν, which has the force of a present in Pind Pyth. 4, 181.

‡ See Greg. Cor. in Att. 78. with the quotations there made by Koen.; and Phryn. Appar p 35, 24.

a preference given (the Attic usage is sometimes exclusive), in the active voice to the infin. ἐνεγκεῖν, the part. ἐνεγκών, ἐνεγκόντος, and the 2. sing. imper. ἔνεγκε, all from the aor. 2.; while the others together with the whole of the middle are taken from the aor. 1., e.g. ἤνεγκαν, -κατε, -κατο, ἐνεγκάτω, -κάσθαι, -κάμενος, &c.: imperat. midd. ἔνεγκαι. Perf. ἐνήνοχα; pass. ἐνήνεγμαι, ἐνήνεγξαι, ἐνήνεγκται (e. g. Corp. Inscr. i. 76, 4.) and ἐνήνεκται; aor. 1. pass. ἠνέχθην; fut. pass. ἐνεχθήσομαι and οἰσθήσομαι: verbal adj. οἰστός, οἰστέος (poet. φερτός).—Midd.

In the aorist the Ionics have ἤνεικα, conj. ἐνείκω, infin. ἐνεῖκαι, &c., midd. ἠνεικάμην, &c., and pass. ἐνήνειγμαι, ἠνείχθην. The most simple theme which can be adopted for these forms is ΕΓΚΩ, whence by redupl. ἤνεγκον, like ἤγαγον, ἀλαλκεῖν, &c.* The relation of the aor. 1. to ἤνεγκον is the same as that of εἶπα to εἶπον as described at p. 9. under εἶλα. Let us now suppose ΕΓΚΩ lengthened to ΕΝΕΚΩ (compare ὀρέγω ὀργυιά, ἀλκή ἀλέξασθαι), then ἐνήνοχα (see κέκλοφα under Κλέπτω), ἐνήνεγμαι and ἠνέχθην are quite regular. The Ionic ἤνεικα appears to have been produced from ἤνεγκα by a mere change of pronunciation, and the same formation was then extended by a false usage to other forms, e. g. to ἠνείχθην, ἐνήνειγμαι, and to the pres. συνενείκεται in Hes. Scut. 440.; still however we find the perf. ἐνήνεγκται in old Attic inscriptions: see Corp. Inscr. Græc. to. 1. Inscr. Att. no. 71. p. 116.

The old Aorist, of which the imper. οἶσε and infin. οἰσέμεν are the only remaining tenses, was mentioned at the beginning of this article and in the note there subjoined. If this οἶσε and the other imperatives quoted below be considered as isolated instances of an imperative future, such a supposition is at variance with all usage, for strictly speaking either all imperatives are futures, or none are so. Hence it is more agreeable to analogy to suppose a new theme arising out of the future from which these aorists may be formed; compare ἀείσεο, λέξεο, ὄρσεο, βήσεο, and ἐδύσετο, δύσεο, p. 73. This aorist occurs also with the common termination of the aor. 1.; of which the surest instance is found in Herodotus, but with an unusual lengthening of the radical syllable, in the compound ἀνῷσαι (1, 157.); and this lengthening is again found in another form, in which it is quite as extraordinary, ἀνώ-

* Compare also ἀνάγκη, which is evidently a reduplication from the stem ἄγχειν.

ἰστοι (6, 66.), both words having the same sense of *sending* (*referre*) to consult an oracle*. Suspicious examples of the aorist οἶσαι from succeeding writers, and genuine ones of a very late period may be seen in Lobeck Parerg. p. 733. We find in Lucian Parasit. 2. a solitary instance of the perf. pass. προοῖσται, in which for the sake of perspicuity the οι is left unchanged, and the augment therefore can only be recognised by means of the accent.

The few forms coming immediately from φέρω, which are in general use are the following; the imperf. ἔφερον like ἐφερόμην from φέρομαι; the syncopated Epic imper. φέρτε for φέρετε, Il. ι, 171.; the 3. sing. φέρησι as from φέρημι, Od. τ, 111.; the Ion. 3. sing. imperf. φέρεσκε, and 3. plur. φέρεσκον, Od. ι, 429. κ, 108.; and the poetical verbal adj. φερτός. From φέρω was formed φορέω†, like τρομέω from τρέμω, δομέω from δέμω; see last note, p. 61.: but this latter has the more precise sense of *being in the habit of carrying, of wearing generally*. Of this verb we find an Epic infin. pres. φορήμεναι and φορῆναι for φορεῖν: compare γοήμεναι, καλήμεναι, ποθήμεναι, &c. See Φρέω below.

Φεύγω, *I fly*: fut. φεύξομαι and φευξοῦμαι‡; perf. πέφευγα; aor. 2. ἔφυγον. There is no passive voice. Verbal adj. φευκτός, φευκτέος.

The perf. pass. πέφυγμαι is a passive in form only, as the Epics use the part. πεφυγμένος in the active sense of *having escaped*, Od. α, 18§. On the υ of this perf. see note under Χέω.

The Epic language uses the verbal adj. φυκτός: whence ἄφυκτος came into the common dialect.

For the Homeric part. πεφυζότες see λελειχμότες under Λιχμάομαι.

* Reiz, Schneider in his Lexicon voc. ἀνώϊστος, and Lobeck, Parerg. p. 733. consider both as corruptions and read ἀνοῖσαι, ἀνοιστος; and certainly in Herodot. 7, 149. we find the fut. ἀνοίσειν in a similar sense (*referre* ad populum) without any various reading. Hermann on the contrary conjectures it to be an old Ionicism, and he has this in his favour; that Aretæus, who affects the Ionic dialect, has (2, 11.) ἀνώϊστος from ἀναφέρω, consequently an imitation of Herodotus. But errors are frequently found even in works of great antiquity; and as we meet with this incorrect form in this compound only, the mistake was perhaps caused by the similar sound of the other ἀνώϊστος, *unexpected*, which is correctly formed from ἀ and (οἴομαι) ὀϊστός, like ἀνώνυμος, ἀνώμαλος, &c. And why should not the gloss of Suidas, ἀνοῖσαι, although explained only by the general expression κομίσαι, refer to the above passage of Herodotus? Still however greater certainty is requisite before we alter the text of Herodotus.

† Of this verb we find an instance (φορέσαι) as early as Isæus; in the later authors it is more frequent.

‡ [Φευξοῦμαι is properly Doric, but is found in Aristoph. Ach. 203. and elsewhere in that writer. Very late authors have a fut. 2. φυγῶ.—Passow.]

§ We may compare this participle with δεδακρυμένος; in both verbs the perf. pass. expresses the completion of an action belonging rather to the middle voice, *having shed a flood of tears, having conveyed himself to a place of safety*. See also ἀλιτήμενος.

Φημί, *I say*: φής, φησί, &c., imper. φάθι*, opt. φαίην, conj. φῶ (3. sing. φῇη, Hom.), infin. φάναι, part. φάς; imperf. ἔφην; fut. φήσω; aor. 1. ἔφησα. Of the midd. were used the following forms, viz. the infin. and part. pres. φάσθαι, φάμενος; both used by Homer, the latter by the Attics also; and the imperf. ἐφάμην. Of the passive we find some perfect forms, as the part. πεφασμένος, Il. ξ, 127. and the imperat. πεφάσθω. Verbal adj. φατός, φατέος, and the Hesiodic φατειός.

This verb is the only genuine instance of a dissyllable in -μι (beginning with a consonant) without the reduplication. The radical form is ΦΑΩ. The indicative present, with the exception of the 2. sing., is enclitic, i. e. throws back the accent on the word preceding. In the formation of this 2. sing. φῄς there is no ground for the *ι subscriptum*, and the acute accent instead of the circumflex is unusual, but both are supported by very strong tradition†.

This verb has a twofold meaning, viz. 1. the general idea of *I say*, and 2. the more precise one of *I assert, maintain, assent, allow*; with its converse οὔ φημι, *I dissent, deny*. The present φημί has both senses; but the first is limited by the general usage of the pure Attic writers to the pres. and imperf. active through all their moods, the remaining tenses being supplied from the anomalous εἰπεῖν. On the other hand the fut. and the aor. 1. are generally found in the second sense; in which also the imperfect with the infin. and part. present, in order to avoid ambiguity, are generally expressed by φάσκειν (which does not otherwise occur in prose), and by the midd. φάσθαι, φάμενος; e. g. ἔφη σπουδάζειν, *he said he was in haste*, but ἔφασκε σπουδάζειν, *he maintained that he ....*; φάσκων, *asserting, maintaining*; οὐ φάμενος, *denying*.

In the 2. sing. of the imperfect we generally find in the Attic writers ἔφησθα; see Thom. Mag. p. 397.: the simple ἔφης becomes more frequent in the later authors; see Lobeck ad Phryn. p. 236. This ἔφην is commonly used as a complete aorist, synonymous with εἶπον; and

* The Grammarians are at variance on the accent of this form: see Schol. Aristoph. Equ. 22. Lobeck (ad Phryn. pp. 60. 172.) unhesitatingly rejects φάθι, but I prefer it to φαθί, as this imperative is not enclitic like φημί.

† Matthiæ in his Grammar directs that the 2. sing. indic. should be written without the ι *subscriptum*, like ἵστης, but the conjunctive with it. Passow however in his Lexicon says expressly φῄς (not φής or φῇς): the latter he restricts to the 2. sing. imperf. Ion. for ἔφης, Hom. See the Etym. M. voc. φῄς and Chœrobosc. MS. ap. Bekk. p. 345. v.—Ed.]

to this imperfect we may add the infin. φάναι, which is confined so entirely to express *past* time only (φάναι τὸν Περικλέα, *that Pericles has said*) that as soon as an infin. pres. is wanted, λέγειν or φάσκειν is used*. The same holds good of the imperf. with the infin. and part. pres. of the middle voice. With regard to the statement of the Grammarians that there was also a particular aor. 2. ἔφην, which retained the η in the plural, and had φῆναι or φᾶναι in the infinitive, it is entirely unfounded. If we find φᾶναι occasionally in the text of some authors, it is either an error of transcription, or if correct (as it is in Eubul. ap. Athen. p. 8. c.) it is a poetical licence like τεθνᾶναι.

By aphæresis the following forms have arisen from φημί in the language of common conversation; ἠμί, *say I* (*inquam*), in a quick repetition in Aristoph. Nub. 1145. Ran. 37.; and again in the imperf. ἦν δ' ἐγώ, *said I*, ἦ δ' ὅς, *said he*, (for ἔφην, ἔφη,) in the conversational narrative of Aristoph. Equ. 640. and Plato; to which belongs also the Epic ἦ, *he spake*, Il. α, 219.

[In the Homeric usage we find the 1. plur. opt. pres. φαῖμεν for φαίημεν; the 3. conj. φήῃ for φῇ; the imperf. φῆν, φῆς, φῆ for ἔφην, ἔφης, ἔφη, and the 3. plur. ἔφαν, φάν for ἔφασαν; also the imperat. midd. φάο for φάσο, Od. π, 168. σ, 170.—Passow.]

Φθάνω†, *I get before, anticipate*: fut. φθήσομαι; aor. 2. ἔφθην, opt. φθαίην, conj. φθῶ, infin. φθῆναι, part. φθάς; perf. ἔφθακα. The aor. 2. is preferred by the Atticists to the aor. 1. ἔφθασα; but this latter is used by the best Attic writers, e. g. by Thucyd. 3, 49. and from the time of Xenophon is the more usual form of the two.

The fut. φθάσω is found only in the later writers, e. g. in Dio Chrys. 12. p. 195.; and an aor. 1. pass. ἐφθάσθην occurs in Joseph. Ant. 8, 6. A part. aor. midd. φθάμενος is used by the Epic poets synonymous with φθάς, like φάς, φάμενος from φημί. We find also a Doric fut. φθάξω, aor. 1. ἔφθαξα. Παραφθαίησι in Il. κ, 346. is a lengthened aor. opt. not conj.; as the αι would be an unheard of diphthong in the conjunctive of ἔφθην, and the -σι is admissible in lengthening the optative, though less usual than in the conjunctive.

Φθέγγομαι, *I sound*, depon. midd.; fut. φθέγξομαι; aor. 1. ἐφθεγξάμην. The active φθέγγω never occurs.

* However, in Plat. Hipp. Maj. p. 289. 9. φάναι is considered as a genuine present in the Attic writers; and in the later authors common; see Jacob. Anthol. Poet. p. 884.—Passow.]

† [The α is long in the Epic, but short

Φθείρω, *I corrupt*, is regular: thus, fut. φθερῶ (Epic φθέρσω, Il. ν, 625.); perf. ἔφθαρκα; perf. 2. ἔφθορα; perf. pass. ἔφθαρμαι; aor. 1. pass. ἐφθάρην; verbal adj. φθαρτός. The perf. 2. ἔφθορα, διέφθορα had originally the intransitive sense, *I am become corrupt, am destroyed, undone*; this is its meaning at Il. ο, 128., and it was so used by the Ionics and by all the later writers from Theophrastus. The pure Attics on the contrary gave it a transitive sense, and used intransitively the pass. ἔφθαρμαι, ἐφθάρην. See Lobeck ad Phryn. p. 160. Still however we find the perf. 1. ἔφθαρκα in the early Attic writers: see the old instances collected in Piers. ad Mœr. p. 127.

The fut. of the neuter meaning is generally φθαρήσομαι, for which the Ionics have the fut. 2. midd. (with the change of vowel to α;) διαφθαρέομαι, Herodot. 8, 108. 9, 42*.

Φθίνω and φθίω, *I pass away, come to an end, perish.* This verb is generally poetical, and the pres. φθίω with its imperf. ἔφθιον are exclusively Epic. The intransitive meaning (*I pass away*) is by much the prevailing one in the present tense, indeed there occurs no instance of φθίω with the causative sense of *I bring to an end, consume*: for the imperfect in Il. σ, 446. φρένας ἔφθιεν is to be understood intransitively, as is also φθίῳ at Od. β, 368. ὥς κε δόλῳ φθίῃς. The transitive meaning of φθίνω is found in Soph. El. 1414. and Theocr. 25, 122. In general this form has the neuter sense, in which it is used in prose also, still however only in certain expressions which do not proceed from the present. The remaining forms, which the poets use in an intransitive sense, are taken from the midd. of φθίω, as the fut. φθίσομαι, the perf. ἔφθιμαι, and the pluperf. ἐφθίμην, which last form is at the same time (see ἐκτάμην in note under Κτείνω) a syncopated aorist, e. g. in Eurip. Hipp. 839. Soph. Œd. T. 962. 970., and in this respect it has its own moods, as opt. φθίμην, (φθῖο), φθῖτο, Od. κ, 51. λ, 330†; conj. φθίωμαι, shortened to φθίομαι, φθίεται; infin. φθίσθαι; part. φθίμενος.

On the other hand the transitive meaning is established in the fut. act. and aor. 1. φθίσω, ἔφθισα: see note under Μείρομαι, and compare ἐγήρασα under Γηράω.

* Διεφθαρέατο in Herodot. 8, 90. would be 3. plur. aor. 2. midd., of which tense however there is no other instance whatever. Some manuscripts have the imperfect, but we must adopt, with Hermann, the pluperfect διεφθάρατο.

† In the latter passage the reading of the text was until lately φθεῖτο, arising from a false conception of the unusual form φθῖτο.

The quantity of the ι (both in the present in -ιω and in the tenses formed from φθίω) is the same as that of τίνω, long in the Epic poets, but short in the Attic writers: e. g. compare φθίνω, Od. λ, 182. ξ, 161. with Soph. Ant. 695. Eurip. Alc. 201.; and φθίσω, &c. Il. π, 461. χ, 61. with Soph. Trach. 709. Aj. 1027. On the contrary the perf. pass., and consequently the syncop. aor. also, together with the derivatives φθίσις, φθιτός, have always the ι short. Compare the υ short in λέλῠμαι and ἐλύθην while it is long in λύω, λύσω.

The neuter φθίνω came into more general use in the later writers, who formed for themselves a new inflexion in -ήσω: thus φθινήσαντες (having perished), Lucian. Parasit. 57., καταφθινήσας καὶ τιμωρηθεὶς ἀπέθανεν, Plut. Cons. ad Ap. κατεφθινηκότες, Vit. Cicer. 14.

In a verse thrice repeated (Od. ε, 110. 133. η, 251.) Ἔνθ' ἄλλοι μὲν πάντες ἀπέφθιθον ἐσθλοὶ ἑταῖροι, this reading ἀπέφθιθον, as from a theme in -θω (compare ἀμύναθον, p. 22.) has always maintained its ground in the text against ἀπέφθιθεν: and yet it is decidedly incorrect. The latter is found in the best sources; and in the Etym. M. p. 532, 43. it is quoted as the established and only reading. If the former is supposed to be an imperfect, that tense does not suit persons *suddenly* perishing by shipwreck; if an aorist be required, nothing is more natural than ἔφθιθεν. The perf. ἔφθιμαι (without σ, and with ι short) is quite sufficient ground for an aorist ἐφθίθην.

Φιλέω, *I love*, is regular.

The Epic language has from the stem of this verb an aorist in the middle voice with ι long, ἐφίλατο, imperat. φῖλαι. The analogy of τίλλω, ἔτῖλα enables us to form a correct opinion of this old form. In Hes. θ, 97. and Hom. Hymn. 25. (see Hermann on that passage) we find the conj. of this aorist φίλωνται corrupted in the text to φιλεῦνται; while in Hymn. Cer. 117. Wolf has restored it from φίλονται, and v. 487. from φιλῶνται.

Φλέγω, *I burn*, transit.: fut. φλέξω. The aor. 2. pass. is ἐφλέγην: see note under Βλέπω.

Φλέω, *I am full to overflowing*: used only in pres. and imperf. This verb is connected by Onomatopœia with φλύω, *I overflow*; *chatter*: ἀνὰ δ' ἔφλυε, Il. φ, 361; φλῦσαι, Æschyl. Prom. 504.: which was formed also φλύζω, φλύξαι*. But φλύω, *I singe, burn*, is quite distinct from the above; of which we find περιφλύει in Aristoph. Nub. 395. with υ

* [Μανίης ὕπο μυρία φλύζων, Nicand. Alex. 214.—Schneid. Lex.]

long, instead of which Herodotus (5, 77.) has the diphthong περιπεφλευσμένος.

Φοβέω, *I terrify*: fut. φοβήσω; aor. 1. ἐφόβησα, &c.; aor. 1. midd. imperat. φόβησαι. Pass. φοβέομαι, *I am terrified*: [fut. midd. φοβήσομαι and fut. pass. φοβηθήσομαι, without any difference of meaning, Xen. Cyr. 1, 4, 19. 3, 3, 30. 6, 7, 15.; aor. 1. pass. ἐφοβήθην; perf. pass. πεφόβημαι.—Passow.]

[The perf. pass. has particularly the sense of *to be put to flight, to fly*, Il. and Herodot. 9, 70. The aor. 1. midd. ἐφοβησάμην belongs to the latest and worst period of the language; e.g. Anacr. 3, 11.—Passow.]

Φορέω. See Φέρω.

Φράζω, *I say, point out*: fut. φράσω; aor. 1. ἔφρᾰσα; perf. πέφρακα. Pass. (in Herodotus) *I perceive, observe*: imperf. ἐφραζόμην, Herodot. 3, 154.; aor. 1. ἐφράσθην, part. φρασθείς, ib. 1, 84. 5, 92. 7, 46. 9, 19.; perf. πέφραδμαι or πέφρασμαι. Midd. (in the Epic poets) *I perceive, observe*; also *I consider, reflect, consult, plan*: fut. φράσομαι; aor. 1. midd. ἐφρασάμην.

The active voice has in the Epic poets a reduplicated aorist πέφραδον (see Κάμνω), or with the augment ἐπέφραδον (compare ἐκέκλετο under Κέλομαι), Il. κ, 127., particularly used in the 3. sing. πέφραδε; dual πεφραδέτην, Hes. θ, 475.; infin. πεφραδέειν and πεφραδέμεν, Od. η, 49. τ, 477.; optat. πεφράδοι. The part. perf. pass. with a δ, and in a passive sense, occurs in Hes. ε, 653. In a fragment in Athen. 11. p. 465. f. φράδη is a false reading, instead of which there is a various reading φράσθη.

[The active of this verb is frequent in Xenophon; otherwise it is not often found in prose: the middle occurs only in the Epic poets and in an oracle in Herodotus 3, 57.—Passow.]

Φράσσω, Att. φράττω, (in the later writers φράγνυμι also), *I fill, stop up, place close together, fortify*: fut. φράξω; aor. 1. ἔφραξα; aor. 1. pass. ἐφράχθην; aor. 1. midd. ἐφραξάμην; perf. pass. πέφραγμαι; aor. 2. pass. (in the compound) ἀπεφράγην, Lucian. Dial. Mort. 28, 2.

Φρέω, *I suffer to pass*: fut. φρήσω. This verb is used

only in composition, e. g. ἐκφρέω, εἰσφρέω, διαφρέω, *I let out, in, through*: in addition to which we find a decompound ἐπεισφρέω in Eurip. Herc. Fur. 1267. and Seidl. Eurip. El. 1028*. Midd. *I suffer to pass to myself, take to myself, admit*; e. g. εἰσεφρούμην, Eurip. Tro. 647, to which belongs the fut. εἰσφρήσεσθαι, Demosth. Cherson. p. 93, 18. : for the fut. act. (ἐκφρήσω, εἰσφρήσω, διαφρήσω, Aristoph. Vesp. 156. 892. Av. 193.) is in common use. The aor. 1. pass. ἐκφρησθῆναι occurs in Ælian. ap. Suid. in voc.

The Grammarians mention also an imperat. εἴσφρες, ἔκφρες, which belongs to the syncopated formation of πῖθι, κλῦθι, σχές from πίνω, κλύω, ἔχω; but we know not any passage where it really occurs†. Ἐξεφρείομεν in Aristoph. Vesp. 125. is a very singular form‡. Whether the unusual present πιφράναι belongs to φρέω, by a change of the radical vowel (compare δειπνέω and πίμπλημι), is uncertain: see Schneider in Ἐμπίφρημι§, and on Aristot. H. A. 5, 5. Schæf. on Gregor. p. 521. not.‖

Φρίσσω, Att. φρίττω, *I shudder*: fut. φρίξω; aor. 1. ἔφριξα; perf. (its pure characteristic letter is κ, as in the subst. φρίκη,) πέφρικα.

The Doric part. πεφρίκοντας (Pind. Pyth. 4, 326.) is either a perfect formed according to the analogy of the present, like κεκλήγοντες under Κλάζω, and ἐρρίγοντι under Ῥιγέω, or it is a present from a form πεφρίκω. Compare also ἀνεστάκουσα, Archim. and see Greg. Cor. in Ætol. 56. Maitt. p. 239.

* Ἐπεισφρεῖς is also quoted by Hermann from Eurip. Phaëth. 2, 50.

† This form is mentioned by all the Grammarians and in Stephan. Thesaur. in voc., but I know not from what writer it is taken. The simple φρές is in the Etym. M. p. 740, 12. This compound surely could not have found its way into such general tradition, (as there is nothing elsewhere to lead to it,) had it not been in actual use at some earlier period. I almost think that ἔκφρες must have been the original reading in Aristoph. Vesp. 162. instead of ἔκφερε, which cannot be the true one.

‡ [Passow has Ἐκφρείω Poet. for Ἐκφρέω.]

§ [In Schneider's Lexicon we find Ἐμπίφρημι, like ἐμφράττω, *I thrust in, in order to fill up an aperture*, Aristot. H. A. 5, 6. ἐμπιφράναι εἰς τὸν μυκτῆρα. But the word is suspicious.—Passow omits it altogether in his Lexicon.]

‖ Φρέω has been most improperly reckoned among the sister-forms of φέρω: for though it may be wished to class it etymologically with that verb, still its totally distinct meaning requires a grammatical treatment equally distinct.

Φρύγω, *I roast*: fut. φρύξω; aor. 1. ἔφρυξα; aor. 1. pass. ἐφρύχθην, infin. φρυχθῆναι, Hom. Epigr. 14, 4. aor. 2. pass. ἐφρύγην, infin. φρυγῆναι.

ΦΥΖ–, See Φεύγω.

Φυλάσσω, Att. φυλάττω, *I watch*: fut. φυλάξω, &c.—MIDD. *I stand on my guard, guard myself against, take heed of.*

The imperative Νηὸν δὲ προφύλαχθε (Hymn. Apoll. 538.) in whatever way we explain it, is a very anomalous form. If we suppose it to be the perf. pass. for προπεφύλαχθε, the immediate context δέδεχθε δὲ φῦλ' ἀνθρώπων, seems greatly in favour of that supposition, particularly as the imperat. perf. was also in use, e.g. in Hes. ε, 795. πεφύλαξο: but this form, as well as the whole of the middle voice, has always the definite sense of *to be on one's guard*, and with the accus. *to be on one's guard against, watch against*; whereas the simple meaning of *watching over* is expressed by the active only, φυλάσσω, προφυλάσσω; there is no reason, therefore, why we should adopt in this case the great anomaly of dropping the reduplication. Nor can it be the syncopated aorist, because, as we have just said, the passage requires the common meaning of the active voice, and a tense which shall strictly express duration. As we are reduced, then, to the necessity of supposing it to be some anomalous form, it appears most reasonable to preserve a regularity in the meaning. I consider therefore προφύλαχθε to be a syncopated form of the pres. act. like φέρτε, consequently for προφυλάσσετε, formed from the stem or root ΦΥΛΑΚ–, yet instead of the termination -κτε taking that of -χθε, like ἄνωχθε*.

Φύρω, *I mix*, particularly by adding moisture; whence, *I knead*; and in Homer, *I wet, moisten, stain*: it has in the older language a fut. φύρσω; aor. 1. ἔφυρσα, &c.: but in prose it changes to the inflexion of -άω, as fut. φυράσω, and in Hippocr. Diæt. 2, 8, 10. φυρήσω; aor. 1. ἐφύρασα; aor. 1. midd. ἐφυρασάμην (infin. φυράσασθαι, Aristoph. Nub. 979.); aor. 1. pass. ἐφυράθην (part. φυραθεῖσα, Plat. Theæt. p. 147. c.); see Lobeck ad Phryn. p. 205. In the perf. pass. both πεφύραμαι and πέφυρμαι† were in use; the latter

* In Xen. Cyr. 8, 6, 3. διαπεφυλάκασι is a false reading for -λάχασι.

† Whether both were used in Attic prose, is still a question. In Thucyd. 3, 49. criticism has declared in favour of πεφυραμένος: but the exclusive usage of πεφυρμένος in succeeding writers, e.g. in Lucian, Plutarch, and others, leads us to

in Homer and Xenophon; compare Od. ι, 397. and Xen. Ages. 2, 14.

Lucian has the aor. 2. pass. ἐφύρην (συναναφυρέντες, Epist. Saturn. 28.): on the other hand the present φυρῶ, φυρᾷν appears not to have been in use, except perhaps among some of the later writers. The formation of φύρσω always remained in the language of poetry; and Pindar (Nem. 1, 104.) has also the fut. 3. (paullo-post) πεφύρσομαι; which rather confirms than opposes the observation made in my Grammar, "that verbs with λ, μ, ν or ρ as their characteristic letter, seldom have a third future, if they are inflected regularly:" for φύρω, by its inflexion in -σω, no longer preserves its analogy with those verbs.

Φύω, *I beget**, is inflected regularly. But the perf. πέφυκα and the aor. 2. ἔφυν, infin. φῦναι, part. φύς (see note p. 53. and note p. 238.) have the immediate meaning of *to spring up*, *be produced* or *begotten*†, to which belong also the pres. pass. φύομαι, and fut. midd. φύσομαι, e. g. Xen. Cyr. 5, 2, 32. θάρσος δὲ ἐμφύσεται. Compare Δύω and the statement there made of this verb.

The moods of ἔφυν correspond also with those of ἔδυν. The conj. φύω (probably with υ long) is found in Xenoph. Hier. 7, 3. οἷς δ' ἂν ἐμφύῃ......ἔρως. The 3. sing. opt. φύη occurs in Theocr. 15, 94. If this optative had followed strictly the analogy of verbs in -μι, the optatives in -είην, -αίην, -οίην would have required the corresponding termination to be -υίην: but as this diphthong is never found before a consonant, the passive optative could not be -υίμην, -υῖτο, but became -ύμην, -υτο, and therefore to preserve conformity the active was written φύην, not φυίην. Compare ἐκδῦμεν for ἐκδυίημεν p. 73. and Buttm. Lexil. p. 425. with note‡.

Beside ἔφυν, an aor. 2. pass. was formed with the same sense, viz. ἐφύην, conj. φυῶ, infin. φυῆναι, &c., which was in use as early as the time of Hippocrates, and among the later writers became the common form. To this belongs also a fut. φυήσομαι, of which we find the infin. ἀναφυήσεσθαι in Lucian. Jup. Trag. 19.

conjecture that there were older precedents for this latter. See Valck. ad Schol. Eurip. Phœn. 1201.

* [This verb is not confined to the above sense; it has the general meaning of *to produce*, *bring forth*, and is used of plants, trees, the hair, the teeth, &c.; and in Porson. Eurip. Phœn. 34. of a mother. —Passow.]

† In the later writers φύς, οἱ φύντες is used in the causative sense; see Bekker on Phot. Bibl. p. 17. a. (Appian.)

‡ [Passow is however of opinion that φύην still remains very doubtful.]

Instead of πεφύκασι we find in Homer the Epic πεφύασι, and instead of the part. πεφυκώς, -ότος, the Epic πεφυώς, -ῶτος, fem. πεφυυῖα: on the omission of the κ, see βεβαώς p. 37. and on the length of the oblique cases see γεγαώς, γεγαῶτος with note p. 51. or Τρίζω. In the pluperf. Homer always uses the mere reduplication without the augment; while Hesiod (ε, 151. α, 76. θ, 152, 673.) has in a particular instance restored the augment, and formed a 3. plur. ἐπέφῡκον (for ἐπεφύκεσαν) like the imperf. of a pres. πεφύκω: see Μηκάομαι.

[Parmenides has ventured to use φῦν for φῦναι; but the 3. plur. aor. 2. ἔφῡν for ἔφυσαν is principally Epic.—Passow.]

Φώσκω See Φαύσκω.

X.

Χάζομαι, ἀναχάζομαι*, *I retire, retreat*: depon. midd.

The prose usage of this verb is known only from Xenophon, who has the imperf. ἀνεχαζόμην, Anab. 4, 7, 7. and Cyr. 7, 1, 17. (24.): but he has also in the same sense an instance of the unusual active voice of this same verb, ἀναχάζοντες, Anab. 4, 1, 12. (16.) We find also ἄγχαζε quoted from Soph. in Lex. Seguer. 6. p. 340. In the older language the active voice of this verb had also the causative sense of *I cause to retire, drive back*: see Pind. Nem. 10, 129. where the reading ἔχασσαν is given, it must be confessed, by only one Codex, and yet both metre and sense leave no doubt of its being the true one.

Homer has an aor. 2. κέκαδον, and in the midd. a. 3. plur. κεκάδοντο, with a fut act. κεκαδήσω formed from it. These forms came by an old Ionicism (compare τετυκεῖν) from ἔχαδον, which usage has retained in this unchanged shape under the cognate verb χανδάνω. Hence κεκάδοντο (Il. δ, 497.) is precisely the same as ἐχάσαντο; but the active forms (Il. λ, 334. Od. φ, 153.) with the genitive have the sense of *to deprive*, in which lies the same causative sense as in ἀναχάζω, *I make a person yield* or *retire from anything*, expressed more simply in Latin by *cedere facio*. On κεκαδήσομαι see Κήδω.

Χαίνω. See Χάσκω.

Χαίρω, *I rejoice*: fut. χαιρήσω; aor. 2. (from the passive voice) ἐχάρην; and from this aorist was formed again a perf. κεχάρηκα or κεχάρημαι, with the force of the present increased, *I am rejoiced*: compare Ἀνδάνω ἕαδα, Θάλλω τέθηλα, Κήδομαι κέκηδα, Πείθομαι πέποιθα. On the for-

* [There is no instance of the simple χάζω in the active voice.—Passow.]

mation of the perfect from the aorist see ἀκαχήσω and note p. 12.

The perfect κεχάρηκα is found in Aristoph. Vesp. 764.; the part. κεχαρηκώς, *rejoiced*, is of frequent occurrence in Herodotus, and without the κ (κεχαρηότα, &c.) in the Epic poets: the perf. pass. κεχάρημαι occurs likewise in Aristoph. Vesp. 389. and its part. κεχαρημένος in Hom. Hymn. 6, 10. Both the futures formed with reduplication from these perfects are found also in Homer, e.g. κεχαρησέμεν, Il. ο, 98., κεχαρήσεται, Od. ψ, 266.

Of the regular inflexion, we find in the poets (from an Epic aor. 1. midd. ἐχηράμην) the 3. sing. χήρατο, Il. ξ, 270.: compare Jacob. Anthol. Poet. p. 262. and (from a reduplicated aor. 2. midd. κεχαρόμην) the 3. plur. κεχάροντο with the optatives κεχάροιτο, κεχαροίατο, Il. and Od. The part. perf. κεχαρμένος, *rejoiced*, occurs in Eurip. Or. 1122. El. 1077. and other tragedies of the same writer. The verbal adj. is χαρτός.

The aor. 1. ἐχαίρησα is found in the later writers, e.g. in Plut. Lucull. 25.*. The fut. χαρήσομαι which occurs in the LXX., although formed analogically from ἐχάρην, like ἀκαχήσω from ἤκαχον (see note p. 12.), is decidedly a form to be rejected: see Thom. Mag. [The pres. midd. χαίρομαι was a notorious barbarism, Aristoph. Fr. 291.: nor were χαιρέω, χαρέω or χάρω ever in use.—Passow.]

Χαλάω, *I loosen, relax*: fut. χαλάσω, Dor. χαλάξω, &c. This verb has α short in the inflexion, and takes σ in the passive; e.g. perf. pass. κεχάλασμαι.

Χανδάνω, *I contain*: fut. χείσομαι (Od. σ, 17.); aor. ἔχαδον; perf. (synonymous with the present) κέχανδα. This future is generally placed by mistake with a theme ΧΕΙΩ, although it is evident that χείσομαι bears exactly the same relation to ἔχαδον as πείσομαι to ἔπαθον. It comes therefore from the root ΧΑΝΔ–, with a change of the radical vowel. See Buttm. Lexil. p. 181.

Χάσκω, *I open* (intrans.), *open my mouth, gape*: imperf. ἔχασκον. This verb borrows from χαίνω (which is not used

* Lobeck (ad Phryn. p. 740.) is wrong in speaking of this reading as suspicious. The expression οὐ χαιρήσεις, "you shall have cause to rue it," was so common, that the transition to the aorist became quite natural, and it is at the same time very conceivable that οὐκ ἐχάρη would have given a somewhat different meaning. Hence I cannot but think it a question worth considering, whether the earlier writers would not have used the same expression in this case, and whether Plutarch had not some precedent for his use of it.

by any of the older writers) a fut. χανοῦμαι*, an aor. ἔχανον, and a perf. (synonymous with the pres.) κέχηνα†, *I am open, have my mouth open.*

Lucian (Dial. Mort. 6, 3.) is the earliest writer in which we find any instance of the pres. χαίνω‡.

In the passage of Aristoph. Ach. 133. ὑμεῖς δὲ πρεσβεύεσθε καὶ κεχήνατε, Herodian found κεχήνετε written, (see Chœrobosc. in Bekk. Anecd. III, p. 1287. where Ὄρνισιν is a corruption,) which he considers to be an inflexion of the indicative for -ατε. For that some of the older authors preferred writing the perf. act. of the verb with ε, is clear from Apollon. Synt. 1, 10. (p. 37, 9. Be.): see also Ἀνήνοθα and note p. 25. In the Attic language, indeed, this inflexion is inadmissible, but for that very reason the reading of Herodian is most probably the true one, misunderstood by the Grammarians above mentioned. Κεχήνετε is the *imperative*, which mood is most suitable to the context of that passage; and the rarity of its occurrence misled the commentators: see κεκράγετε under Κράζω.

Χέζω, *caco*: fut. χεσοῦμαι; perf. κέχοδα; aor. ἔχεσα and ἔχεσον; perf. pass. κέχεσμαι (part. κεχεσμένον, Aristoph. Ach. 1185.).

I have some doubt whether the aor ἔχεσον be a genuine form; and I may say the same of the infin. χεσεῖν which is found in Aristoph. Thesm. 570. As the word is only a vulgar term, individual forms do not occur often enough to enable us to speak of the two aorists with any degree of certainty. In the Attic language they appear to be confounded, as they are in εἰπεῖν and ἐνεγκεῖν; compare ἔπεσον and ἔπεσα, and see ἐδύσετο pp. 73. 74. Aristophanes (Eccles. 320. Nub. 174.) has the part. aor. 1. χέσας, καταχέσαντι; but the form χέσαιτο (Equ. 1057.) proves as little in favour of the aor. 1. as it does of the middle voice of this verb, for it is used in that passage in a play on the word.

Χείσομαι. See Χανδάνω.

Χέω, *I pour*: fut. χέω, χεῖς, χεῖ; fut. midd. χέομαι; aor. 1. ἔχεα (see ἔκηα under Καίω), imper. χέον, χεάτω;

* [Buttmann, in his Lexil. p. 181 supposes another fut. χήσομαι, of which the 3 sing. χήσεται may be read in a corrupted passage of Hom, Hymn. Ven 253]

† [According to Ap. Dysc there was also a perf κέχαγκα — Passow]

‡ The mention by Chrysoloras in his Grammar that χαίνω was not in use, shows that the older Grammarians had before taught the same.

conj. χέω, infin. χέαι; aor. 1. midd. ἐχεάμην; perf. κέχῠκα; perf. pass. κέχῠμαι; aor. 1. pass. ἐχύθην*.—MIDD.

The forms χεύσω, ἔχευσα appear to have never occurred†, but are only supposed to have existed from the derivative χεῦμα and the shortness of the υ in κέχυκα, &c. That χέω is fut. as well as pres. was first remarked by Elmsley, and proved by the following examples: κάρα τε γάρ σόυ ξυγχέω .... ῥανεῖ τε ...., Eurip. Thes. Fr. 1. οὐ κατορύξεις καὶ .... μύρον ἐπιχεῖς, Aristoph. Pac. 169....παραχέων ἔρχομαι, Plat. Com. ap. Athen. p. 665. c. To which we may add χεόμενον (said of pouring out the libation,) καὶ ἐναγιοῦντα, Isæus 6. p. 61.: which passages had been previously explained sometimes as harshness of syntax, at others as harshness of contraction. And thus ἐγχεῶ in Jerem. VI, 11. and Act. Apost. II, 17., which has been hitherto cited as a barbarous form of the biblical writers, differs only in accent from the pure Attic ἐγχέω‡.

The Epic language has an aor. ἔχευα, conj. χεύω (χεύωσιν, Il. η, 86.), midd. ἐχευάμην; and at Od. β, 222. Il. η, 336. we read χεύω, χεύομεν, which may be the conj. aor. supplying in Homer's usage the place of the future, quite as well as the Epic fut. χεύω answering to the Attic fut. χέω (compare δήω, κείων, κέων, σώω); both which views are in syntax fundamentally the same. Again δάκρυσι χεύω, Eurip. El. 181. (where I proposed on a former occasion to read the false form χεύσω,) is, as far as regards the verb, quite correct. Χεύω in that passage is not the present, (it never occurs as a present even in the Epic language, the metre being satisfied by χείω: see Od. ι, 10. Hes. θ, 83.) but it is the Epic future of Homer which suits the lyric stanza, and may be joined with κρούσω in the preceding verse, without offending against μέλει in the following one.

The Epic language has also the syncop. aor. pass. ἐχύμην, ἔχυτο, χύμενος (*to be poured out*,) formed after the perfect.

* Some verbs change the diphthong ευ of the radical syllable in the perf. pass. to υ; e. g. τεύχω τέτυγμαι, φεύγω πεφυγμένος, σεύω ἔσσυμαι, πεύθομαι πέπυσμαι. Χέω, as one of the verbs in -έω which take ευ in the inflexion, follows the same analogy. In all these perfects the υ is short.

† Whatever appearance there was in Homer of these forms, has now been changed on the best authority to the Epic formation mentioned above in the next paragraph.

‡ Elmsley very correctly compares this future with τελέω, whose fut. τελέσω, by the Ionic omission of the σ, becomes again τελέω, Attic τελῶ, the only difference is, that the shorter word did not admit the contraction in ῶ, οῦ, as it does in the present. But that χέω, χέσω was the original formation is shown by the aorist ἐχέθην, which remained in common use to quite a late period an additional cause for the other formation without the σ, was the coincidence of the fut. and aor. of χέω with those of χέζω.

On the aor. 1. pass. ἐχέθην, χεθῆναι, which was very common in the later writers, see the preceding note, and Lobeck ad Phryn. p. 731.

ΧΛΑΔ–, whence an Ionic perf. κέχλᾱδα*, of which Pindar (Ol. 9, 3. Pyth. 4, 319.) has the part. κεχλᾱδώς, gen. κεχλάδοντος, *swelling*: compare πεφρίκοντας under Φρίσσω. [We find also in Pind. Fr. 18. a perf. infin. κεχλάδειν for κεχλαδέναι.—Passow.]

Χόω, *I heap up* (generally, *a mound of earth*): fut. χώσω, &c.; infin. pres. χοῦν, part. χῶν. The passive takes σ, e. g. perf. κέχωσμαι; aor. 1. ἐχώσθην, infin. χωσθῆναι.

The above formation is frequent in Herodotus, while the pres. χώννυμι belongs to the later writers. Χώομαι may be found in its alphabetical place.

Χραισμεῖν, *to help*, infin. of a defective aorist ἔχραισμον, from which again came a fut. χραισμήσω and aor. 1. ἐχραίσμησα: compare ἀκαχήσω and note p. 12. See also Buttm. Lexil. pp. 541—8.

Χράω. To this stem belong many verbs with particular meanings; all those, however, which are used in prose may be easily traced to the same idea, *commodare*, *to give*, *lend*†. All have the inflexion with the η, e. g. χρήσω, &c., and that even in the Doric dialect. The contracted forms take also η as the vowel of contraction, as in ζάω, κνάω, σμάω, &c., while this peculiarity is also to be remarked, that the Ionic dialect here takes ᾱ as the vowel of contraction, as in κνᾶν, σμᾶται, &c., Herodot. 9, 110. We will now describe five forms which are used in prose.

1. Χράω, *I give an oracle, foretel*: fut. χρήσω; aor. 1. ἔχρησα. Pass. χράομαι; fut. midd. χρήσομαι; perf. pass.

* If we suppose a present from which to form this perfect, it must be χλήδω (like πλήθω πέπληθα); which is connected with χλιδή, but not with καχλάζω, a term signifying sound; nor is it akin to κλάζω, partly because the stem of this latter has γγ, partly because analogy gives us the change of χ to κ (in κεκαδών and the like), but not the converse of κ to χ which would be required in this case. [Passow, however, forms this perfect from a present χλάζω, Dor. χλήζω, which he makes exactly synonymous with its compound καγχλάζω (Pind. Ol. 7, 2. καγχλάζοισα), supposing both to mean *the bursting forth of water from a spring* or *any confined place*, or *the bubbling of boiling water*.]

† Some other old deviations of meaning in this verb come from the idea of *to lay hold on*: see χράω, ἐπιχράω, χραύω, and χραίνω, in Schneider's Lexicon; where, however, there are no striking peculiarities of deviation. It appears to me evident that all these and the meaning of *to give*, &c., come etymologically from χείρ, χερός.

κέχρησμαι; aor. 1. pass. ἐχρήσθην. Thus the passive takes σ. See also χρήζω.

In the Attic tragedians we find the present and imperfect contracted in η: thus χρῇ is 3. sing. pres. for χρᾷ, Herm. Soph. El. 35. ἐξέχρη is 3. sing. imperf., Soph. Œd. C. 87. On the other hand Herodotus has frequently the 2. sing. χρᾷς, 3. sing. χρᾷ, and in the infin. χρᾷν; and he is followed by the later writers, as Lucian, &c. In the Ionic dialect χράω is sometimes changed to χρέω, whence the part. pres. χρέουσα, Herodot. 7, 111.; and in the Epic poetry it becomes χρείω, whence the part. χρείων, Od. θ, 79.

In many passages of Herodotus all the manuscripts have the perfect passive with the σ: in others the σ is wanting: see Schweigh. Lex. Herodot. It is easily seen that uniformity must be preserved by adopting it in all cases; κέχρημαι belongs to χρῆσθαι only.

In the middle voice the meaning of this verb approaches very nearly to that of the common χρῆσθαι, as in the expression χρῆσθαι μαντείῳ, which appears to be exactly the same as χρῆσθαι μαντικῇ in Xenophon; sometimes however it stands absolutely, as χρῆσθαι περὶ πολέμου: so that χρῆν, *to foretell*, answers correctly to χρῆσθαι, *to consult an oracle*. See Od. θ, 79, 81. κ, 492.

2. Χράομαι, *I use*, depon. midd.: fut. χρήσομαι; aor. 1. ἐχρησάμην; perf. (without σ) κέχρημαι. The present and imperf. are contracted in η instead of the regular α, thus χρῶμαι, χρῇ, χρῆται, infin. χρῆσθαι, &c., Lobeck ad Phryn. p. 61. Κέχρημαι is sometimes used in the strict sense of a perfect, e. g. in Xen. Cyr. 3, 1, 30. (24.) ὁ πολλάκις αὐτῇ κεχρημένος: but it has generally the sense of the present, as in Xen. Equ. 4, 5. κεχρῆσθαι ταῖς ὁπλαῖς, and in most instances the force is increased, *I am always using* and therefore *I have**. Verbal adj. χρηστός, χρηστέον, Plat. Gorg. 136.

In the Epic language κεχρῆσθαι has the meaning of *to be in need of*†; hence in Homer and Hesiod κεχρημένος is used as an adjective in the sense of *needy*. Τίνος κέχρησθε; Theocr. 26, 18. Fut. κεχρήσεται, id. 16, 73. Compare χρή and the note under Χρήζω.

* See Ἀνδάνω ἕαδα, θάλλω τέθηλα, Κήδομαι κέκηδα, Πείθομαι πέποιθα.

† [This meaning properly belongs to the Epic poets, but there are instances of it in the Attic also, e. g. in Elmsl. Eurip. Heracl. 801.—Passow.]

In the unusual case of a passive tense being formed from this middle verb (compare βιάζομαι), the aorist has the σ (as in χράω, *I foretell*), αἱ νῆες .... ἐχρήσθησαν, Herodot. 7, 144. again, καταχρησθῆναι, *to be put to death* (from καταχρῆσθαί τινα), Herodot. 9, 120. with which the verbal adjective agrees.

In this verb the forms of the Ionic dialect are difficult to be ascertained with any degree of certainty: for sometimes the passages and manuscripts of Herodotus give the contractions χρᾶται, χρᾶσθαι, χράσθω, &c ; at other times the α is changed to ε in the same forms, as χρέεται, χρέεσθαι: in some passages we find χρέωνται, in others χρέονται*. In the imperative Herodotus (1, 115.) has, according to all the manuscripts, χρέω, while Hippocrates frequently uses χρέο shortened from χρέεο, like ἐκλέο, which see under Κλέω.

3. Κίχρημι, *I lend*: fut. χρήσω; aor. 1. ἔχρησα, &c.; infin. pres. κιχράναι. Midd. κίχραμαι, *I borrow*.

It has been correctly remarked, that χρῆσαι in Herodotus means simply *to give, grant* (see Herodot. 7, 38. and Schweigh. in Lex.). But a present χράω never occurs in this sense; we place, therefore, the present κίχρημι instead of it, although in the instances where it occurs in Demosthenes and others, it has the proper meaning of *to lend*. The aor. 1. midd. ἐχρησάμην was avoided by the Attic writers in this sense: see Antiatt. Bekk. p 116.

4. Χρή, (*oportet*) *it is necessary*; an impersonal verb: opt. χρείη, conj. χρῇ, infin. χρῆναι, part. (τὸ) χρεών. Imperf. ἐχρῆν, or in prose χρῆν. Fut. χρήσει.

The indicative of this verb may be considered as the 3. sing of χράω —χρῇ, with the tone or accent shortened. The participle also comes exactly, according to analogy, from χράον, like ναός, Ion. νηός, Att. νεώς (compare the subst. χρέως and the neut. part. τεθνεώς): but it has the anomalous accent of ἰών and the Ionic ἐών: It is indeclinable; that is to say, it occurred so seldom in any construction requiring other

* All the above-mentioned forms are undoubtedly pure Ionic; and this uncertainty of usage is not otherwise than surprising, even in a dialect That the same writer should have had a twofold usage in the same form, is an unreasonable supposition. Undoubtedly, therefore, the variation in the forms of this verb in Herodotus arose entirely from the uncertainty of tradition, and from the different Grammarians who employed themselves on the text. Whoever examines the passages and their various readings with the help of Schweighæuser's Lexicon Herodot., will find it most probable that Herodotus always contracted in α the forms which were grounded on αε, while those in αο were changed to εω. To decide between εω and εο is much more difficult. There can be, however, no hesitation in rejecting from the text of Herodotus such forms as χρῆσθαι and ἐχρῆτο.

than the nominative or accusative case, that the other cases became obsolete. It is found sometimes as a genitive, e. g. in Eurip. Hippol. 1256. Herc. Fur. 21. Joseph. Ant. 8, 284. but there is perhaps no instance of its being used as a dative, τῷ χρεών.

In the other three moods (opt., conj., and infin.) this verb follows the formation of verbs in μι, retaining, however, the η in the infinitive, and ει instead of αι in the optative, as in a similar case under Πίμπλημι.

We find twice in Euripides (Hecub. 258. Herc. Fur. 828.) τὸ χρῆν, which Thom. Mag. in voc. affirms to be a poetical infinitive; therefore contracted for χρῆν. At the same time it is not to be denied that the participle χρεών, which is preferred by some critics, and which may be pronounced as a monosyllable, would suit both passages better.

The imperfect, whether it followed the conjugation of contracted verbs or of those in μι, would be ἔχρη: therefore ἐχρῆν or χρῆν (the only forms ever used) are to be compared with the 3. sing. ἦν, Ion. ἔην from εἰμί. But the accent of the augmented form is so strikingly anomalous that we should be forced to consider it incorrect, did not the vain attempts of the Grammarians to explain it show (see Eustath. ad Od. κ, 60.), that it was founded firmly on tradition*.

In the older language this verb had also the meaning of *opus est; one has need, I have need*; and in this sense it was afterwards used or rather misused personally: e. g. ὧ χρῄς, *of which thou hast need*, Cratin. ap. Suid. v. χρή; οὐ χρῆσθα, *thou hast no need*, Megarensis ap. Aristoph. Acharn. 778. compare Δέω. From this verb Herodotus (3, 117.) has a middle voice with a similar meaning in the form χρηΐσκομαι. Compare κέχρημαι above, and note on Χρήζω below.

5. Ἀπόχρη, *is sufficient*. This verb has the anomaly of the preceding one in this 3. sing. pres. indic. only, inasmuch as it is shortened from ἀποχρῆ; in all its other forms it follows regularly χράω, &c.: thus 3. plur. ἀποχρῶσιν; infin. pres. ἀποχρῆν; imperf. ἀπέχρη; fut. ἀποχρήσει; aor. 1. ἀπέχρησεν, &c. Midd. ἀποχρῶμαι, *I have enough*; infin. ἀποχρῆσθαι. In this voice it is inflected like χράομαι, 2.

The Ionics have also the regular 3. sing. pres. indic. ἀποχρᾷ. In the same or a similar sense Herodotus has other compounds, καταχρᾷ, ἐκχρήσει, ἐξέχρησε, ἀντέχρησε.

This verb is not an impersonal, although, like other personal verbs, it

* Perhaps the shorter form χρῆν had become so general in common life, that the augmented one was made by degrees to conform to it.

is sometimes used impersonally; on the contrary, in many instances its subject stands plainly before it, and hence it has the plural ἀποχρῶσι: but as things or objects in the third person are its most natural subject, the other persons became obsolete; yet not entirely; see Epicharmus in Heindorf's Note on Plat. Gorg. 131. εἷς ἐγὼν ἀποχρέω, *I alone am sufficient*. See a similar appearance in Μέλω, where however the 1. and 2. person have remained in use somewhat more than in this verb. A solitary irregularity occurs in the middle voice in ἀπεχρέετο (Herodot. 8, 14.) used impersonally for ἀπέχρα; compare μέλεται for μέλει*.

Χρήζω, *I desire, wish*†. The Attics use it in present and imperfect only.

In the Ionic dialect it is χρηΐζω: whence the more precise Grammarians write the common form χρῄζω, like ᾄττω: see Greg. Cor. in Ion. 42. The Ionics have also other tenses, as χρηΐσω, ἐχρήϊσα (Herodot. 7, 38. 5, 20. 65.), because in this form no confusion can possibly be made with the tenses of χράω. But in the printed text all these are constantly written with η in Herodotus also. Χρήζω in the sense of χρᾷν, *to foretell*, see in Schneid. Lex.‡.

Χρίω, *I besmear, anoint*: fut. χρίσω, &c.; perf. pass. κέχρισμαι; but the perf. part. (without the σ) κεχριμένος is found in Com. ap. Athen. 13. p. 557. f.—Midd.

This verb has also the meaning of *to sting*, as spoken of insects and the like; on which Phrynichus (Appar. p. 46.) gives the following rule, that in this latter sense the perfect passive is written κεχρίσθαι, in the former κεχρεῖσθαι. In this last incorrect form (although in that writer the diphthong ει is expressly named,) we must look for nothing more than the correct form κεχρῖσθαι; and the direction given by Phrynichus must necessarily be extended thus: χρίω, ἔχρῖσα, χρῖσαι, κεχρῖσθαι, *I anoint*: χρίω, ἔχρῐσα, χρίσαι, κεχρίσθαι, *I sting*.

Χρώννυμι or Χρώζω, *I colour*: fut. χρώσω, &c.

* Such an irregularity could arise only from the original meaning of the expression being entirely forgotten. In these compounds the active χράω is used exactly in its true sense. The thing *supplies* us with what we need; in ἀποχρᾷ, ἐκχρᾷ it *supplies* us to the extent of our need; in ἀντιχρᾷ it *supplies* us by acting in opposition to our need. The similarity of the German expression to the Greek illustrates this in a most striking manner in German *dar*reichen means *to reach* (anything) *forward, offer*; *hin*reichen, *to reach* or *extend to any certain point*, and also *to be sufficient*.

† This meaning arises from those forms of χράω which have the meaning of *I need*, in which sense, however, the verb χρῄζω itself occurs in the later writers only: see Stephan. Thesaur.

‡ [Schneider quotes χρῄζω in this sense from Æschyl. Choeph. 338. Soph. Œd. C. 1426 Eurip. Hel. 523.]

In Eurip. Phœn. 1619. we find χρώζω and in Med. 497. κέχρωσμαι, but in both passages with the meaning of *to touch*, and the collateral idea of a *polluting* touch. Perhaps in the old Attic language this was the only meaning of χρώζω, and κέχρωσμαι belonged to this present only: for according to the analogy of ζώννυμι and σώζω, we might expect the perfect passive of χρώννυμι in the old Attic to be κέχρωμαι, which appears merely as the various reading of κέχρωσμαι, e. g. in Aristot. De Color. 3. But in Eth. Nicom. 2, 3. all the manuscripts have ἐγκεχρωσμένος.

Χώννυμι. See Χόω.

Χώομαι, *I am angry*, depon. midd.: fut. χώσομαι; aor. 1. ἐχωσάμην.

Χωρέω, *I yield, go*: fut. midd. χωρήσομαι, but sometimes also χωρήσω: see Poppo Obs. Crit. in Thucyd. p. 149. and Buttmann's Notes in the Auctarium ad Plat. Theæt. 117. Ed. 2.

Ψ.

Ψαύω, *I touch*: fut. ψαύσω, &c.; perf. pass. ἔψαυσμαι; aor. 1. pass. ἐψαύσθην.

[It is generally joined with the genitive, sometimes with the dative, whether with an accusative depends on Soph. Ant. 858. 962.—Passow.]

Ψάω, *I rub*: fut. ψήσω, &c., like κνάω, σμάω; see also Πεινάω. The passive fluctuates between the formation with and without the σ; as, perf. ἔψημαι, ἔψησμαι; aor. 1. ἐψήθην, ἐψήσθην.

See Lobeck ad Phryn. p. 254. The sister-form ψήχω (compare σμάω, σμήχω) has the more precise sense of *to rub down* (a horse), *to rub in pieces*; to the latter of which belongs κατέψηκται in Soph. Trach. 698.

Ψέγω, *I blame, reproach*: fut. ψέξω, &c.; perf. ἔψογα; aor. 2. pass. ἐψέγην (see Βλέπω).

Ψεύδω, *I deceive, cheat*: fut. ψεύσω, &c.; perf. pass. ἔψευσμαι; aor. 1. pass. ἐψεύσθην. Midd. *I deceive, lie*: οὐκ ἐψεύσαντο τὰς ἀπειλάς, *they did not make their threats false, made them good*, Herodot. 6, 32.

Ψήχω. See Ψάω.

Ψύχω, *I cool*: fut. ψύξω; aor. 1. pass. ἐψύχθην; aor. 2. pass. ἐψύγην, and ἐψύχην, Lobeck ad Phryn. p. 318.

Ω.

Ὠθέω, *I push*: fut. ὠθήσω and ὤσω. All the other tenses are formed from ΩΘΩ, and with the syllabic augment, e. g. imperf. ἐώθουν; aor. 1. ἔωσα, infin. ὦσαι; perf. ἔωκα; perf pass. ἔωσμαι; aor. 1. pass. ἐώσθην. Pors. Eurip. Med. 336. Plat. Tim. p. 79. e —Midd.

Ὠνέομαι, *I buy*, depon. midd.: fut. ὠνήσομαι, &c. This verb has also the syllabic augment, e. g. imperf. ἐωνούμην; aor. 1. ἐωνησάμην, infin. ὠνήσασθαι: but instead of this aorist the pure Attic writers used ἐπριάμην, πρίασθαι.

[This verb was seldom or never used as a passive in the sense of *to be sold*, yet we find in Plat. Phæd. p. 69. b. the part. ὠνούμενα, where Heindorf's reading ὠνούμεθα appears to be unnecessary. The pluperf. ἐώνητο occurs in Aristoph. Fr. 1175. On the aor. 1. pass. infin. ἐωνηθῆναι and ὠνηθῆναι see Markl. Lys. p. 720. Isæus De Philoct. Hered. 19. A part. perf. act. ἐωνηκώς is quoted by the Grammarians from Lysias.—Passow.]

THE END.

INDEX.

N. B.—The following Index is intended to assist the Student, where the alphabetical arrangement of the work may fail him: consequently those forms only will be found here, which do not begin with the same letter or syllable as the verbs to which they respectively belong. Nor has it been thought necessary to mention all the persons, moods, participles, &c. which occur in the work; in most cases the 1. pers. sing. of the indicative (if that form be in use,) will be found a sufficient guide to all the other moods and persons of any particular tense. The references are to pages.

A.

H.

P.

Σ.

END OF THE INDEX.

Printed by Richard & John E. Taylor, Red Lion Court, Fleet Street.